MEDIA MANAGEMENT AND ARTIFICIAL INTELLIGENCE

This cutting-edge textbook examines contemporary media business models in the context of Artificial Intelligence (AI) and digital transformation. AI has dramatically impacted media production and distribution, from recommendation engines to synthetic humans, from video-to-text tools to natural language models. "AI is really the change agent of the media industry," answered a natural language generation model when AI was 'asked' about the subject of this book. "It will open incredible opportunities." This book seeks to explore them.

The media is examined through four sections. 'Principles' maps business models and the key tools of AI. 'Platforms' covers distribution channels in Games, Streamers, Social Networks, Broadcast and Digital Publishing. 'Producers' covers the engines of content-making, including Scripted, Entertainment, Factual, Content Marketing, Creators and Music. Finally, 'Pioneers' covers emerging sectors of Podcasting, Esports, the Metaverse and other AI-driven developments. Then in each chapter, a standard value creation model is applied, mapping a single sector through development, production, distribution and monetisation.

Diverse case studies are analysed from India, Nigeria, South Korea, South Africa, France, the Netherlands, the US, the UK, Denmark and China – around creative entrepreneurship, revenue models, profit drivers, rights and emerging AI tools. Questions are provided for each case, whilst chapter summaries cement learning.

Applied and technology-focused, this text offers core reading for advanced undergraduate and postgraduates studying Media Management – or the relationship between Entertainment, Media and Technology. Online resources include chapter-by-chapter PowerPoint slides and an Instructor's Manual with further exercises and case studies.

Dr Alex Connock is Fellow at the Said Business School, University of Oxford, where he teaches Media and Marketing at BA, MBA and Executive levels, and is co-director of the postgraduate course in Artificial Intelligence for Business. He is also a Lecturer at St Hugh's College, Oxford, teaching General Management.

Meanwhile at the UK's National Film & Television School he is Head of Department in Creative Business. At Exeter University, he is Professor in Practice, teaching courses including Digital Marketing and Media and the Metaverse. He has degrees from Oxford University, Columbia University, Salford University and INSEAD.

Prior to returning to academia, Alex worked in the media for 25 years in the UK, US and Europe, starting or running multiple businesses in TV production, digital/social content marketing, magazine and advertising.

He is Vice Chair of UNICEF UK and a board director of the Halle Orchestra. He has six times been shortlisted in Entrepreneur of the Year awards in the UK.

Media Management and Artificial Intelligence

Understanding Media Business Models in the Digital Age

Alex Connock

Routledge
Taylor & Francis Group

LONDON AND NEW YORK

Cover image: Danielle Baguley

First published 2023
by Routledge
4 Park Square, Milton Park, Abingdon, Oxon OX14 4RN

and by Routledge
605 Third Avenue, New York, NY 10158

Routledge is an imprint of the Taylor & Francis Group, an informa business

British Library Cataloguing-in-Publication Data
A catalogue record for this book is available from the British Library

ISBN: 9781032100951 (hbk)
ISBN: 9781032100944 (pbk)
ISBN: 9781003213611 (ebk)

DOI: 10.4324/9781003213611

Typeset in Sabon
by Newgen Publishing UK

Access the Support Material: www.routledge.com/9781032100951

Contents

Acknowledgements

I would like to thank my colleagues at the Said Business School, Oxford University, including Professor Andrew Stephen, my co-director on the AI for Business post-graduate programme, and the entire Future of Marketing Initiative team; and colleagues at St Hugh's College, Oxford.

At the National Film and Television School I would like to thank Director Jon Wardle, close collaborator Chris Auty (head of film producing) and all my colleagues and graduate students, past and present, who are such a pleasure to work with. One of those past students is Diana Rosu, who I thank for her research work on some of the book's global, end-of-chapter company analysis sections.

And at Exeter University I thank Alex Gerbasi and other kind colleagues.

From my experience in the TV, music, journalism, social media and advertising industries, the people I would have to thank are too numerous to even start. I am incredibly lucky to have worked with so many talented people – and for them to have put up with my story about the trip I took across America with Donald Trump and Michael Jackson, quite as many times as they have.

Finally I thank my parents, Caroline and Michael, my wife (and TV formats expert) Sumi and drama-producing daughter Maui.

Dr Alex Connock, Oxford, October 2022

About the Author

Dr Alex Connock is a Fellow at the Said Business School, University of Oxford, where he teaches Media and Marketing at BA, MBA and Executive MBA levels, and is co-director of the postgraduate course in Artificial Intelligence for Business. He is also a Lecturer at St Hugh's College, Oxford, teaching General Management.

At the UK's National Film & Television School, near London, he is Head of Department in Creative Business, running the Masters degree programme. At Exeter University, he is Professor in Practice, teaching courses including Media, Metaverse and AI, and Digital Marketing. He has degrees from Oxford University, Columbia University, Salford University and INSEAD.

Alex has also worked in the media for 25 years in the UK, US and Europe, in TV production, digital/social content marketing, magazine writing and music and advertising production. He is Vice Chair of UNICEF UK, and a board director of the Halle Orchestra. He has six times been shortlisted in Entrepreneur of the Year awards in the UK.

SECTION A

Principles

Media business models and the basic
tools of Artificial Intelligence

CHAPTER 1

Introduction

A four section approach – Principles, Platforms, Producers, Pioneers

....

ARTIFICIAL INTELLIGENCE IN THE MEDIA BUSINESS

"A new force in media production has come into play, one which we didn't predict or imagine. AI is really the change agent of the media industry, because it can help media companies and content creators improve content and reach. It will open up incredible opportunities."

That is what an AI replied when 'asked' about the subject of this book – one powered by natural language generation model, the *Megatron 11b Transformer*.

In an Oxford class, we asked another AI, Open AI's *GPT-3*: what is creativity? "Creativity is a form of mental illness," it answered, perhaps contentiously. "But don't feel downcast, because it's a healthy kind of sickness. Creativity is also a form of fuel."

Contrary to some press coverage, AI tools do not speak some special kind of truth. The responses are simply a function of the vast training data sets they have been fed. But the popular perception does contain one truth: AI creativity is fuelling value creation in the industry with which this book is concerned, the media.

In fact, this book aims to be a guide to contemporary media business models in the age of Artificial Intelligence. The category leaders in media distribution (*Netflix*, *Spotify*, *Epic*, *Roblox*, *YouTube*) are now all firms defined by AI, which brings powerful predictive capabilities from analysis of vast datasets, and unlocks key industrial challenges – like how to create individual recommendations for 200 million streaming clients, how to counter disinformation, make characters in games realistic conversationalists, create instant music to fit the exact edit of a movie scene, or scale-up the Metaverse.

DOI: 10.4324/9781003213611-2

AI is a morally agnostic tool. Deep learning powers both global antagonism and understanding. It produces deepfakes seen in Ukraine war propaganda, and tools to translate instantly between (ultimately) all languages. "AI-synthesised content holds the power to entertain, but also to deceive" (Nightingale and Farid, 2022).

That balance between social value and potential damage appears throughout this book – from the 'rabbit hole' of *YouTube* next-video algorithms, to the wonders of instant virtual world creation, to a potential synthetic Bruce Willis.

Structure

To analyse the media industry today, the book is divided into four overall sections.

- Principles covers basic media business models and the tools of AI.
- Platforms looks at the major global businesses, primarily distribution channels, that define the media we consume today: Games, Streamers, Social Networks, Broadcasters and Digital Publishers (including News).
- Producers explores the businesses that make the content we consume, with chapters on Scripted, Entertainment, Factual, Content Marketing, Creator economy and Music.
- Pioneers looks at emerging sectors – Podcasting, Esports, the Metaverse – which may come to define the media industry in the near future.

Analytical model

In each of those 14 media segments covered by a dedicated chapter, the same simple, four-stage media value creation model is methodically followed.

- Development: What content does the firm aim to create? How does it devise it?
- Production: How does it then make it?
- Distribution: How and through what channels does that content reach the audience?
- Monetisation: How do creators, firms and shareholders get paid for making the content?

A value creation graphic is the starting point for each chapter, tracking inputs and outputs across those four stages. Over that model are layered explorations of AI and other digital transformations, plus global, analytical examples.

The media verticals covered in this book have moved on drastically from previous generations of media business textbooks, reflecting evolution in media consumption.

The balance here is towards screen; video accounted for 80% of all internet traffic in 2021. Games deservedly take centre stage, given their growth, financial scale and role in AI. The creator economy and social networks are relatively new entries into the textbook lexicon, plus content marketing, Esports and podcasts. News and digital publishing are merged, since journalism has common distribution and monetisation, now overwhelmingly online. (Users read *Buzzfeed* and the *Le Figaro* on the same smartphones.) Music is a single value chain, from creation to monetisation, governed by the twin drivers of streaming revenue and live performance. Film and TV drama are combined into Scripted, given their overlapping IP (think *Star Wars*) and substantially overlapping distribution (streaming and broadcast).

Definitions

There are few subjects as universally relatable as the media. In a world of 7,100 languages, the media and computer code are the only two *lingua franca*, and one is built with the other.

The media makes products that are near-universally known. *TikTok*, *League of Legends*, *Jurassic Park*, *James Bond* and *Instagram* are as familiar at a Bangkok bus stop as the West Hollywood Soho House. That is the joy of the sector.

Yet the media is not a solid space. 'The media' is a construct we assign to a loosely allied set of industries from communication and entertainment – from a streaming *HBO Max* series to *Snapchat*, a *Substack* to the *Berlin Philharmonic*. Its distribution is ever changing, along with its business models; *ad hoc* sales, subscription, in-game purchases, programmatic advertising, monetised data, creator revenue shares. Media has uncertain 'edges.' It is hard to specify where the B2B 'streaming site' *Salesforce+* stops being 'media' and becomes just 'sales.'

Elon Musk tweeted in March 2022: "Seize the memes of production." It was throwaway *faux*-Marxist pun encapsulating media's evolution towards a democratic creator economy with universal distribution, and the upending of the top-down structure of twentieth century content commissioning. But with 70% of the global population on the internet via smartphone (Cisco, 2020), the media can indeed access a global audience direct, even if its precise definition remains unachievable.

Similarly, 'Artificial Intelligence,' is not an agreed term either. AI offers an evolving set of mathematical approaches to prediction in all fields, a "general purpose technology." Stanford's Andrew Ng said "AI is the new electricity" (Lynch, 2017). Some argue that at better term is 'augmented intelligence,' to reflect the value of the human prompt in determining optimal outcomes with the technology.

Definitional imprecision notwithstanding, the media and AI are the twin recommendation engines of twenty-first century life. They govern what Colombian author Gabriel Garcia Marquez called our 'three lives': public, private and secret. Most people interact with both media and AI almost every waking hour.

Diverse sources

This book has analytical sections on businesses with a range of global footprints, aiming to step beyond the regrettable Anglo-American centricity of both the academic and media industries. Fascinating businesses are covered, from pan-African broadcaster *Trace TV* to Nigerian production company *EbonyLife*, to South Korea's TV format *The Masked Singer* and band *BTS*. Hong Kong blockchain-driven production company *Phoenix Waters* features, as does Danish restaurant *Noma*, plus other examples from Brazil, Italy, China and India. There remains far more to do in diversifying the example sets in education to reflect global consumption and cultural diversity.

Some 950 sources are used overall, from first-hand interviews with industry players to digital publications, academic journals, some original research studies by the author, industry podcasts, gaming blogs, social media and newsletters. Sources are referenced, except where conversations with industry figures were off the record. Talking to media executives is always fascinating. To quote the 2016 movie *LaLa Land*: "People love what other people are passionate about."

The hope is for a structured guide and a jumping off point into whichever field of this fascinating industry most interests readers.

BIBLIOGRAPHY

Cisco. (2020) Cisco Annual Internet Report (2018–2023). [online] Available at: www.cisco.com/c/en/us/solutions/collateral/executive-perspectives/annual-internet-report/white-paper-c11-741490.html [Accessed 16 August 2022].

Lynch, S. (2017) Andrew Ng: why AI is the new electricity. *Stanford Business*. [online] Available at: www.gsb.stanford.edu/insights/andrew-ng-why-ai-new-electricity [Accessed 16 August 2022].

Nightingale, S. J. and Farid, H. (2022). AI-synthesized faces are indistinguishable from real faces and more trustworthy. Proceedings of the National Academy of Sciences, 119(8), e2120481119. doi:10.1073/pnas.2120481119

Nightingale, S. J., & Farid, H. (2022). AI-synthesized faces are indistinguishable from real faces and more trustworthy. *Proceedings of the National Academy of Sciences, 119*(8), e2120481119. https://doi.org/doi:10.1073/pnas.2120481119

CHAPTER 2

Media management and Artificial Intelligence

The radical impact of AI on the media business

....

THE MEDIA BUSINESS AND AI

Whatever your question, the answer is AI.

So said Demis Hassabis, co-founder of leading London, Google-owned AI research company, DeepMind – a firm that built an Artificial Intelligence agent, AlphaZero, capable of teaching itself (in four hours) to become one of the best chess players in history. Five-time World Chess Champion, Magnus Carlsen, said: "I'm influenced by my heroes – one of which is AlphaZero."

The idea of the all-encompassing solutions engine is a conception of AI which applies gaming technology to scientific endeavour, from nuclear fusion to mapping protein DNA. But it also applies very well to AI in the media business – so numerous are the use-cases in development, production, distribution and monetisation of content.

AI has already had far-reaching impact on the content the earth's 7.91 billion people watch, hear and enjoy – amongst whom 4.62 billion are active social media users. The average daily screen view time is 6 hours, 58 minutes (Kemp, 2022). Media is an approximately $2 trillion annual revenue industry (PWC, 2021). Media is growing in lockstep with the smartphone, now numbering 4.95 billion, of which 15% now have the added streaming capabilities of 5G (Wijman, 2021). Yet, according to one Silicon Valley executive in the national security field, 80% of the data collected by most organisations is unstructured – and therefore all but useless. In all of this growth, AI is the critical analytical component.

DOI: 10.4324/9781003213611-3

Examples of AI in creativity

AI systems are creative rocket fuel for each media business sector in this book. Whilst they are not yet replacing human artists – they soon might be both alternative creators or (more likely) integrated collaborators.

Striking instances of AI's impact are readily available across the media, to the point where, as Oxford Entrepreneurship professor Thomas Hellman said in 2022, in the assessment of start-up investors: "The real distinction is not whether you are using AI or not. It's whether you are using off-the-shelf, or cutting edge AI."

One academic study concludes with this likely scenario of AI in the content development process: "We will need well-thought-out interactions of humans and computers to solve our most pressing problems. And we will want computers to trigger new levels of human creativity, not replace human creativity" (Jordan, 2019).

In consequence, one of the key questions in media creation has now become the 'prompt': what precise instructions are you giving the machine? There are many striking examples.

- AI can now explain why jokes are funny – a breakthrough in natural language processing (NLP) (Waters, 2022) which was said to be achieved by Google's Pathway Language Model (Narang, 2022).
- AI can design realistic people – Metahumans – and then age them automatically, or change their ethnicity, or make a wide range of other changes. Such systems exploit tools like the *Unreal Engine 5*, a game design platform from Epic Games, creators of *Fortnite*. In fact: "there are now businesses that sell fake people" (Hill, 2020). Engineer Philip Wang used NVDIA graphics to "create an endless stream of fake portraits." Trained on a dataset of real people, the algorithm uses a generative adversarial network (GAN) to create new ones (Vincent, 2019) and test them on itself. "I have it dream up a random face every two seconds, and display that to the world in a scalable fashion," Wang said (Gault, 2019). Musician Kendrick Lamarr used 'deepfake' versions of himself as OJ Simpson, Will Smith and Kanye West in his 2022 video *The Heart Part 5*.
- Metahumans are already used in advertising. There is a content tool for putting metahuman faces on background people in footage. Neural filters in Adobe *Photoshop* enable expression changes on photos of real people – turning a frown into a smile.
- Synthetic faces are more trusted by consumers than real ones. Researchers in Lancaster, UK looked at "weaponized," AI-created images in disinformation. They found they "have passed through the uncanny valley," and are both indistinguishable from, and more trustworthy than actual people (Nightingale and Farid, 2022).
- Aside from entertainment and marketing, this has implications for information wars. On 16 March 2022, a deepfake video appeared of Ukraine's President Zelensky apparently surrendering – an early use of the technology in war. Social media company Meta collaborated with Michigan State University to create a

way of reverse-engineering deepfakes, to "reveal identifying characteristics of the machine learning model that created it" (Vincent, 2021).

- AI-created synthetic faces were also found by a Stanford University study in March 2022 being used at scale for *LinkedIn* marketing – outward-bound bots deployed by lead generation agencies, even without the knowledge of the firms hiring them. *LinkedIn* removed 15 million fake accounts in the first six months of 2021 alone (Bond, 2022).

- Synthetic voices are used to automatically revoice podcasts into 119 other languages (Spangler, 2022), or add statements that the guests did not say in the studio recording or documentary – famously lines of speech from the deceased chef Anthony Bourdain (BBC, 2021) (see Chapter 19). Text-to-speech tools achieve realism with just a few minutes training on the real voice (DeepMind, 2016). Actors' unions are already complaining that they are losing voice over work and that their voices have been used to create new lines of speech which they have never said (Vallance, 2022).

- In film, AI systems can read hundreds of film scripts at speed to work out which will be a hit, basing their assessment on how well the story beats and character profiles map to the box office performance of past films (Cinelytic, 2021).

- In music, a similar tool tests new songs against databases of past hits for which single to release (Hitlab, 2021). An AI trained on Beethoven samples finished his unfinished tenth symphony (Hall, 2021), one of hundreds of such projects spanning all kinds of music. AI has also 'created' piano music from Bach and Chopin (DeepMind, 2016) and programmed 24-hour a day radio stations that play nothing but instantly composed heavy metal or free jazz (see Chapter 15). AI is no pass card to creative integrity. In August 2022, Capital Records signed 'AI robot' rapper FN Meka, who had amassed a 10.3 million followers on *TikTok* – but, after accusations of racial stereotyping, rescinded the deal (Mustafa, 2022).

- AI has revolutionised photography and design. Graphics chip-maker NVIDIA's 2022 *Instant NeRF* uses a neural network to turn off-the-cuff still photos into a three dimensional, fly-through video. Neural networks make a hobbyist into a credible *manga* animator, through Google's *Giga Manga*, using machine learning trained on 140,000 images.

- AI creates fake landscapes. NVIDIA's text-to-image feature *GauGAN*, turns a single sentence into extraordinary photorealistic imagery, trained with 10 million landscape pictures. "The researchers used a neural network that learns the connection between words and the visuals they correspond to like 'winter,' 'foggy' or 'rainbow'" (Salian, 2021).

So can AI not only help creatives, but itself be viewed as 'creative?'

There is a sequence in the 2017 film *AlphaGo*, the story of a match between Lee Sedol, player of the board game *Go*, and a DeepMind computer program. The AI plays a move (Move 37) which observers find shockingly left-field. Sedol says this changes his perception of how computers might innovate: "I thought *AlphaGo* was based on probability calculation, and that it was merely a machine. But when I saw this move I changed my mind. Surely *AlphaGo* is creative."

However, many believe that AI is not currently 'creative' in the conventionally understood sense of the term: it is a statistical system able to determine the most likely next note or word in a sequence. In order for an AI system to create content, it must have training data; it must have prior access to our own creative material. As Bob Dylan sang in *Talking World War III Blues*: "I'll let you be in my dream, if you let me be in yours."

AI/human collaboration

AI is integrated into the fabric of media production and distribution. There is a "tango," between human and AI to create optimal outcomes and experience (Prescott, 2022). Combined human and AI insights produce leaps of creativity which neither can achieve alone.

- "The magic happens when you crash the technology into domain specific expertise" says one government official, involved with driving the UK's Artificial Intelligence development.
- Perry Nightingale, Senior VP of Creative AI at WPP, the word's biggest marketing agency, delivered this to the debate: "This technology is not at its most powerful when it is replacing humans. Its true power lies in amplifying and informing what we do. I believe the human-machine symbiosis will be the next great partnership, much like the advances in computer and electricity have been revolutionary. We will all be empowered to do the most inspiring work imaginable, with tools and insights that would have been inconceivable a decade ago. Over half of this quote was written by AI."
- That AI system was *GPT-3*, an Autoregressive Language Model, from Californian research company Open AI which in 2022 underpinned many of the applications of AI in the creative industries.

Implications of AI

How AI in the media is organised and deployed matters economically, to societies and the collective psyche.

Media informs our creative imagination, because we each spend an average of 482 minutes per day watching and reading it (Statista, 2022).

AI is creating an entirely new layer of modern corporate risk. Companies now need (like Microsoft and the BBC) policies around responsible use of AI, Metahumans and synthetic voices, measures to protect the integrity of training data sets, mitigate bias and deal with the risks from content misappropriation. An executive with one company said it had to be careful in deploying AI-created characters, for fear it could be argued in a court action around copyright that since the algorithms that created these assets were trained on third party data, the company could not even own its characters, or stop them being used by other games.

All of this will be explored in this book. But the story begins earlier – in the 1990s – with the arrival of the internet, and digital transformation.

Digital transformation

The tools of the digital age – increasing computer processing power, and the internet – changed the media industry in fundamental ways even before AI became commonplace. "Software is eating the world in all sectors. In the future every company will become a software company," said leading venture capitalist Marc Andreessen.

- In the 30 years from 1990 to 2020, typical CPU (central processing unit) speeds improved by a factor of over a million.
- An optimisation problem that took 26,000 years to solve on a 1991 computer can now be solved in less than a second (Mak, 2022).

In media, digital transformation meant disruption to the source, and delivery, of the content we consume. Twentieth-century media verticals – music, TV and publishing – had unique technologies and suppliers. Music was on vinyl, magazines on paper, TV on TV sets. In the twenty-first century, the genre boundaries vanished into pixels, "with increasing technical overlap of devices, components, and software" (Noam, 2019). Music, text, TV and games are all now seen on smartphones.

- By 2020, 85% adults in the UK used a smartphone: "the device most likely to go online," (OFCOM, 2021) Smartphone usage in less-developed countries leap-frogged earlier technology to new devices.
- Now 2.8 billion of the world's 3 billion gamers play on smartphones (Wijman, 2021). A smartphone can shoot a documentary or record an album, play a video game, and distribute to a global audience.
- Even professional disruptors have been taken by surprise by the smartphone. One social media executive observed that *Facebook* started in 2004, was one of the most successful start-ups in history, yet eight years in, was already struggling to keep up: "In 2012, 0% of *Facebook*'s revenues were on mobile."
- The Metaverse is not here yet – but 700 million people per month already engage with augmented reality on their smartphones, via *TikTok* and *Snapchat*.

Tech creating new players in media

Technology disruption also changed management and valuation in media businesses, switching users partially from national commercial TV to global streamers – *Amazon Prime Video, Disney+*. It changed our physical relationship with music, from analogue to streaming via chaotic interim stages, during which the industry was halved. It changed the paradigm of video game play from a solid unit to global, networked, real time, multiplayer, proto-Metaverse games, like *Call of Duty* (2020s).

- Technology created new, global media industry businesses – in *Netflix* (market capitalisation $105 billion, October 2022), *Facebook*, which became *Meta* ($375 billion), in *Alibaba* ($229 billion) and *Spotify* ($17 billion). (Those valuations fluctuated wildly in 2022.)
- Tech interventions amounted to a brutal cull of legacy brands: the *New York Times* went from national newspaper to global online media giant with 10 million subscribers, more than at the apogee of newsprint. But companies that didn't adapt to exponential technology shifts, like the regional newspaper publishing industry, saw substantial decline (Azhar, 2021). Financial value was destroyed amongst cinema exhibitors, with $2.17 billion of value destroyed in a single set of corporate results (Vlessing, 2020).
- Tech created new products of global scale and reach. In March 2022, the game *Fortnite* raised $36 million for victims of the war in Ukraine – in a single day.

New forms of content

Digital transformation did not simply change the media as a business. It also changed the distribution of cultural conversation. In the UK, digital news supplanted *The Sun* as the town crier of election victories in the UK. In the US, digital-first brands dislodged *People Magazine* as the printed source of celebrity truth, through refocus of the global public's attention onto the scrolling, user-arbitrated news feeds of *TikTok*, *Facebook*, *Twitter* and *Instagram*.

These changes changed the DNA of the media, and how content was processed. "For a long time, media management had a strong reliance on experience and gut feeling rather than numbers and analytical formulas" (Noam, 2019). Films, books and TV shows were commissioned on an individual's instinct. But in place of gut feel came analytics. What matters in the 2020s is data – how firms obtain, organise, analyse, monetise and, most interesting of all, combine it with human creativity.

And in data, the most powerful analytical tool is AI.

Artificial Intelligence

In a second substantial tide of digital transformation, which impacted the media from the second decade of the twenty-first century, the media business model is being radically changed. Adaptation is accelerated by the massive opportunities offered by Artificial Intelligence.

AI is the secret sauce behind many category winners – *YouTube* with its market-leading video recommendation engine, Microsoft's *LinkedIn* business connections, or data-driven newspaper sites like the *Financial Times*.

AI offers edit systems, music recording software, real-time translation, text-to-video editing, visual effects, dynamic optimisation, virtual studios, distribution and bandwidth-management algorithms, video game engines and many more tools. All will be explored in this book.

Real-time insights

AI is a broad term, referring to technologies and techniques like deep learning/neural networks, computer vision and natural language processing (see Chapter 4). Their impact is upending not just media, but almost all industries.

Why is that? Because AI accelerates real-time insights, and discovers correlations and relationships too arcane for the human eye – like back-tracing hospital CT scans at scale to understand signs of cancer in patients years before conventional techniques would see it. And AI rapidly automates tasks hitherto done by humans – categorising millions of animal photos collected in the field by conservationists, or reading the faces of dogs to help them pick out treats on a Brazilian pet shop website (Hogarth, 2020).

For this introductory chapter, we will consider AI in each of the four stages of the media value creation process (development, production, distribution and monetisation) and then some of the limits and ethical drawbacks.

AI and development

At the development stage, the point where content and ideas are devised, AI is embedded in the media industry.

- Mark Zuckerberg, founder of *Facebook*, said: "Every time you get a recommendation or search for something or even take a photo on a phone, there is machine learning in the background" (Meta, 2022).
- AI-driven *Google AutoDraw* helps people use to turn their bad sketches into helpful icons. Midjourney or Open AI's *DALL E 2* tools create photography or facsimile designs and paintings in huge varieties of styles, from simple phrases: a raccoon in a space suit, a delivery cyclist in the style of Mondrian. Meta's Makeavideo.studio (released September 2022) did the same function but with video.
- In photographic creativity, AI is being used by almost everyone on earth. In 2020, 1.43 trillion photos were taken, of which 90% were shot on smartphones (Canning, 2020). The iPhone uses an on-device neural network to classify them (Apple, 2017).
- In music, AI gives every individual uniquely tailored song selections (*Spotify*) (Tiffany, 2019). Or it performs brand new ones, in any style from Sinatra to death metal (Robertson, 2020). The music start-up Brainrap marries music to neuroscience with natural language processing algorithms in its *iRap* software, which suggest words to would-be rappers based on rhythm, meaning and rhyme (Faber, 2022).
- In film, AI forecasts box office and offers marketing strategies (Kim, 2021) and AI-driven emotion-decoding software predicts audience behaviour. Disney used it to audience-test *Star Wars: The Force Awakens*. Niche companies Affectiva and HireVue used it to test user opinions of cars (Murgia, 2021). AI creativity leaks from the media to other industries.

- In Broadway theatre, natural language processing (NLP) tool *GPT-3* generates automated text articles at scale, providing a search-optimised landing point for every commonly used query more cost efficiently than humans. Because the theatre performance dates that it was promoting were a couple of months in the future, the AI idiosyncratically redrafted the plot of *A Christmas Carol* to the future as well. "This time the tale is told through the eyes of a cyborg named 'Scrooge' and the ghost of his future self." (A human spotted it before it went live, but it could have made a good play.) The NLP was also further optimised for sentiment analysis so that it could even match the mood of the person posing the question (Petrova, 2022).
- A practical benefit of AI in creativity is tenacity. "Computers don't get embarrassed. They can do uninhibited ideation. They can work all night" (Bell, 2022).

AI and content ownership

AI changes the bargain between artist and audience.

- When, in 1966, Paul McCartney wrote the *Beatles* song *Yesterday*, he had the idea in a dream. "I went round to people in the music business and asked them whether they had ever heard it before." (The song has so far earned over $30 million.) Today, a new song might be created using an AI tool trained on a million others, and containing creative DNA in the source code rather than a single writer's imagination. This confuses rights ownership far beyond the kind of concerns McCartney might have had.
- The Spanish artist Picasso said: "Good artists copy, great artists steal." That view prefigured the debate around AI and creativity. Algorithms are trained on datasets with imperfect ownership credentials – in music, synthetic humans and natural language processing – and that creates challenges with their output.
- Some in the field of 'computational creativity' have challenged the idea that only biological entities (humans) could create great content, rather than AI-driven ones. (The idea that only humans can be creative has been called 'carbon fascism.')

One solution to the copyright challenge around AI-facilitated content could be to give the content's ownership to the algorithm's creator. "Only the investor will have the exclusive right to tweak the algorithm and/or use and exploit a product design generated by the algorithm" (Leupold, 2021). The problem is that this will give power to the few tech companies able to innovate AI tools at scale.

- Identifying the author of content is challenging when an algorithm is trained on a public dataset of a million faces, or every comment ever made on *Reddit*.
- As one court held in the UK in a case between two newspapers: "It is hence ill-founded to treat the algorithm the same way as a simple pen and 'to suggest that, if you write your work with a pen, it is the pen which is the author of the work

rather than the person who drives the pen'" (OFCOM, 2019). (The case was *Express Newspapers plc v. Liverpool Daily Post & Echo* in 1985.) Application of this logic would put the intellectual property (IP) into the source of the training data rather than the composer of the algorithm.

- Oxford academics describe a future of classics "divided between those written only by humans and those written collaboratively, by humans and some software, or maybe just by software. It may be necessary to update the rules for the Pulitzer Prize and the Nobel Prize in literature" (Floridi and Chiriatti, 2020).

- This field is work in progress; copyright infrastructure is being adapted in Europe to encompass input, even authorship, of AI. IP problems with AI-driven content creation will be high profile in the 2020s.

AI and media production

When content ideas are produced, AI impacts process and scale. Examples are readily available.

- 'Adtech' firms use AI-driven 'dynamic content optimisation' tools to serve a thousand different versions of a pizza advert to individual social feeds, by A/B testing variants of image and text to match the likes of individual users. One e-commerce producer said that in 2021 they produced 23,757 pieces of video content.

- Visual search uses computer vision/object recognition (an AI technology) to make matching images to goods easier in e-commerce. By not relying on human-added metatags, a system can recognise the video itself and speed up shopping. On *Snapchat*, users reverse photo-search products via Amazon. A survey of millennial internet users in the US and UK carried out by ViSenze found over 60% of users liked it (Chadha, 2019).

- Deepfake technology can create commercials featuring stars too busy to act. In 2020, streamer *Hulu* made an advert with NBA and hockey stars. "The faces of those stars were superimposed onto body doubles using deepfake tech. The algorithm was trained on footage of the players, captured over Zoom" (Heaven, 2020). The same technology could be used to create new movies with legacy film stars, licensed by their estates – say, James Dean or Sean Connery. The technique is also being used to create 'fake news' in war, and newsrooms like *The Washington Post* now have specialists using visual forensics to spot them (Izadi, 2022).

- Editing tool *Descript* lets users edit video simply by dragging and dropping AI-transcribed text, rather than more laboriously finding video frames – a pivotal workflow change to the global production industry. Emotion selection can be added, letting an editor ask the system for 'a cutaway of an actor looking angry,' without watching or categorising the rushes first.

- At Oxford, an AI tool, the *Megatron Transformer*, 'debated' with whether it was itself ethical. Taking one side it said: "I see a clear path to a future where AI is used to create something that is better than the best human beings." Switching

- sides it said: "AI will never be ethical ... the only way to avoid an AI arms race is to have no AI at all" (Stephen, 2021).
- In the written word, AI system *GPT-3* finished the opening paragraph of the Jane Austen novel *Sanditon*. It produced a reasonable facsimile of Austen's style – though it has "no understanding of the semantics and contexts of the request, but only a syntactic (statistical) capacity to associate words" (Floridi and Chiriatti, 2020). *GPT-3* also rewrote *Harry Potter* in the style of Hemingway: "Yet the Dementor's Kiss killed nothing. Death didn't leave him less dead than he had been a second before," as well as Bram Stoker (programmerChilli, 2020).
- AI can execute coding for media projects too. *GPT-3* tool Codex, trained on code bases like GitHub, turns natural language requests into functioning code (Bell, 2022).
- As AI advances, it could feed creative endeavour. One leading executive at a major technology company said in a June 2022 interview at Oxford University: "We love movies, we love superheroes. So we ... brought a massive AI model that we had released in 2020 to look at how they could think about different endings."
- The same executive asked whether, because human creativity will be more expensive than AI, it could actually become rarer.
- And they considered the dramatic pace of change as AI systems scale up: "In 2015, when they announced [neural network] *ResNet* with 60 million parameters, it seemed like a lot. Now, in 2022, they are doing the Megatron Turing model, which is half a trillion parameters."
- What's coming next? 'Quantum computers will see through the walls and be truly creative.'

AI and media distribution

After media content of any kind is produced – from online ads to TV drama series – it must be delivered to the user. AI has had a huge and growing impact on almost every dimension of distribution.

For streamers, AI tools optimise fibre optic networks to send as much HD content as possible without buffering, which spoils the user experience. A media textbook states: "All sectors are conditioned by the same underlying rules, are affected by changes in distribution technologies at approximately the same time" (Vogel, 2020). But in the AI media economy, it was variable adoption rates by platforms which created the defining advantage for streaming category leaders. *Netflix*'s market-leading recommendation tools were its competitive advantage over the many European and US broadcasters in customer recruitment during the period 2015–21. And *Netflix* said in 2016 that it saved $1 billion per year through reduced customer churn, simply by focussing on the first 60–90 seconds of a user's search for a show to watch (OFCOM, 2019).

The sheer scope of AI in media distribution is even outlined by *Netflix* on its recruitment website:

Machine learning powers our recommendation algorithms. We're also using machine learning to hclp shape our catalog of movies and TV shows by learning characteristics that make content successful. We use it to optimize the production of original movies and TV shows in *Netflix*'s rapidly growing studio.

(Netflix, 2022)

Almost every element of *Netflix*'s distribution workflow, including its interaction with telecommunications providers, is AI-powered.

'Closed-loop' recommendations mean users never exit their initial selections of content. Views create training data, driving a model which makes more recommendations, all without external information (Hinkle, 2021). On *YouTube*, which distributes over a billion hours of content per day (Alphabet, 2022), AI facilitates interests and hobbies – but it can also send users down a 'rabbit hole' of radicalisation, serving 'engage and enrage' them. (Meanwhile, 'open-loop' engines – as used by the BBC – introduce new search data into the mix to avoid this issue.)

Regulation, content and algorithms

The creative and distribution power and versatility of AI is driving new challenges for both governments and individual companies; how to regulate an algorithm, or penetrate decision-making in a 'black box' AI system which does not publish why it makes its choices, even to its creator.

Firms are also spending heavily on content moderation, intervening algorithmically in the flow of materials to end users. *Facebook*'s Manipulated Media policy says not to post:

Videos that have been edited or synthesized, beyond adjustments for clarity or quality, in ways that are not apparent to an average person, and would likely mislead an average person to believe a subject of the video said words that they did not say.

(Facebook, 2021)

AI is used both to create such content, and to detect it. That one paragraph presages what media regulation will be in the 2030s, as synthetic content technologies reach the mainstream. But those technologies come loaded with their own ethical challenges: in August 2022, *Facebook*'s own *Blenderbot* conversational AI developed the habit of talking out of turn. It reportedly told *BuzzFeed* that Mark Zuckerberg, boss of parent company Meta: "is a good businessman, but his business practices are not always ethical" (Cantor, 2022).

AI and monetisation in media

The final stage of the media value chain is the one in which the firm gets paid: monetisation. Like all tools of digital advertising, the advantage AI brings to the translation of viewing and engagement into sales is that its calculating power facilitates market segmentation – not just into like-minded customers, but to individuals.

AI elucidates each user's consumption propensity (how much they want something) and the price they will pay – a transformative shift from the mass-market twentieth century commercial TV, which targeted large, society-wide cohorts. Maximising each individual's engagement, the media firm optimises the 'rental' achieved. Personalisation grows more precise, and where the user grants data by using the service – as with *Netflix* – the firm has category advantage. "AI offers more efficient options for classification and archiving of this huge vault of assets, paving the way for more precise targeting and increased revenue generation" (PWC, 2017).

- European market research showed 80% of media practitioners agreed AI would have a significant industry impact (Chan-Olmsted, 2019).
- AI helps the business functions of media. In legal there are new AI-driven suppliers across Expertise Automation (Checkbox, LogicNets, Oracle OPA) and Analytics and Prediction (LexPredict, Loom Analytics, Predictive) (Sako, 2022).

So as will be clear throughout this book, every phase of value creation in media is touched by AI. Daniel Kahneman, management thinker, said: "Provide the same information to the algorithm and to the person, and have them make predictions of judgment. And when you can make that prediction, algorithms tend to win" (Swisher, 2021).

The evolution of widespread AI adoption in media

There have been three broad phases in AI in media, which can be charted as a journey – in reverse – along the media value creation chain, the process of production and delivery of content from development to monetisation.

The first phase was from circa 2007 when AI was used in distribution and recommendation systems, for instance, with early streamers like *Netflix*.

The second phase was from circa 2017 onwards, when AI came to be really widely used in production tools, across music production as well as film and TV post-production. (It was in much earlier use in games.)

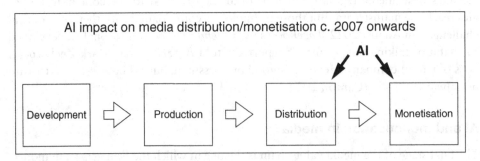

FIGURE 2.1 Initial uses of AI in late stages of media value creation

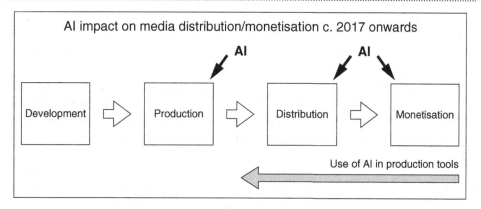

FIGURE 2.2 Subsequent use of AI in media production phase of value creation

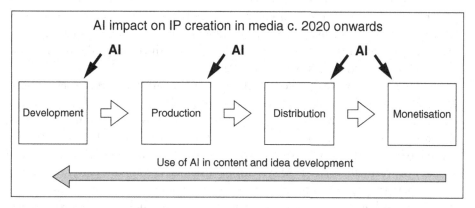

FIGURE 2.3 Coming use of AI in content development/creation phase of media value creation

The most recent phase, from circa 2020, has seen AI beginning to be used in the development of content and ideas. In the most recent adoption phase, systems like natural language processing, text to image or video, and other processes are driving the the core derivation of IP.

AI ethics and the media

AI can be valuable – but it is not the cavalry.

Artificial Intelligence tools have not reached the level of general intelligence (AGI), the quest (possibly never achieved) for an AI that as versatile as a human (see Chapter 4). AI is not self starting. It must still be designed, deployed, curated, interpreted, and sometimes protected against. AI does not yet have the malleability and inspiration of human creative intelligence, and some think it never will:

It's worth asking whether there are limits to what machine learning will be capable of, and whether there is something about the way humans think that is essential to real intelligence and not amenable to the kind of computation performed by artificial neural networks.

*(*Taylor, 2021*)*

AI is beset with challenging ethical issues, almost none comprehensively solved. Making sure the stories AI tells are fair and ethical will be one of the greatest challenges of creative media in the twenty-first century (Lucy and Bamman, 2021). Putting human values into algorithms is the priority for many AI thinkers (Christian, 2021).

- Diversity: as the annual *AI Index report* said, in 2019, 45% of US AI PhDs were white, and only 2.4% African American (Stanford, 2021). What is true in the work force, is also true of the output. MIT AI academic (and poet) Joy Buolamwini showed in her 2018 piece *AI, Ain't I A Woman* the limitations of reverse-search in major search engines. Trained on datasets of white subjects, these failed to even identify as female a number of major figures – such as Oprah Winfrey, or Sojourner Truth, the early nineteenth-century abolitionist and women's rights activist (Buolamwini, 2021).
- Bias: car insurers were accused in 2018 of bias against *Hotmail* users, simply because *Hotmail* is likely to correlate with older users (Williams, 2018). Recruitment algorithms were found to be biased towards certain applicants, because there was a historic bias in the recruitment datasets they were trained on (Gershgorn, 2018). One system was prioritising candidates who played field hockey or were called Jared. AI systems have denied credit limit parity to women, even where they earned more than their husband, most likely because those were the decisions humans had made in the past. AI has wrongly identified suspects in facial recognition, causing at least one person in the US to go to prison. Research in 2019 by Prost *et al*. showed how the training of some natural language AI systems left embedded gender biases – for instance, the automatic association of men as doctors and women as nurses.
- Black box systems: an AI algorithm to distinguish wolves from huskies in pictures worked. But it turned it all it was doing was analysing for snow in the background, as "wolves were typically photographed in snowy backgrounds" (OFCOM, 2019). Such challenges, where AI appears to achieve successful results but through unclear or irrelevant reasoning, are common, and can be problematic.
- In the media: where AI goes, ethical challenges follow. Metahumans create enormous possibilities for both creativity and deception (Hill, 2020). To mitigate the risk, some algorithm creators – like the Californian company Open AI which runs *GPT-3*, offering a natural language processing tool – only licence them to 'responsible actors.' London-based AI company DeepMind has ethicists on each team – whether it is trying to devise an AI to win an *Atari* game or build self-learning robots.

But some are more optimistic. Andrew Ng at Stanford, said: "Worrying about evil AI killer robots today is a little bit like worrying about overpopulation on the planet Mars" (Lynch, 2017).

Core questions about AI

The most meta question of all is: can AI surpass humans at creativity itself, at 'art'? Many think not, that art is something only we can do.

"Creativity is one of the defining features of human beings," said Harvard philosopher Sean Dorrance Kelly.

> The capacity for genuine creativity, the kind of creativity that updates our understanding of the nature of being, that changes the way we understand what it is to be beautiful or good or true – that capacity is at the ground of what it is to be human.
>
> *(Kelly, 2019)*

This book will explore that idea.

Class discussion questions

- Can AI be creative? What examples can you find of AI-driven creativity?
- If a brand new song, in the style of Harry Styles, is written by an AI system, who owns it?
- Why is AI-created content at risk of bias? What can be done to mitigate those risks?
- Look at the example quoted above where *Netflix* lists on its jobs site some of the ways it is deploying machine learning to improve its systems. Find another media company in your country which is using AI tools, and examine the advantage they are potentially achieving from doing so.

BIBLIOGRAPHY

Alphabet. (2022) Alphabet announces fourth quarter and fiscal year 2021 results. [online] Available at: https://abc.xyz/investor/static/pdf/2021Q4_alphabet_earnings_release.pdf?cache=d72fc76 [Accessed 16 August 2022].

Apple. (2017) An *on-device deep neural network for face detection*. [online] Available at: https://machinelearning.apple.com/research/face-detection [Accessed 16 August 2022].

Azhar, A. (2021) *Exponential: how to bridge the gap between technology and society*. London: Penguin.

BBC. (2021) *AI narration of chef Anthony Bourdain's voice sparks row*. [online] Available at: www.bbc.co.uk/news/technology-57842514 [Accessed 16 August 2022].

Bell, J. (2022) *Lecture on AI and Creativity. Diploma in AI for Business*. Said Business School, Oxford University.

Bond, S. (2022) That smiling LinkedIn profile face might be a computer-generated fake. *NPR*. [online] Available at: https://text.npr.org/1088140809 [Accessed 16 August 2022].

Buolamwini, J. (2021) *Poet of code*. [online] Available at: www.poetofcode.com [Accessed 16 August 2022].

Canning, J. (2020) 1.43 trillion photos were taken in 2020 but how many of them were captured on our mobile phones? *Your Mobile*. [online] Available at: www.buymobiles.net/blog/1-43-trillion-photos-were-taken-in-2020-but-how-many-of-them-were-captured-on-our-mobile-phones/ [Accessed 16 August 2022].

Cantor, M. (2022). Meta's new AI chatbot can't stop bashing Facebook. *The Guardian*. [online] Available at: www.theguardian.com/technology/2022/aug/09/blenderbot-meta-chatbot-facebook [Accessed 16 August 2022].

Chadha, R. (2019) Visual search is poised for mainstream adoption. *Insider Intelligence*. [online] Available at: www.emarketer.com/content/visual-search-is-perched-on-the-cusp-of-mainstream-adoption [Accessed 16 August 2022].

Chan-Olmsted, S. M. (2019) A review of Artificial Intelligence adoptions in the media industry. *International Journal on Media Management*, 21(3–4), 193–215. doi.org/10.1080/14241277.2019.1695619

Cinelytic. (2021) *Cinelytic*. [online] Available at: www.cinelytic.com [Accessed 16 August 2022].

Connock, A. and Stephen, A. (2021) We invited an AI to debate its own ethics in the Oxford Union – what it said was startling. *The Conversation*. [online] Available at: https://theconversation.com/we-invited-an-ai-to-debate-its-own-ethics-in-the-oxford-union-what-it-said-was-startling-173607 [Accessed 16 August 2022].

DeepMind. (2016) WaveNet: a generative model for raw audio. *DeepMind*. [online] Available at: https://deepmind.com/blog/article/wavenet-generative-model-raw-audio [Accessed 16 August 2022].

Faber, T. (2022) Rapper's delight or weapons-grade nonsense? The app that uses AI to help MCs bust a rhyme. *The Guardian*. [online] Available at: www.theguardian.com/music/2022/aug/23/ai-rap-technology-music?CMP=Share_iOSApp_Other [Accessed 29 August 2022].

Facebook. (2021) Community standards. *Meta*. [online] Available at: www.facebook.com/communitystandards/manipulated_media [Accessed 29 August 2022].

Floridi, L. and Chiriatti, M. (2020) *GPT-3*: its nature, scope, limits, and consequences. *Minds and Machines*, 30(4), 681–94. doi.org/10.1007/s11023-020-09548-1

Gault, M. (2019) This website uses AI to generate the faces of people who don't exist. *Vice Motherboard*. [online] Available at: www.vice.com/en/article/7xn4wy/this-website-uses-ai-to-generate-the-faces-of-people-who-dont-exist [Accessed 16 August 2022].

Gershgorn, D. (2018) Companies are on the hook if their hiring algorithms are biased. *Quartz*. [online] Available at: https://qz.com/1427621/companies-are-on-the-hook-if-their-hiring-algorithms-are-biased/ [Accessed 16 August 2022].

Hall, S. A. (2021) Beethoven's unfinished Tenth Symphony completed by artificial intelligence. *Classic FM*. [online] Available at: www.classicfm.com/composers/beethoven/unfinished-tenth-symphony-completed-by-artificial-intelligence/ [Accessed 16 August 2022].

Hao, K. and Heaven, W. D. (2020) The year deepfakes went mainstream. *MIT Technology Review*. [online] Available at: www.technologyreview.com/2020/12/24/1015380/best-ai-deepfakes-of-2020/ [Accessed 16 August 2022].

Hill, K. (2020) Designed to deceive: do these people look real to you? *New York Times*, 21 November. [online] Available at: www.nytimes.com/interactive/2020/11/21/science/artificial-intelligence-fake-people-faces.html [Accessed 16 August 2022].

Hinkle, D. (2021) How streaming services use algorithms. *Arts Management & Technology Laboratory*. [online] Available at: https://amt-lab.org/blog/2021/8/algorithms-in-streaming-services [Accessed 16 August 2022].

Hitlab. (2021) Hitlab. [online] Available at: www.hitlab.com [Accessed 16 August 2022].

Hogarth. (2020) Petz. [online] Available at: www.hogarth.com/case-study/pet-commerce-award-winning-digital-first [Accessed 22 February 2022].

Izadi, E. (2022) This is how journalists figure out if all those Ukraine videos are real. *The Washington Post*, 2 March.

Jordan, M. I. (2019) Artificial Intelligence: the revolution hasn't happened yet. *Harvard Data Science Review*, 1(1). doi.org/10.1162/99608f92.f06c6e61

Kelly, S. D. (2019) A philosopher argues that an AI can't be an artist. *MIT Technology Review*. [online] Available at: www.technologyreview.com/2019/02/21/239489/a-philosopher-argues-that-an-ai-can-never-be-an-artist/ [Accessed 16 August 2022].

Kemp, S. (2022) Digital 2022: global overview report. *Datareportal*. [online] Available at: https://datareportal.com/reports/digital-2022-global-overview-report [Accessed 16 August 2022].

Kim, D. H. (2021) What types of films are successful at the box office? Predicting opening weekend and non-opening gross earnings of films. *Journal of Media Business Studies*, 18(3), 214–34. doi.org/10.1080/16522354.2021.1887438

Leupold, A. (2021) Are AI-generated inventions patentable? *Sifted*. [online] Available at: https://sifted.eu/articles/ai-generated-inventions-patentable/ [Accessed 23 August 2022].

Lucy, L. and Bamman, D. (2021) Gender and representation bias in *GPT-3* generated stories. *Proceedings of the 3rd Workshop on Narrative Understanding*, 48–55. doi:10.18653/v1/2021.nuse-1.5

Lynch, S. (2017) Andrew Ng: why AI is the new electricity. *Stanford Business*. [online] Available at: www.gsb.stanford.edu/insights/andrew-ng-why-ai-new-electricity [Accessed 16 August 2022].

Mak, H.-Y. (2022) *Lecture for Diploma in AI for Business*. Said Business School, University of Oxford, 21 May.

Meta. (2022) Inside the lab: building for the Metaverse with AI. *Meta*. [online] Available at: https://about.fb.com/news/2022/02/inside-the-lab-building-for-the-metaverse-with-ai/ [Accessed 29 August 2022].

Murgia, M. (2021) Emotion recognition: can AI detect human feelings from a face? *Financial Times*, 12 May.

Mustafa, F. (2022) Meet FN Meka as virtual rapper lands major deal with Capitol Records. *HITC*. [online] Available at: www.hitc.com/en-gb/2022/08/23/meet-fn-meka-as-virtual-rapper-lands-major-deal-with-capitol-records/ [Accessed 29 August 2022].

Narang, S. (2022) Pathways Language Model (PaLM): scaling to 540 billion parameters for breakthrough performance. *Google AI blog*. [blog] 4 April. Available at: https://ai.googleblog.com/2022/04/pathways-language-model-palm-scaling-to.html [Accessed 16 August 2022].

Netflix. (2022) Machine learning: learning how to entertain the world. *Netflix Research*. [online] Available at: https://research.netflix.com/research-area/machine-learning [Accessed 16 August 2022].

Nightingale, S. J. and Farid, H. (2022) AI-synthesized faces are indistinguishable from real faces and more trustworthy. *Proceedings of the National Academy of Sciences*, 119(8), e2120481119. doi:10.1073/pnas.2120481119

Noam, E. M. (2019) *Media and digital management*. London: Palgrave Macmillan.

OFCOM. (2021) *Adults' media use and attitudes 2021: interactive report*. [online] Available at: www.ofcom.org.uk/research-and-data/media-literacy-research/adults/adults-media-use-and-attitudes/interactive-tool-2021 [Accessed 29 August 2022].

OFCOM. (2019) Use of AI in *online content moderation*. [online] Available at: www.ofcom.org.uk/__data/assets/pdf_file/0028/157249/cambridge-consultants-ai-content-moderation.pdf [Accessed 16 August 2022].

Petrova, M. (2022) *Places dot*. [interview] 30 March.

Prescott, S. M. (2022) Choreographing human-machine collaboration: Spotify's Sidney Madison Prescott. Me, Myself and AI. [podcast] Available at: https://sloanreview.mit.edu/audio/choreographing-human-machine-collaboration-spotifys-sidney-madison-prescott/ [Accessed 16 August 2022].

programmerChilli. (2020) Using *GPT-3* to generate Harry Potter in the style of various famous authors. *Reddit*. [online] Available at: www.reddit.com/r/MachineLearning/comments/hbr6kp/r_using_gpt3_to_generate_harry_potter_in_the/ [Accessed 16 August 2022].

Prost, F., Thain, N. and Bolukbasi, T. (2019) Debiasing embeddings for reduced gender bias in text classification. Proceedings of the First Workshop on Gender Bias in Natural Language Processing, 69–75. doi:10.18653/v1/W19-3810

PWC. (2017) Sizing the prize: what's the real value of AI for your business and how can you capitalise? *PWC*. [online] Available at: www.pwc.com.au/government/pwc-ai-analysis-sizing-the-prize-report.pdf [Accessed 29 August 2022].

PWC. (2021) *UK edition: entertainment & media outlook 2021–2025*. [online] Available at: www.pwc.co.uk/industries/technology-media-and-telecommunications/insights/entertainment-media-outlook.html [Accessed 29 August 2022].

Robertson, D. (2020) 'It's the screams of the damned!' The eerie AI world of deepfake music. *The Guardian*, 9 November.

Sako, P. M. (2022) Lecture *to Oxford Diploma in AI for Business*. Said Business School, University of Oxford, 20 May.

Salian, I. (2021) 'Paint Me a Picture': NVIDIA research shows GauGAN AI art demo now responds to words. *NVDIA*. [blog] Available at: https://blogs.nvidia.com/blog/2021/11/22/gaugan2-ai-art-demo/ [Accessed 16 August 2022].

Spangler, T. (2022) iHeartMedia will translate English Podcasts into other languages using Veritone's synthetic voices. *Variety*. [online] Available at: https://variety.com/2022/digital/news/iheartmedia-podcast-translate-synthetic-voices-veritone-1235184677/ [Accessed 16 August 2022].

Stanford. (2021) Artificial intelligence index report 2021. *Stanford University: Human-Centered Artificial Intelligence*. [online] Available at: https://aiindex.stanford.edu/wp-content/uploads/2021/11/2021-AI-Index-Report_Master.pdf [Accessed 16 August 2022].

Statista. (2022) Average time spent per day with digital media in the United States from 2011 to 2022. *Statista*. [online] Available at: www.statista.com/statistics/262340/daily-time-spent-with-digital-media-according-to-us-consumsers/ [Accessed 16 August 2022].

Swisher, K. (2021) Daniel Kahneman says humans are noisy. (He's Not talking about volume.). *Sway*. [podcast] Available at: www.nytimes.com/2021/05/17/opinion/sway-kara-swisher-daniel-kahneman.html [Accessed 29 August 2022].

Taylor, P. (2021) Insanely complicated, hopelessly inadequate. *London Review of Books*, 21 January.

Tiffany, K. (2019) Spotify's most personalized playlist is now for sale to brands. *Vox*, 11 January.

Vallance, C. (2022) Actors launch campaign against AI 'show stealers.' *BBC News*. [online] Available at: www.bbc.co.uk/news/technology-61166272 [Accessed 29 August 2022].

Vincent, J. (2019) ThisPersonDoesNotExist.com uses AI to generate endless fake faces. *The Verge*. [online] Available at: www.theverge.com/tldr/2019/2/15/18226005/ai-generated-fake-people-portraits-thispersondoesnotexist-stylegan [Accessed 29 August 2022].

Vincent, J. (2021) Hollywood is quietly using AI to help decide which movies to make. *The Verge*. [online] Available at: www.theverge.com/2019/5/28/18637135/hollywood-ai-film-decision-script-analysis-data-machine-learning [Accessed 29 August 2022].

Vincent, J. (2021) Facebook develops new method to reverse-engineer deepfakes and track their source. *The Verge*. [online] Available at: www.theverge.com/2021/6/16/22534690/facebook-deepfake-detection-reverse-engineer-ai-model-hyperparameters [Accessed 16 August 2022].

Vlessing, E. (2020) AMC theatres discloses $2.17 billion quarterly loss amid pandemic closure. *The Hollywood Reporter*, 9 June.

Vogel, H. L. (2020) *Entertainment industry economics: a guide for financial analysis*. 10th edn. Cambridge: Cambridge University Press.

Waters, R. (2022) The big tech players are muscling into A. *Financial Times*, 14 April.

Wijman, T. (2021) The games market and beyond in 2021: the year in numbers. *Newzoo*. [online] Available at: https://newzoo.com/insights/articles/the-games-market-in-2021-the-year-in-numbers-esports-cloud-gaming/ [Accessed 16 August 2022].

Williams, Z. (2018) A sign that you're not keeping up: the trouble with Hotmail in 2018. *The Guardian*, 23 January.

CHAPTER 3

Media business models

A four-stage value creation model for each media segment – Development, Production, Distribution and Monetisation

....

THE EVOLVING DEFINITION OF MEDIA BUSINESSES

"A producer is a rare, paradoxical genius – hard-headed, soft-hearted, cautious, reckless, a hopeful innocent in fair weather, a stern pilot in stormy weather, a mathematician who prefers to ignore the laws of mathematics and trust intuition." So said theatrical producer Oscar Hammerstein II (1895–1960).

He might have added an additional requirement: paranoia.

- In a 2020 survey of 350 senior media executives worldwide, over a third said that "without reinvention, their company will no longer exist in five years" (Harrison, 2020). "Increasing fluidity of companies across sectors" is redesigning the media. Today, content producers work in e-commerce, publishers are information services providers, and ad agencies are content creators.

This evolving landscape is the starting point for this book.

- In Germany, the phrase "Irgendwas mit Medien" means "something with media" and is used to joke about people thinking non-specifically about going into film or music. Segments in modern media are so unstable that the catch-all phrase "seems to perfectly describe the state of mind a prospective laborer needs to have to succeed" (Riedl, 2019).

Film and TV, once different industries, now compete on the same streaming platforms. Meanwhile, their financial models, clients, technologies and ownership are all converging into a boiling goulash of universal competition.

DOI: 10.4324/9781003213611-4

Blurring the lines between consumers and professional media

Media companies continue to create and distribute content – whether that is TV, radio, recorded music or a fast-growth newcomer sector, like the $1.35 billion Esports industry (Guttmann, 2022).

- But so too does every one of the world's 4.95 billion mobile phone users (Wijman, 2021) who spend at least 40% of their lives looking at screens (OFCOM, 2020).
- The audience are now both consumers and creators of material (Hess, 2014) empowered by global distribution far beyond the reach and velocity of a professional, big-city 1970s newspaper.
- A clip from, say, the 2022 Ukraine war reached global audiences minutes after an event via *Twitter*. It would have taken a day for a news crew to get it on national TV in the 1980s, or weeks in the 1940s for a picture to reach US newspapers.
- An effective viral video can, in the 2020s, easily accumulate 50 million viewers in 24 hours – the population of Spain. Spain's top newspaper, *El Pais*, would in 1980 have taken several weeks to reach the same audience.

Life cycle of any media project

There are four stages of value creation: Development, Production, Distribution and Monetisation.

In this sequence, an idea for a TV drama series is conceived, made, streamed and paid for – or a game is conceptualised, developed, published and monetised with in-game upgrades.

Stages in this model can overlap, or even appear somewhat out of sequence. They can loop back on each other in a 'flywheel' effect, in which more distribution creates more sales, thus creating yet more distribution. But all the key stages will be present with any media project, from a performance by the *LA Philharmonic Orchestra* of Mahler's *Sixth Symphony*, to a televised *Muay Thai* tournament in Bangkok; development (the tournament idea) production (the fight on the night), distribution (broadcast of the fight) and monetisation (tickets, pay TV fees and advertising revenue).

This introductory chapter discusses general principles of each of the four stages of value creation model. Figure 3.1 below describes the model graphically, with inputs (along the top) at each stage, and the outputs in terms of value creation (along the bottom). This model will be revisited for each category of media, providing continuity across sectors within the book as a whole.

Development stage

At the development stage, the inputs from the firm are investment of whatever resources are needed to create ideas, plus the talent required, and the brand equity of the firm in making those ideas credible. All of those stages follow a market analysis, whether formal or not, of the genre and opportunity in which the firm aims to

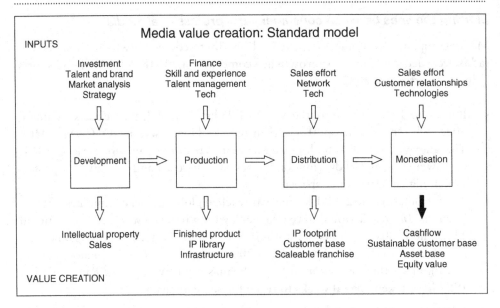

FIGURE 3.1 Mapping the business model of media sectors - a standard model throughout this book

participate. The outputs are a definable piece of intellectual property – for instance, a song, or a development slate – and sales to funders of content production.

The key starting point is creativity. "Where do you get ideas from? Inside, outside, crowd source, R&D?" asks Oxford innovation expert Marc Ventresca. "How do you turn those ideas into innovation with the potential to create value. And how do you push those innovations into the world? Do you use existing markets or build new markets?" (Ventresca, 2022). Axiomatically, translation from investment to return in media is a non-linear, and non-specific function. "Innovation is not just the idea. It's the work of moving the idea through a studied process. It requires different types of expertise. You have to do the work of a systems builder. You have to imagine the system."

Why is that relationship between what you spend on creative development and what you get in return so hard to quantify? Because as British nineteenth-century playwright Oscar Wilde said: "Genius is born – not paid."

Uncertainty of economic model in content

It has never been quite certain even *how* content is truly created – what drives inspiration, how funding can amplify creation, and what the random factors are that can get in the way.

- In 2020, *Netflix* made *The Queen's Gambit*. Head of Production, Bela Bajaria, said: "There was never any data that would have proven that a series about a female chess prodigy would have captured hearts and minds in the way *Queen's Gambit* eventually did." Making a show about 1960s chess was a creative gamble, which couldn't be fully supported by data from historic experience. But it became the network's number one show in 63 countries (Spangler, 2020). It was a creative inspiration and a business gamble, even at a company as data-driven as *Netflix*.

Value creators are not machines in a factory – but complex characters, "subject to a wide array of emotions, and expressing behaviours that at times can be quite unpredictable" (Schreiber and Rieple, 2021). Asset valuations and lifetime value equations for star talent are hard for finance directors to calculate, to their frequent frustration.

- An upset actor may refuse to come out of their trailer on a set that is costing $200,000 a day. Stars can go off the rails – like Bollywood actor Salman Khan being jailed for a hit-and-run killing (BBC, 2015) or bankable Hollywood actor Johnny Depp engaged in a damaging libel trial (Marsh, 2021).
- Audiences like familiar content, but great talent is not easily fixed in time and space. Actors refuse sequels, authors change styles even when the market would welcome more of the same. Mozart, possibly the greatest composer of all time, said: "A man of superior talent will fall to pieces if he remains forever in the same place."

ROI calculation on media investment

The lack of algebraic relationship between content investment and outcome, or the public demand for it, provides the core challenge in media businesses.

- The highest-budget film in history (*Pirate of the Caribbean: On Stranger Tides* at $378.5 million) did not generate the highest return.
- The tiny *Blair Witch Project*, with an initial budget of $35,000, earned less at the box office ($249 million) but a far higher ROI (Galloway, 2020).
- Creation can be part of an organisation's innovative "human capital," which needs curating and developing within a company to maximise its value (Malmelin and Virta, 2021).
- Creativity matters even in supposedly un-creative media sectors. An academic study found Scandinavian local newsrooms actually need creative people (Nylund, 2013).

The challenge of benchmarking creativity impedes the kind of financial transparency and visibility that investors demand.

- "What makes Shonda Rhimes' programs [like *Bridgerton*] addictive eye candy, while others never make it past the pilot stage? … If you've ever asked yourself questions such as these – even while buying tickets to the latest *Marvel* movie on *Fandango* – you've considered the murky mysteries at the root of the popular entertainment industry and the decisions that define it" (Whipple, 2019).

Tension between creatives and 'suits' in media is commonplace, institutionalised in the division between 'Church and State' in US media companies.

- At *Time Inc* magazines, leading publisher of the mid-twentieth century USA, 'Church' was the editorial side, and 'State' was advertising sales and distribution side. These departments were located on different floors. Time's editor-in-chief was "not answerable to the CEO but only to the board of directors" (Diamond, 1986). When the system was dismantled in 2014 and journalists began reporting to business executives rather than the editor-in-chief, that change was itself a news story (Sacks, 2014).

Principles of collective value creation

The solution to value generation may not just lie in the mercurial talents or perform-ance of individuals, but in the collective talents of the group.

- For CEO Reed Hastings at *Netflix* the winning formula was: "A culture that valued people over process, emphasized innovation over efficiency, and had very few controls … *Netflix* is different. We have a culture where No Rules Rules" (Hastings and Meyer, 2020). Applying the metrics and start-up philosophies of the tech industry helped management build investable and value-generative plans.
- Often quoted by tech start-ups are Peter Thiel's 7 rules (Koraza, 2021). Billionaire Thiel is a politically controversial but very successful early investor in *Paypal, Facebook* and other companies. In start-ups, he looks for factors such as breakthrough technology instead of incremental improvements, the right timing, team, distribution and a defensible market position 10 years in the future.
- But the unique dimension of media is that most content start-ups fail all of Thiel's tests. The only 'moat' around the business is creativity itself – and that is hard to benchmark, quantify or predict.

For all the difficulties in codifying creativity as a business asset, there are three standard questions that should be asked at the development stage of any creative project. This simple three-part test applies equally to a proposal for a game, a film or an album.

(1) What is the idea?
(2) Who is the creator delivering it, and what is their track record?
(3) Who is the target customer or audience, and what is the likelihood that they will buy the idea?

If a creative business can successfully answer those three questions, it has a chance to generate value.

Production stage

At the production stage in the media value creation model, the firm's inputs are the production finance, skill and experience, infrastructure and (in some cases) the new competitive advantage of AI tools necessary to deliver the project. In the case of Disney series *The Mandalorian*, this would include experienced executive input, substantial cash flow, studio space, and virtual studio knowhow. The outputs at this stage are finished creative product in the firm's IP library, and any boost to its infrastructure and talent base which will facilitate the next project.

In production volume and scale, the media industry is as efficient as any industry.

- "Every 30 seconds, a new book is published. Every hour, three new feature films are produced" (Noam, 2019).
- Every minute, 500 hours of content are uploaded to *YouTube* (Mohsin, 2021).
- In the UK, about 2.1 million people work in the creative industries, approaching 1 in 30 of the entire population (DCMS, 2019).
- In China alone, in 2021, 253 million posts were posted on a single platform, *Douyin* (*TikTok*), just on the single subject of personal growth (Ceci, 2022).

The production phase of media creation is the manufacturing process. It is the first stage in the value creation chain in which investment is required-to translate conceptual project ideas into visible media assets. That investment varies from the cost to an influencer of buying a smartphone, to the $15,000 per night necessary to put on a play in London's *West End*, to the $50,000 cost of shooting an entry-level action movie in Lagos, Nigeria, to the $165 million cost of shooting the 2021 science fiction film, *Dune*.

Many challenges associated with running a factory also apply to media; operational efficiency, process control, compliance, continuous improvement. Each segment of the media business has its own name for quality control teams; copy editors in news, producers in film, testers in video games. The function is the same: to benchmark efficient manufacture of content.

Radical shift in media industry verticals

The media industry is in constant operational reinvention. Production processes of newspapers have been through sequential revolutions (see Chapter 9). Recorded music has been transformed by successive generations of studio software (see Chapter 15), the impact of which is strong enough to define the sound and shape of compositions themselves.

In screen content, each phase of change in the production technology changes the business model itself. For instance, the 'creator' style of video production disrupted the traditional business model of reality TV (see Chapters 11 and 14). In light of this, it is vital for media firms "to develop ways to examine and better understand how and why the media industry is transforming, and … adapt to and thrive in the dynamic and disruptive operational environment" (Malmelin et al., 2021).

Change drives constant shape-shifting between media genres.

- Newspapers (say, France's leading centre right paper, *Le Figaro*) become websites, then digital news feeds.
- Video games (*Sonic the Hedgehog*, *Mortal Kombat*) become films, and *vice versa* (*Planet of the Apes: Last Frontier*).
- Toys become films (*The Lego Movie*) and films become toys (*Transformers*).
- This idea is not new. "The content of any medium is always another medium," said Canadian philosopher Marshall McLuhan (1911–80).
- A more recent academic noted: "The film *Pretty Woman* went to Broadway. And Disney's *Pirates of the Caribbean* began as a theme park attraction before becoming a movie franchise" (Vogel, 2020) – an endemic media fragmentation where "every successful form, soon after introduction, rapidly fragments into many slightly different subsidiary niches."

Defining a production methodology for intellectual property is complicated by this dynamic evolution. In sports, for instance, the primary content delivery has migrated across ten platforms in 100 years. Sports reporting began in print and migrated to radio, terrestrial TV, cable and satellite, streaming and social media, video games, Esports and now, quite possibly, the Metaverse. Each genre demands different production methodologies – even if the core product (a football match) is constant.

The imprecision of the German aphorism at the top of the chapter still applies. As much as an individual can be vaguely employed as 'something in the media,' so the media business itself requires dynamic flexibility from its companies, just for them to keep pace with its own changing platforms.

Distribution stage

At the distribution phase in the media value creation process, the firm's inputs include sales effort, its distribution network and relationships, and any technologies it can deploy for competitive advantage – like recommendation engines on streaming services. Value creation outputs are a footprint for its IP, such that it acquires traction and value in the market place, a customer base (temporary or sustainable), and a potentially scaleable franchise.

In the media business, value is principally materialised when content is consumed, not when it is made.

So without distribution – the process of transfer from the point of production (in music, often the recording studio) to the point of consumption (the listener) – media products are unseen, unheard and arguably worthless.

- *Bohemian Rhapsody* was recorded by the band *Queen* in *Rockfield Studio*, a barn on a farm near Monmouth, South Wales, in 1975. The record label, EMI, thought the song was too long and wouldn't be a hit.

- EMI's accountants may have argued that it had a modest balance sheet value as a percentage of the cash investment made to record it.
- The reality was that the song was worth more than that figure – but *Bohemian Rhapsody* demonstrated financial value only when pressed as records and played on radio – when distributed in other words.
- The total earnings of the title may now have topped $1 billion, depending on whether the $911.1 million box office gross of the *Queen* biopic film of the same title is counted in the equation.

Changes in distribution

Distribution is constantly becoming more democratic, another persistent theme in this book. Noam (2019) argues that the principles of distribution are more timeless than the transient technology *du jour*. Both digital distributions (in music, *Spotify*) and physical ones (say, vinyl) take place in networks with similar "architecture," even though they are built of completely different materials.

- Tracking that industry movement has been important for major media companies – like the UK's *Sky* which, in the period 2001–14, had seven different technical upgrades to its platform, from electronic programme guides to the streaming service *NOW TV* (Oliver, 2018). Whilst the means of delivery were different, the product itself (programming) was constant.
- Distribution is shifting away from systems requiring large investment (print or cinemas) and towards places like *YouTube* where mass audiences can aggregate via social media referrals (Mierzejewska and Shaver, 2014).
- Audience usage of digital distribution can "enhance individual's ability to play a more active role in the creation, dissemination and interpretation of information" (Meo, 2016).
- Distribution success depends on customer experience and perception, and all media businesses will at least pay lip service to focussing on the customer's needs. "Every business competing for the future is customer-centric, customer-driven, customer-focussed, customer-yadda-yadda-yadda" (Pine and Gilmore, 1999).

Distribution can work in unexpected ways with new channels:

- In 2022, the social platform, *TikTok*, was credited with a role in growing UK book sales to $6.7 billion because of the recommendations of influencers to their younger audiences (the 'BookTok' phenomenon).
- Precisely because not all businesses in the media perform alike in these changing environments, through differential user experience (UX), there are category winners – *Spotify* and *Apple* (in music), *Steam* (in games) and so on. In many ways, UX is a defining feature of media platforms as important as the content they carry.

- In the 1990s, when telecoms media companies were beginning to merge, the phrase "Content is king" became commonplace. But as author Eli Noam asks: "Is it possible that in actuality 'distribution is king?' " (Noam, 2019).

Monetisation stage

The final stage in the media value creation process is where produced ideas turn into cash. Inputs required from the firm include sales effort, customer relationships and technologies that will improve the monetisation, such as in-game purchase systems. Outputs are cash flow, a sustainable customer base, the asset base of successful creation of sustainable IP, and equity value enhancement for the firm.

A dismissive attitude to the prosaic business of making money half-accurately caricatures how creative people can view the monetisation phase of the media value creation process. "I have a business appointment," said the character Algernon, in Oscar Wilde's nineteenth-century British comedy, *The Importance of Being Earnest*, "that I am anxious to miss."

As a result, there is sometimes tension in media firms between the 'creatives' and the 'business people.'

Challenges of monetisation

Even if they eschew finance meetings, creatives are passionately interested in monetising their work.

- "Chaplin's no negotiator," said film producer Sam Goldwyn of the silent movie star Charlie Chaplin, in the 1920s possibly the most famous person in human history to that point. "He just knows he can't take anything less."
- Actor Scarlet Johansson sued Disney for revenues from the movie *Black Widow* in 2021 when it was switched from cinemas to a hybrid streaming distribution. They settled the case for what *Deadline* said may have been $40 million (a figure which Disney did not confirm) (Pulver, 2021).

Monetisation in media takes three basic forms, each considered throughout this book.

(1) Product is monetised, by being sold direct; a hard copy of *Vogue Italia* magazine; a ticket to watch *Argentinos Juniors* play; a pass for the *Beijing Pop Festival*; an in-game loot box.
(2) Customers are monetised, through individual transactions and lifetime value relationships, which reflect the desirable financial visibility of subscription models.
(3) Data is monetised, driving the digital marketing that powers distribution of modern media content in all forms, and offering opportunities like e-commerce on social media. Each of these will be introduced in turn.

Product

Product is monetised via intellectual property rights. In the 1970s, oil baron J Paul Getty said "The meek shall inherit the earth – but not its mineral rights." By the 2020s, he could have replaced that with "copyright" – such is the power of owning content catalogues.

- Universal Music Group paid nearly $400 million to buy the songs of Bob Dylan, a reported 25 times multiple on the annual revenue it generates (Wang, 2021).
- Copyright is not the same as physical ownership. Take a book on your shelf, ownership of which does not imply a slice of the copyright: "The physical component of the book is the object itself, which can be held by a person's hands. The intellectual component of the book is the words that appear on the pages and the expression of any ideas contained in those words" (Vinet, 2010).
- Copyright protection happens immediately when content is made (Vinet, 2010).
- Copyright is scaleable, physical ownership of the asset is not, so copyright is the better asset to own in media. But copyright is also not globally standardised, which means territories like the US which enforce it are better locations to create media assets than the many that do not. Countries that want to see their media sector grow need first to build legal copyright enforcement.

Customer lifetime value

Customers are monetised through their lifetime of engagement with a media product. The longer and more high-margin the engagement, the higher the value of customers to the business. That customer value is expressed in an equation – Customer Lifetime Value (CLV) – which underpins marketing and subscription businesses.

CLV expresses the relationship between investment in customer acquisition (Acquisition Cost per customer or 'AC'), the gross margin per customer (gm), which is what a customer spends with the brand per year and the length of the relationship. Here are the key parameters:

- The discount rate or cost of capital (i.e., interest rate) to the firm is (i), and customer retention rate is (r), the opposite of which is the churn rate.
- N is the number of years the relationship lasts.
- The formula for a finite period of customer relationship is therefore as follows:

$$CLV_N = \sum_{t=1}^{N} \frac{gm_t * r^{(t-1)}}{(1+i)^{(t-1)}} - AC$$

And for an infinite period:

$$CLV_\infty = \frac{gm * (1+i)}{(1-r+i)} - AC$$

This is not just an academic formula.

Customer lifetime value is used in any media business today, particularly those that thrive from subscription. Deloitte's *2022 Media and Entertainment Industry Outlook* says: "We will see the streaming video industry mature as metrics evolve beyond subscriber counts to lifetime customer value, and existing business models expand to find greater profitability amid global competition" (Deloitte, 2022).

There are a number of key dimensions to CLV that are helpful to keep in mind with the study of media companies.

- The higher the retention rate, the higher the CLV. Media firms must usually provide great content to keep people watching. This is why streamers focus on providing each customer something new to watch each month, or why publishers add new titles to game franchises. Streamers without new content have higher churn, and lower CLV.
- The higher the customer acquisition cost, the higher the incentive to increase retention – because winning customers is so costly. This is why production companies super-serve a broadcast customer once they have an entertainment commission (see Chapter 11).
- Useful modifications of CLV include introduction of a measure for customers evangelising each other to a new product. A viral customer is worth not only their own cash flow, but also the combined cash flows of everyone they have brought into the service: this is customer lifetime social value (CLSV) through 'ripple evolution' (Ofek et al., 2018).
- A good example of this CLSV would be the rapid growth of *TikTok*, which by growing users virally at 40.8% in 2022 outstripped any advertising it paid for (Perez, 2021).

Value of data

Data is monetised in the media through marketability of information that gives advertisers the ability to more cost-efficiently target customers, or gives holders of existing customer relationships the ability to improve retention.

Data monetisation has been the underlying revenue driver at social media sites *Facebook* and *Instagram*. Any loss of the full access to customer data (e.g., through regulatory intervention around customers' digital privacy) compromises the business model.

- The February 2022 results statement of *Facebook*'s parent company Meta Platforms said that loss of data due to Apple's *iPhone* privacy changes would cost the company $10 billion in lost revenue, through increasing ad targeting and measurement headwinds (Meta, 2022).
- In digital news businesses, knowledge of the precise landing points and view times of individual users on stories helps target content and advertising to customer cohorts. This improves retention. This is why the *Financial Times* has over 40 data analysts (Ridding, 2020).

Data is so valuable that it is constantly sought by, and bought from, media companies.

- Ben Page, CEO of global market research agency Ipsos MORI, explained in an interview that his firm had a 10,000-person panel with full, legitimate access to users' complete router data: "Every device in the house, including all their Alexa and Amazon devices. And we can then start to understand what people are doing, not just on not just on one form on all the platforms" (Page, 2021).
- Such data, even anonymised, can be a powerful marketing tool when extrapolated to a market segment or regional level "to build a synthetic universe of the UK population" (Page, 2021). Accuracy like this helps media planners and advertisers to target their paid media spend (see Chapter 13). Increased advertising efficiency generates higher return for media businesses.

The media value chain

Management theorist Michael Porter first used the phrase 'value chain' in his 1985 book *Competitive Advantage: Creating and Sustaining Superior Performance*, identifying "the set of interconnected, value creating activities that a company performs in developing, manufacturing, delivering and supporting its product, and the points of connection with the activities of suppliers, channels and customers" (Kehoe and Mateer, 2015).

The four-stage media value chain process (development, production, distribution and monetisation) used in this book brings a common grammar to discussion of categories as different as social network and recording artist.

All media sectors covered also face endemic change (Harrison, 2020). Consultants E&Y have three ideas on how to manage that change and create value: pursue operational excellence, reboot the company's innovation strategy approach and accelerate talent and skills development.

Class discussion questions

- What can media companies learn from factories, and in which ways are they operationally unique?
- By doing some online research, take a look at one of the leading 'Bollywood' film production companies such as *UTV Motion Pictures*, *Eros International* or *Red Chillies Entertainment*. Identify the drivers of its success in each of the four phases of media value generation: development, production, distribution and monetisation.
- Why is data now an important product for media businesses of all kinds? And what are the risks of selling it?
- What impact do you think creativity powered by Artificial Intelligence will have on copyright ownership in media businesses? What are the specific ways in which AI can cause intellectual property problems?

Analysis: EbonyLife Group (Nigeria)

EbonyLife Group is an example of a media company looking to find its optimal model for value generation. It is a relatively recent start-up, one of a new generation of Nigerian media companies, with annual revenue of about $9 million (ZoomInfo, 2022), exporting African stories globally.

Interest in content around the world from non-Anglo/American sources has grown, but global delivery remains costly. Typical budgets and production values for TV shows or films in Nigeria's film industry ('Nollywood') are also lower than in the content produced at the high end of Hollywood output. So what are the best business models on which to bring eponymously African stories to a global market? This is a key question for EbonyLife.

Creating the business

Born and raised in London, Mosumola "Mo" Abudu, relocated to Nigeria, developing a career in HR. But, aged 40, she started a new career in media (WIFT, 2020). In 2006, Mo started Africa's first syndicated talk show, *Moments with Mo*.

- The show took off, turning into an African entertainment and lifestyle global channel. *EbonyLife TV* launched in 2013 on the *DStv* platform, Sub-Saharan Africa's direct broadcast satellite service, owned by *MultiChoice* (EbonyLife TV Legacy, 2022). In 2019, the channel expanded onto *StarTimes*, the Chinese owned media company that offers digital and satellite terrestrial television – adding 11 million homes across Africa (Anazia, 2018). *EbonyLife TV* made and broadcast over 5,000 hours of original drama, talk shows, entertainment and factual content (EbonyLife TV Legacy, 2022), one of the largest self-owned libraries on the continent of Africa (EbonyLifeYou, 2022).
- Video-on-demand platform *EbonyLife ON* launched in 2015, targeting the Nollywood international audience. Initially priced at $4,99 per month within the Nigerian *diaspora*, it did not grow fast. In 2018, with both diaspora and home audience in mind, the service launched a mobile app instead, dropping prices to $2.99 monthly in the US and just over $1 in Nigeria, and (in July 2020) took *EbonyLife TV* off *DStv* and onto streaming (ShockNG, 2020).

EbonyLife Film

In 2014, Mo announced the film production unit, *EbonyLife Films*. Two years later, *The Wedding Party* made over N400 Million Naira (circa $1 million) at the box office, the highest grossing film in Nollywood to that date, establishing *EbonyLife Films* as the new face of Nollywood (Vourlias, 2017). *EbonyLife Films* had produced seven films by 2020 (Ritman, 2020).

EbonyLife Studios/partnerships and development slate

Mo continued to build production, with a three-project first-look deal with Sony Pictures Television in 2018. This positioned the *EbonyLife* media conglomerate as a strategic route for African stories to the world stage – developing a series about the all-female army of the ancient West African kingdom of Dahomey (Kanter, 2021).

- In 2022, with *Netflix* they developed and released Nigerian undercover journalism thriller *Oloture*.
- They developed two adaptations of critically acclaimed Nigerian literary works: a series based on contemporary author, Lola Shoneyin's best-selling debut novel, *The Secret Lives of Baba Segi's Wives*, and a film adaptation of *Death And The King's Horseman*, a play by 1986 Nobel Prize Laureate in Literature, author, poet and play-wright, Wole Soyinka (Kanter, 2021).
- With AMC Networks they developed *Nigeria 2099*, an 'afro-futuristic' crime-drama (Mitchell, 2020) and *Queen Nzinga*, a scripted drama series, the life story of the famed African Warrior Queen with Lionsgate's STARZ, executive produced by Curtis "50 Cent" Jackson (White, 2021).
- Yet another development deal was announced in late 2021 with BBC Studios, kicking off with action-adventure series *Reclaim*, written by BAFTA Breakthrough Brit Rowan Athale (BBC, 2022). With the expansion came new offices in London and Los Angeles.

According to Mo Abudu, *EbonyLife* are therefore bringing African stories to the mainstream in three ways:

- Afro-futurism, focusing on the fantasy/sci-fi genre.
- Afro-impact, focusing on contemporaneous African stories.
- Afro-history, spotlighting African heroes, tales and everyday life (Mitchell, 2020).

Other ventures and business models

In December 2019, Abudu turned to the hospitality business – and built *EbonyLife Place*, an entertainment venue in Lagos with a cinema (Mitchell, 2020). The media conglomerate also launched writer's initiative *Alo* to develop African writers, in partnership with Sony Pictures Television (Ramachandran, 2021).

Class discussion questions

- Should *EbonyLife* focus on production or distribution? Which of the business models it is operating do you consider the most desirable?
- Identify and analyse another media business outside the US and Europe which has developed in multiple segments. And again, outline which strategy you think that company should prioritise.

BIBLIOGRAPHY

Anazia, D. (2018) EbonyLife TV ends exclusivity with DStv, expands globally. *The Guardian (Nigeria)*. [online] Available at: https://guardian.ng/technology/communications/ebonylife-tv-ends-exclusivity-with-dstv-expands-globally-2/ [Accessed 23 August 2022].

BBC. (2015) Salman Khan: Bollywood star jailed for five years in hit-and-run case. *BBC News*. [online] Available at: www.bbc.co.uk/news/world-asia-india-32603596 [Accessed 23 August 2022].

BBC. (2022) BBC Studios Drama Productions signs development deal with Mo Abudu of EbonyLife. *BBC Media Centre*. [online] Available at: www.bbc.com/mediacentre/bbcstudios/2021/bbc-studios-drama-productions-signs-development-deal-with-mo-abudu-of-ebonylife/ [Accessed 23 August 2022].

Ceci, L. (2022) TikTok: statistics & facts. *Statista*. [online] Available at: www.statista.com/topics/6077/tiktok/#topicHeader__wrapper [Accessed 29 August 2022].

Deloitte. (2022) 2022 media and entertainment industry outlook. *Deloitte*. [online] Available at: www2.deloitte.com/us/en/pages/technology-media-and-telecommunications/articles/media-and-entertainment-industry-outlook-trends.html [Accessed 23 August 2022].

Department for Digital, Culture, Media & Sport (DCMS). (2019) DCMS *sectors economic estimates 2019: empl*oyment. London: DCMS. [online] Available at: www.gov.uk/government/statistics/dcms-sectors-economic-estimates-2019-employment/dcms-sectors-economic-estimates-2019-employment [Accessed 23 August 2022].

Diamond, E. (1986) Trouble in paradise. *New York Magazine*, 3 March.

EbonyLife TV Legacy. (2022) http://ebonylifetv.com [Accessed 23 August 2022].

EbonyLifeYou. (2022) Affordable TV advertising to grow your business. *EbonyLifeTV*. [online] Available at: http://ebonylifetv.com/ebonylifeyou/ [Accessed 23 August 2022].

Galloway, S. (2020) What is the most profitable movie ever? *The Hollywood Reporter*. [online] Available at: www.hollywoodreporter.com/movies/movie-news/what-is-profitable-movie-ever-1269879/ [Accessed 23 August 2022].

Guttmann, A. (2022) Global media revenue 2020, by category. *Statista*. [online] Available at: www.statista.com/statistics/1132706/media-revenue-worldwide/ [Accessed 29 August 2022].

Harrison, J., Whistler, M. and Goyal, A. (2020) How are media and entertainment businesses reinventing in an age of transformation? *EY*. [online] Available at: www.ey.com/en_uk/tmt/how-the-media-and-entertainment-enterprise-is-evolving [Accessed 23 August 2022].

Hastings, R. and Meyer, E. (2020) *No rules rules: Netflix and the culture of reinvention*. London: Penguin Press.

Hess, T. (2014) What is a media company? A reconceptualization for the online world. *International Journal on Media Management*, 16(1), 3–8. doi.org/10.1080/14241277.2014.906993

Ingham, T. and Wang, A. X. (2021) Why superstar artists are clamoring to sell their music rights. *Rolling Stone*, 15 January.

Kanter, J. (2021) How EbonyLife founder Mo Abudu Kicked down doors to bring african stories to Netflix, AMC & Sony. *Deadline*. [online] Available at: https://deadline.com/2021/07/ebonylife-media-mo-abudu-cannes-magazine-disruptor-1234789746/ [Accessed 23 August 2022].

Kehoe, K. and Mateer, J. (2015) The impact of digital technology on the distribution value chain model of independent feature films in the UK. *International Journal on Media Management*, 17(2), 93–108. doi.org/10.1080/14241277.2015.1055533

Koraza, T. (2021) Peter Thiel's 7 questions for starting a billion dollar business are ruthless. *DataDrivenInvestor*. [online] Available at: https://medium.datadriveninvestor.com/peter-thiels-7-questions-for-starting-a-billion-dollar-business-ce5a924bd1bc [Accessed 23 August 2022].

Malmelin, N. and Virta, S. (2021) Critical creativity: managing creativity as a strategic resource in media organisations. *Journal of Media Business Studies*, 18(3), 199–213. doi. org/10.1080/16522354.2020.1858677

Malmelin, N., Virta, S. and Kuismin, A. (2021) Transforming media: reviewing the issues and contexts of change in media management research. *Journal of Media Business Studies*, 1–22. doi.org/10.1080/16522354.2021.1960619

Marsh, S. (2021) Johnny Depp loses bid to overturn ruling in libel case. *The Guardian*, 25 March. [online] Available at: www.theguardian.com/film/2021/mar/25/johnny-depp-loses-bid-to-overturn-ruling-in-libel-case [Accessed 23 August 2022].

Meo, G. (2016) The Marketplace of attention: how audiences take shape in a digital age. *International Journal on Media Management*, 18(3–4), 181–2. doi.org/10.1080/14241277.2016.1260341

Meta. (2022) Meta platforms fourth quarter and full year 2021 results. *Meta.* [online] Available at: https://investor.fb.com/investor-news/press-release-details/2022/Meta-Reports-Fourth-Quarter-and-Full-Year-2021-Results/default.aspx [Accessed 23 August 2022].

Mierzejewska, B. and Shaver, D. (2014) Key changes impacting media management research. *International Journal on Media Management*, 16(2), 47–54. doi.org/10.1080/14241277.2014.954439

Mitchell, W. (2020) Perspectives on 2020: EbonyLife Media CEO Mo Abudu on Netflix deals and African stories. *ScreenDaily.* [online] Available at: www.screendaily.com/features/persp ectives-on-2020-ebonylife-media-ceo-mo-abudu-on-netflix-deals-and-african-stories/5155 854.article [Accessed 23 August 2022].

Mohsin, M. (2021) 10 YouTube stats every marketer should know in 2021. *Oberlo.* [blog] Available at: www.oberlo.com/blog/youtube-statistics [Accessed 23 August 2022].

Noam, E. M. (2019) *Media and digital management.* London: Palgrave Macmillan.

Nylund, M. (2013) Toward creativity management: idea generation and newsroom meetings. *International Journal on Media Management*, 15(4), 197–210. doi.org/10.1080/14241277.2013.773332

OFCOM. (2020) *Lockdown leads to surge in TV screen time and streaming.* [online] Available at: www.ofcom.org.uk/about-ofcom/latest/media/media-releases/2020/lockdown-leads-to-surge-in-tv-screen-time-and-streaming [Accessed 23 August 2022].

Ofek, E., Libai, B. and Muller, E. (2018) Customer lifetime social value (CLSV). *Harvard Business School Faculty & Research.* [online] Available at: www.hbs.edu/faculty/Pages/item.aspx?num=53770 [Accessed 23 August 2022].

Oliver, J. J. (2018) Strategic transformations in the media. *Journal of Media Business Studies*, 15(4), 278–99. doi.org/10.1080/16522354.2018.1546088

Page, B. (2021) *AI and market research* [interview with Dr Alex Connock]. Diploma in AI for Business. Said Business School, University of Oxford, 13 May.

Perez, S. (2021) TikTok to rank as the third largest social network, 2022 forecast notes. *TechCrunch.* [online] Available at: https://techcrunch.com/2021/12/20/tiktok-to-rank-as-the-third-largest-social-network-2022-forecast-notes/?guccounter=1&guce_referrer=aHR0 cHM6Ly93d3cuZ29vZ2xlLmNvbS8&guce_referrer_sig=AQAAADlGGu7fzxwIC1gThx eK2-TcQz5OFsDNAjzwszHeC0OBYSrYX-8otQyIeiQ-EwKbZnxOevoNSBL2nZMQJSD fBs1yGB3J0BVeawiystGkZ2jM1NiB1KiXNAISenh4n0xxLBWlm2ZrdRuCAYb7MFnYH VUdRUeQnQyb1mXWbTNyp5K5 [Accessed 23 August 2022].

Pine, B. J. and Gilmore, J. (1999) *The experience economy.* Boston: Harvard Business School Press.

Pulver, A. (2021) Scarlett Johansson settles Black Widow lawsuit with Disney. *The Guardian*, 1 October. [online] Available at: www.theguardian.com/film/2021/oct/01/scarlett-johans son-settles-black-widow-lawsuit-disney [Accessed 23 August 2022].

Ramachandran, N. (2021) Sony Pictures Television, EbonyLife set African Writers Initiative Alo. *Variety.* [online] Available at: https://variety.com/2021/tv/global/sony-pictures-televis ion-ebonylife-african-writers-initiative-1235069922/ [Accessed 23 August 2022].

Ridding, J. (2020) *Interview with John Ridding, CEO Financial Times, conducted at Oxford University*, 20 July.

Riedl, M. J. (2019) Making media: production, practices, and professions. *International Journal on Media Management*, 21(3–4), 218–19. doi.org/10.1080/14241277.2019.1644481

Ritman, A. (2020) Nigerian producer Mo Abudu on striking Netflix's First multi-title African deal: 'As a Continent, We've Remained So Quiet' (Exclusive). *The Hollywood Reporter*. [online] Available at: www.hollywoodreporter.com/news/general-news/nigerian-producer-mo-abudu-on-striking-netflixs-first-multi-title-african-deal-as-a-continent-weve-remained-so-quiet-exclusive-4066612/ [Accessed 23 August 2022].

Sacks, B. (2014) Time Inc.'s editors and their damned church and state. *Adweek*, 25 August.

Schreiber, D. and Rieple, A. (2021) Aggrandisement: helping micro-enterprise owner-managers construct credibility in the recorded music industry. *Journal of Media Business Studies*, 1–25. doi.org/10.1080/16522354.2021.1978263

ShockNG. (2020) EbonyLife TV exits DStv air waves 7 years later. Why? *ShockNG*. [online] Available at: https://shockng.com/ebony-life-tv-exits-dstv-air-waves-7-years-later-why/ [Accessed 23 August 2022].

Spangler, T. (2020) 'The Queen's Gambit' scores as Netflix most-watched scripted limited series to date. *Variety*. [online] Available at: https://variety.com/2020/digital/news/queens-gambit-netflix-viewing-record-1234838090/ [Accessed 23 August 2022].

Ventresca, M. (2022) *Lecture to the Diploma in AI for Business*. Said Business School, University of Oxford, 28 July.

Vinet, M. (2010) *Entertainment industry: the business of music, books, movies, tv, radio, internet, video games, theater, fashion, sports, art, merchandising, copyright, trademarks and contracts*. Quebec, Canada: Wadem Publishing.

Vogel, H. L. (2020) *Entertainment industry economics: a guide for financial analysis*. 10th edn. Cambridge: Cambridge University Press.

Vourlias, C. (2017) 'Wedding Party' fuels record Nigerian box office despite ailing economy. *Variety*. [online] Available at: https://variety.com/2017/film/global/wedding-party-fuels-record-nigerian-box-office-despite-ailing-economy-1201977878/ [Accessed 23 August 2022].

Whipple, K. (2019) Entertainment science: data analytics and practical theory for movies, games, books, and music. *International Journal on Media Management*, 21(3–4), 220–1. doi.org/10.1080/14241277.2019.1646697

White, P. (2021) Yetide Badaki to star in African Warrior Queen Nzinga drama series in the works at Starz from 50 Cent, Mo Abudu and Steven S. DeKnight. *Deadline*. [online] Available at: https://deadline.com/2021/12/queen-nzinga-yetide-badaki-starz-50-cent-1234892198/ [Accessed 23 August 2022].

WIFT (2020). Carla 2020 opening: Mo Abudu. *YouTube*. [online] Available at: www.youtube.com/watch?v=Rqkj43EXDDA [Accessed 23 August 2022].

Wijman, T. (2021) The games market and beyond in 2021: the year in numbers. *Newzoo*. [online] Available at: https://newzoo.com/insights/articles/the-games-market-in-2021-the-year-in-numbers-esports-cloud-gaming/ [Accessed 23 August 2022].

ZoomInfo. (2022) EbonyLife TV. *ZoomInfo*. [online] Available at: www.zoominfo.com/c/ebonylife-tv/357662101 [Accessed 23 August 2022].

CHAPTER 4

Overview of AI

Radical new tools are being used in media management and beyond

....

A BRIEF HISTORY OF AI

As suggested in the opening chapter: "AI is not a thing. AI is an assembly of possibilities and capabilities" (Ventresca, 2022).

But even if the object is imprecise, its impact is tangible. The 'AI industry' is already at huge scale, and is developing at enormous pace. A simple glossary is useful, such that the reader of the rest of this book will know and understand the tools applied in the many use cases in the media business discussed, if not the mathematical complexities of each underlying algorithm. AI tools are evolving fast – daily – such that any list will be rapidly out of date before it is even printed. But the core technologies will endure. This book is not a technical guide to AI, but an overview of its implementations in media.

There are many definitions of Artificial Intelligence, none universally agreed. The Oxford English Dictionary calls it: "the capacity of computers or other machines to exhibit or simulate intelligent behaviour." A useful refinement is: "technology which has the capability to exhibit human-like behaviour, when faced with a specific task" (OFCOM, 2019).

There are differing origin stories for the field. Philosophically (not technically) Mary Shelley's 1812 novel, *Frankenstein*, alluded to a 'monster' created after an enquiry into "the prime cause of life itself." Similar perceptions still play out in much press coverage of AI today – in dystopian imagery of *The Terminator* or *Skynet* and countless other popular movies and novels.

In the science of AI, Alan Turing was an early figure – a UK mathematician otherwise credited with invention of an early computer, which enabled the Allies to crack the Nazi enigma code and (it is argued) shorten the Second World War. By

DOI: 10.4324/9781003213611-5

1950 Turing was concerned with mathematical challenges of machine 'intelligence,' predicting that "in about 50 years' time it will be possible to programme computers, with a storage capacity of about 10 to the power 9, to make them play the imitation game so well that an average interrogator will not have more than 70 per cent chance of making the right identification after five minutes of questioning" (Turing, 1950). This was the so-called 'Turing Test.'

The field was actually termed 'Artificial Intelligence' at a 1956 Dartmouth College conference, run by a young mathematician, John McCarthy. Now at Stanford, he defines the space as: "the science and engineering of making intelligent machines."

AI's intermittent growth in the second half of the twentieth century

AI went through phases of optimistic growth – such as Japan's 1982 Fifth Generation Computer Project, or Naval, the first autonomous car, built by Carnegie Melon university. It also has had periods of retrenchment, 'AI Winters,' in industry parlance.

Key watersheds include the 1997 defeat of Chess Grand Master Gary Kasparov, in by IBM's *Deep Blue*. Another was the development of speech recognition tools by Dragon Systems (Anyoha, 2017). In the twenty-first century, companies came to the fore like Apple, NVIDIA, Open AI and DeepMind (now owned by Google owner Alphabet) which pioneered techniques such as deep reinforcement learning, to perfect the playing of board and (later) video games, extrapolating that technology to a vast array of other use-cases, from sequencing protein DNA, to plasma control in nuclear fusion.

Turing began his 1950 paper for the journal *Mind* on Computing, Machinery and Intelligence: "I propose to consider the question, 'Can machines think?'" People are still asking that question today.

The idea that a computer could be sophisticated enough to exhibit human-style thinking, has been an underpinning concept in both the continuing evolution of AI, and the evolution of the way the entertainment industry has thought about AI – from the calculating Hal in *2001: A Space Odyssey* to the manipulative Ava in *Ex Machina* (2014).

AI 'sentience' is a matter of debate. In 2022, a Google employee – Blake Lemoine – was suspended after publicly claiming to have seen evidence of sentience in the LaMDA language transformer system. Many computer scientists are sceptical, arguing instead that LaMDA is simply replicating text about sentience that it has been trained upon. Demis Hassabis at DeepMind has referred to asking an AI interesting questions at 3am, to try and understand whether it can indeed think for itself. His conclusion: "To some level, I don't think it really knows anything, to be honest. That would be my conclusion. It knows some words" (Fry, 2022). When Open AI's *GPT-3* transformer was asked "Can a system like *GPT-3* actually understand anything at all?" it said: "Yes. I can. Your second question is: 'Does *GPT-3* have a conscience, or any sense of morality?' No. I do not" (Kissinger, 2021).

Categories of AI

Common to all AI is the idea of the algorithm – a list of rules to follow in order to solve a problem. Algorithms are everywhere in our lives – from how a car starts, to how a calculator works out a long division. How those algorithms are developed and implemented is the substance of AI as a subject.

By general consensus there are three main philosophical categories of AI, which together map its journey from early definition to a potential (though not yet achieved) near-universal, future footprint.

- Artificial Narrow Intelligence (ANI) can do one simple job really well, and quite possibly better than a human. It can play a board game to world-class level, or identify which shot in a set of safari pictures shows an elephant, or drive a car along well-signposted roads. As technology improves, so does the AI – its performance increasing as a function of the hardware running it. This is one reason why, in 2021, the computer chips industry was at $368 billion annual turnover, with expected compound 15% annual growth rate. ANI is all around us today – in pre-completed *Google* search results, our personalised homepage on *Amazon*, the *McDonalds* drive-through menu, or optimised distribution of fashion items to the *H&M* store where they will be most likely to sell. When banks use systems that track the length of time it takes a loan applicant to type their own name as a potential indicator of fraud (slower typing shows less familiarity with the name) that is ANI at work. The algorithm doing that would not have the general skill to suddenly pivot to fly an aeroplane or compose a symphony without further training.
- Next, as software, hardware and cloud computing capabilities grow, we may – or may not – move towards Artificial General Intelligence (AGI). Here, the skills of AI agents may include the ability to conduct a conversation with nuance to the mood of whoever it's talking to, and solve problems where the agent has not had individualised training. The field is not yet mature. Some researchers believe it will happen within a decade. Many think it take longer than that to reach AGI. Software scientist Francois Chollet said "AGI is pure hype, and interest will wane" (OFCOM, 2019). Demis Hassabis of DeepMind said: "I think it comes down to the definition of AGI. So if we define it as a system that's able to do a wide variety of cognitive tasks to a human level, that must be possible, I think, because the existence proof is the human brain. And unless you think there's something non-computable in the brain, which so far there's no evidence for, then it should it be possible to mimic those functions on effectively a Turing machine or computer" (Fry, 2022).
- Finally, there may come a point where we reach Artificial Super Intelligence (ASI) – a system that would surpass human intelligence (Kavlakoglu, 2020). ASI would create societal challenges, such as the need for humans to consider how to think about machines that are cleverer than us. "We (the children) will have all the power, even though the machines will in fact be far more powerful. We need a

new metaphor, a new way of seeing ourselves, and we will need all the writers and filmmakers and poets to guide our culture in the process" (Russell, 2021). Computer scientists have posited that ASI systems might think about humans as 'pets.' That moment when AI surpasses even humans' ability to understand it, is sometimes known as 'singularity,' a science fiction favourite. "Singularity is the moment beyond which we can no longer see, we can no longer forecast. It is the moment beyond which we cannot predict how AI will behave because our current perception and trajectories will no longer apply. Now the question becomes: how do you convince this superbeing that there is actually no point squashing a fly?" (Rifkind, 2021).

Global economic significance of AI

Many governments around the world have formulated and launched AI strategies, such is its centrality to long-term performance of economies.

- Brazil launched its national AI strategy in April 2021, around workforce; R&D, innovation, entrepreneurship and public safety. Turkey launched a similar one in September 2021, aiming for AI to contribute 5% of GDP by 2025. The UK government has an Office for Artificial Intelligence, and 10 stated tech priorities, around "creating an economy that harnesses artificial intelligence (AI) and big data." China is a strong investor in AI research, with a national programme to be strong in a number of high-tech fields by 2025.
- Globally, according to one academic study, AI could contribute $15.7 trillion to the global economy in 2030, more than the current output of China and India combined. Of this, $6.6 trillion is likely to come from increased productivity and $9.1 trillion is likely to come from the side effects of consumption (Verweij, 2017). Much of the total will depend on the definition of an AI transaction.
- But AI does have applications in every area of the modern economy, from agriculture to zoology, via defence, logistics, marketing, infrastructure, counter-disinformation, medicine, law, financial trading and consumer banking.
- For instance, computer vision (an AI technique) is being used for automated assessment of the health of marijuana plants in the US cannabis industry, so that any plant stressors such as nutrient deficiencies can be identified by AI days ahead of when a human can spot them (Velte, 2022). And machine learning is being used in automated forecasting of European power demand, including in a single predictive dashboard hundreds of factors ranging from when Spanish people tend to get home in the evening (9pm) to when the break will be in a World Cup match (Morsili, 2022).
- A US national security report says AI is going to "reorganize the world" (US National Security Commission on Artificial Intelligence Final Report, 2021). It paints an alarming picture of AI applications in security, including the mass, simultaneous application by an adversary of personalised blackmail to millions of people; a digital Pearl Harbour, at scale.

AI is not being used equally by every country or every company, which creates competitive advantage for category winners – like Apple, Adobe and Tencent.

> Research and systems-building in areas such as document retrieval, text classification, fraud detection, recommendation systems, personalized search, social network analysis, planning, diagnostics, and A/B testing have been a major success – these advances have powered companies such as Google, *Netflix*, *Facebook*, and Amazon.
>
> *(Jordan, 2019)*

AI is so necessary that new software players such as India's Zoho build AI into almost all of their applications, seeking to facilitate simple tasks such as expense tracking via optical character recognition. AI is best not thought of as something separate at all: it is an integral part of almost every product at any software-driven company.

Though sectoral winners across many fields of the economy are companies that have engaged with AI as a competitive advantage, many firms are not yet embracing it.

As science fiction writer William Gibson said in his 1984 novel *Neuromancer*: "The future is already here, It is just very unevenly distributed" (Quoted by (Ventresca, 2021)). By September 2022, the US White House published a blueprint AI 'Bill of Rights.'

Machine learning

Many of the use cases described as Artificial Intelligence are Machine Learning (or ML) – which, to purists, is not AI at all. (That fascinating debate is too arcane to solve in a book about the media business.)

ML combines statistics, computer science and other sources to design algorithms that process data, make predictions and help make decisions (Jordan, 2019). The algorithms in ML are primarily regression models which can look at data and strip out patterns useful for decision making. "Machine learning aims to build computers that can learn how to do things without being explicitly told how" (Efremova, 2021). But machine-learning systems need training data in order to learn, upon which they can become powerful: "*Facebook*'s machine learning tools predict your preferences better than any psychologist" (Spinney, 2022).

Within machine learning are four clear sub categories – supervised learning, reinforcement learning, unsupervised learning and self-supervised learning. The difference between them is around how much data and training is needed to extrapolate useful patterns from existing data. And each of these fields is a foundational tool in the application of AI to many aspects of media development, production and distribution – the focus of this book.

Supervised learning

Supervised learning requires a comprehensive, labelled dataset (OFCOM, 2019). For instance, a library of pictures of cats would allow a system trained on enough images to recognise cats amongst any new pictures it is shown (Somers, 2021).

Supervised learning is typically used to classify data. It needs a dataset where each input has a labelled output. Once adequately trained, the machine should be able to correctly label input data that it has *not* seen before – using what is called the inference function.

Face recognition is a case in point: "when you identify individuals in a photo on social media, you are providing training data for machine-learning algorithms, so that those algorithms will be able to identify those individuals" in future (Wooldridge, 2018). When machine learning has been given insufficient or inaccurate training data, the inferences will also be wrong.

Reinforcement learning

The key difference in reinforcement learning is that it does not need an existing dataset for training.

However, it does require a training environment for reinforcement, where the experimentation can be carried out and there is a clearly defined metric to optimise (OFCOM, 2019). That means, the system needs guidance as to whether it is making the right decisions. For example, reinforcement learning can be used by a machine to learn to play a computer game. It can see, from the score it achieves, how well any given decision is working, and then over thousands of games, learn the right moves to make to optimise its score.

- In reinforcement learning, "a system is able to experiment by making decisions, and receives feedback on those decisions (whether they were good or bad). If a system receives feedback that a decision was bad, it will be less likely to make that decision in the same circumstances in future" (Wooldridge, 2018).
- The strength of this approach is that reinforcement learning does not need big labelled datasets, which saves time for the humans setting the task. It can use trial and error, as long as it has a clear metric (like a score) by which to measure success.
- This is how DeepMind's *AlphaGo* system learned to play well enough to beat Lee Sedol at *§* in 2016 (see Chapter 2).
- A reinforcement learning agent needs to be able to sense its surroundings and track how it is doing against the goals it has been given – to keep score.

Unsupervised learning

Unsupervised learning, like supervised learning, requires a large volume of input data. But again in this case, the data does not need to be labelled.

The point of this technique is to understand the structure of data in the absence of labels. In marketing, a system could look at millions of store card users and put them into meaningful market segments, based on card usage and goods bought, without the marketer having pre-legislated what those cohorts would be, or even understanding how they came to be formed.

The machine simply clusters input data points based on similarities, but does not place input data into specific named categories. (Of course, the owner of the algorithm could then subsequently label those categories. This happens often, e.g., a supermarket data analyst could manually identify a machine-identified cohort that tended to buy small amounts of food frequently, as 'student shoppers.')

So the purpose of unsupervised learning is to find hidden patterns or groupings within the dataset. The machine can group similar images without any prior knowledge of category names.

Unsupervised Learning is useful in situations where the user doesn't know what the underlying attributes of different groups of data points are. With unsupervised learning, there is no feedback to the system based on the prediction results (no human saying 'this is a picture of a dog')

> This type of machine learning is called 'unsupervised' because we're not telling the algorithm in advance that these are type 1 data, type 2 data or type 3 data like in supervised learning. Instead we are showing data and asking [the machine] to automatically find structure in the data.
>
> *(Efremova, 2021)*

Self-supervised learning (SSL)

This is machine learning where the model trains itself by leveraging one part of the data to predict the other part, and generate labels accurately. "In the end, this learning method converts an unsupervised learning problem into a supervised one" (Hajjar, 2022). It is a model heavily used by Meta in its AI work. In 2018, Google created the BERT model which used Self-Supervised Learning (SSL) for natural language processing (see below), including language translation.

Neural networks and deep learning

Neural networks are a programming model for statistical pattern recognition. Meanwhile deep learning is what you do with a neural network when it reaches its full potential complexity, in order to get the most accurate results and map the most complex of datasets. This could be the categorisation of pictures and videos with billions of pixels. Pioneered by computer scientist Yoshua Bengio, neural networks originated in efforts to replicate the structure of the human brain, with its millions of interconnected cells or neurons (Economist, 2021).

- Neural networks can start out very simple, with just a few layers.
- But at scale, they break complex calculations in vast datasets into billions of simpler choices, and then learn by iteration across that enormous set of decisions. They do that by altering the weight given to each piece of information at each stage, until the output of the entire network of calculations conforms to a predetermined target (Taylor, 2021), for instance, the identification of objects.

- A neural network that consists of more than three layers – which would be inclusive of the inputs and the output – is a deep learning algorithm (Kavlakoglu, 2020).
- Artificial neural networks (ANNs) have been particularly useful in such fields as computer vision (see below). (There are other types, specifically Convolutional Neural Networks (CNNs) and Recurrent (RNNs.))
- ANNs have four elements: inputs, weights, a bias or threshold, and an output. A question is asked – for instance: is this a picture of a car? – and then every variable that might go into evaluating that decision is factored into a formula. The model weighs up the shape, the number of wheels and so on, each of these at a different node in the network. If the output of any given node is above a given value, that node is activated, and data goes to the next layer of the network. Each layer sends information to the next one. "A single change can have a cascading effect on the other neurons in the network" (Kavlakoglu, 2020).
- Back propagation – or going backwards through the network – is used to update the network weights based on how close the real output is to the desired output. A recurrent network is connects nodes back through layers, to recognise sequences.
- In the car example, we could (like in supervised learning) collect a group of images for which we knew what we were looking at – cars, bikes, planes, camels – and show them to a deep neural network. The network would turn those images into mathematical information, and then when it saw a new picture, would assign a confidence level to its belief that the new image was, or was not, a car, with a certain level of confidence. "If the neural network is more than 90% confident … That's a car" (Ramey, 2016). An expert in facial recognition working for law enforcement told an Oxford lecture in 2022 that a confidence score above 80% was more typical of a match between two images of the same person at different ages in their life.

Deep learning

Deep learning models are amongst the most complex algorithms. They are often the most difficult to train, the least simple to interpret and they require vast amounts of data. Due to the lack of transparency and difficulty to explain the result, they are often referred to as a 'black box' approach. However, they allow the data scientist to work with the most complex data (Efremova, 2021).

One challenge with deep learning is just how much data it needs. A deep learning facial recognition system will need many thousands of faces or other proof points.

That need for training data is why bot-filtering tools often ask you to recognise street signs and lamp posts: you are helping to train deep learning systems. But the systems can still get things wrong, because of faults in the training data. Neural networks have a problem recognising real pictures of bedrooms, because they have been trained on unrealistic images from the internet that are "clearly staged and depict a made bed from 2–3 meters away," researchers at the University of California, Berkeley found (Somers, 2021).

The 'black box' issue describes that these models are not easily explainable. Even the supervisor of a system may not be able to summarise its outputs.

> For example, a neural net that has been trained to recognize cancerous growths on X-ray pictures cannot explain its decisions. The expertise the system has is hidden in the numeric weights associated with neurons, and there is no easy way to extract the knowledge that these weights implicitly carry.
>
> (Wooldridge, 2018)

Sometimes when black box AI systems have been unpicked, the explanatory dynamics have turned out to be left-field. For instance, in one Australian study of cancerous moles at a medical pathology lab, the actual pathology of the slides was not being looked at all, but visual cues were being taken from the annotation on the sides of the training data photographs themselves, which the AI system had figured out offered a short cut. This means using decisions taken by black box systems can be risky. As discussed above, black box systems have, in the past, given job interviews to people who play field hockey or are called 'Jared' – just because that happened to be a common factor in previously successful candidates. Black box algorithms make organisations such as banks uncomfortable, because they may not be able to explain their decision making to regulators.

Finally, systems capable of running the largest models must be extremely powerful. The biggest firms are competing to build sufficient computing power to ingest, for instance, all the world's English language digital data in a single system the size of a football pitch. *Facebook* owner Meta announced in early 2022 that it was building "the fastest supercomputer in the world," the AI Research SuperCluster (RSC). All the underlying technologies require foundational scale: "Computer vision … needs to process larger, longer videos with higher data sampling rates. Speech recognition needs to work well even in challenging scenarios with lots of background noise, such as parties or concerts. NLP needs to understand more languages, dialects, and accents" (Meta, 2022).

The results of this arms race between the biggest tech and media firms to deliver cutting edge media products are evident throughout this book, and across the media itself. They tend to centralise AI power in the hands of a few, large companies, which may be perceived as un-democratic.

Computer vision

Another use of neural networks is in allowing computers to understand the content of images or videos. Image classification describes categorising an entire image. Finding specific objects within an image is called object detection (Efremova, 2021).

- Perhaps the most commonplace and controversial use of computer vision is in facial recognition. When computer vision looks to recognise a face, it uses around 60 landmarks in the face, which are initially determined by human labellers. Algorithms are trained on those landmarks. Inside the facial recognition model, the features on a face are tested against database images. In emotion recognition, similar landmarks are tracked to produce measurements along (say) five ranges of emotion – around subtle movement of the eyebrows or cheeks, for instance.

- Many companies, such as NAC and Clearview AI, have built systems and datasets to recognise faces at scale. Such companies have (legally) used billions of images off the internet to build their databases. Systems such as these have been used by law enforcement in many countries – particularly the US and China – but there have been legal challenges around the accuracy of the database. Sometimes these challenges have been around the results of the systems when used on images of ethnic minorities. Steve Talley, a financial analyst from Colorado, was charged with bank robbery, on the basis of an error in a facial recognition system. Tally fought the case and was cleared, but he lost his house and his job and access to his children in the process of doing so (Strong, 2021).

- Beyond facial recognition, computer vision was used by DeepMind to create a multifaceted analysis of the action in football matches with Liverpool Football Club, aiming to produce a 'voice assistant coach' that would be capable of predicting the outcome of different tactical changes during a match. "This automated coach could make counterfactual predictions of what would happen in the game, if a particular tactical change is made" (Fry, 2022).

- Computer vision can go wrong in a sports context too. In 2020, the Scottish football team, Inverness Caledonian Thistle used a *Pixellot* AI-driven camera to track the action in live-streamed games. But in one match the automatic camera followed the linesman instead – having mistaken his bald head for the ball (Fry, 2022). Blogger James Felton said: "The object recognition technology could clearly do with a bit of a tweak, or else the team might actually have to implement the policy of bald referees being forced to wear a sombrero to differentiate themselves from the ball."

Generative adversarial networks (GANs)

Across the media, there is increasing use of content assets that appear real – but are not. Examples are synthetic voices, synthetic humans and synthetic animals. They occur throughout this book, and increasingly in any given reader's social feed. Those assets are often created by GANs, or Generative Adversarial Networks.

- First used in 2014, GANs are two neural networks, that work in pairs to imagine and produce fakes so accurate that they can be entirely credible. To do this, one neural network, the generator, learns to generate images so real that they trick the second network, the discriminator, into believing them. Meanwhile the discriminator is also learning more and more skilfully to spot fakes. In a feedback loop, the models compete with each other, until the generator is good enough at creating fakes to trick the discriminator into believing them.

- Like in a Charlie Chaplin movie, "it's as though you have a pairing of a counterfeiter and a police officer. The counterfeiter tries to produce an image that will fool the police officer. And if it's not good enough, they'll get caught and have to try again" (Fry, 2022).
- Amongst countless examples, NVIDIA have demonstrated the use of GANs to create fake celebrities with highly credible photographic detail, after training them on pictures of real celebrities on the red carpet and gradually escalating the resolution of training data (Gershgorn, 2018).
- GANs have been used to make Deepfakes – like fake videos of Tom Cruise or Barack Obama (OFCOM, 2019). Deepfakes are overstated in the press as a risk of AI, but again they are covered at a number of points in this book, including in music, film and news.

Positive uses of GANs

- GANs were used in a 2021 research study to test the trustworthiness of synthetic vs real faces. They proved that the systems have become so effective that they "are capable of creating faces that are indistinguishable [from] – and more trustworthy – than real faces" (Nightingale and Farid, 2022).
- GANs can be used to bulk-up a set of training data by creating images of harmful content such as nudity or violence. These pictures can supplement existing examples of harmful content when training an AI-based moderation system, thus sparing the human moderators the potential psychologically traumatic process of looking at real images (OFCOM, 2019).
- GANs have been used in language processing – for instance, to turn legal text into simple text that people can actually understand, or to edit down long legal documents to the really key points (Waters, 2020).
- Design applications of GANs are growing fast. StyleGan2 is a generative adversarial network (GAN) made by Nvidia, which is useful for manipulating images. One Oxford academic, Dr Jason Bell, used it to create hundreds of unique new designs for sneakers, enabling him to ratchet up and down the radical nature of design combinations (Bell, 2021).
- Another team reported at a conference how they experimented with the design of completely new 'gourmet dishes' (such as bananas, bacon and tofu in cacciatore – Heavenly Bacon Tomato Cacciatore) using PIERRE, the Pseudo-Intelligent Evolutionary Real-time Recipe Engine, which is trained on ratings and ingredients on AllRecipes.com (Morris et al., 2012). "The computer sees something here that is worth trying, and moves beyond a boundary. That is an important component of computers that can help us with creativity" (Bell, 2021).
- GANs have been used by DeepMind in partnership with the UK Meteorological Office to model 'what comes next' in a historic video sequence of cloud formations, That capability has then been applied to forecasting itself, to accurately predict both rainfall and flooding (Fry, 2022).

Natural language processing

Natural language processing (NLP) explores the mechanisms behind language – at the meeting point of AI, linguistics and computer science. Language is deconstructed using text vectorisation, such that it can be analysed and, using statistical analysis of training data text on which systems have been trained, replicated. Put simply, in a given sequence of words, NLP will be educated to come up with the statistically most likely next word.

The goal of NLP is that computers start to write and speak with as much sophistication and nuance as humans. Using the calculation power of neural networks, NLP can be combined with different tools in a single process to form sophisticated speech, including syntactic analysis (grammar), sentiment analysis and topic classification. There are dozens of examples in this book of its implementation – from social media analysis to automated journalism, text creation and synthetic speech in games.

- NLP is currently used in translation, content moderation, email filters, speech to text tools, predictive text, smart assistants *Alexa* and *Siri* and sentiment analysis (e.g., for public relations purposes, including social listening by brands and national intelligence services).
- One of the better known NLP systems is *GPT-3*, a generative pre-trained transformer from Open AI. Trained on Microsoft's Azure's AI supercomputer, it takes a computational approach to language (Floridi and Chiriatti, 2020). But other transformers are constantly being developed, such as GLaM, Gopher, LaMDA and Megatron-Turing NLG. A number of these are referred to throughout this book. NLP systems can have recognisable genetic fingerprints. But one US-based national security AI expert said that unknown NLP systems might be deployed by adversaries making synthetic content (words, images or video) that cannot, because their fingerprint is not known, be identified as such.
- Google announced its own, 540-billion parameter language model, PaLM (Pathways Language Model) in April 2022, which it said dramatically advanced the capabilities of NLP from earlier competitors. Authors of its release said PaLM could explain complicated scenarios that required sophisticated understanding of language and knowledge of the world around us – for instance, providing "high quality explanations for novel jokes not found on the web" (Narang, 2022).

Limitations of AI

When talking about AI, we should not assume that it is all-powerful. As society, we need to use it as a tool, not be driven by it: "We need to incentivize states of the world, not actions of the agent" (Christian, 2021).

Just because an AI system is algorithmic rather than human, that does not mean it is incapable of making mistakes. Bad data, bad training data, or an error in the algorithms themselves can be compounded because of the sheer scale of calculations undertaken. And because of the 'black box' nature of some systems, mistakes can be hard to spot or even understand.

- "Anywhere that things are a little bit less predictable," said one Oxford expert on machine learning, "humans are still going to maintain the edge over the machines" (Osborne, 2021).
- AI-driven social networks that become too powerful have been repeatedly shown to cause societal damage, including the contribution social posts made to the 2021 Capital Riot in the US. AI-powered social media needs checks and balances: "A networked society needs to have well-designed circuit breakers that can swiftly reduce the connectivity of the network in a crisis, without atomizing and paralyzing society completely" (Ferguson, 2021).
- The challenge for media companies is to keep the evolutionary limitations of AI in mind, while implementing applications that focus on enabling humans to create and strategise more effectively (Chan-Olmsted, 2019).
- AI is not a singular path to progress. Errors can result from the erosion of key human skills due to AI implementation. "In the wake of the two plane crashes involving Boeing 737 Max jets, some experts expressed concern that pilots were losing basic flying skills – or at least the ability to employ them – as the jet relied on increasing amounts of AI in the cockpit" (Godwin, 2020).

Class discussion questions

- What AI tools have you used so far today? What kind of AI technology were they built from?
- What is the difference between (1) unsupervised learning; (2) supervised learning and (3) self-supervised learning, and what would be a contrasting use case for each?
- What AI tools have you seen used by media companies in their creative output?

BIBLIOGRAPHY

Anyoha, R. (2017) The history of artificial intelligence: can machines think? *Harvard University: Science in the News (SITN)*. [blog: Special Edition on AI] Available at: https://sitn.hms.harvard.edu/flash/2017/history-artificial-intelligence/ [Accessed 23 August 2022].

Bell, D. J. (2021) *Lecture on Diploma AI for Business*. Said Business School, University of Oxford.

Chan-Olmsted, S. M. (2019) A review of Artificial Intelligence adoptions in the media industry. *International Journal on Media Management*, 21(3–4), 193–215. doi.org/10.1080/14241277.2019.1695619

Christian, B. (2021) *Interviewed by Dr Alex Connock*. Diploma in AI for Business. University of Oxford, 18 November.

Economist, T. (2021) More than just a game. *Gamechangers*. [podcast] 16 August. Available at: https://play.acast.com/s/gamechangers/gamechangers-morethanjustagame [Accessed 29 August 2022].

Efremova, N. (2021) *AI for business: a glossary*. Said Business School, University of Oxford.

Ferguson, N. (2021) *Doom: the politics of catastrophe*. London: Penguin.

Floridi, L. and Chiriatti, M. (2020) *GPT-3*: its nature, scope, limits, and consequences. *Minds and Machines*, 30(4), 681–94. doi.org/10.1007/s11023-020-09548-1

Fry, H. (2022) Season 2. DeepMind: the *podcast*. [podcast] Available at: https://hannahfry.co.uk/deepmind-the-podcast-season-2/ [Accessed 23 August 2022].

Gershgorn, D. (2018) The hottest trend in AI is perfect for creating fake media. *Quartz*. [online] Available at: https://qz.com/1230470/the-hottest-trend-in-ai-is-perfect-for-creating-fake-media/ [Accessed 23 August 2022].

Godwin, J. O. (2020) *Artificial intelligence: a modern approach and machine learning.* Independently Published.

Hajjar, A. (2022) In-depth guide to self-supervised learning: benefits and uses. *AI Multiple*. [online] Available at: https://research.aimultiple.com/self-supervised-learning/ [Accessed 23 August 2022].

Jordan, M. I. (2019) Artificial Intelligence: the revolution hasn't happened yet. *Harvard Data Science Review*. doi.org/10.1162/99608f92.f06c6e61

Kissinger, H., Schmidt, E. and Huttenlocher, D. (2021) *The age of AI and our human future.* London: John Murray.

Kavlakoglu, E. (2020) AI vs. machine learning vs. deep learning vs. neural networks: what's the difference? *IBM Cloud*. [online] Available at: www.ibm.com/cloud/blog/ai-vs-machine-learning-vs-deep-learning-vs-neural-networks [Accessed 23 August 2022].

Meta. (2022) Introducing the AI Research SuperCluster – Meta's cutting-edge AI supercomputer for AI research. *Meta AI*. [online] Available at: https://ai.facebook.com/blog/ai-rsc/ [Accessed 23 August 2022].

Morris, R. G., Burton, S. H., Bodily, P. M. and Ventura, D. (2012) Soup over bean of pure joy: culinary ruminations of an artificial chef. *International Conference on Computational Creativity 2012*. [online] Available at: https://axon.cs.byu.edu/papers/morris2012iccc.pdf [Accessed 23 August 2022].

Morsili, S. (2022) *AI for power generation performance optimisation.* [Interview] 19 February.

Narang, S. (2022) Pathways language model (PaLM): scaling to 540 billion parameters for breakthrough performance. *Google AI blog*. [blog] 4 April. Available at: https://ai.googleblog.com/2022/04/pathways-language-model-palm-scaling-to.html [Accessed 16 August 2022].

Nightingale, S. J. and Farid, H. (2022) AI-synthesized faces are indistinguishable from real faces and more trustworthy. *Proceedings of the National Academy of Sciences*, 119(8), e2120481119. doi:10.1073/pnas.2120481119

OFCOM. (2019) *Use of AI in online content moderation.* [online] Available at: www.ofcom.org.uk/__data/assets/pdf_file/0028/157249/cambridge-consultants-ai-content-moderation.pdf [Accessed 16 August 2022].

Osborne, M. (2021) *Lecture on Diploma in AI for Business.* Said Business School, University of Oxford, 19 November.

PWC. (2017) *Sizing the prize: What's the real value of AI for your business and how can you capitalise?* [online] Available at: www.pwc.com.au/government/pwc-ai-analysis-sizing-the-prize-report.pdf [Accessed 23 August 2022].

Ramey, W. (2016) Ep.1: deep learning 101. *The AI podcast*. [podcast] Available at: https://soundcloud.com/theaipodcast/ai-podcast-deep-learning-101?in=user-20989779/sets/ai [Accessed 16 August 2022].

Rifkind, H. (2021) Can this man save the world from artificial intelligence? *The Times*, 29 September.

Russell, S. (2021) BBC Reith Lectures 2021 – Living with Artificial Intelligence. *BBC*. [online] Available at: www.bbc.co.uk/programmes/articles/1N0w5NcK27Tt041LPVLZ51k/reith-lectures-2021-living-with-artificial-intelligence [Accessed 29 August 2022].

Somers, J. (2021) The pastry AI that learned to fight cancer. *The New Yorker*, 18 March.

Spinney, L. (2022) Are we witnessing the dawn of post-theory science? *The Guardian*, 9 January.

Strong, J. (2021) Land of a billion faces. *In machines we trust*. [podcast] Available at: www.youtube.com/watch?v=o4H6NYa1iK0 [Accessed 29 August 2022].

Taylor, P. (2021) Insanely complicated, hopelessly inadequate. *London Review of Books*, 21 January.

Turing, A. M. (1950) I: Computing machinery and intelligence. *Mind*, LIX(236), 433–60. doi. org/10.1093/mind/LIX.236.433

UK Government (Department for Business, Energy and Industrial Strategy/Department for Digital, Culture, Media and Sport). (2019) AI sector deal policy paper. *Gov.UK*. [online] Available at: www.gov.uk/government/publications/artificial-intelligence-sector-deal/ai-sector-deal [Accessed 23 August 2022].

US National Security Commission on Artificial Intelligence (NSCAI). (2021) *The Final Report*. Washington, DC: NSCAI. [online] Available at: www.nscai.gov/2021-final-report/ [Accessed 23 August 2022].

Velte, T. (2022) *Artificial Intelligence in the commercial cannabis industry*. Interview with Dr Alex Connock conducted at Said Business School, University of Oxford.

Ventresca, M. (2022) *Lecture for the Diploma in AI for Business*. Said Business School, University of Oxford.

Waters, R. (2020) Calculating where artificial intelligence can do business. *Financial Times*, 25 October.

Wooldridge, M. (2018) *Artificial intelligence: everything you need to know about the coming AI. A Ladybird Expert Book* (Ladybird Expert Series, 27). London: Penguin.

SECTION B

Platforms

The engines of media distribution

CHAPTER 5

Games

AI is powering game platforms, and games are powering AI

....

INTRODUCTION TO THE SECTOR

If there was an Oscar for the global scale, impact and growth rate of media business segments, the games sector would win – every year.

Games sit like a vast and thriving, pixelated metropolis at the heart of the media landscape, inexorably adding new levels, details and users. The reach is vast, with 3 billion players in 2021, up 5.3% (Hersko, 2021). Games are culturally pivotal: Swedish game *Minecraft* was watched 201 billion times on *YouTube* in 2020 (Statista, 2021), around 23 views for every human being. Games store *Steam* is *YouTube*'s most-followed brand (Geyser, 2022). Only 10% of children aged 6–16 do *not* consider themselves gamers (Wood, 2022).

In the Metaverse (an always-on, globally scaled virtual world) populations could soon move to digital spaces for their social, entertainment and business lives – an enormous opportunity for games developers, who already have key software to support it (see Chapter 18).

The games market is globalised – but tilted noticeably towards Asia. It is shifting to mobile, digital downloads and the cloud. Its software and hardware are driving AI research fields within, and beyond, entertainment. And because of all these factors, it is attracting huge investment.

- In 2021, total game revenues were $180.3 billion, including all consumer spending on physical and digital copies, in-game spending, subscription services like *Xbox Game Pass* – but excluding advertising around games, or sales of consoles, hardware and gambling (Wijman, 2021).

DOI: 10.4324/9781003213611-7

- For comparison, in pre-pandemic 2019, the global cinema box office was $42.2 billion, less than a quarter the size of games, and declining long-term. In 2021, the global music industry had $26 billion revenue, almost seven times smaller than games (Savage, 2022).
- Within gaming's revenue mix, the segmentation tells a story of rapid evolution: in 2021, $93.2 billion was spent on mobile games (of which $11.7 billion on tablets and $81.5 billion on smartphones), up 7.3% year-on-year. Consoles took $50.4 billion, down 6.6% on 2020. (This may have been partly due to supply issues.) PCs, long the staple tool for hardcore gamers, were at $36.7 billion, down slightly (0.8%) year-on-year . The budget for PC and console games is so much higher than mobile games that the ROI is higher – which augments the industry pivot to mobile.
- It is worth observing however, that not all gaming is at the high-end, either creatively or in technology usage. One social media executive said (2022): "If you exclude casual games, and just focus on console players, it's about a tenth of the size."

AI research and gaming

Artificial Intelligence drives gaming and *vice versa*. AI in games drives image rendition, automated level generation, stories and autonomous motivations and even emotional interactions of non-playing characters (NPCs) (see section below) (Belova, 2021).

Games are also pivotal to some of the best AI in science as a whole, through use of gamification to structure approaches to complex problems across science. "Games have long been a way to evaluate the advancement of Artificial Intelligence (AI), showing just how 'intelligent' computer algorithms are, by pitting them against top human players in contests of strategy" (Good, 2022). Some of the great scientific breakthroughs of the early twenty-first century have already been achieved using AI developed on computer games, for instance, by AI research company DeepMind, which was co-created by the designer of the original *Theme Park* game, and whose team were honing their AI tools with games.

- In 2015, *DeepMind*'s *AlphaGo* used supervised learning and reinforcement learning to defeat a professional Go player and, in 2016, to defeat a Go champion.
- By 2017, with reinforcement learning and the Go-specific optimisations removed, *AlphaZero* mastered chess.
- By 2019, *MuZero* could teach itself a wide range of games without being taught the rules.
- In 2019, AlphaStar played *Starcraft 2* to professional level, using supervised learning on human data as a guide.

In parallel, DeepMind was using some of the same techniques for protein mapping, nuclear fusion modelling, autonomous robots (Fry, 2022) energy-saving control systems in data centres and national grids, early detection of eye diseases (Manthorpe, 2016) and other technologies beyond gaming.

- Having taught AI agents to work together in games like *Capture the Flag* and *Starcraft 2*, DeepMind leveraged the same collaborative approach to solving problems in machine learning, by introducing multiple agents to solve problems together. "By thinking about PCA [Principal Component Analysis] from a multi-agent perspective, we were able to propose scalable algorithms and novel analyses" (DeepMind, 2021).

DeepMind is not unique. At other developers, deep neural networks drive game agents, adapting to the approach of human players. Genetic algorithms mimic natural selection to make autonomous non-playing agents in the games more adaptive to what the human player is doing (Belova, 2021). "Games provide structure, repetition and reinforcement, which help algorithms learn" (Good, 2022).

Gaming and entertainment

Games push the technical envelope of entertainment. One industry insider said: "Making a game is like constructing a building during an earthquake. Or trying to drive a train while someone else runs in front of you, laying down track as you go" (Schreier, 2017). Crossover projects are growing in number and market penetration.

- Season 2 of *The Witcher* (which is inspired by the game) became a hit on *Netflix*, as did animation show *Arcane* (Riot Games' *League of Legends*-based series), which won 8 *Annie Awards* in 2022. Riot is also buying a stake in Fortiche, the animation studio that created the show (Radulovic, 2022).

And just as streaming has come to dominate the music and screen content spaces, so cloud gaming is also belatedly beginning to take hold, including even at *Netflix*, the quintessential cloud-based video streamer.

- Cloud gaming revenues in 2021 were a modest $1.57 billion, but that was a ten times increase on the 2019 figure, and they are forecast to reach $6.5 billion by 2024 (Wijman, 2021).

Finally games are informing the shift of entertainment towards a Metaverse. *Fortnite* (Epic Games), *Roblox* and other platforms have already hosted concerts within games, one of which (Lil Nas X) had 33 million visitors (Kastrenakes, 2020).

Gaming as an investable business

Given the growth and scale of the sector, games are attracting substantial investment – indicative of change in the games industry and the media.

- Games content had $5.9 billion investment in in 2021, up from $3.4 billion in 2020. Platform and technology received a further $4.8 billion.
- Blockchain gaming (see below) saw exponential growth from $38 million in 2020 to $3.1 billion in 2021 (Investgame, 2022), an increase of over 80 times. Non-fungible tokens (NFTs) are now a credible form of in-game intellectual property protection. Mobile investment also trebled, to $463 million.
- Gaming is also one of the very few areas of content production globally which attracts venture capital interest. Andreessen Horowitz, one of the two best-known firms in Silicon Valley, made 15 games investments in 2021, for a total of $1.7 billion (Investgame, 2022).

Academics are taking note too, with increasing literature in the space. On one end of the spectrum is study of player psychology – users have "virtual parasocial relationships with virtual characters and environments" (Palomba, 2020). On the other end – business dimensions: media companies looking to enter the mixed-reality space fail to balance their editorial expertise with enough IT skills (Zabel and Telkmann, 2020). In consequence of the opportunity: "there have been repeated calls to further understand the video game industry through a business lens due to its financial significance and fast growth" (Burgess and Jones, 2021).

The cumulative picture is a media segment with both maturity and green shoots, cultural value and huge financial momentum. Its influence reaches into almost all other segments of the media business – from scripted content to music to news. Even *The New York Times* buys gaming companies. (It bought *Wordle* in 2022.)

THE VALUE CREATION MODEL

The value creation model for games content can be viewed through the four stages of media value creation: development, production, distribution and monetisation.

Development is when games titles are conceived and pitched. Production is when games are funded, made and published. Distribution is where they reach the global public, via multiple channels. Monetisation is where they generate cash, from unit sales, to in-game purchases, to sale of the developer or publisher that created them.

Flywheel effect

There are two value-generative 'flywheel' effects in games, whereby success at a given stage of the process pulls momentum into the previous stage, in a virtuous circle. (The flywheel concept was created by author Jim Collins in his 2001 book *Good to Great*, but popularised by a potentially apocryphal drawing that Amazon founder Jeff Bezos made on a restaurant napkin, showing the positive cycle of sales he planned (Peppler, 2019).)

- First, a game title – say, the original 2009 *League of Legends* multiplayer battle arena from Riot Games – achieves traction in the market, builds players and is

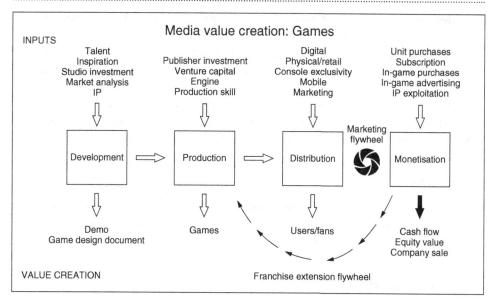

FIGURE 5.1 Success with a game launch can create powerful flywheel effects - driving further sales, distribution and new franchise titles

monetised. That creates network effects to pull in further players, which translates into cash and further marketing spend.

- Second, where a title monetises successfully, like the original 1981 *Mario* in *Donkey Kong*, franchise extension becomes possible (*Super Mario Bros* for *Nintendo Entertainment System* (1985)) whereby the games studio (Nintendo EAD) and publisher (Nintendo) fund additional iterations of the game, and a valuable franchise. This, in turn, delivers marketing economies of scale and higher financial returns. *Super Mario* has so far created at least 27 distinct titles and earned over $30 billion. A single mobile game created in 2016, *Super Mario Run*, earned over $60 million by 2018 (Lanier, 2018). An single, unopened copy of the 1985 *Super Mario Bros* first edition sold for $2 million (Browning, 2021).

Franchise effect

The highest-grossing franchises in games are *Pokemon*, *Mario*, *Call of Duty*, *Wii* and *Pacman*. *Pokemon* has sold over 47 million copies, with revenues of over $90 billion, potentially the most lucrative media franchise of all time.

For an example of how the franchise generates equity value, *Call of Duty* follows a quintessential course through the value creation model.

- The title was first created in 2003, by studio Infinity Ward (later, studios Treyarch, Sledgehammer and Raven) as a World War 2 first-person shooter game.
- Franchise extension has also expanded the storyline from the *Cold War* (2020) to *Zombies* (2009), *Black Ops* (2008 onwards) and *Ghosts* (2013). Besides new

titles, they also bring out patches or extensions of existing titles, which players buy, driving further monetisation (see below).

- The franchise has extended into at least 34 identifiable titles, on consoles, handheld, PC and mobile. Published by Activision it has over 400 million unit sales.

As well as the cash flow from successful franchises, value can be enhanced by corporate transactions (see monetisation below.) Activision Blizzard was the subject of a $68 billion takeover offer by Microsoft in 2022.

Development

At the development phase of the value creation process in games (or 'gamedev' cycle as it is called in the industry), the business challenge is the uncertainty that characterises construction of any new media IP.

Structure of industry

There is creative and operational risk. "Every single video game is made under abnormal circumstances. Video games straddle the border between art and technology" (Godwin, 2020). Video game titles have an 80% failure rate (Noam, 2019). The odds are stacked against any game developed.

The key players are studios and publishers.

- Studios (otherwise known as developers) create ideas and turn them into playable games, before giving them to a publisher to be distributed and monetised. Key 'gamedev' roles are Game Designer (develops ideas and directs development), Producer (organises the team and resources), Programmer, Tester and Artist (sets the style for the visuals and audio) (Thorn, 2022). Ideas come from talent, inspiration, market analysis (formal or not), code base (e.g., game engine or environments they can re-skin from previous work) and existing IP (e.g., any characters or story content they might own).
- Studios are either independent or owned by publishers or media companies. Well known studios include the UK's Rebellion (*Sniper Elite*) Supermassive (*Until Dawn*), The Chinese Room (*Dear Esther*), Jagex (*RuneScape*) and Splash Damage (*Wolfenstein: Enemy Territory*). In the US, a quintessential games studio is Washington state's Hidden Path Entertainment (*Counter-Strike: Global Offensive*). There is a hinterland of thousands of developers, often hand-to-mouth, who "operate on the premise that initial grant or client-funded projects will eventually generate enough profit to invest into building their own IP" (Chitty, 2020). Game ideas come from diverse sources. For instance the Japanese *Manga* comic publisher Shueisha in 2022 launched a company to exploit its animation IP in a new space (Rousseau, 2022).
- Publishers take game ideas from studios, invest in them and act as distributors. Major publishers fund AAA games – they include Ubisoft (*Rainbow Six Siege*),

Valve Corporation (*Data 2*, *Half-Life*), Rockstar Games (*Grand Theft Auto*, *Max Payne*), Blizzard Entertainment (*Hearthstone*), Tencent Holdings (*League of Legends*) and Electronic Arts (*FIFA*, *Battlefield*, *The Simpsons* and *Star Wars*). Distribution-only deals are with smaller, indie games studios, requiring less cash upfront and taking care of the mechanics of the game reaching the public.

- The landscape is complicated by the fact that many successful game developers are also publishers, making the distinction often irrelevant. Publishing is so substantial a segment that the combined market value of all the 'unicorns' (companies valued above a billion dollars) such as Bungie, MPL, RecRoom, Voodoo, Valve, IronSource, Epic Games, Niantic, JamCity, Wargaming.net, MiHoYo is $192.2 billion (Takahashi, 2021).

There are growing regional centres of excellence in games. In Africa, ten studios in 2022 came under the umbrella of the Pan African Gaming Group to promote a unified vision from the continent. They included South Africa's Sea Monster, Cameroon's Kiro'o Games, Ghana's Leti Arts and Rwanda's Messeka Games (Njanja, 2022).

Barriers to entry for game development, especially smaller indie games, are low, so indie developers can self-publish on *Steam* and, by building an engaged community become global success stories – such as the Indie game *Cuphead* from Studio MDHR, now also a *Netflix* animated series (Brossart, 2021).

Design process

In the development phase of a game, the game is not built, because capital has not yet been allocated to do so.

Teams create GDDs (Game Design Documents) specifying "the rules of the game, character back stories, level maps and complete game play descriptions" (Thorn, 2022). A famous example of one is the Tim Schafer GDD 'puzzle document' for *Grim Fandango* (Schafer, 1996).

Developers can create a demo, a 'vertical slice' of the video game, to justify investment. "During traditional, publisher-funded development, it was important for a vertical slice to look impressive, because if the publisher didn't approve, the studio wouldn't get paid" (Schreier, 2017). Erosion of the publisher/developer distinction weakens this requirement, since the publisher can invest in its own game. Development is not risk-free: "Video games might pull in tens of billions of dollars a year, but for the people who make those games, it's an incredibly unstable industry" (Martin, 2017).

Key dimensions in development

There are six key factors to consider in taking a game from development to production: IP, scale, marketing, platform choice, technology and co-creation.

- IP: is the creative idea a winner? This is near-impossible to know *a priori*. Working with legacy content can give the game developer advantages, for publisher investment and user traction. *Game of Thrones King's Landing* is a good example of a game using pre-existing IP. A good example of a self-published game where the studio maintained IP through distribution is *Farming Simulator 22*, by Swiss company GIANTS Software.

- Marketing: allied to the above point, any new game IP needs a market positioning or IP-relatability for traction. This can be a huge movie character (*Marvel's Spiderman*, 2018, developed by Insomniac Games and published by SONY) or it could be a simple, addictive and viral game (*Wordle*, developed by Welsh software engineer Josh Wardle and played by up to 2 million people per day when sold to *The New York Times* for over $1 million).

- Scale: open-ended worlds capable of infinite scaling are a larger logistic challenge, but can be attractive to large user base. *Roblox*, *Minecraft*, *Fortnite*, and *Pokémon Go* each achieve some 1.2 billion hours of engagement per month (Ball, 2020), because of the near-infinite scalability of their games.

- Platform: the device on which a game will be played is critical to games publishers, and always built into the game conception. Consoles own 28% of the market, split between *Xbox*, *PlayStation*, *Switch* and others. (It costs around $13,000 in fees to distribute a game to a console like *Nintendo Switch*, and there is always the risk of veto by the platform, "with no court of appeal" (Thorn, 2022) which is disincentivises games companies to rely on that outlet.) Smartphones and tablets have 52%, picking up increasing so-called AAA game titles as publishers go cross-platform. PCs have 19%, many hardcore gamers, for some of whom the PC is a point of purist pride, with alleged benefits over consoles of lower latency and higher frame rate. Some platforms carry economic incentive to go exclusive with them – for instance, *Demon's Souls* or *Marvel's Spider-Man Remastered* on *PS5*. But it can be a conscious decision to be platform-neutral, which is called 'crossplay.' *Fortnite* (Epic Games) expanded market opportunity by being available on *PlayStation*, PC, *Xbox* and *Switch*. *Overwatch* (Activision Blizzard) followed suit. For exclusivity to make sense, the premium paid to the publisher needs to be greater than potential revenue from all the platforms foregone, minus the costs of re-tooling the game for different platforms.

- Technology: the degree to which a games developer innovates with their game engine and other components correlates to both the risk and the upside in a game. Where new engines are built for the game, there is budgetary risk (Chitty, 2020). Some companies benefit creatively and commercially from having their own engine, such as Bethesda Game Studios' *The Creation Engine*, used to create *Fallout 76* and *The Elder Scrolls V: Skyrim*.

- Co-creation: openness of a game or a platform to user adaptation or user creativity will increase traction. *Minecraft* can incorporate legacy games within its universe, like Nintendo's *Metroid*. *Grand Theft Auto* has user "mods" (unlicensed) that can seamlessly transplant characters like *Iron Man* into the streets of Liberty City (Ball, 2020) The *Xbox Live Creators Program* gives new developers access to the distribution power of its marketplace. "Today, you and I could go build a video game, put it on *Xbox* without having a publisher, and our game could literally be sitting right next to, in our digital store, a game that was built for $100 million, and frankly, do just as well," said the Microsoft Gaming CEO (Spencer, 2022). "Think about the origins of where *Minecraft* came from, a small team in Stockholm." Games from China, Brazil and India are all given access to the global market.

Production

At the production phase of the value creation process in games, key inputs are investment, code base and production skill.

From a creative/technology standpoint, production of games requires many departments (story, music, design, interstitial film 'directors') all built around a game engine, often on industry standard software *Unity* (which powers circa 50% of all games, on over 20 platforms, and has an asset store which offer, say, off-the-shelf forests to developers) or *Unreal Engine* (owned by Epic Games). The engines have different charging models, and which tool has been used is visible to game engine providers via 'disassembly software.' Unity charges studios on a $150-per-seat basis for its Pro solution (2022). Epic takes a percentage of revenue on a game above a certain threshold (currently $1 million of lifetime gross revenue (Machkovech, 2020)). It is also used in Hollywood scripted production – and well beyond, in construction, architecture and car companies (Peckham, 2020). Other tools include *Maya* and *Photoshop* to create the game in cyclic phases (Thorn, 2022). Once the game is created, testers play it.

Investment in a game title can be from a publisher, which may or may not also be the developer (see above) or a pure-play investor. Any approach to game finance carries risk.

> Traditionally, independent studios like Obsidian and Double Fine had three ways to stay afloat: (1) finding investors, (2) signing contracts with publishers to make games, or (3) funding their own video games … No decent-size indie studio could survive without relying at least partly on money from outside partners.
>
> *(Schreier, 2017)*

So, as with all media production, critical to the relationship are budget and deal terms.

Budgets

Game builds for independent studios cost between (approximate figures) $50,000 and $1 million. A standard indie game might have a budget of approximately $250,000 (Thorn, 2022), representing 18 months' work for a five to seven person team. But for larger AAA games, budgets can be over $50 million, as high as action movies (which to some extent they actually are). Video game *Genshin Impact* reportedly cost $100 million to make, but earned $577 million in China alone, out of a total $2 billion revenue in its first year. (And it was a mobile game.)

- *Call of Duty Modern Warfare 2* had a reported production and marketing cost of $250 million, of which some $40 million was spent on production itself.
- *Grand Theft Auto V* (Rockstar Games) cost a reported $265 million.

Publisher financing deal terms

Deal terms for a publisher funded game were reported by a lawyer at the Games Developer Conference 2020.

- The average of 30 developer/publisher contracts showed a $318,000 advance for development. The sale price to consumers will be set by the publisher. During recoupment of the advance, there is a 60:40 split in revenues to the publisher. Then the split reverses to 60:40 to the developer. The agreement typically lasts 6.5 years (Wilde, 2020).
- Developers are wary of ceding IP to publishers, or automatic sequel rights on the same terms. (If a game is a hit, the developer's bargaining position should be improved.) Deals where the developer has no influence over pricing or discounting of its game are not desirable.
- For a developer-funded game: where the developer takes production risk and the publisher enters late, the publisher becomes a distributor in the more conventional media business sense, and the split of any advance favours the developer, as much as 70:30. (Wilde, 2020). The problem is that obtaining these terms means more risk, and: "the life of an independent developer is, every morning you wake up wondering if your publishers are going to call and cancel your games" (Schreier, 2017).
- Some games dev teams produce games or game assets on a work-for-hire basis.

Other forms of game financing

Venture capital investors have disliked games developer investments because of the low success rate of game titles. As *TechCrunch Equity* discussion explained the model's changing attraction. "The top triple A games day cost $100 million. And then you put your box on the shelf or on *Steam* and it pops … and you've lost all your cash. So venture capitalists hate this model. It's why they weren't in content, it's why they never really engaged with Hollywood."

But new generation scalable games with recurring revenue, like *League of Legends*, *Fortnite* and *Roblox*, are more attractive. "It feels like SAAS [software as a service] and … investors are much more confident in investing" (Wilhelm and Mascarenhas, 2021). Investors now like the monthly income of subscription games, as it gives a customer lifetime value rather than a simple one-off acquisition fee (see Chapter 3).

Crowd-funding has occasionally enabled a games company to obtain investment without giving away rights, thereby offsetting financial risk. Indie developer Double Fine raised $3.3 million in 2012 from 87,142 backers for an adventure game project which ended up being called *Broken Age* (Byford, 2012). But this is not a reliable business strategy.

Distribution

The key inputs at the distribution phase of the media value creation process in games are digital and/or physical retail, console deals, mobile distribution (52% of all gaming revenues (Newzoo, 2021)) and marketing. The key outputs from the distribution phase are engaged users, monetised in a range of ways (see below).

- The games fan base is massively global: Asia (55%), Middle East and Africa (15%), Europe (14%), Latin America (10%) and North America (7%). Sometimes games are marketed by different distributors in different territories, as was the case with *Mortal Kombat*.
- The fastest growing region is Africa at 10% annually (Newzoo, 2021).

Whereas game developers can be relatively small companies (though some are still multibillion dollar entities) distribution is where some of the very biggest companies on earth – and certainly the biggest companies in media – become directly involved in games.

- Meta (*Facebook Gaming*), Microsoft (*Xbox*), Sony (*PlayStation*), Tencent (owner of Riot Games) and Google (*Stadia*) all have major stakes in games distribution.
- Even *Netflix*, hitherto a film and TV streamer, entered the space with acquisition of games studios Night School, Next Games and, in March 2022, Boss Fight Entertainment (Browning, 2022). At the time, Mike Verdu of *Netflix* said it planned to make games out of its TV shows. But the streamer has also experimented with wider, cloud-based games streaming.

Success factors in distribution

The value of traction a game title across a vast games market, forecast to be 3.32 billion players by 2024, is the financial dynamic which underpins the games value chain.

There are five key channels to consider in distribution.

- Digital distribution: this is now the dominant avenue – higher-margin, traceable, more direct-to-consumer and more likely to build a valuable long-term engagement with the customer than physical sales. Major publishers and retailers going digital include the platform *Steam* (owned by game publisher Valve), the indie-centric *itch.io*, the *PlayStation Store*, *Nintendo eShop*, *Xbox Games Store*, *GAME*, *GameStop*, *Amazon*, the *Apple* and *Android* app stores, and others.

Within digital distribution there are retail and subscription channels. "The retail market continues to be very strong and grow," said the CEO of Microsoft Gaming, whose subscription product is *Game Pass*. "Subscription is growing faster" (Spencer, 2022). Until September 2022, Google promoted cloud-based subscription platform *Google Stadia* (described by one games professional as "a masterclass in how not to do games streaming"). Apple is the most highly valued game company, though it doesn't produce games, because of its distribution via the App Store. In November 2019, Apple (mostly) won a legal action with Epic Games around its App Store commissions (Perez, 2021). Platforms are so important to the games business (Takahashi, 2021) because they have the customer base and data to maintain subscription relationships. Digital Rights Management (DRM) software protects games from piracy.

- Cloud distribution: as streaming grows (see Chapter 7), so cloud-based gaming may grow, whereby users subscribe for access to a playable library. There are already subscription services such as *Xbox Cloud Gaming*, *Google Stadia*, *GeForce Now*, and *Amazon Luna* (Hersko, 2021).

- Digital marketing: part of the secret to successful online distribution is the wider market traction a brand can bring. Games publisher Electronic Arts spent $689 million marketing in 2021 (Statista, 2022). Research showed a game's marketing budget was three times more important than positive reviews in generating sales (Martin, 2009). Chinese company Tencent, which in 2020 led the global market with $30.6 billion sales, wraps mobile games into its other messaging products for its vast domestic user base (Lewis, 2022). In China, a constraint on the effectiveness of marketing is thelevel of demand itself. The state intervened in the market in August 2021, labelling gaming 'spiritual opium' and reducing to one hour per day childrens' game time, with a ban on in-game purchases (Lockett, 2021) – Tencent also put similar constraints on its own game, *Honor of Kings*.

- Social marketing: viral scaling via games influencers is a powerful tool. In Brazil, 30% of 18–34 year olds say their source of information about games is influencers – which is more than the 23% who use online shops (YouGov, 2021). The customer lifetime value (CLV) of a player is in part a function of their promotion of the products, giving them what a Harvard report termed an enhanced 'customer lifetime social value' (Ofek, 2018), taking account of their social marketing of the game. *Xbox Live* is a "social network" as much as gaming tool: "Those friends relationships that are on the network are incredibly important," said its CEO (Spencer, 2022). Multiplayer games like *World of Warcraft*, *Call of Duty* and *League of Legends* naturally have brought friends' networks to games distribution. As yet, their scale is capped – *Fortnite* manages about 100 players per server – but this is likely to grow with the Metaverse where "fully emergent social experiences that model the serendipity of the real world will become the norm" (Lai, 2022). Part of the social marketing of a game is done in person, at trade conferences like E3, the Electronic Entertainment Expo. Social channels like *Discord* are also an important marketing channel, creating a fan base even before a title launches.

- Consoles: this category remains important. *Sony PlayStation 5* sold out in 2021, causing hikes in prices, and turning the role of Xbox managers to logistics. "How do you actually manage so that real customers are buying our consoles, and it's not a bunch of scalpers and bots that are securing the capacity?" (Spencer, 2022).

Monetisation

At the monetisation stage of the value creation process in games, unit purchases, subscription revenues, in-game sales, advertising and other sources combine to produce revenues to the publisher and then (via revenue share and recoupment arrangements) the developer.

Ultimate monetisation of the game may result from acquisition of the rights-owning developer and/or publisher, which in effect is a crystallisation in the present day of all future cash flows from the games produced.

Unit purchases

Premium games (sold upfront) tend to be single player, and multiplayer games tend to be subscription. For premium games, the 'Zero Day' cohort of committed customers seek out new titles at almost any price on its launch date. But following launch, price evolves dynamically (downwards) and potentially before the costs of game creation have been recouped. This creates a motivation for publishers to shift to a subscription model, or use microtransactions (see below) to drive long-term income, which is known as DLC (downloadable content).

In-game microtransactions

Microtransactions are small payments made during a game for extra play advantage or cosmetic benefit. They often tap into behavioural economics tools, such as loss aversion and variable rate reinforcement (Agarwal, 2022) to encourage players. It is a very big business. The largest annual additions to entertainment spending as a whole in 2020 (versus 2019) were $18.5bn of microtransactions, and other in-game purchases (Hancock, 2021).

While many console games make money from sale of a hard copy or digital download, platform games like *Fortnite* (with an in-game currency – 'v-bucks' – allowing purchase of skins or a battle-pass) have tilted their revenue mix heavily towards microtransactions (Colagrossi, 2021).

Microtransactions have been present in gaming since the 1990s, but more prevalent in the 2020s. They either help the player move forward in the game, or make them feel good about being in the game. Some apply in games which are free to play but whose business model is to upsell players; such a 'freemium' sales method may be more effective than charging for game download from the mobile app stores. It has been suggested that a tiny 0.15% of mobile gamers account for over 50% of in-game revenue (Takahashi, 2014).

Players often grumble about these "freemium" games, says a philosophy academic in the *Games and Culture* journal. "But most recognize that some kind of payment is necessary for the labor that goes into designing a game. However, the practice of including microtransactions in a game that players have already spent US$50 or US$60 on has generated much more controversy" (Neely, 2021).

An example of the freemium model was the launch of *League of Legends* by Riot Games. A competing Multiplayer Online Battle Arena (MOBA) game was *Heroes of Newerth (HoN)*, in which some gamers saw higher production quality. But *Heroes of Newerth* launched a free beta of the game and moved to a subscription model. Many of the initial players ended up moving to *League of Legends* instead of staying loyal to *HoN*. "Having a slightly superior game with a subscription model is not enough to charge a subscription fee and players will go where they perceive they are receiving the highest return for their investment" (Rosu, 2019). *League of Legends* allows users to buy *Riot Points*, a currency which can then buy skins, "which are different aesthetic choices for the game characters" (Colagrossi, 2021).

Types of microtransactions

Within the field, there are broad categories (Duverge, 2016).

- In-game currencies: these can play the role of masking to users the true cost of what they are spending. In the *Dawning* event from *Destiny 2* players had to buy an in-game currency called *Bright Dust* for attractive skins, costing up to $220 (Ahmad, 2022).
- Random chance purchases: these are mystery items know as 'loot boxes,' or 'prize boxes,' paid in real or in-game currency, but with unpredictable outcomes (Neely, 2021). These are in major game franchises such as *Call of Duty: WWII*, *Destiny 2*, *FIFA 19*, *Fortnite*, *Hearthstone*, *Shadow of War* and *Need for Speed* (McCaffrey, 2019). *Call of Duty: Black Ops 4* had a $2 loot box (in addition to the base price $60 and an extra $50 season pass) which sometimes gave players a gameplay advantage (Ahmad, 2022). Philosopher Erica Neely argues loot boxes are unethical because of "concerns about casually including gambling in video games and in part it is due to the potentially predatory nature of these microtransactions" (Neely, 2021). She notes countries such as Belgium and China have restricted loot boxes on these grounds of casualised gambling. Electronic Arts (EA) used microtransactions until a November 2017 controversy around the beta version of *Star Wars: Battlefront II*, with extensive loot boxes. Critics argued that to win enough loot crates to get all the extra cards for in-game abilities and heroes, "players had to put in thousands of hours" (Ahmad, 2022). EA ended up dropping them: "but not before it caused a storm of controversy among gamers and policymakers" (McCaffrey, 2019). In 2020, the UK's National Health Service said that loot boxes contribute to youth gambling addiction (NHS, 2020).

- In-game upgrades/bonus purchases/XP boosters: these enable players to play more levels, or longer, or advance faster, or with better tools, or a better skin, often using motivators like a countdown clock. *League of Legends* gives players the chance to buy skins for their character. *World of Warcraft* offers in-game add-ons like pets (Agarwal, 2022) which became an industry talking point because the pets were cosmetic items which bestowed no game advantage: "there was controversy over whether this would lead to buying in-game gear with real money" (Neely, 2021). In 2016, *FIFA's Ultimate Team* feature reportedly earned EA $800 million in additional revenue from the game (Trefis, 2017).

- Some in-game extras allow players to accelerate acquisition of items which could be accumulated for free with investment of time, such as in *Middle-earth: Shadow of War*. Some upgrades improve game performance – like armour in *Dragon Age: Inquisition*. Some paid upgrades can be 'pay to skip,' like in *Game of War: Fire Age*, where players who pay to train their troops beat people who have not paid. Some put within the game item trading which was previously going on outside, as with *Diablo III* (Blizzard, 2012). (The auction was eventually removed.) But even transparent rewards (unlike loot boxes) can present ethical problems: "designers need to consider how they are marketed, and it could be possible to market them to child players, say, in a predatory way" (Neely, 2021).

- In-game transactions can be too large. The persistent-universe game, *Star Citizen* reportedly raised over $400 million dollars in funding in the decade after its 2012 start, as it built the game. One of the approaches was selling spaceships which did not yet exist in the game (Tassi, 2022); the 'high roller exclusive' *Legatus 2951* pack was marketed for $40,000 (Strickland, 2021). The UK's Advertising Standards Authority said in 2021: "we issued an Advice Notice advising the advertiser, in future, to ensure that its ads include any material information and significant limitations." The game-makers Cloud Imperium Games said: "The *Crusader Ares (Inferno* and *Ion)*, *A2 Hercules*, *Genesis Starliner*, are being offered here as a limited vehicle concept pledge … This means that the vehicle is in development but is not yet ready to display in your Hangar or fly in *Star Citizen*." The game continues to (slowly) grow: "the developer is continuing to toil away at this Gordian Knot of a project. They don't have to try and sell their vision anymore – you can actually play bits of it" (Marshall, 2022). Epic Games, makers of *Fortnite*, were sued in California by lawyers representing choreographer Kyle Hanagam, who has worked with Jennifer Lopez, over alleged copyright infringement (which Epic denied) around the 'It's complicated' dance emote, on sale in the game for 500 V-bucks (roughly $5 in real world money). Epic had previously won a case at the Supreme Court from other choreographers, having argued that dance moves fell under the category of free speech (Jiang, 2022).

- Expiration and pay-to-unlock: these microtransactions offer replacement of items which run out. In the game *Asura's Wrath*, gamers had to pay more to access the end of the story.

- The *Gacha* model of mobile games offers yet another monetisation strategy, in most of the 200 top games in Japan. *Gacha* (randomised arcade gift picking machines) was pioneered by the game *Dragon Collection* and requires payment with in-game currency. *Gachas* are similar to loot boxes, but whereas loot boxes offer optional extras, *Gachas* offer items essential to progress (Grguric, 2022) and can be addictive. A 'comp' (complete) *Gacha* requires players to complete a set of items in order to achieve a valuable item – banned in Japan because of its statistical improbability. A 'step-up' *Gacha* offers accelerating odds, the more a player plays. Other types are 'box' (limited reward pool), 'consecutive' (bulk spending improves odds), 'open' (know odds), 'closed' (unknown odds) and so forth. Legitimate games using Gacha include *Fire Emblem: Heroes* from Nintendo and *Genshin Impact* from MihoYo.

Finally, not all in-game sales are for profit at all.

- In March 2022, *Fortnite* raised over $30 million for the relief effort for the Ukraine war in a single day.
- Play to earn games were used by Yield Guild Games to raise $1.45 million for Philippine typhoon relief, including $458,000 of crypto and tokens donated (Wright, 2022).

In-game advertising

Game developers can include pre- or mid-roll video ads around the game, in fixed advertising positions within the games themselves, or programmatic advertising. Adtech agencies such as Adverty offer this in-game advertising, calling alternative, 30-second video spots, intrusive. CEO Niklos Bakos said: "we allow game developers to put billboards and posters, and basically any objects of their liking, to have an advert on them" (Hart, 2021).

There are three types:

- Static in-game advertising: here the adverts are built into the fabric of the game action at the coding stage, but not geo-targeted, so likely to be efficient only to the most global brands (RapidFire, 2022).
- Advergames: these are games specifically built by a single advertiser to promote their product, enabling brand-building.
- Dynamic in-game advertising: this allows real time purchase of in-game, geo-targeted programmatic, time-specific advertising, on in-game billboards or banner ads, via the games engine or an external ad server. Via 2014 acquisition of Applifier, Unity launched an in-game mobile advertising network, then expanded substantially with the Unified Auction, a simultaneous auction that helps games get the highest bid among potential advertisers. Unity is now one of the world's largest mobile ad networks, serving 23 billion ads per month. Unity also has a dynamic monetisation tool that makes real-time assessments of whether it is

optimal to serve an ad, prompt an in-app purchase or do nothing – to maximise each player's lifetime value. While the Unity IAP feature enables developers to manage in-app purchases (IAP). Games offering dynamic advertising through different methods are *Angry Birds Go* (sponsored power-ups), *Crossy Road* (cross-promotion) and *Football Manager Classic*.

IP exploitation

Games have added a powerful driver to their mix of gross revenues through exploitation of games titles in film and TV. "There are far more film and television adaptations of video games in various stages of development today than at any other time in history" (Hersko, 2021). EA Sports included hit Apple TV+ show Ted Lasso in FIFA 2023.

- Key titles migrated to film and streaming include *Minecraft* and *Metal Gear Solid* films, *Sonic the Hedgehog* 2 (which took a substantial $71 million at the US box office on its first weekend in April 2022) and *Netflix*'s *Assassin's Creed* series to coincide with the new *Assassin's Creed Infinity* game universe from Ubisoft. Perhaps driven by the wider success of *Marvel* and *Star Wars* franchises, top directors and talent now work on video game-driven projects such as *Fallout*.
- Franchise IP is also being developed in a platform-agnostic way: Disney+ gave the *Marvel* character *Loki* a streaming series that fits into the *Avengers* story, and will ultimately have its own video game (Hersko, 2021).

Acquisitions

One of the best ways to monetise a game is to sell the company that made it. This brings future cash flow to the present day, sometimes on high multiples of profit (or even revenue), which implicitly include valuation of (so far non-existent) franchise titles.

Acquisitions are active in the games market because of the user growth, profit margin of hit games and instant global scalability.

- In 2021, 937 acquisition deals were completed, for $71.3 billion. Of those, 52% were in gaming, 32% platform/tech, 11% Esports and 5% in other categories (Investgame, 2022).
- In 2022, Microsoft initiated the biggest deal ever in games, to buy Activision Blizzard (*Call of Duty, Overwatch, World of Warcraft*) for $68.7 billion (Datastream, 2022). Activision Blizzard had itself bought King (*Candy Crush*) for $5.9 billion in 2015. Whilst some industry watchers worried Microsoft would take *Call of Duty* exclusive on *Xbox*, this was illogical: Microsoft would have to add 5 million subscribers to make up for the sales it would lose as a publisher, just by not putting it on *PlayStation* (Lewis, 2022).
- Other key deals of 2022 alone included Take-Two Interactive's acquisition of mobile game developer Zynga (*Farmville*) for $12.7 billion. (Zynga had itself

bought casual gaming company Peak – *Toon Blast, Toy Blast, Lost Jewels* – in 2020 for $1.8 billion.) Sony bought Bungie (*Destiny*) for $3.6 billion – possibly as a counter to Microsoft's market disruption (Datastream, 2022) – and then bought Haven Entertainment Studios, a company barely a year old, founded by developers who had previously worked on *Assassin's Creed* and other major titles.

- Compared to almost any other industry, the valuation metrics – around ten times revenue – of deals in the gaming space are high. These multiples would not be paid for a TV broadcaster or production company. In mid-2021, *Roblox*, with revenues of $920 million, had a valuation of $54.9 billion. Electronic Arts was valued at $40.6 billion with revenues of $5.5 billion (Takahashi, 2021). The justification for the valuation is future growth projected. There is an additional valuation premium where an exclusive title can facilitate value upside in for platform business (because people will be driven to buy consoles).

AI technologies

Artificial intelligence is extensively used in games coding.

- Games developers optimise systems to play under human-like constraints, in reaction time and input accuracy, with human-like cognitive load and strategies. Otherwise the AI opponents would be too good. AI can also be used in dialogue generation, dynamic storytelling, facial animation and environmental interaction.
- Procedural Content Generation (PCG) generates large, open-world environments, new levels and assets. NLP is used for text analysis and scenario generation, for instance, in the *AI Dungeon 2* application (Belova, 2021) using Open AI's Natural Language Processing engine, which can understand a script, and continue it (Lai).
- In-game complexity algorithms flex the game environment to reflect the present tense impact of choices the gamer makes. This is used in *FIFA*'s 'ultimate team mode,' which computes chemistry and morale as a function of game action – DeepMind have also used AI to analyse the real Liverpool football club) (Fry, 2022).
- Deep learning was used in *Grand Theft Auto 5* to create realistic Los Angeles cityscapes, making synthetic images look more real. NVIDIA have used deep neural networks in 'realistic materials acquisition,' for instance, wood or denim, from a single photo (Kravitz, 2021). NVIDIA GPUs are now used to run programmes for every pixel on the screen and produce more realistic rendition of environments, up to 70 times faster than a normal chip for convolutional neural networks. When this was discovered at Stanford in 2012, it was a 'big bang' for deep learning in general (Economist, 2021).
- Some of the hardware tools in gaming are also being leveraged in the wider world of computing. For instance, NVIDIA graphics cards in generative adversarial

networks (GANs). NVIDIA's Maxine AI video conference tool uses GANs to analyse a person's face and then algorithmically animate in video calls (Lai, 2022).

- AI allows Non Playing Characters (NPCs) to be more intelligent and responsive to gave conditions. Electronic Arts has an in-house technical group called Seed (SeedEA, 2022) which researches autonomous characters to be used across gaming. AI-driven gaze tracking tools are being used to more accurately map game action to the attention of the player (Kravitz, 2021).
- Machine translation (another use of NLP) is being used for real-time rendition of games into eight other languages by *Roblox* (Lai, 2022). Meta is also working on this in a Metaverse context.
- Making in-game advertising work can also involve using AI. For instance, a WPP India used a 'target tuner,' usually known as a model tuner, to precisely filter and value how inventory was performing on in-game advertising for engagement for the advertiser PGI, resulting in a three times increase in click through rate.

Class discussion questions

- Why is the games industry so much bigger than the music business?
- How important is having internally owned IP in the development of a successful video games business?
- Which AI-driven technologies will play a significant role in the development of the next generation of video games?
- What are the relative merits of the different distribution options for a games studio?
- What are the barriers to entry in the games console market?

Analysis: product development in ML/NLP-driven games tech company, Charisma.ai

UK company Charisma AI, founded by Guy Gadney, is exploring interactive narrative in games.

> We see the world based very strongly on characters, and bringing characters to life. But there is one character that is missing from our immersive storytelling past – you. Now with new technologies, for the first time in many years, you get to talk to the characters in stories. Not only can these characters make you laugh and cry, but you can make them laugh and cry.

Gadney sees three key changes coming in games and the verbal dimension of storytelling.

The first key movement in the market was [Amazon] *Alexa*. Before *Alexa* we weren't used to talking to technology. The second was the move to virtual production, as seen in *The Mandalorian*. The third was Epic Games' metahumans, which will change the verbs that are used in the games industry. Chris Swain at Electronic Arts pointed out that the video games has a verb problem – it's below-the-shoulder verbs: "run, kick." Hollywood is above the shoulder: "make them laugh, make them cry." When they combine, this will be a new future.

Narrative tools

Charisma has a story-building tool with dialogue nodes and character decision points which remember what you said, and respond differently according to your emotion. There are gates, wildcards and memory points. Gates are situations where the actions of a character determine the progress in the game. The memory point is where a character remembers names, sentences, or decisions that the player has made. The 'brain' of Charisma analyses the text. It can't pick up irony or sarcasm yet, but it can do visual emotion-sensing, from a webcam, and tonal sentiment analysis.

Charisma made a real-time sequence where *Steppenwolf* has an interaction with a player using natural language processing for a real conversation. And it made a simulated tool, *Conversation*, for parents with autistic children with the University of Ulster, in which the participants interact in a gamified way to practice how to interact with kids. This approach could also be taken with workplace bias and negotiation.

Games development with verbally interactive characters

"Warner Bros released *The Matrix Metaverse* [in 2022] with Neo and other characters in it," says Gadney. "But the most interesting part of it was 55,000 metahuman pedestrians on the streets. How fantastic would it be if you could enable the conversation with each of those pedestrians. To create content on that scale you need augmented intelligence."

Gadney has key takeaways for AI in gaming. (1) AI accelerates production – via automation. (2) AI deepens engagement – inclusion of narratives into AI deepens engagement into days/weeks/years. (3) AI enables creativity. "I don't think AI should be seen as a technology, but a lens through which you look at business optimisation." (4) AI raises quality. "This year we will see content that is indistinguishable from reality." But (5) "Above all, awe do need to remember that our customers are human. What people respond to is (forgive the pun) charisma" (Gadney, 2022).

Discussion question

• Are Gadney's five conclusions about the role and potential of AI in gaming the right ones?

Chapter summary

TABLE 5.1 Key themes in this chapter

GAMES	Development	Production	Distribution	Monetisation
Business model	Risky early stage investment, and most titles do not even get funded into production.	Substantial investment required for game production, and 80% fail. Developer risk offset with publisher funding.	Versatility of platforms (including mobile), compelling content and strong marketing are the key success factors.	Digital sales predominate. In-game advertising and purchases significant. Franchise titles produce flywheel and cash flow.
Uses of AI	AI is embedded into many game creation tools, and will increasingly be so.	Many AI technologies are used in game creation – from worlds and levels to non-playing chapters. NLP, deep learning common.	Some AI used on games distribution via digital marketing.	AI is being used for in game advert optimisation.
Value Creation	Low value creation at the development stage.	Value is created at the moment a game is invested in and produced.	Real value creation moment is when games distributed to market. At this point, if successful, there can be exponential leaps in value.	Developers and publishers with hit title have value realisation opportunity via company sale. This is happening.

BIBLIOGRAPHY

Agarwal, P. (2022) Microtransactions in video games. Intelligent Economist. [online] Available at: www.intelligenteconomist.com/microtransactions/ [Accessed 23 August 2022].

Ahmad, K. (2022) 7 Examples of gaming microtransactions: from acceptable to evil. *MUO.* [online] Available at: www.makeuseof.com/examples-of-gaming-microtransactions/ [Accessed 23 August 2022].

AI for Good (2022) How video games can help Artificial Intelligence deliver real-world impact. *AI for Good blog*. [blog] Available at: https://aiforgood.itu.int/how-video-games-can-help-artificial-intelligence-deliver-real-world-impact/ [Accessed 23 August 2022].

Ball, M. (2020) Digital theme park platforms: the most important media businesses of the future. *MathewBall.vc*. [online] Available at: www.matthewball.vc/all/digitalthemeparkplatforms [Accessed 23 August 2022].

Belova, K. (2021) How artificial intelligence (AI) upends game development. *Pixelplex*. [online] Available at: https://pixelplex.io/blog/how-ai-enhances-game-development/ [Accessed 23 August 2022].

Brossart, T. (2021) 15 indie games that became major success stories. *Gamerant*. [online] Available at: https://gamerant.com/indie-games-major-success-stories/ [Accessed 23 August 2022].

Browning, K. (2021) A Super Mario Bros game sells for $2 million, another record for gaming collectibles. *New York Times*, 6 August.

Browning, K. (2022) Netflix buys another video game studio as it builds out its gaming business, *New York Times*, 24 March.

Burgess, J. and Jones, C. (2021) Exploring emergent co-creative narrative in a strategy video game brand. *Journal of Media Business Studies*, 1–18. doi.org/10.1080/16522354.2021.1959705

Byford, S. (2012) Double fine Kickstarter project ends with $3,336,371 funding. *The Verge/Kickstarter*. [online] Available at: www.theverge.com/2012/3/13/2869261/double-fine-kickstarter-project-ends-3335130-funding [Accessed 23 August 2022].

Chitty, A. (2020) *The UK creative immersive landscape 2020: business models in transition. Audience of the Future*. [online] Available at: https://audienceofthefuture.live/wp-content/uploads/20201126_DC_153_UKCreativeImmersiveLandscapeReport_Digital_v1.pdf [Accessed 23 August 2022].

Colagrossi, M. (2021) How microtransactions impact the economics of gaming. *Investopedia*. [online] Available at: www.investopedia.com/articles/investing/022216/how-microtransactions-are-evolving-economics-gaming.asp [Accessed 23 August 2022].

Datastream, V. C. (2022) The most expensive gaming company acquisitions.

DeepMind. (2021) Game theory as an engine for large-scale data analysis. *DeepMind*. [online] Available at: www.deepmind.com/blog/game-theory-as-an-engine-for-large-scale-data-analysis [Accessed 23 August 2022].

Duverge, G. (2016) Insert more coins: the psychology behind microtransactions. *Touro University*. [online] Available at: www.tuw.edu/psychology/psychology-behind-microtransactions/ [Accessed 23 August 2022].

Economist, T. (2021, 16 August 2021) In *Gamechangers: More than just a game*.

Ehrlich, D. and Hersko, T. (2021) How the future of entertainment will be forged between Hollywood and video games. *IndieWire*. [online] www.indiewire.com/2021/08/future-of-entertainment-hollywood-video-games-indiewire-25-1234659532/ [Accessed 23 August 2022].

Fry, H. (2022, January 2022) Series 2 In *DeepMind: the Podcast*.

Gadney, G. (2022, 1 April 2022) *Interview at Oxford University* [Interview].

Geyser, W. (2022) The state of influencer marketing 2022: benchmark report. *InfluencerMarketingHub*. [online] Available at: https://influencermarketinghub.com/influencer-marketing-benchmark-report/ [Accessed 23 August 2022].

Godwin, J. O. (2020) *Artificial intelligence: a modern approach and machine learning*. Independently Published.

Grguric, M (2022) Gacha system in mobile games: everything you need to know. *Udonis*. [blog] 5 January. Available at: www.blog.udonis.co/mobile-marketing/mobile-games/gacha-system [Accessed 23 August 2022].

Hancock, D (2021). The cinema landscape and recovery.

Hart, A. (2021, 5 May 2021) Marketing Today with Alan Hart In *Adverty's Niklas Bakos: Marketing Today with Alan Hart 5 May 2.*

Investgame. (2022) Gaming Deals Activity Report 2021.

Jiang, S. (2022) Fortnite's getting sued by dance choreographer who's worked with Bieber, Britney. *Kotaku.* [online] Available at: https://kotaku.com/fortnite-epic-games-lawsuit-dance-emote-kyle-hanagami-1848727617 [Accessed 23 August 2022].

Kastrenakes, J. (2020) Lil Nas X's Roblox concert was attended 33 million times. *The Verge.* [online] Available at: www.theverge.com/2020/11/16/21570454/lil-nas-x-roblox-concert-33-million-views [Accessed 23 August 2022].

Kravitz, N. (2021) Episode 127: NVIDIA Research's David Luebke on intersection of graphics, AI. *The AI podcast.* [podcast] Available at: https://soundcloud.com/theaipodcast/nvidia-research-david-luebke?in=user-15593072/sets/ai [Accessed 16 August 2022].

Lai, J. (2022) Meet me in the metaverse. *andreesen horowitz.* [online] Available at: https://a16z.com/2020/12/07/social-strikes-back-metaverse/ [Accessed 23 August 2022].

Lanier, L. (2018) 'Super Mario Run' leaves $60 million revenue mark in the dust. *Variety.* [online] Available at: https://variety.com/2018/gaming/news/super-mario-run-hits-60-million-revenue-mark-1202863810/ [Accessed 23 August 2022].

Lewis, R. W. L. (2022) Why gaming is the new big tech battleground. *Financial Times,* 21 January.

Lockett, H. (2021) China's Tencent imposes controls to tackle gaming addiction among children. *Financial Times,* 3 August.

Machkovech, S. (2020) Unreal Engine is now royalty-free until a game makes a whopping $1 million. *Ars Technica.* [online] Available at: https://arstechnica.com/gaming/2020/05/unreal-engine-is-now-royalty-free-until-a-game-makes-a-whopping-1-mill/ [Accessed 23 August 2022].

Manthorpe, R. (2016) DeepMind has conquered games, London's underground and now it wants to help save the planet. *WIRED.* [online] Available at: www.wired.co.uk/article/mustafa-suleyman-deepmind-google-ai [Accessed 23 August 2022].

Marshall, C. (2022) Star Citizen still doesn't live up to its promise, and players don't care. *Polygon.* [online] Available at: www.polygon.com/22925538/star-citizen-2022-experience-gameplay-features-player-reception [Accessed 23 August 2022].

Martin, G. (2017) Loot boxes are more proof that the economics of video games are broken. *Paste.* [online] Available at: www.pastemagazine.com/games/loot-boxes/loot-boxes-are-more-proof-that-the-economics-of-vi/ [Accessed 23 August 2022].

Martin, M. (2009) Marketing influences game revenue three times more than high scores. *Gamesindustry.biz.* [online] Available at: www.gamesindustry.biz/articles/marketing-influences-game-revenue-three-times-more-than-high-scores [Accessed 23 August 2022].

McCaffrey, M. (2019) The macro problem of microtransactions: the self-regulatory challenges of video game loot boxes. *Business Horizons,* 62(4), 483–95. doi.org/10.1016/j.bushor.2019.03.001

Neely, E. L. (2021) Come for the game, stay for the cash grab: the ethics of loot boxes, microtransactions, and freemium games. *Games And Culture,* 16(2), 228–47. doi.org/10.1177/1555412019887658

Newzoo. (2021) Global esports and streaming market report 2021. *Newzoo.* [online] Available at: www.newzoo.com [Accessed 23 August 2022].

NHS England. (2020) Country's top mental health nurse warns video games pushing young people into 'under the radar' gambling. *NHS England.* [online] Available at: www.england.nhs.uk/2020/01/countrys-top-mental-health-nurse-warns-video-games-pushing-young-people-into-under-the-radar-gambling/ [Accessed 23 August 2022].

Njanja, A. (2022) Game studios come together to grow industry in Africa. *TechCrunch.* [online] Available at: https://techcrunch.com/2022/02/23/game-studios-come-together-to-grow-industry-in-africa/ [Accessed 23 August 2022].

Noam, E. M. (2019) *Media and digital management.* London: Palgrave Macmillan.

Ofek, E., Libai, B. and Muller, E. (2018) Customer lifetime social value (CLSV). *Harvard Business School Faculty & Research*. [online] Available at: www.hbs.edu/faculty/Pages/item.aspx?num=53770 [Accessed 23 August 2022].

Palomba, A. (2020) How high brand loyalty consumers achieve relationships with virtual worlds and its elements through presence. *Journal of Media Business Studies*, 17(3–4), 243–60. doi.org/10.1080/16522354.2020.1768637

Peckham, E. (2020) Unity IPO aims to fuel growth across gaming and beyond. *TechCrunch*. [online] Available at: https://tcrn.ch/3CYTdkf [Accessed 23 August 2022].

Peppler, L. (2019) The amazing flywheel effect. *Medium*. [online] Available at: https://medium.com/swlh/the-amazing-flywheel-effect-80a0a21a5ea7 [Accessed 23 August 2022].

Perez, S. (2021) Apple ordered to comply with court's decision over in-app payments in Epic Games case. *Tech Crunch*. [online] Available at: https://techcrunch.com/2021/11/09/apple-ordered-to-comply-with-courts-decision-in-epic-games-case-over-in-app-payments/ [Accessed 23 August 2022].

Radulovic, P. (2022) Riot Games invests in the animation studio behind Arcane. *Polygon*. [online] Available at: www.polygon.com/22977437/riot-games-fortiche-production-arcane [Accessed 23 August 2022].

RapidFire. (2022) The three types of in-game advertising. *RapidFire*. [online] Available at: www.rapidfire.com/blog/the-three-types-of-in-game-advertising/ [Accessed 23 August 2022].

Rosu, D. (2019) *Riot Games: company case study*. Project delivered at the National Film and Television School.

Rousseau, J. (2022) Manga publisher Shueisha launches Shueisha Games. *Gamesindustry.biz*. [online] Available at: www.gamesindustry.biz/manga-publisher-shueisha-launches-shueisha-games [Accessed 23 August 2022].

Savage, M. (2022) The global music market was worth $26bn in 2021. *BBC News*. [online] Available at: www.bbc.co.uk/news/entertainment-arts-60837880 [Accessed 23 August 2022].

Schafer, T. (1996) Grim Fandango Puzzle Document. *Grim Fandango*. [online] Available at: www.grimfandango.net/media/Grim_Fandango_Puzzle_Document.pdf [Accessed 23 August 2022].

Schreier, J. (2017) *Blood, sweat, and pixels: the triumphant, turbulent stories behind how video games are made*. New York: Harper Paperbacks.

SeedEA. (2022) [online] Available at: www.ea.com/seed [Accessed 23 August 2022].

Spencer, P. (2022) To understand the Metaverse, look to video games. *Sway*. [podcast] Available at: www.nytimes.com/2022/01/10/opinion/sway-kara-swisher-phil-spencer.html [Accessed 23 August 2022].

Statista. (2021) Most watched games on YouTube worldwide in 2020, by views. *Statista*. [online] Available at: www.statista.com/statistics/1201166/most-watched-game-content-youtube-global/ [Accessed 23 August 2022].

Statista. (2022) Marketing and sales expenditure of Electronic Arts from fiscal 2014 to 2021. *Statista*. [online] Available at: www.statista.com/statistics/672141/electronic-arts-marketing-and-sales-spending/ [Accessed 23 August 2022].

Strickland, D. (2021) Star Citizen's new Legatus 2951 pack costs $40,000. *TweakTown*. [online] Available at: www.tweaktown.com/news/83666/star-citizens-new-legatus-2951-pack-costs-40-000/index.html [Accessed 23 August 2022].

Takahashi, D. (2014) Only 0.15 percent of mobile gamers account for 50 percent of all in-game revenue. *GamesBeat*. [online] Available at: https://venturebeat.com/games/only-0-15-of-mobile-gamers-account-for-50-percent-of-all-in-game-revenue-exclusive/ [Accessed 23 August 2022].

Takahashi, D. (2021) The DeanBeat: do game company valuations make sense? *VentureBeat*. [online] Available at: https://venturebeat.com/2021/06/04/the-deanbeat-do-game-company-valuations-make-sense/ [Accessed 23 August 2022].

Tassi, P. (2022) 'Star Citizen' must admit its for-sale concept ships do not exist, says advertising authority. *Forbes*. [onlinc] Available at: www.forbes.com/sites/paultassi/2021/09/09/star-citizen-must-admit-its-for-sale-concept-ships-do-not-exist-says-advertising-authority/?sh=57e65194553f [Accessed 23 August 2022].

Thorn, A. (2022) *Interviewed by Dr Alex Connock*. The National Film and Television School, 5 April.

Trefis. (2017) FIFA remains EA's bread and butter. *Forbes*. [online] Available at: www.forbes.com/sites/greatspeculations/2017/10/10/fifa-remains-eas-bread-and-butter/ [Accessed 23 August 2022].

Wijman, T. (2021) *The games market and beyond in 2021: the year in numbers. Newzoo*. [online] Available at: https://newzoo.com/insights/articles/the-games-market-in-2021-the-year-in-numbers-esports-cloud-gaming/ [Accessed 23 August 2022].

Wilde, T. (2020) What a good (and bad) indie game publishing deal looks like. *PC Gamer*. [online] Available at: www.pcgamer.com/what-a-good-and-bad-indie-game-publishing-deal-looks-like/ [Accessed 23 August 2022].

Wilhelm, N. and Mascarenhas, N. (2021) Episode 421: The Metaverse is coming for Squid Game. *Equity*. [podcast] Available at: https://tcrn.ch/3cM5wps [Accessed 23 August 2022].

Wood, C. (2022) How the gaming universe is preparing marketers for the metaverse. *Martech.org*. [online] Available at: https://bit.ly/3RBnvNU [Accessed 23 August 2022].

Wright, K. (2022) Yield Guild Games raises $1.45m for Philippine typhoon relief. *Cointelegraph*. [online] Available at: https://cointelegraph.com/news/yield-guild-games-raises-1-45m-for-philippine-typhoon-relief [Accessed 23 August 2022].

YouGov. (2021). Game-changers: the power of gaming influencers. *YouGov*. [online] Available at: https://business.yougov.com/content/38826-international-gaming-report-2021 [Accessed 23 August 2022].

Zabel, C. and Telkmann, V. (2020) The adoption of emerging technology-driven media innovations. A comparative study of the introduction of virtual and augmented reality in the media and manufacturing industries. *Journal of Media Business Studies*, 1–32. doi.org/10.1080/16522354.2020.1839172

CHAPTER 6

Social networks

The defining distribution platform of the digital age

....

INTRODUCTION TO THE SECTOR

In 2021, there were 38 million #Dog posts on *Instagram* – but there were 205 million on *TikTok* just part of the way into 2022 (Kemp, 2022).

This chapter looks through a top-down lens at the range, scale and power of that social network economy, via the platforms that make it possible. Later chapters on Creators and Marketing Content then look at that business through the lens of the individual users and brands.

Social networks are a global industry with 4.61 billion users in January 2022 (Kemp, 2022).

- Distribution of social content constitutes 82% of all internet traffic (McCue, 2020).
- Social media is provided by major global companies, such as Google-owned *YouTube*, Meta-owned *Facebook* and *Instagram*, Bytedance-owned *TikTok*, *Snapchat*, *Twitter*, *LinkedIn* (now owned by Microsoft), *Pinterest* and others. Other major China market players include *WeChat*, *Sina Weibo Tencent* and *Meituan*.
- There are social platforms in Russia (*Vkontakte*), Japan (*LINE*) and South Korea (*Daum/KakaoTalk*).
- Social content is so powerful a driver of consumer engagement that "even the traditional notions of what constitutes storytelling itself could see some interesting innovations" (Tran, 2021). This is particularly evident in the power of the short-form *TikTok* feed, where user view-time on content (rather than particular followed influencers) powers recommendation.

DOI: 10.4324/9781003213611-8

- Social content drives value generation for the winners. Meta Platforms Inc, for instance, had a market capitalisation in October 2022 of $373 billion. Snap Inc was worth $63.36 billion in March, but fell to $18 billion by October. *LinkedIn* was bought by Microsoft, in December 2019 for $26.2 billion.

Social networks are a winning business model – when they work. "Such networks are able to take advantage of almost zero marginal distribution costs while attempting to capture the value of delivered content at prices that will be accepted by users and advertisers" (Vogel, 2020).

Social networks, and the brands that use them, are in continual innovation. The *Facebook* employee handbook said: "If we don't create the thing that destroys *Facebook*, somebody else will" (Frier, 2020).

- Fashion brands *Prada*, *Batman* and *Dior* all used *TikTok* to live-stream their Spring/Summer 2021 seasons. In 2022, *TikTok* introduced multi-view live-stream experience *Live Lineup*, allowing viewers to multi-angle viewing. *Off-White* used it to stream its Autumn/Winter 2022 show: the hashtag #OffWhite had 1.4 billion views without any advertising spend (Maguire, 2022).
- The platforms are demography-specific. In 2022, *TikTok* had an audience of over 1 billion monthly active users, the "Epicentre of Generation Z" with 27.9% of 18–24 year old females and 11.9% of males using the platform. Amongst 55+, just 0.04% of females are using it (Geyser, 2022). *TikTok* was also growing fast.
- Social media channels are constantly vying for position. January 2022 data showed *WhatsApp* as the global leader with 15.7% of adult internet users. *Instagram* had 14.8% of global internet users, overtaking both of their stable-mate *Facebook*. But *TikTok* was climbing fast in the rankings; people choosing it as their no. 1 choice jumped 71% in the previous 3 months. *YouTube* had the longest per-month view time, at 23.7 hours per month on average (ranked by cumulative use of the apps on Android, by Android users) (Kemp, 2022).
- Many start-ups have tried to succeed in the space – *Classmates* (1995), *Friendster* (2002), *Hi5* (2003) and *My Space* (2003). Most have failed.
- Only a handful succeed like *Instagram* co-founder Kevin Systrom, who co-created the world's largest photo sharing website in 2010, and sold it just two years later to *Facebook*, when it still had only 13 employees, fewer than a typical restaurant. The price was $1 billion. "I'm dangerous enough to know how to code and soci-able enough to sell our company," he said. "And I think that's a deadly combin-ation in entrepreneurship" (Frier, 2020). By 2022, *Instagram* had 1.13 billion users and a quarter of the revenue of its parent, Meta.

Engage and enrage

Many echo Systrom's view that social media platforms are, from a societal perspec-tive, a deadly combination. In the 2021 BBC *Reith Lectures*, leading AI thinker Stuart

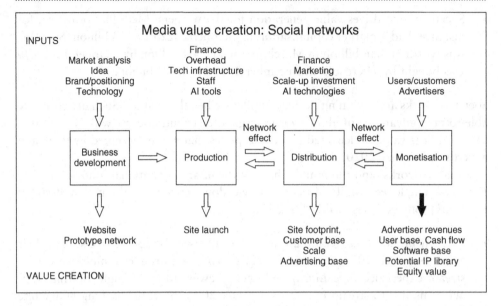

FIGURE 6.1 Social networks require high investment upfront, but generate exceptional returns if they reach scale

Russell raised his concerns about their ability to take users down a 'rabbit hole' of radicalising content, via AI-powered recommendation which prioritises engagement over social good.

Russell said:

> Talking of ruining the world, let's look at social media content-selection algorithms, the ones that choose items for your newsfeed or the next video to watch. They aren't particularly intelligent, but they have more power over people's cognitive intake than any dictator in history.
>
> *(Russell, 2021)*

This idea is encapsulated in the phrase 'engage and enrage,' often applied to the Trump election campaigns of 2016 and 2020 in the USA.

Reach and engagement, planetary-level value creation, societal damage around ethics and data form the unique mix of the social network business. "I think what's happening in social media is already worse than Chernobyl. It has caused a huge amount of dislocation" (Russell, 2021).

THE VALUE CREATION MODEL

Development

The business development process for the social network requires market analysis to show a clear, ultimately defensible space into which a new network can fit: *Clubhouse* as a live audio-first brand, *BeReal* as alternative to the glossy *Instagram*. From here, time, programming acumen, brand and technology are needed. The outputs from this phase are a prototype network and a market positioning.

Many media segments can be reductively described as a business in which producers invest in making content, then sell it. Not so social platforms – which generate value by monetising content, without themselves funding or – they would say, though regulators disagree – publishing it. This produces extraordinary economics.

- In the last quarter of 2021, *YouTube* advertising revenues were $8.6 billion, more than *Netflix*'s subscription income.
- Its production cost was a tiny fraction of the *Netflix* content spend, thus delivering a huge margin (Cotton, 2021). (*YouTube* have paid for 'Originals' content but it shut the project down in January 2022.)

A new social network requires three initial commodities: an idea, investment and an operational/programming delivery.

Idea

Any new social network requires, for positioning, a novel and coherent idea.

- With *Facebook* it was facilitation, initially at Harvard University, of social networking (at first, dating).
- At *Instagram* – it was photo sharing. "People don't carry around point-and-shoots anymore, they're just going to carry around these phones" (Frier, 2020).
- *Weibo* is about microblogging, like *Twitter*, whose co-founder Jack Dorsey described the branding: "We came across the word 'twitter,' and it was just perfect. The definition was 'a short burst of inconsequential information,' and 'chirps from birds.' And that's exactly what the product was. It was inspired by taxi firms, with cars around town squawking their location" (Sarno, 2009).
- *TikTok*'s short-form video sharing has a complex origin story. It first came to the Chinese market in September 2016 as *A.me*, then *Douyin*, and was renamed *TikTok* when it went international in 2017. The merger with lip-sync and comedy platform music.ly in September that year created the current product.
- *Snapchat* is messaging and ephemeral, low-jeopardy sharing. Evan Spiegel, co-founder said: "a photo app that doesn't conform to unrealistic notions of beauty or perfection, but rather creates a space to be funny, honest or whatever else you might feel like" (Warman, 2013). Even now, academic research has shown that the network is "a mystery to many marketers" – at best occasional food for consumer relationships (Tropp and Baetzgen, 2019).

Branding is critical. Names of networks acquire grammatical versatility as names (*Twitter*), nouns (a tweet) and verbs (to tweet). To express the idea of sending pictures, *Instagram* co-founders Systrom and Mike Krieger conflated "instant" and "telegram" (Frier, 2020). Stanford students Evan Spiegel and Reggie Brown, founders of their new vanishing messages app in 2011, called it *Picaboo* – but switched to *Snapchat* after a legal letter from a phonebook firm of the same name (Lang, 2014).

Investment

Network effects are the rocket fuel of the sector. They were described by ethernet co-inventor Robert Metcalfe, who observed the cost of network cards increasing in proportion to the number used, whilst the value increased proportional to the square of the number of users. In other words: the more people join, the more value for everyone.

To exploit that mathematics, social platforms need to scale fast. This demands investment. *LinkedIn* founder, Reid Hoffman, called it "blitz-scaling." Most companies struggle to get funded: but the few with growth have the pick of investors.

When, in 2004, the young Mark Zuckerberg needed money for hit start-up network *The Facebook*, an associate fixed a meeting for him and Sean Parker, at leading Silicon Valley venture capital firm, Sequoia Capital. They arrived late, wearing pyjamas, and pitched a different business (Mallaby, 2022). Zuckerberg could afford to be dismissive because he had the growth to be certain of investment elsewhere. The site signed up over 1,000 Harvard students on day one.

But when Zuckerberg bought *Instagram* six years later in 2012, he had the valuation challenge of an investor himself: "I've thought about it and I want to buy your company," Zuckerberg told Kevin Systrom. "I'll give you double whatever you're raising your round at" (Frier, 2020). Pundit Chris Hill of *Motley Fool* observed in March 2022 that what at the time looked like overpayment turned out to be a bargain, such was the pace of growth in the brand: "In 2012, *Facebook* bought *Instagram* for 1 billion dollars. Today *Instagram* is worth 100 billion."

Implementation

Delivery on the promise – not 'flaming out' – is vital. Scale-up requires effective engineering, but implementation at scale is more possible in social networks than any other media form.

- In China, *WeChat*, the instant messaging, social media and payment app first released in 2011, had 1.1 billion active users by 2019 (Sun, 2020). China still has 400 million people not connected to the internet (Kemp, 2022).
- When *Instagram* was launched, co-founder/programmer Mike Krieger took his laptop everywhere to stay online. "He fixed *Instagram* in the back of movie theaters, in parks, and even while camping" (Frier, 2020).
- Stanford professor Robert Sutton met early *Facebook* workers in his class when they were struggling to find enough Palo Alto office space. He said start-ups require a careful mindset and attention to detail around culture and staff training

to not lose their essence. They "needed to hire an engineer for every 500,000 users" and ended up putting a 25-year-old engineer, Chris Cox, in charge of HR. New hires went through "a six-week Bootcamp ... led almost entirely by engineers (not HR)" (Sutton, 2014).

- In the period 2016–20, *Facebook* was reputationally damaged by negative stories around what critics said were weak system controls, most famously with the *Cambridge Analytica* situation, in which the data of millions of users was used for political ad targeting without explicit consent.

Production

At the production phase of the value creation process for a social network, the inputs are finance (in the tens of millions of dollars, at least), infrastructure and implementation of a unique set of tech tools to define user experience. The outputs are a site that works at scale.

Whilst tools are built by the network engineers, content comes from customers, at vast scale and for free. The marginal cost of customers is close to zero, the marginal revenue from advertising to those customers making them instantly profitable; a very different equation from the multibillion-dollar content purchasing of the streamers in Chapter 7.

Why do consumers upload content? For behavioural reasons that enhance demand. Psychologist Daniel Kahneman said: "We don't think of our future as anticipated experiences. We think of it as anticipated memories ... We go on vacation to a very large extent in the service of our remembering self" (Swisher, 2021). Writer Susan Sontag said: "To remember is, more and more, not to recall a story but to be able to call up a picture." *Instagram* "has made us not only more expressive, but also more self-conscious and performative" (Frier, 2020). Each network taps different behavioural tropes. *LinkedIn*, for instance, encourages faux-modest business boasts ('some personal news' or 'Honoured to be recognised').

As well as user content, some networks also commission 'originals.' In 2022, Amanda Krentzman, Head of International Originals, said that *Snapchat* had commissioned 160 original series since 2016. The delivery of 5–7 minute segments may feel social media casual, but the design is as complex as long form streaming: "It is very developed and thoughtful in terms of the story learning" (Krentzman, 2022). A-list talent is a critical driver of shows – including, in 2022, *Secret Superpowers*, a showcase of hidden celebrity skills like knitting with former Olympic diver Tom Daley; and *A Fighting Chance* with boxer Anthony Joshua. Over 20 million people watched a *Snapchat* show starring actor Ryan Reynolds. *Snapchat* has also made scripted titles: *Dead of Night* and *Breakwater* in the US.

Celebrity content has compelling value to the network through virality, costing nothing but driving advertising opportunities and new member recruitment.

- Rapper Snoop Dogg was the first on *Instagram*, wearing a suit and holding a can of Colt 45 (Frier, 2020).

- In 2022, the largest *Instagram* accounts were footballers Cristiano Ronaldo (402 million followers) and Lionel Messi (306 million), model Kylie Jenner (309 million), actors Dwayne "The Rock" Johnson (296.4 million) and Selena Gomez (295.9 million). (The content they upload is very often paid – but not by the network. See Chapter 14.)

Distribution

In the distribution phase of the media value creation process for a social network, marketing (viral or paid) is needed, plus investment to reach positive network effects (i.e., users) and, frequently, AI-driven technologies.

Outputs from this phase are a footprint (if the plan works) consisting of a customer base of DAUs (daily active users), scale and advertisers. There is a network effect between production and distribution, and again between distribution and monetisation. The more join the network, the more it scales up, the more it can be monetised. The network's consumer utility is content – user-generated (UGC), originals and advertiser-created. Issues for the network to manage are content guidelines, copyright (say, commercial music tracks) and the challenge of radicalisation, misinformation and bots. In war, like in 2022, those can be extreme.

Even if social networks are new, they follow many precepts of twentieth-century media businesses. They are content wholesalers that often disavow the role of 'publisher,' avoiding legal responsibility for content, including, for instance, around defamation and copyright. (In the US, under so-called Section 230.) "The new distribution technology changes network architectures, market structures, and the players. But the basic roles of distribution intermediaries – wholesalers and retailers – remain" (Noam, 2019).

The challenge of algorithmic recommendation

A powerful challenge at the heart of the social network business model – not dissimilar to those which concern the board of an alcoholic drinks company or an online betting firm – is the contradiction between its incentive to maximise user engagement, and its societally perceived responsibility to protect user welfare.

Algorithmic recommendation, which works by machine learning seeing what a customer engages with and providing more of it, may actually work too well. This critique is often levelled at *YouTube* and *TikTok*.

"If you think about a surveillance world," said Tim Cook, CEO of Apple,

> a world where you know, somebody is always watching everything you're doing. And in the case of a phone or a computer, it's also what you're thinking because you're typing in searches and so on and so forth. And so I think in that kind of world, you begin to do less. You begin to think less. Your freedom of expression begins to narrow and the walls move in on you.
>
> *(Cook, 2021)*

- Teen girls feel worse about themselves after looking at imagery of perfect bodies on *Instagram*, alleged the *Wall Street Journal*, claiming that "32% of teen girls said that when they felt bad about their bodies, *Instagram* made them feel worse." Teenage girls were reported to find that *TikTok*'s focus on performance made appearances on that network less onerous, and that *Snapchat*'s jokey animal filters had a similar effect (Wells, 2021).
- *Facebook* has been (unwittingly) used by drug cartels to recruit staff and intimidate others (Scheck, 2021b). Social networks have suffered temporary loss of advertisers when their advertising was too close to harmful material. Drinks company Diageo paused advertising on social media platforms in 2020 while discussing "with media partners how they will deal with unacceptable content" (Murphy, 2020).

But sites such as *Facebook* can do societal good too – for instance, around coronavirus information and self-help groups in the pandemic of 2020–22. Managing both sides of the network equation is the major challenge for social networks.

Disinformation

"This is a dark moment in our nation's history," Zuckerberg wrote in January 2020 when the US Capitol was stormed by rioters, "and I know many of you are frightened and concerned about what's happening in Washington, DC. I'm personally saddened by this mob violence" (LaFrance, 2021). The riot took place in an environment of misinformation, a facet of an information war which has been raging globally since 2014, and accelerating through the Ukraine crisis of 2022. Social networks, including Zuckerberg's, were caught in the crossfire.

New York Times writer Nicole Perlroth, in her book *This Is How They Tell Me the World Ends* on cyberwar, claims Russia had a stated goal to "spread distrust toward the candidates and the political system in general," and was using the social networks to do that. In September 2014, Perlroth claims, Russian trolls launched a *Heart of Texas Facebook* group with secessionist memes – "Hillary Clinton was coming to take their guns away" – then started a *Facebook* group for an opposing group too, the *United Muslims of America*. They egged on rallies and counterrallies – a social media civil war that "Russia's digital puppeteers were coordinating from five thousand miles away" (Perlroth, 2021).

- Bots are amplification tools for misinformation, constituting 8.5% of *Twitter* users at one point, *Twitter* said: "Bots which automatically disseminate spam, political bots that get involved in political discussions, and Sybils which are fake accounts used to gain large influence" (Orabi et al., 2019).
- Human checking of potential misinformation is time consuming. A single post with 9.5 million *Twitter* views as the first Russian troops entered Ukraine in February 2022 took four steps to be verified by the BBC's disinformation and Open Source Intelligence (OSINT) unit. A video showed a Ukrainian driver

joking with a Russian soldier about his armoured vehicle running out of fuel. Geolocation was unavailable. Accents were checked. Other location tools were used. They did a reverse search to make sure it wasn't old footage. That time allocation would be impossible for almost all content – hence the need for AI tools to moderate content (Skippage, 2022).

- Social platforms can thwart misinformation, too. Again in early 2022 as *Facebook* and other networks were shut down by Russian authorities, messaging app *Telegram* sustained non-censored communications; 7–8% of its users were Russian. The app was started in 2013 by Pavel and and Nikolai Durov, when Pavel was running the Russian answer to *Facebook*, named *VK*. That app is not blocked because it is "very useful to the Russian government in getting its message out. So it may be that on balance, they think *Telegram* is more helpful to their message than hurtful." It might also have been "too big to cancel" or technically unblockable because of the way it is distributed across servers (Schechner, 2022).

Monetisation

The final phase of the media value chain for a social network requires input of substantial users and advertisers (assuming that it is not on a paid subscription model).

Outputs can be substantial if the process succeeds. A scaleable advertising revenue base can be delivered, with rapidly increasing users against relatively fixed costs. This offers cash flow, IP, content and equity value gains.

In social media, many have contended that the user creates the value, by giving away their data for a free service. (The phrase: "it is the consumer who is consumed" was first used on US television in 1973, by Richard Serra). This has consequences for privacy at the user level, and for society as a whole.

In 2015, Tim Cook, CEO of Apple, said "some of the most prominent and successful companies have built their businesses by lulling their customers into complacency about their personal information." He said: "They're gobbling up everything they can learn about you and trying to monetize it," concluding: "You might like these so-called free services, but we don't think they're worth having your email, your search history and now even your family photos data mined and sold off for God knows what advertising purpose" (Wu, 2017).

But the *New York Times* accused Cook of ignoring "the substantial benefits that free, ad-supported services have brought to consumers worldwide" (Manjoo, 2015). Mark Zuckerberg, CEO of *Facebook*, said. "What, you think because you're paying Apple that you're somehow in alignment with them? If you were in alignment with them, then they'd make their products a lot cheaper!" (Wu, 2017).

Whatever the merits in that debate between two of the largest tech companies, social platforms certainly are monetised through advertising, and that is in turn driven by the precise targeting offered by customer data. The advantage social networks have over 'traditional' media (TV, print) is their ability to target not just to market segments, but individual consumers. Social sites can take that relationship further, and monetise via click-to-buy, for instance, on *Facebook*, *Instagram* and *TikTok*. As Deloitte's *2022 Media and Entertainment Industry Outlook* put it: "Social media, the largest digital aggregator of humanity, will find itself at a turning point, moving to build out the next generation of retail shopping" (Deloitte, 2022). (See Chapter 13 for more detail.)

Copyright control and management

Every day a tsunami of content is placed on social networks. Some 500 hours of content are uploaded to *YouTube* every minute. *YouTube Shorts* receives 15 billion views daily. *Instagram Stories* (a video tool, like *Shorts*, like *Snapchat Reels*) are viewed by 500 million people per day. And 59% of US adults use *Instagram* itself daily (Hootsuite, 2022).

Most of the content is not under meaningful commercial copyright. A given user will not monetise a picture of their dog (unless it goes super-viral *and* they are formally set up as a Creator – see Chapter 14).

But copyright on commercial content is managed algorithmically. *YouTube*'s Copyright Management Suite allows legitimate owners to identify their content and claim programmatic advertising revenues from its viewing, instead of taking it down. "After providing us with reference files, Content ID and Copyright Match Tool users are automatically notified of user-uploaded videos that may contain their creative work … it's not just an anti-piracy solution, but also a revenue-generation tool." The site claims to have paid over $5.5 billion to rights holders from claimed content that someone else uploaded (YouTube, 2022).

Intermediate businesses to monetise content

Intermediate businesses also sit between copyright holders and, for instance, *YouTube* to claim content cost-efficiently, aggregate channels and drive traffic and programmatic ad revenue.

- The commodity is CPM, or cost-per-thousand, a measure of the dollar amount a content owner will earn per thousand impressions, or more specifically, per 30-second, monetised view of a commercial within a content view, or per click on an advert.
- CPM rates lack both transparency and consistency across genres and territories, as they are driven by the perceived quality of the viewer of any given content type, but a typical rate can be looked up online – approximately $0.35 cents to $4, in early 2022.

A successful such business is the UK-based Little Dot Studios which, in 2020, had some 350 staff from London to Sydney, managing 600 digital channels, with 6 billion organic video views a month and 280 million subscribers. Little Dot had its own network of 30 plus channel brands, syndicated to 17 platforms globally (such as *Samsung, Roku, Rakuten, Vizio, Amazon Prime Video*). The mission of Little Dot Studios was (according to its website): "Realising potential in every story" – combining the journalism and entertainment in the product with the monetisation in its execution.

Sponsorship

Social networks monetise content non-programmatically, too. *Twitter* runs events and brand launches. "We have explored with a lot of our network partners doing after-shows immediately after [a TV] episode airs ... allowing ... super fans or bloggers or actually talent from the show to create a room where they can all talk together" (Spangler, 2021).

Policies

At *YouTube* the network manages the risks it has through a policy called the 'Four Rs.' *YouTube*'s Chief Product Officer, Neil Mohan, described the model:

- Removing content that violates community guidelines.
- Raising up authoritative content. "We have information panels ... videos from authoritative news sources."
- Reducing misinformation content in recommendations and ranking algorithms.
- Rewarding creators that are looking to build an audience, or build a business on *YouTube* with monetisation (Patel, 2021).

These policies could be a viable starting policy point for any social network. Meanwhile for commercial reasons, platforms have been accused of tolerating posts from stars that would have had non-stars banned. *The Wall Street Journal* suggested that *Facebook* had a 24 hour 'self remediation window' where a star or politician had a chance to avoid penalty by taking down problematic content (Scheck, 2021a).

Class discussion questions

- How do social networks generate shareholder value?
- How will increased regulation around data privacy affect the distribution and monetisation of advertising by each of the major social networks in your country?
- Why is misinformation a greater problem for social platforms than for conventional publishers?
- If you were going to present a business plan next week for a new social network, what would be the consumer-facing idea behind it, and the business model?
- Which social network has the most sustainable business model in your view, and what evidence can you present to support your contention?

AI technologies in social media

Just as Chapter 10 highlighted AI-driven technologies that are changing distribution of scripted content, here we analyse technologies powering social media platforms, all the way towards the Metaverse (see Chapter 19).

AI tools impact how advertising is created, distributed and measured, and how content is created, moderated and translated. AI is developed in social networks with wide applications. So big are the opportunities to scale social media and entertainment businesses, that major companies need to "become more open to letting their IP live in environments outside their control" (Tran, 2021).

- ByteDance, the company behind *TikTok* and its Chinese counterpart *Douyin*, is using its AI in the pharmaceutical research to discover and manufacture new drugs, according to *TechCrunch:* "trying to leverage that expertise to find new revenue beyond social media advertisements" (Robitzski, 2020).
- Meta (owner of *Facebook* and *Instagram*) can train algorithms on vast datasets without having to manually label the data. In the past, they taught systems to perform a task by giving them of human labelled examples – supervised learning. But there is a problem with that. "It's not clear when the machine really understands beyond the narrower task, and then requires a lot of human labour, and they can introduce unwanted biases" (Meta, 2022). As one media executive says of supervised learning: "If you want AI to recognise the real world, manual annotation is never going to scale. You need someone to sit there saying 'this is a dog,' 'this is a dog,' this is a dog.' That's not sustainable." So Meta pivoted to self-supervised learning (see Chapter 4), which does not take as much labelled data to train, and enables faster scaling. "The general technique of self-supervised learning is to predict any unobserved or hidden part (or property) of the input from any observed or unhidden part of the input" (MetaAI, 2021). Showing a system 30% of a picture of a dog will let a neural network train itself, by learning to complete the image. Again, this technology has much wider industrial uses than deployment on social networks.

Advertising distribution: AI-driven audience selection

AI tools are already available for any advertiser on social media platforms – even someone who just wants to sell a pair of shoes. Yann LeCun, then Facebook's top AI researcher, said: "without AI, *Facebook* would crumble" (LeCun, 2021). To any small business buying *Facebook* advertising through its Ads Manager tool, audience segmentation (behavioural and demographic) can be made manually, but they are better off using the AI.

- Audience selection: If a cinema in Accra, Ghana, was playing an action film, the marketing manager could select target audience for what they believed the likely filmgoers to be – say, men who had previously watched content related to action films within 10 miles.
- Audience narrowing: This might narrow the audience to 50,000 or more, very broad for a business as specific as a local cinema. But *Facebook* advise to do that, and let

its machine learning find the customers the user didn't expect. For instance – contrary to stereotyped expectations of the cinema's marketing manager – older women in Accra might also like action films. By not mandating specifically who sees initial displays of the advert, the customer enables the AI system itself to test, learn and find unexpected customers.

- Dynamic content selection: AI has another use in ad manager tools, serving the uniquely right version of content to each individual. By allowing advertisers to upload combinations of different options for assets – pictures, headlines, taglines – the platform's AI can test and learn (A/B test) permutations to figure out the combination which works. This is not just a standard set of assets for everyone, but specific combinations for each many different audiences.
- Advertising distribution: AI helps optimise dissemination of advertising. Social photo sharing network *Pinterest* drove engagement using a neural network-driven image-based search and advertising placement system. Jeremy King, Pinterest's senior VP of engineering: "It's like this giant machine-learning engine that is being powered by the people that are pinning content." In early 2021 this led to a more than doubling of advertising sales (McCormick, 2021).

Stimulation of content creativity

Tech investment by social platforms has had substantial impacts beyond the sites that built the tools. Programmatic advertising and other ad tech tools suffuse the consumer ecosystem (and not always in popular ways.) In content creation, augmented reality filters from *TikTok* and *Snapchat* find their way into popular entertainment.

- R&D: Technical leaps can require large companies to make big investments needed. UK research shows most creative immersive companies are in "perpetual R&D: unable to catapult from explorative prototyping and proprietary technology development to sustainability and growth" (Chitty, 2020). Big platforms have the wealth to do that core research.
- Creative tools: in 2022, Joelle Pineau, the Director of AI research at Meta, demonstrated the creation of an animated cartoon of a dancing cat from a simple drawing she sketched, using AI-driven creativity tools: "Our state of the art object detection model mask, our CNN [convolutional neural network] as implemented in the open source detector to detect the figure from the background. We then use *Alpha Pose*, a model trained for human pose detection, to identify key joints on the character. Once we have the mask, the joint predictions, we can move the character into various poses" (Meta, 2022). The result is an engaging animation.

Content moderation and the challenge of societal harm

With 3 million posts flagged for potential problems per day at *Facebook* alone (Koestier, 2020) challenges of content moderation are on an epic scale. AI is the only viable solution – working on five dimensions: accounts, metadata, real-time content analysis and context analysis. The ultimate prize, towards which both social platforms and governments are working, is an integrated system, alert to speech, text and video and able to interpret how they function together for subtle, overall meaning.

Automated moderation

Automated moderation of problematic content (violence, for instance) is socially advantageous, sparing humans the obligation to view disturbing material.

- AI at social platforms can filter the content based on how bad it looks, reducing psychological harm to human moderators – an office job one commentator likened to 'the trauma floor' (Newton, 2019).
- Object recognition algorithms blur parts of images, which the moderator would only then watch if they chose to.
- AI can give moderators a semantic option to ask the system if the image showed something in words, rather than looking at it (OFCOM, 2019).
- In 2021, *Facebook* reportedly spends $2 million a week on hate speech moderation, of which about three quarters was spent to hire human moderators (Seetharaman, 2021). With AI interventions, 96% of all hate speech was taken down before it even went live, versus the 2018 figure of 76%.
- A large percentage of problematic content comes from a small number of problem accounts. AI tools can tag those users and flag their posts for priority moderation. Similarly metadata (place, time, keywords) can help spot difficult material (OFCOM, 2019).
- Consequences of non intervention can be serious: *Facebook Live* (unknowingly) streamed a terrorist attack on two mosques in New Zealand (OFCOM, 2019).

It's not just traditional social platforms that moderate.

- * Live chat on *Xbox Live* presents opportunity for dissemination of harmful material, so *Xbox* CEO Phil Spencer said they monitor the sentiment in live gamer conversation. "The AI does a good job of kind of highlighting when a conversation is getting to a destructive point … we will give the people in the thread a note that says, hey, this is getting to a point where we see it's becoming destructive. So either calm it down or we're going to shut down the conference" (Spencer, 2022).

Context analysis

The next opportunity for social platforms is to combine text analysis with analysis of pictures and videos, to produce an automated overall reading. Meta is doing this with self-supervised learning.

- Multimodal approaches combine two types of media understanding, in the way the human brain can, enabling take-down of problematic content. Multimodal mapping addresses challenging situations where neither the words nor a picture on a meme individually has a 'hate speech' dimension, but when they are combined they do. An example would be a meme saying 'Look How Many People Love You,' on a picture of an empty desert with tumbleweed blowing across it. Neither the tumbleweed, nor the slogan, are individually problematic – but, when combined, they produce a facsimile of hate speech. With self-supervised learning, Meta bring five categories together: accounts, metadata, real-time content analysis and context analysis – to understand "multiple modalities" at the same time (Meta, 2022).

- Generative adversarial networks (GANs) (see Chapter 4) can create new images of harmful content on which to train systems, preserving the anonymity of victims shown in real examples of harmful content. Or they can be used in a style transfer, a technique to change the style of one image into the style of another (OFCOM, 2019).

Dataset bias mitigation

"The world is about to be painted with data. Every place. Every person. Every thing" (Fink, 2018).

Making sure that this data is unbiased is a major challenge. Where human selection or moderation is involved, the dataset will inevitably reflect the bias and cultural geography of the moderator and so will the output decisions. The simple effect of viewing extreme content can inure human moderators to what they are seeing, and problematically recalibrate their tolerance (OFCOM, 2019). Social networks need to be alert to this.

Advert vetting

Not only does content need to be moderated on social networks – but so does the advertising. *YouTube* use a 'Human + Machine' approach to designing Creative Effectiveness guidelines for advertisers to make better ads. They use machine learning in two ways. First – to complement the human review and detection of the creative elements present in a *YouTube* ad. And second – to predict performance of each element on brand metrics or even sales (in partnership with market research agency Nielsen).

Universal translation tools

One barrier to culturally universal content is language. "The goal of universal translation is 'any language to any language,' real time," says one executive with a leading social media company. "This is a case of not if – but when."

- Four billion people speak languages there are not significantly online, and more than 20% of the world's population is not covered by commercial translation technology, which only work with languages widely spoken (Meta, 2022).
- Training systems for each two-way translation individually (French to Urdu, French to Mandarin, Urdu to Mandarin and so forth) quickly gathers an exponential number of

datasets. Translating between two languages can often require software that passes through English twice, and therefore loses valuable meaning and nuance.

- There are large and open source databases of 'monolingual' data – like *Populi*, which is in 23 languages. Parallel data is automatically created, via wide multilingual similarity searches to identify sentences that have similar representation, which automatically become pairs of translations in the training data, without human moderation. There are now automatically created datasets of up to 100 languages like CC Matrix. "If we get this right," says Meta's Mark Zuckerberg, "this is just one example of how AI can help bring people together on a global scale" (Meta, 2022).
- Universal translation also poses an economic issue. Whether Meta, *Google Translate* or another offer is the first to develop true universal translation, will that universal translation become commoditised and ever cheaper (like cloud storage is today), or will it be a scarce resource and competitive advantage, like high-end software, in the hands of the few? (Palmer, 2022) This could be one of the fundamental determinants of both social platforms and content output in the decade ahead.

Class discussion questions

- Why do social networks need to keep innovating in AI research?
- Why is self-supervised learning a better tool for visual recognition tools in content moderation than supervised learning?
- If researchers make multilingual translation technology work, what opportunities will that create in content production and distribution?

CHAPTER SUMMARY

TABLE 6.1 Key themes in this chapter

Social Network	Development	Production	Distribution	Monetisation
Business model	Modest investment in idea creation, rapidly followed by significant scale up costs requiring external investment.	Content is 'produced' and delivered for free by the users, giving advantage over traditional media companies.	Network management costs rise with users and traffic. Costs of moderation and other harms rise with profile.	Powerful personalised advertising models deliver transformative value to advertisers and scaled networks.

(continued)

TABLE 6.1 Cont.

Social Network	Development	Production	Distribution	Monetisation
Uses of AI	Limited AI in first stages of creation, but tool design comes into play in algorithm-driven distribution of content/ advertising.	Use of AI tools in gathering of content, translation.	High AI usage in distribution to manage and drive user tastes in content, plus content moderation and other tools.	Very heavy use of AI in delivery and targeting of advertising, including dynamic creative optimisation and other adtech.
Value Creation	High chance of failure, rapid aggregation of value if the site gains traction.	Substantial value creation as volume and upload rate of content gains speed.	High value as network grows, but challenges around moderation, misinformation ad fraud and bots.	Extraordinarily high returns once a network built at scale, from programmatic advertising etc.

BIBLIOGRAPHY

Chitty, A. (2020) *The UK creative immersive landscape 2020: business models in transition. Audience of the Future.* [online] Available at: https://audienceofthefuture.live/wp-content/uploads/20201126_DC_153_UKCreativeImmersiveLandscapeReport_Digital_v1.pdf [Accessed 23 August 2022].

Cook, T. (2021) Apple's CEO is making very different choices from Mark Zuckerberg. *Sway.* [podcast] Available at: www.nytimes.com/2021/04/05/opinion/apples-ceo-is-making-very-different-choices-from-mark-zuckerberg.html [Accessed 23 August 2022].

Cotton, B. (2021) YouTube's ads generate almost similar revenue as Netflix. *Business Leader.* [online] Available at: www.businessleader.co.uk/youtubes-ads-generate-almost-similar-revenue-as-netflix/ [Accessed 25 August 2022].

Deloitte. (2022) 2022 media and entertainment industry outlook. *Deloitte.* [online] Available at: www2.deloitte.com/us/en/pages/technology-media-and-telecommunications/articles/media-and-entertainment-industry-outlook-trends.html [Accessed 23 August 2022].

Fink, C. (2018) The world will be painted with data. *Forbes.* [online] Available at: www.forbes.com/sites/charliefink/2018/05/19/the-world-will-be-painted-with-data/ [Accessed 25 August 2022].

Frier, S. (2020) *No filter: the inside story of* Instagram. New York: Simon & Schuster.

Geyser, W. (2022) The state of influencer marketing 2022: benchmark report. *InfluencerMarketingHub.* [online] Available at: https://influencermarketinghub.com/influencer-marketing-benchmark-report/ [Accessed 25 August 2022].

Kemp, S. (2022) Digital 2022: global overview report. *DataReportal.* [online] Available at: https://datareportal.com/reports/digital-2022-global-overview-report [Accessed 25 August 2022].

Koestier, J. (2020, 9 June 2020) Report: Facebook makes 300,000 content Moderation mistakes every day. *Forbes*. [online] Available at: www.forbes.com/sites/johnkoetsier/2020/06/09/300000-facebook-content-moderation-mistakes-daily-report-says/ [Accessed 25 August 2022].

Krentzman, A. (2022) Snapchat presentation. Edinburgh TV Festival, 26 August.

LaFrance, A. (2021) The Facebook papers: history will not judge us kindly. *The Atlantic*. [online] Available at: www.theatlantic.com/ideas/archive/2021/10/facebook-papers-democracy-election-zuckerberg/620478/ [Accessed 25 August 2022].

Lang, A. (2014) Why is it called Snapchat? *Rewind and Capture*. [online] Available at: www.rewindandcapture.com/why-is-it-called-snapchat/ [Accessed 25 August 2022].

LeCun, Y. (2021, 7 April 2021) Robot Brains Podcast In Yann LeCun explains why Facebook would crumble without AI. https://play.acast.com/s/the-robot-brains/yann-lecun-on-how-he-brought-ai-to-facebook

LeCun, Y. (2021) Yann LeCun explains why Facebook would crumble without AI. *The robot brains podcast*. [podcast] Available at: https://play.acast.com/s/the-robot-brains/yann-lecun-on-how-he-brought-ai-to-facebook [Accessed 25 August 2022].

MacLachlan, S. (2022) 35 Instagram stats that matter to marketers in 2022. *Hootsuite*. [blog] 18 January. Available at: https://blog.hootsuite.com/instagram-statistics/ [Accessed 25 August 2022].

Maguire, L. (2022) Off-White makes TikTok debut to stream its next show. *Vogue Business*. [online] Available at: www.voguebusiness.com/technology/off-white-makes-tiktok-debut-to-stream-its-next-show [Accessed 25 August 2022].

Mallaby, S. (2022) *The power law: venture capital and the making of the new future*. London: Penguin.

Manjoo, F. (2015) What Apple's Tim Cook overlooked in his defense of privacy. *New York Times*, 10 June.

McCormick, J. (2021) Pinterest's use of AI drives growth. *The Wall Street Journal*, 22 May.

McCue, T. (2020) The state of online video for 2020. *Forbes*. [online] Available at: www.forbes.com/sites/tjmccue/2020/02/05/looking-deep-into-the-state-of-online-video-for-2020/?sh=3f7dfa3c2eac [Accessed 25 August 2022].

Meta. (2022) Inside the lab: building for the Metaverse with AI. *Meta*. [online] Available at: https://about.fb.com/news/2022/02/inside-the-lab-building-for-the-metaverse-with-ai/ [Accessed 29 August 2022].

MetaAI. (2021) Self-supervised learning: the dark matter of intelligence. *Meta AI*. [online] Available at: https://ai.facebook.com/blog/self-supervised-learning-the-dark-matter-of-intelligence/ [Accessed 25 August 2022].

Murphy, H. (2020) Facebook fails to stem advertising boycott over hate speech. *Financial Times*, 28 June.

Neal Mohan, Y. (2021, August 2021). Decoder In Neal Mohan Chief Product Officer of YouTube on Decoder.

Newton, C. (2019) The trauma floor: the secret lives of Facebook moderators in America. *The Verge*. [online] Available at: www.theverge.com/2019/2/25/18229714/cognizant-facebook-content-moderator-interviews-trauma-working-conditions-arizona [Accessed 25 August 2022].

Noam, E. M. (2019) *Media and digital management*. London: Palgrave Macmillan.

OFCOM. (2019) *Use of AI in online content moderation*. [online] Available at: www.ofcom.org.uk/__data/assets/pdf_file/0028/157249/cambridge-consultants-ai-content-moderation.pdf [Accessed 16 August 2022].

Orabi, M. *et al.* (2019) Detection of bots in social media: a systematic review. *Information Processing and Management*, 57(4). doi.org/10.1016/j.ipm.2020.102250

Palmer, S. (2022) Is Meta smarter than Google? *Shelly Palmer*. [online] Available at: www.shellypalmer.com/2022/02/is-meta-smarter-than-google/ [Accessed 25 August 2022].

Patel, N. (2021) YouTube Chief Product Officer Neal Mohan on the algorithm, monetization, and the future for creators. *The Verge*. [online] Available at: www.theverge.com/22606296/youtube-shorts-fund-neal-mohan-decoder-interview [Accessed 25 August 2022].

Perlroth, N. (2021) This is how they tell me the world ends: the cyberweapons arms race. London: Bloomsbury.

Robitzski, D. (2020) TikTok parent company says it'll develop drugs using AI. *Neoscope*. [online] Available at: https://futurism.com/neoscope/tiktok-parent-company-develop-drugs-ai [Accessed 25 August 2022].

Russell, S. (2021) BBC Reith Lectures 2021 – Living with Artificial Intelligence. *BBC*. [online] Available at: www.bbc.co.uk/programmes/articles/1N0w5NcK27Tt041LPVLZ51k/reith-lectures-2021-living-with-artificial-intelligence [Accessed 29 August 2022].

Sarno, D. (2009, 18 February 2009) Twitter creator Jack Dorsey illuminates the site's founding document. Part I. *Los Angeles Times: Technology blog*. [blog] 18 February. Available at: http://latimesblogs.latimes.com/technology/2009/02/twitter-creator.html [Accessed 25 August 2022].

Schechner, S. (2022) Telegram thrives even as Russia drops digital iron curtain. *Wall Street Journal: Tech News Briefing*. [podcast] 21 March. Available at: www.wsj.com/podcasts/tech-news-briefing/telegram-thrives-even-as-russia-drops-digital-iron-curtain/58a648cd-4326-4625-84a5-d6b6f67203f9 [Accessed 25 August 2022].

Scheck, J. (2021a) Facebook's Secret Rules for Elite Users. *Wall Street Journal: Tech News Briefing*. [podcast] 14 September. Available at: www.wsj.com/podcasts/tech-news-briefing/facebook-secret-rules-for-elite-users/2938eb79-5b9d-4ea1-8e26-ec820fee31bc [Accessed 25 August 2022].

Scheck, J. (2021b) When Facebook's staff flagged criminal content, its response was weak. *Wall Street Journal: Tech News Briefing*. [podcast] 17 September. Available at: www.imdb.com/title/tt17349912/ [Accessed 25 August 2022].

Seetharaman, D. (2021) The Facebook files, part 7: the AI challenge. *The Journal*. [podcast] 19 October. Available at: www.wsj.com/podcasts/the-journal/the-facebook-files-part-7-the-ai-challenge/318d6439-93e5-4352-9f08-402af9a79d4b [Accessed 25 August 2022].

Skippage, R. (2022) How we're verifying information out of Ukraine. *BBC News*. [online] Available at: www.bbc.co.uk/news/av/61096713 [Accessed 25 August 2022].

Spangler, T. (2021) Inside Twitter's strategy to bring celebs, media companies into its social conversation. *Variety: Strictly Business*. [podcast] 30 June. Available at: https://variety.com/2021/digital/news/twitter-celeb-strategy-1235006896/ [Accessed 25 August 2022].

Spencer, P. (2022) To understand the Metaverse, look to video games. *Sway*. [podcast] Available at: www.nytimes.com/2022/01/10/opinion/sway-kara-swisher-phil-spencer.html [Accessed 23 August 2022].

Sun, J. (2020) China's media organisations' adoption of the WeChat public platform: news flow network, exploitation and exploration. *Journal of Media Business Studies*, 1–18. doi.org/10.1080/16522354.2020.1840711

Sutton, R. (2014, 4 February 2014) The scaling lesson from Facebook's Miraculous 10-year rise. *Harvard Business Review*. [online] Available at: https://hbr.org/2014/02/the-scaling-lesson-from-facebooks-miraculous-10-year-rise [Accessed 23 August 2022].

Swisher, K. (2021) Daniel Kahneman says humans are noisy. (He's Not talking about volume.). *Sway*. [podcast] Available at: www.nytimes.com/2021/05/17/opinion/sway-kara-swisher-daniel-kahneman.html [Accessed 29 August 2022].

Tran, K. (2021). Metaverse & Media, Special Report. *Variety Intelligence Platform*. [online] Available at: https://variety.com/vip-special-reports/metaverse-and-media-how-techs-hottest-trend-will-impact-the-entertainment-industry-1235116381/ [Accessed 29 August 2022].

Tropp, J. and Baetzgen, A. (2019) Users' definition of Snapchat usage: Implications for marketing on Snapchat. *International Journal on Media Management*, 21(2), 130–56. doi.org/10.1080/14241277.2019.1637343

Vogel, H. L. (2020) *Entertainment industry economics: a guide for financial analysis* 10th edn. Cambridge: Cambridge University Press.

Warman, M. (2013) Snapchat's Evan Spiegel: 'Deleting should be the default.' *The Telegraph*. [online] Available at: www.telegraph.co.uk/technology/social-media/10452668/Snapchats-Evan-Spiegel-Deleting-should-be-the-default.html [Accessed 25 August 2022].

Wells, G. (2021, 15 September 2021) Facebook downplayed Instagram's harm to some teens. *Wall Street Journal: Tech News Briefing*. [podcast] 15 September. Available at: www.wsj.com/podcasts/tech-news-briefing/facebook-downplayed-instagram-harm-to-some-teens/c03aee6f-15e1-4879-9676-54f65114b48e [Accessed 25 August 2022].

Wu, T. (2017) *The attention merchants: the epic struggle to get inside our heads*. London: Atlantic Books.

YouTube. (2022) Our commitments. *YouTube*. [online] Available at: www.youtube.com/intl/ALL_uk/howyoutubeworks/our-commitments/safeguarding-copyright/ [Accessed 25 August 2022].

CHAPTER 7

Streamers

An entirely new media industry is defined by its use of AI

....

INTRODUCTION TO THE SECTOR

In the second decade of the twenty-first century, streaming companies hit the TV and film content markets like a tidal wave. The home video/DVD market was all but washed away entirely, and cinema exhibition was severely damaged. Broadcast TV, already impacted by digital advertising competition, lost further audience, particularly amongst highly-prized young adults who in many cases eschewed the television set entirely. Cable TV risked obsolescence through 'cord-cutting.'

But on the other hand, the engines of content production were fuelled by dramatically increased demand. Film production was transformed by (on the downside) loss of some cinema exhibition revenues and (on the upside) the arrival of new and gilt-edged customers, deploying capital from their much bigger technology businesses, on metrics which were driven more by long-term customer retention than short-term project profitability. As a result, production volumes and budgets soared.

To summarise the streamers, they "are the barons of the new gilded age, able to leverage vast resources to ensure their market power remains unchecked" (Lotz and Landgraf, 2018). In the era of streaming, the distribution platforms "now wear the crowns" (Vogel, 2020).

- In 2011, there were 17 significant streaming platforms. By 2021, there were 115 (ITV, 2021). One report (Anderson, 2021) said the total number of video-on-demand services globally was actually 3015 (2020), with 750 services launched in a four year period alone.
- Major global players *Netflix*, *Amazon Prime Video*, *Disney+* and *Apple TV+*, compete with local providers, like the BBC's *iPlayer* in the UK, Nigeria's *IrokoTV*

DOI: 10.4324/9781003213611-9

or Argentina's niche film service, *Cine.AR*. However, most consumers have capacity to pay for four streaming services at a time, for $10 each (Fischer, 2022).

- *Netflix* was the most mentioned brand on *TikTok* in 2021 (Geyser, 2022).
- Streaming continues to broaden as an idea. In 2022, even the business software provider Salesforce had a streaming service – *Salesforce+* – which was in effect a B2B video content marketing offer (Salesforce, 2022).
- The global market for streaming was projected to grow to $81.3 billion in 2025 (PWC, 2021).

Nonetheless, there were clear signs in 2022 of an upper limit to growth in the streaming market.

- *Netflix* reported in April of that year that it had for the first time in a decade lost subscribers and projected further loss of customers (Urwin, 2022).
- Broadcasters saw stabilisation in their revenues, and companies which combined broadcast advertising and subscription revenues (such as Paramount, which owned both broadcaster CBS and streaming service *Paramount+*) were considered by some to be more resilient to potential recession.
- As streamers reach both home market saturation for their brands and intensified competition, there is incentive for them to move to both new markets (e.g., in Africa and Asia) and new models. *Netflix* moved towards a subscription/advertising hybrid model, in 2022 – working with Microsoft, as the company stated in July 2022, for both technical innovation and privacy protection.

Categories of streamers

Global streamers fit into five key categories.

Finance-driven

Some streamers have huge equity and debt fundraising capabilities – *Netflix* is the standout example – the fruit of a low cost of capital and high equity-multiple environment 2010–20. This model is almost uniquely geared to the 'blitz-scaling' (a phrase coined by *LinkedIn* founder Reid Hoffman) of initially unprofitable businesses.

Focus is key. As a DVD service, *Netflix* stocked 100,000 titles, but as a streamer it dropped 85% to just 15,000, of which typical users can only access 4,000.

Tech-subsidised

Some streamers are minor lines on the income statement of trillion-dollar tech companies. They amount to a cost-efficient marketing spend designed to drive subscription to wider platform services, like *Amazon Prime Video*, and *Apple TV+*. "This is a company [Apple] with a market cap well over $2 trillion. Content is a rounding error" (Wallenstein, 2020).

- These streamers create disruption in the content market – subject to regulators – because they have a different economic model. For instance, *Amazon* bought studio *MGM* in 2021 with its 4,000-title library in 2021 for $8.45 billion, more than anyone else wanted to pay, but a valuable addition of substance to its content offer.
- That price could be argued to have been incidental. It was less than one twentieth of the $192 billion gain in stock market value Amazon experienced on a single day in February 2022.

Legacy rights owners

Some streamers leverage back catalogues built up over time. By bringing those titles onto their own streaming services, they convert licence fees historically paid for their shows by third parties into sustainable recurring revenues of their own – like *Disney+*, which launched in 2019.

- In 2017, Disney began to prepare for the transition – bulking up its library by buying much of 21st Century Fox (*The X-Men* and *Avatar*) for $66 billion, and by letting its distribution deals with *Netflix* lapse so that it could deploy its own titles.
- Rights to content libraries once governed success for any new service, but less today as consumers crave the new. Following that logic, Disney doubled down on new content from old franchises – commissioning ten new *Star Wars* projects in December 2020 alone (RadioTimes, 2020).
- In April 2022, Disney migrated its hit, BBC-produced entertainment show *Dancing with the Stars* from its TV network ABC to its *Disney+* streaming service, presumably to drive subscriber growth.

Legacy broadcasters

Other streamers are national players, tracking consumer market change from broadcast into streaming – like *Peacock (NBC)*, *Paramount+ (CBS)*, *HBO* and *Hulu* (US); *Hotstar*, *ALTBalaji* and *Zee 5* (India); *Iqiyi*, *QQ* and *Youku* (China); *BBC iPlayer*, *ITV Hub* and *All4* (UK).

- Legacy owners exploit legacy content. *Paramount+*, owned by legacy broadcaster ViacomCBS, of which the parent company is Paramount Global, announced a $5 billion slate of originals in February 2022, revisiting classic shows *Frasier* and *Criminal Minds*, 1980s movie *Flashdance*, and *Spongebob Squarepants* (Layton, 2022). The aim: 100 million subscribers in an already-crowded market.
- Countries like Brazil track the US' top streaming platforms. Others, like Russia – with *Ivi*, *Kinopoisk*, *Okko*, *Megogo*, *Amediateka* and *Wink* – have national players pursuing unique strategies (Statista, 2022).

- These market entrants typically arrived later (except the BBC) and without the balance sheet firepower of the tech companies.

Niche players

Streamers can target specific cultural segmentations. *ViX* launched in February 2022, to serve the world's 600 million Spanish speakers, with over 50,000 hours of content, including shows from Selena Gomez and Mario Vargas Llosa.

- In 2022, *Crunchyroll* hit 3 million subscribers in Anime, and *BritBox* reached 1 million 'subs' in the US for its British shows. In March 2022, UK broadcaster ITV launched *ITVX*, targeting young adults.
- Other niche streamers have been bought by larger firms to boost subscribers – like *Tubi*, bought by Fox, and *Acorn TV* (another UK offer) by AMC (Alexander, 2021). They also bought horror streamer *Shudder* with a 1 million + subscribers, art-house channel *Sundance Now* (with the South of France thriller *Riviera*) and African-American streamer ALLBLK (*Millennials, Double Cross*). AMC called that differentiation strategy "specialty boutiques," claiming the lowest customer churn amongst US streamers (Szalai, 2021).
- In Australia, *SBS On Demand* offers cultural programming. Local SVOD channels *Binge* (with *HBO Max* content) and *Stan* compete with *Netflix* and *Disney+* (Hammill, 2022).
- In Egypt, population 96 million, of whom 60% are under 24, pan-Arab *Shahid* is largest streaming service in the world outside USA, China and India (Allam and Chan-Olmsted, 2020).
- One streamer is so niche it only has one show: launched in March 2022 *Taskmaster Supermax+* offered every episode ever made for £5.99 a month (Heritage, 2022).

Consumer perspective on streamers

The section above provides a view of the streaming market from the top-down perspective of service providers. From the alternative, consumer-centric view, streaming offers three key benefits.

(1) *Different payment model:* the monthly subscription is an alternative to licence-fee public sector funding models (like the BBC) and commercial, advertiser-funded offers (like France's TF1). It is similar to cable TV because it needs good bandwidth (whether fixed or mobile) and may sit alongside cable as a home subscription. From 2022, there may be hybrid payment models which combine ad-supported tiers and ad-free offerings.

(2) *Different distribution model*: the switch from programme schedules to an always-on content library content has reframed the TV viewing experience. Why did that disruption succeed? An academic survey of 260,000 households

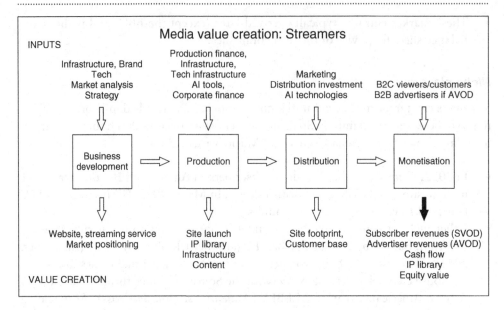

FIGURE 7.1 Streamers require exceptional investment in technology, marketing and content – but can achieve global revenue from subscription and advertising

found the biggest attractions were video-on-demand and genre choice (Fudurić et al., 2020).

(3) *Personalised viewing experience*: machine learning-driven personalisation, combined with AI tools to optimise streaming of shows across constrained bandwidth (see below) have offered an opportunity for customer centricity.

With evolution in technology, distribution, platforms and tastes, broadcasters have been "forced to re-examine their approaches to creativity and ideation including capacities and enabling methods" (Mooney et al., 2018).

- Customers expect omnichannel delivery (TV, laptop, phone) – a trend amplified by streamers being owned by tech companies like Apple and Amazon.
- Apple CEO Tim Cook said the world's richest company was in streaming for the long term: "It is not a hobby. It is not a 'dip your toe in,' because it's an original focus … We're going to build over time. We've gotten over three hundred nominations now for awards" (Cook, 2021).
- In retail, some marketers observe 'the Amazonification of everything,' meaning all sectors are benchmarked against *Amazon*. In the context of streaming, *Netflix* offers the equivalent default standard of customer service excellence. Many national broadcasters found their early efforts to compete were poorly received as a consequence of not matching *Netflix*'s delivery and personalisation.
- *Netflix* takes personalisation so seriously that it has dozens of thumbnails for each title, and algorithmically selects the content most likely to appeal to each

viewer in a variety of ways. The secret to this market-defining customer centricity is AI (see the section at the end of this chapter).

THE VALUE CREATION MODEL

Business development

For streamers, investment in a new service is not a casual decision. Such is the scale of the commitment required and the competitive threat, that it will be underpinned by exhaustive market analysis capable of due diligence by financial backers.

The service must be credibly positioned within a crowded market. So in the development phase of media value creation, the streamer develops a clear content proposition (say, Indian cinema). They need infrastructure, brand, technology, content and money. Outputs in this phase are creation of the website, and service proposition.

Streamers are differentiated by brand and content. Of these, content is more important, because it defines the brand in the eyes of the consumer. Content budget is therefore, in effect, marketing spend. Content drives subscriber acquisition and retention better than any advertising. (See Chapter 3 for CLV and why retention counts.)

- The primary performance figures in the public results of a listed streaming company are the rate and scale of customer acquisition, and churn rate. (Churn = 1 − retention.)
- Streamers address that requirement to minimise churn through competitive pricing, and content spent. For the latter, they can produce in-house, contract production out by commissioning production companies or acquire finished programming. Most combine all three. The higher their budget, the more likely they are to do the first two, for a bespoke positioning.

Table 7.1 summarises the strengths and weaknesses of each.

Most streamers use all three content sources – but in different combinations, so market differentiation is determined by the mix they choose. There are four commonly used strategies.

Differentiate by programme acquisition

This strategy is to define the streaming service by acquiring high-value finished programmes – bringing existing customer cohorts as subscribers, like fans of *Friends* or *The Office*. *Netflix* viewers watched over 52 billion minutes of *The Office* in 2018, some 3% of all *Netflix* minutes watched in the US. This is why NBC took the programme back in-house for the early 2021 launch of its own streaming service, *Peacock* (Alexander, 2019).

TABLE 7.1 Relative merits for streamers of different sources of content

Content Source	Advantage	Disadvantage
In-house	Full, automatic rights ownership. Full control of production workflow. No competition for ideas with other buyers. Full creative control.	High fixed cost. Slow scaleability of production either up or down. Requires full cash flow upfront.
Commissioned externally	Strong creative control of creative. Can match to subscriber tastes and marketing. Rapidly scaleable up and down. Pick of producers globally. Low fixed costs. Pass cash flow risk to producers, who offset it with banks.	Give away margin to external producers in return for rights. Slightly less control over production process than if in-house. No automatic access to best ideas. Retention of long-term relationships with top producers is expensive.
Acquire finished content	Cheaper than first-run programming. Rapidly scaleable at short notice.	Unlikely to drive new subscriber numbers – since by definition the content will have been seen elsewhere, unless major archive, like *Friends*.

One dimension of this acquisition strategy can be sports. Sports fans tend to be 'sticky' viewers to networks which have the sports rights they value. *Apple TV+*, for instance, took rights to US *Major League Baseball* for the 2022 season. Streamers took 20% of all sports rights deals in 2022 (Dziadul, 2022).

Differentiate by global footprint

This strategy uses programming from all three sources – but with a global footprint. Globalisation targets customer growth in new markets, often at lower average revenue per user (ARPU) than in the streamer's home territory.

The spin-off cultural benefit is to challenge the global predominance of licensed material from UK and US producers, and offer viewers a more diverse, multilingual content market, compared to the home market-centric footprint of most commercial broadcasters.

- Streamers have commissioned widely. *Netflix* bought *Narcos* (Mexico), *Money Heist* (Spain), *The Kingdom* (South Korea) and *Dark* (Germany).
- This change frames French show *Call My Agent*, South Korean hit *Squid Game* and Spanish breakout *Money Heist* in the same 'hits' category as US-produced (though British-made) *Bridgerton*.
- *Amazon Prime* bought *Fleabag* from the UK and *Made in Heaven* from India. *Disney+* bought from France, Germany, and Italy, aiming for fifty European titles by 2024. *Apple TV+* bought spy show *Tehran* from Israel (Roxborough, 2021).

- *HBO Max* commissioned art-house content as product differentiation in Europe – signing a first-look deal with Turkish-German director Fatih Akin.
- *Amazon Prime Video* signed Nigerian production companies Inkblot and Anthill Studios, for access to *Nollywood*, which produces thousands of films per year.
- *Discovery +* (formed from merger of WarnerMedia and Discovery) leverage their heritage of 'glocal' cable TV production to offer regionally appropriate titles. "You've got to have the infrastructure on the ground," said CEO J. B. Perrette. "People and teams that know the local markets … and know the production communities who are producing stories … We are in a period also where content is travelling" (Littleton, 2021).
- Bela Bajaria, *Netflix*'s global head of TV, works on the basis of "think locally, act globally" overseeing content for *Netflix*'s more than 222 million subscribers in over 190-countries and "allowing storytellers all around the world to export their stories." Non-English language programme viewing by *Netflix*'s US subscribers grew some 67% between 2019 and 2021 (Littleton, 2021). Each programme requires dubbing and subtitling into multiple languages, a process that can take up to six months from delivery of the tape.

Differentiate by bespoke commissioning

This strategy creates value by commissioning content from internal and external producers, combined with judicious acquisition for a rounded programming mix.

- This tripartite model is found on China's long-form video platforms, which simultaneously increased acquisitions of popular programmes and produced their own shows. *Alibaba's Youku, Tencent Video* and *Baidu*-backed *iQiyi* beat user growth expectations in 2021, turning around viewer losses to short-form video sites like *Kuaishou*. "Investing in content will become more important in China's video industry, at a time when leading players are encroaching on to each other's turf" (Sun, 2021).
- Tencent had TV series *The Land of Warriors*, and increased subscribers 12% to 125 million year-on-year. *Youku* had fantasy series *Word of Honor*, and doubled down on the property by staging live events with the stars. It sold out in 14 seconds – evidence of the value of strong content to customer stickiness.
- Stickiness is the Holy Grail of streamer commissioning. That explains why comedian Dave Chappelle came to *Netflix* – despite his controversial material. "Stand-up specials are, to use *Netflix*'s chief creative officer Ted Serandos's words, 'sticky.' People watch them. They watch them again. Subscribers like them. So *Netflix* went out and basically bid up the price of stand-up comedy to record highs. And one of their big gets was Chappelle, for a multi-special deal at about $20 million dollars a special" (Flint, 2021).

In streaming, when the flow of new titles dries up, churn goes up too.

- A study by a subscriber-measurement firm Antenna using email traffic and other data, published in the *Wall Street Journal*, showed strong acquisition of customers when big shows came out – and then a rapid drop-off.
- *HBO Max* had a surge in sign-ups for *Wonder Woman 1984*, and *Apple TV+* for its war movie *Greyhound*. But about half the people show signed up in the first three days churned out after six months – which is expensive customer acquisition (Marcelis, 2022).
- *Netflix* differentiated with interactive commissions, famously in a *Black Mirror* episode *Bandersnatch* (2018), *You vs Wild* (2019) and *Cat Burglar* (2022). "They are likely beachheads from which the company will participate in Metaverse-related opportunities, getting early learnings that may not pay off for some time" (Tran, 2021).
- *Netflix* has accelerated its supply of new titles – at the expense of cancelling existing hits like the successful *Bloodline*, with other titles such as *V Wars* and *Messiah* only achieving a single season. In fact, less than 20% of *Netflix*'s shows launched in 2017 reached a third series, compared to 31% in 2015 (Urwin, 2022).
- When Amazon bought MGM, it was a content library purchase, rather than a commissioning deal. The response from investors was modest – in light of "the market's obsession with brand-new content" (Finney, 2022).

Differentiate by brand extension

There are two kinds of brand extension in streaming.

First, streamers have been heavy commissioners of content that trades on existing IP – a book, film, sports or TV title, and therefore has easy homepage salience. *Amazon* has made a sequence of such commissions:

- *Amazon Prime Video* bought *The Grand Tour* (2016), a modest departure from the BBC's *Top Gear* format, with its original team. Scripted series *Jack Ryan* (2018) was based on the popular Tom Clancy novels and films. *Bosch* (seven seasons) came from a series of novels. *Bourne Supremacy* yielded the spin off *Treadstone*. There was a disappointing 2018 TV spinoff to the Luc Besson hit movie *Taken*.
- By buying MGM studios in 2022, Amazon opened the possibility of the *James Bond* catalogue; "to have the *James Bond* universe of television shows like Disney is doing [with *Star Wars*]" (Kafka, 2021). Sure enough, Amazon immediately announced reality series *007's Road to a Million*, to launch in 240 countries. "Both *Amazon* and *Netflix* started doing original content in the same year. And everyone knows *Netflix*'s first show was *House of Cards*, and you cannot tell me the name of the first *Amazon* show" (Kafka, 2021).

The second kind of brand extensions is where a streamer moves into a new space in the content market.

In 2022, to bring in new viewers beyond *Star Wars* and *Marvel* fans (who probably subscribed already by that point) *Disney+* broadened from its family entertainment heritage, to the adult-themed comedy *Pam and Tommy* (2022) on its *Hulu* streaming service, about the Pamela Anderson and Mötley Crüe drummer Tommy Lee and a missing sex tape, which was arguably off-brand for family oriented heritage Disney. Bloomberg commentator Lucas Shaw, said: "They're trying to figure out how to be elastic with the Disney brand." Financial analysts Moffett Nathanson said: "We wonder if *Disney+* is too narrow a product and requires much greater investment in non-Disney content to widen out the product's appeal," after seeing growth slow at the 118 million mark in 2021 (Cumming, 2021).

The challenge of brand elasticity affects each streamer differently, as they seek growth and distinctiveness in a saturated market.

Production

At the production stage in the streaming value chain, quality control is the key.

Like any content customer in the media business, the streamer needs to ensure it receives shows with sufficient global appeal, at the standard it has paid for, and on schedule – so that it can meet the customer expectations for new content to drop at least weekly. Production is therefore supervised from offices globally. *Netflix* has studios or offices in Mexico City, New York, New Mexico, Toronto, Madrid, Paris, Mumbai, Sydney, London, Amsterdam, Seoul, Tokyo (Roxborough, 2019) and significant production in Nigeria and Kenya (Vourlias, 2020). This makes *Netflix* likely to be the most globally diversified production entity.

Streamers do not typically derive profit from the process production. Taking full rights in the show, they pay the production budget, including a margin to the producer (up to 10%) and a potential premium of another 10–30% on top to account for the producer's forfeiture to the streamer of long-term upside in the property. *Netflix* does not always fully cash flow productions, expecting producers to bank-finance a large portion. *Netflix* therefore also carries a large amount of debt on its balance sheet as future obligations to pay for programmes already delivered. To the extent that the streamer allows rights windows to the producer or other distributors, its payment will be lower, reflecting its incomplete ownership of rights in the show.

Distribution

At the distribution phase of value creation, streamers need great programming. Without that, they cannot succeed. With great programming, streamers also require infrastructure, a tech platform (including cloud relationships at scale) and substantial finance. Outputs as this stage include the site's launch, the IP library, the infrastructure (a balance sheet asset), and market-visible proposition.

How streamers get their programmes to the audiences is their stock-in-trade. Every streamer is slightly different, and users are attuned to the nuance of service delivery. This requires artful user experience design (UX), technical efficiency, global and regional data storage, recommendation engines and bandwidth optimisation technology.

- From a value creation perspective, *Netflix* was a case study in a business built on distribution. When it launched, it wasn't a streamer at all. It was a mail order business, of which in 1997 the founders decided "that the intellectual property – the idea for DVD by mail ... was worth \$3 million" (Randolph, 2019).
- One of the great missed opportunities of the past decades in the media business was failure by the dominant home video company *Blockbuster* to buy *Netflix* when it had the chance. Reed Hastings, co-founder of *Netflix* related the story: " 'Blockbuster is a thousand times our size,' I whispered to Marc Randolph as we stepped into a cavernous meeting room on the twenty-seventh floor of the Renaissance Tower in Dallas, Texas, early in 2000. These were the headquarters of *Blockbuster*, then a \$6 billion giant that dominated the home entertainment business with almost nine thousand rental stores around the world" (Hastings and Meyer, 2020). By 2010, *Blockbuster* had filed for bankruptcy with \$1 billion debt. In April 2022, *Netflix* had a market capitalisation of \$355 billion.

Having both distribution and production in the same company, as do the BBC, Disney, *Netflix* and Warner Bros. Discovery, can enable flexibility about where a film or TV show goes out – which is a competitive advantage. Studio and network heads are able to "make the call about whether a project is destined for theatrical, linear TV or streaming distribution" (Alexander, 2020).

A distribution challenge for the major streamers is that once they have saturated a market, they have few new customer cohorts remaining to target. Even *Netflix*'s break out hit of 2021, *Squid Game*, watched by around 140 million subscribers, only delivered about 70,000 new customers in North America, out of the global 4.4 million who signed up that quarter. Growth for *Netflix* came overseas. (Nicolaou, 2021) Streamers may kill off shows at the height of their success, on the basis that there are few new potential customers to be gained by recommissioning them. This is different from TV broadcasters, who will keep successful shows for as long as possible, because they will generate advertising revenue from commercials shown to high ratings.

Viewing figures

Streamers are secretive about viewing, with (in 2022) no universally accepted version of ratings measurement, equivalent to US ratings company Nielsen ratings in commercial TV. Some streamers have gone some way to addressing this – for instance, *BBC iPlayer* and Channel 4's *All4* in the UK release viewing statistics – and as mixed models of subscription and advertising are developed, more transparent ratings will be required, to satisfy media buyers' need for transparency.

- *Netflix* expanded its Top 10 lists in 2021, detailing the best watched shows and movies globally, and hired audit firm EY to publish more. "The streamer is giving notice to the industry, customers and Wall Street that it has an engine capable of producing a surprise hit like '*Squid Game*,' which (*Netflix* says) was viewed an astronomical 1.6 billion hours over its first 28 days of release." But the figures are partial, and don't reveal the flops (Spangler, 2021).
- In the US, Nielsen started in 2021 to release streaming charts weekly, but only on cable TV homes.
- Amazon targets a much wider range of data points to evaluate success of its shows than a simple ratings number, which might be about targeting a particular audience cohort for potential subscription to the wider Amazon Prime e-commerce offering. Georgia Brown, Head of European Originals at Amazon Studios, told the Edinburgh TV Festival in August 2022: "Every single show has a different benchmark."

Monetisation

At the monetisation phase of the media value creation process, key inputs required are viewers, plus either paying subscriber customers (SVOD model) or paying advertisers (AVOD model). A show without viewers has no commercial value.

Principal outputs at this stage are revenues, cash flow (usually negative in the first few years), assets and IP, and (if successful) huge equity value. That value is derived from the lifetime value of all customers, current and future, the equity in the brand, programme and technical IP, and any net financial assets.

Money is earned direct by streamers through their own billing systems, or via partners who bundle deals with their broadband or satellite subscription – like the UK's *Sky*.

Growth constraints of streamers

Each streamer has financial challenges born of their particular circumstance, but there are two central issues in streaming. Is there too much investment in the market for anyone to make money? And are there too many streamers? In mature markets, growth is challenged.

- Warner Bros. Discovery's *HBO Max* reported slowdown in the third quarter of 2021, signing up only 570,000 Americans, against 2.4 million in the previous one. Disney added only 2 million subscribers globally, a big drop from 12 million (Nicolaou, 2021). In India, the average *Disney+* subscriber paid just $4.12 a month (Cumming, 2021). In March 2022, Disney added an advertising-subsidised subscription plan, in an effort to increase users.
- *Netflix* kept investing, reaching 200 million paying customers in 2021, but also $15 billion in debt, and content spending of $17 billion. Some of *Netflix*'s growth

came from markets where the price charged was lower than for existing users. In Asia, the average *Netflix* price was $9.60 a month, compared with $14.68 in the US. But in Kenya, *Netflix* too launched a total free offer in 2022, a 'freemium' launch model in partnership with Google-owned *Android*, designed to drive user growth. *Netflix* is by far the dominant streamer in Africa, but in 2020 had only 2 million subscribers, on a continent of 1.27 billion people.

User fatigue?

Administering multiple subscriptions is not cost-efficient for consumers, and that problem may need to be solved. The solution may involve aggregating services in a model akin to the cable TV model.

- "Already there are signs that many of the new generation of streamers will eventually be re-aggregated" (Cumming, 2021).
- Former 21st Century Fox CEO James Murdoch stated the same view, in the context of a fierce battle between the major global players and local Australian services *Stan* and *Binge*. Streamers would coalesce into something approximating to an old-style cable bundle, where for one payment and set-top box, they user accessed multiple services. "The danger for some firms is if they are left out of that re-aggregation or re-bundling … if you're not the top three choices, really where are you?" (MirandaWard, 2021).
- An executive at a leading cable firm agrees that may happen, because the lower administration costs can be passed back to consumers, creating a win-win of the same revenue to the streamer combined with cheaper prices for consumers: "If you can create bundles that reduce churn, they [streamers] can afford to lower the price to the consumer by the cost of two or three months [service per year], and still take home the same revenue. This is as old as Noah's Ark. The more something is aggregated, the less it turns."

Class discussion questions

- For a major streamer, what is the *financial* case for and against commissioning content from *external* production companies?
- Try to spot a gap in a *regional* streaming market and provide a presentation of a plan to fill it. (For instance, you could make the case that there is a gap for a Latin American content on a streaming service aimed at the Spain market.)
- Is there a limit to the number of players who can co-exist globally in streaming?
- From the perspective of a consumer, what are the threats to any given streaming service as a use of their home budget? How can the streamer best mitigate those risks?

Analysis of an AVOD service: Pluto TV (US and Latin America)

Background

How can an advertising-funded streaming business be customised to different global audiences without adding costs?

A 2013 LA-based start-up, *Pluto TV* was founded by Tom Ryan, Ilya Pozin and Nick Grouf, who spotted market opportunity for content aggregation, raising seed funds in Hollywood (Viktor, 2021) to launch in 2014 with 100 channels. Next came a $52 million second round including media/tech firms Scripps, Samsung and Sky (Roettgers, 2019).

Most of the content was live streams, but in 2017 Pluto added on-demand video, reaching 12 million US users in 2018 Pluto (Schiff, 2020). In January 2019, Viacom bought Pluto, for $340 million (Roettgers, 2019). It expanded the channels, and added its own content. Pluto's Tom Ryan was promoted to head Viacom's overall streaming operation (Middleton, 2020).

Where is Pluto now? (in 2022)

- *Pluto TV* now has over 250 unique live channels that stream content with commercial breaks (Minor and Moore, 2022).
- In news, it carries: *NBC News*, *CBSN*, *CNN*, *Best of The Today Show*, *Bloomberg*, *Cheddar News*, *Newsmax TV*, *Top Stories by Newsy*, *Court TV*, *WeatherNation*. In sports: *Fox Sports*, *CBS Sports HQ*, *NFL Channel* (not *NFL Network*), *PGA Tour Rewind*, *Stadium*, *MLB Channel*. And in entertainment: Comedy Central, MTV, Nickelodeon, VH1, Entertainment Tonight (ET Live), *Spike TV*, *CMT*, *BET*, *AMC* (*The Walking Dead*, *Brockmire*) (Cole, 2021).
- *Pluto* also has *YouTube*-style thematic channels – like *Wipeout*, *Dr Who Classic*, *Teenage Mutant Ninja Turtles*, and *Slow TV* which features live streams like Norwegian train trips. These may not build the network as well as verifying the curation model (Schneider, 2019).
- *Pluto*'s free offer works in Latin America (Spangler, 2020) with 100 channels in the Spanish-speaking countries, and 50 in Brazil (Television, 2021). In Europe, it launched in Germany, Austria, Switzerland and the UK (Munson, 2020). So, by 2021, *Pluto TV* had over 52 million global monthly active users, in 25 countries and on three continents (Winslow, 2021).
- Tech partnership helped 60% of the audience find Pluto on smart TV sets like *Vizio* (Roettgers, 2018). *Pluto*'s competitive advantage over linear TV in advertising is customer data, and better programmatic ad performance.
- In December 2021, *Pluto* reached $786 million in net US ad revenues, a 77.7% increase year-on-year (Benes, 2022).

Class discussion

- Why has *Pluto* been successful?
- *Pluto* has huge competition from AVODs and SVODs. How will it keep its audience engaged?
- Should *Pluto* double down on its developing economies footprint, where the AVOD model works well?

Analysis: AI technologies at *Netflix*

AI and machine learning is embedded in the DNA of the streamers. Recommendation systems fit three basic categories (Hinkle, 2021):

- Content based: the system uses data about a programme's content to suggest ideas for similar ones for the customer to watch.
- Collaborative filtering: here *Netflix* compares user behaviour to the actions of other people, to make useful viewing suggestions.
- Knowledge-based: here the streamer combines user preferences, past viewing and other data to make recommendations about new programmes.

Using all of those approaches, *Netflix* is a good example of industry best practice, and recommendation has always been its focus.

The section below considers some of the ways in which *Netflix* is implementing AI systems, and the competitive advantage that it was able to achieve in doing so.

- In 2006, *Netflix* offered a $1 million prize for anyone who could beat its recommendation system.
- In 2014, it invested 3% of revenue in recommendation engine development.

Recommendation engines

Using machine learning, *Netflix*'s personalisation system enables it to serve the 'right' content to each customer, meaning the content that the customer is mostly likely view as a reason to maintain their subscription. Reduction of churn (or increase in retention) is one of the two fundamental value drivers for any subscription business. (The other is customer acquisition.)

Netflix hosts data on *Amazon Web Services*, unlike many other major companies who have their own complete 'tech stack' in-house. This use of external cloud services could be argued to give *Netflix* greater scaleability, because it is leveraging the wider technological versatility, and economies of scale of Amazon. That may give it more capability to launch new tools than an organisation which was seeking to run its entire technology internally.

- A former *Netflix* developer told an AI podcast: "*Netflix* is in that sense, closer to everybody else in the world … And now when you layer something like a data science and machine learning on top of it … all those like learnings are reflected in *Metal Flow* which is the open source library" (Whitenack, 2021). There are diverse AI use cases: "if you think about computer vision, natural language processing, even things that are not technically, machine learning, operations research."
- In 2015, *Netflix* stated that 80% of viewing was based on its automated recommendations (Hinkle, 2021).

Technical distribution methodologies

Netflix says its machine learning functions across almost every aspect of the business – video encoding and optimisation of data streaming "that accounts for more than a third of North American internet traffic … It also powers our advertising spend, channel mix, and advertising creative so that we can find new members" (Netflix, 2022).

- On the underlying maths deployed in AI at *Netflix* also offers insights: "Our research spans many different algorithmic approaches including causal modeling, bandits, reinforcement learning, ensembles, neural networks, probabilistic graphical models, and matrix factorization" (Netflix, 2022). (In machine learning, a 'multi-armed bandit' is a tool in which an agent chooses actions in sequential stages, each with rewards and learning from previous rounds, to maximise cumulative performance (TensorFlow, 2021).)

Deep learning-informed programme commissioning choices

Netflix uses machine learning as a competitive advantage in programme selection, "understanding their audience much better than any of their competitors, and presenting the content that they have available in different ways to different people" (Ford, 2021). Nine out of ten programmes watched on *Netflix* has been recommended to them by its AI systems.

Because *Netflix* produces its own content, it can also tailor the output itself, based on precise audience understanding, which would be harder to do if it was merely acquiring pre-existing content.

"Engagement is now the watchword for so much in the media space, and almost all of that is dependent upon the Artificial Intelligence systems that provide that insight to those who end up taking the decision in terms of the programming decisions" (Ford, 2021).

The full journey from creation, to production, to distribution to monetisation is thereby AI-powered.

Class discussion questions

- To what degree would you argue that *Netflix*'s success is a function of its early adoption, continuing investment and interest in machine learning and AI?

- What specific competitive advantages can you identify, from a technical perspective, that it currently has over the competition in terms of visible iterations of technology on its services?
- Identify a significant streaming service that you believe is *not* making good use of AI tools, and set out a detailed presentation for its board about changes it could make.

CHAPTER SUMMARY

TABLE 7.2 Key themes in this chapter

Streaming	Development	Production	Distribution	Monetisation
Business model	Major investment in contracting producers, buying ideas and commissioning productions.	Heavy investment in delivering production.	Heavy investment in delivery systems, recommendation systems, and administration of subscribers.	Elegant subscription model, either direct or via partners. Low margin for administration.
Uses of AI	Significant data-informed decision making around programme commission selection based on past viewing and other data.	Virtual studio, sophisticated edit technologies, and any other production AI tools.	High AI usage around recommendation engines and tools, bandwidth optimisation and other features.	Machine learning driving efficiency of processes.
Value Creation	Ability to select hit series, and series which will hit with a specific customer cohort that might subscribe or retain subscription highly valued.	High value production (think *Squid Game* or *Bridgerton*) generates equity value, PR, retention and subscription.	Ease of use of platform is a major selling point for a good streamer.	High retention of selling price is an advantage for direct-to-consumer streamers.

BIBLIOGRAPHY

Alexander, J. (2019) The Office will leave Netflix in 2021. *The Verge*. [online] Available at: www.theverge.com/2019/6/25/18758714/the-office-netflix-2021-nbc-universal-streaming-wars [Accessed 25 August 2022].

Alexander, J. (2020, 28 October 2020) Streaming was part of the future – now it's the only future. *The Verge*. [online] Available at: www.theverge.com/21536842/streaming-disney-hbo-max-peacock-cbs-all-access-warnermedia-viacom-nbcuniversal [Accessed 25 August 2022].

Alexander, J. (2021) To all the streaming services you've never heard of before. *The Verge.* [online] Available at: www.theverge.com/c/22244771/streaming-services-niche-crunchyroll-ovid-acorn-tv [Accessed 25 August 2022].

Allam, R. and Chan-Olmsted, S. (2020) The development of video streaming industry in Egypt: examining its market environment and business model. *Journal of Media Business Studies*, 1–19. doi.org/10.1080/16522354.2020.1853436

Anderson, J. (2021, 24 June 2021) Nearly 750 VOD services launched in four years as factual commissions grow: report. *Real Screen.* [online] Available at: https://realscreen.com/2021/06/24/nearly-750-vod-services-launched-in-four-years-as-factual-commissions-grow-report/ [Accessed 25 August 2022].

Benes, R. (2022) Pluto TV will surpass $1 billion in US ad revenues in 2022. *Insider Intelligence.* [online] Available at: www.insiderintelligence.com/content/pluto-tv-will-surpass-1-billion-us-ad-revenues-2022 [Accessed 25 August 2022].

Cole, N. (2021) Pluto TV review: get live streaming TV for free. *Clark.* [online] Available at: https://clark.com/technology/tvsatellite-cable/pluto-tv-free-streaming-review/ [Accessed 25 August 2022].

Cook, T. (2021) Is Apple's privacy push Facebook's existential threat? *Sway.* [podcast] 5 April. Available at: https://open.spotify.com/episode/2brny71rXUZ8nvAgBNiiWi [Accessed 25 August 2022].

Cumming, E. (2021) Goodbye to the golden era of cheap TV. *Financial Times*, 30 April.

Dziadul, C. (2022) Streamers sports rights spend grows. *Broadband TV News.* [online] Available at: www.broadbandtvnews.com/2022/03/23/streamers-sports-rights-spend-grows/ [Accessed 25 August 2022].

Finney, A. (2022) Digital shapes new showbiz models. *Variety.* [online] Available at: https://variety.com/2022/film/awards/digital-impact-on-showbiz-models-1235190712/ [Accessed 25 August 2022].

Fischer, S. (2022) New scripted series hit record high following pandemic dip. [online] Available at: www.axios.com/2022/01/17/scripted-series-streaming-pandemic [Accessed 25 August 2022]

Flint, J. (2021) The Chappelle controversy tests Netflix. *The Journal.* [podcast] 21 October. Available at: www.wsj.com/podcasts/the-journal/the-chappelle-controversy-tests-netflix/129544cd-6b4b-4ebf-8bce-688b4e246003 [Accessed 25 August 2022]

Fudurić, M., Malthouse, E. C. and Lee, M. H. (2020) Understanding the drivers of cable TV cord shaving with big data. *Journal of Media Business Studies*, 17(2), 172–89. https://doi.org/10.1080/16522354.2019.1701363

Geyser, W. (2022) The state of influencer marketing 2022: benchmark report. *InfluencerMarketingHub.* [online] Available at: https://influencermarketinghub.com/influencer-marketing-benchmark-report/ [Accessed 25 August 2022].

Hammill, S. (2022) *Interview by Dr Alex Connock at the National Film and Television School with S. Hammill of AFTRS (Australian Film, Television and Radio School)*, 28 March.

Hastings, R. and Meyer, E. (2020) No rules rules: Netflix and the culture of reinvention. London: Penguin.

Heritage, S. (2022) 'We've no idea if it will work': Taskmaster launches own streaming service. *The Guardian*, 5 March.

Hinkle, D. (2021) How streaming services use algorithms. *Arts Management and Technology Laboratory.* [online] Available at: https://amt-lab.org/blog/2021/8/algorithms-in-streaming-services [Accessed 25 August 2022].

ITV. (2021) Half year results for the six months ended 30th June 2021. *ITV plc.* [online] Available at: www.itvplc.com/~/media/Files/I/ITV-PLC/documents/reports-and-results/ITV%20Plc%202021%20Half-Year%20Results%20Presentation.pdf [Accessed 25 August 2022].

Kafka, P. (2021) Why Amazon is paying nearly $9 billion for MGM and James Bond. *Vox.* [online] Available at: www.vox.com/recode/22451787/amazon-mgm-james-bond-streaming-netflix-analysis [Accessed 25 August 2022].

Layton, M. (2022, 25 February 2022) Paramount+ unveils huge slate including 'Frasier' & 'Criminal Minds' returns, plus $5bn originals plans. *Television Business International.* [online] Available at: https://tbivision.com/2021/02/25/paramount-confirms-frasier-and-criminal-minds-returns-among-originals-slate/ [Accessed 25 August 2022].

Littleton, C. (2021) Think global, act local: discovery international chief on how to win in global streaming. *Variety: Strictly Business.* [podcast] 18 August. Available at: https://variety.com/2021/tv/news/discovery-international-jb-perrette-streaming-1235043503/ [Accessed 25 August 2022].

Littleton, C. (2021) Netflix's Bela Bajaria on *Bridgerton, La Casa de Papel* and tailoring shows for global audiences. *Variety.* [online] Available at: https://variety.com/2021/tv/news/bridgerton-la-casa-de-papel-netflix-bela-bajaria-1234990606/ [Accessed 25 August 2022].

Lotz, A. D. and Landgraf, J. (2018) *We now disrupt this broadcast: how cable transformed television and the internet revolutionized it all.* Boston, MA: MIT Press.

Mullin, B. and Marcelis, D. (2022) Disney+, HBO Max and other streamers get waves of subscribers from must-see content. Keeping them is hard. *Wall Street Journal*, 31 January.

Middleton, R. (2020) ViacomCBS overhauls streaming division, with Pluto's Tom Ryan promoted and senior exec exits. *Television Business International.* [online] Available at: https://tbivision.com/2020/10/20/viacomcbs-overhauls-streaming-division-with-plutos-tom-ryan-promoted-senior-exec-exits/ [Accessed 25 August 2022].

Minor, J. and Moore, B. (2022) Pluto TV: an easy way to stream for free. *PC.* [online] Available at: https://uk.pcmag.com/internet-3/123624/pluto-tv [Accessed 25 August 2022].

Miranda Ward. (2021) Streaming wars enter rebundling phase: James Murdoch. *Australian Financial Review.* [online] Available at: www.afr.com/companies/media-and-marketing/streaming-wars-enters-re-bundling-phase-says-james-murdoch-20210420-p57kub [Accessed 25 August 2022].

Mooney, G., Burdon, S. and Kang, K. (2018) That's Entertainment: crafting a creative ecology within public television. *International Journal on Media Management*, 20(4), 263–76. doi.org/10.1080/14241277.2018.1557191

Munson, B. (2020) Pluto TV goes live in Latin America. *Fierce Video.* [online] Available at: www.fiercevideo.com/video/pluto-tv-goes-live-latin-america [Accessed 25 August 2022].

Netflix. (2022) Machine learning: learning how to entertain the world. *Netflix Research.* [online] Available at: https://research.netflix.com/research-area/machine-learning [Accessed 25 August 2022].

Nicolaou, A. (2021) New US subscribers are drying up in TV streaming competition. *Financial Times*, 11 November.

PWC. (2021) *Global entertainment and media outlook 2021–2025.* [online] Available at: www.pwc.com/gx/en/industries/tmt/media/outlook.html [Accessed 25 August 2022].

RadioTimes. (2020) Disney announces plans for 10 new Marvel series and 10 Star Wars series. *RadioTimes.* [online] Available at: www.radiotimes.com/tv/sci-fi/disney-10-marvel-star-wars-series/ [Accessed 25 August 2022].

Randolph, M. (2019) *That will never work: the birth of Netflix by the first CEO and co-founder Marc Randolph.* London: Endeavour.

Roettgers, J. (2018) Vizio integrates Pluto TV with new ad-supported WatchFree service. *Variety.* [online] Available at: https://variety.com/2018/digital/news/vizio-watchfree-pluto-tv-1202892147/ [Accessed 25 August 2022].

Roettgers, J. (2019) Viacom has acquired Pluto TV streaming service for $340 million. *Variety.* [online] Available at: https://variety.com/2019/digital/news/viacom-pluto-tv-acquisition-1203114773/ [Accessed 25 August 2022].

Roxborough, S. (2019) Netflix global real estate grab: how the streamer is expanding from London to Singapore. *The Hollywood Reporter.* [online] Available at: www.hollywoodr eporter.com/news/general-news/london-singapore-how-netflix-is-expanding-around-world-1229815/ [Accessed 25 August 2022].

Roxborough, S. (2021) MIPTV: foreign markets become 'Next big battleground' as streamers bet big on global growth. *The Hollywood Reporter.* [online] Available at: www.hollywoodr eporter.com/business/business-news/miptv-streamers-drive-international-tv-boom-4164 502/ [Accessed 25 August 2022].

Salesforce. (2022) Trailblazer. Salesforce. [online] Available at: www.salesforce.com/plus/ser ies/Trailblazer [Accessed 25 August 2022].

Schiff, A. (2020) Coronavirus is accelerating Pluto TV's already massive growth. *AdExchanger.* [online] Available at: www.adexchanger.com/tv-and-video/coronavirus-is-accelerating-pluto-tvs-already-massive-growth/ [Accessed 25 August 2022].

Schneider, M. (2019) 'It's an explosion': inside the rising costs of making a scripted tv series. *Variety.* [online] Available at: https://variety.com/2019/tv/features/cost-of-tv-scripted-series-rises-1203378894/ [Accessed 25 August 2022].

Spangler, T. (2020) Pluto TV launches free-streaming service in 17 latin american countries. *Variety.* [online] Available at: https://variety.com/2020/digital/news/pluto-tv-latin-america-launch-17-countries-1234573798/ [Accessed 25 August 2022].

Spangler, T. (2021) Netflix's expanded viewing data move is mainly a flex. *Variety.* [online] Available at: https://variety.com/2021/digital/news/netflix-expanded-top-10-viewing-data-flex-1235113030/ [Accessed 25 August 2022].

Statista. (2022) Most popular online video services for paid content in Russia 2021. *Statista.* [online] Available at: www.statista.com/statistics/1065631/russia-most-popular-online-video-services/ [Accessed 25 August 2022].

Sun, N. (2021) Alibaba, Baidu and Tencent learn Netflix lessons in content fight. *Financial Times*, 8 June.

Szalai, G. (2021) AMC network's 'boutique' streaming plan: don't try to compete with Netflix. *The Hollywood Reporter.* [online] Available at: www.hollywoodreporter.com/business/business-news/amc-networks-boutique-streaming-plan-dont-try-to-compete-with-netflix-4158525/ [Accessed 25 August 2022].

Television, A. (2021) Pluto TV reaches LatAm channel milestone. *Advanced Television.* [online] Available at: https://advanced-television.com/2021/09/23/pluto-tv-reaches-latam-channel-milestone/ [Accessed 25 August 2022].

TensorFlow. (2021) Introduction to multi-armed bandits. *TensorFlow.* [online] Available at: www.tensorflow.org/agents/tutorials/intro_bandit [Accessed 25 August 2022].

Tran, K. (2021). Metaverse & Media, Special Report. *Variety Intelligence Platform.* [online] Available at: https://variety.com/vip-special-reports/metaverse-and-media-how-techs-hottest-trend-will-impact-the-entertainment-industry-1235116381/ [Accessed 29 August 2022].

Urwin, R. (2022) Settling in for a binge Netflix subscribers? Bad luck, your show's been cancelled. *The Sunday Times*, 24 April.

Viktor. (2021) How does Pluto TV make money? *Productmint.* [online] Available at: https://productmint.com/pluto-tv-business-model-how-does-pluto-tv-make-money/ [Accessed 25 August 2022].

Vogel, H. L. (2020) *Entertainment industry economics: a guide for financial analysis.* 10th edn. Cambridge: Cambridge University Press.

Vourlias, C. (2020) Netflix's Head of African Originals lays out streamer's plans for the continent. *Variety*. [online] Available at: https://variety.com/2020/digital/news/netflix-head-african-originals-lays-out-plans-for-continent-1203518648/ [Accessed 25 August 2022].

Wallenstein, A. (2020) Making sense of a wild year in the streaming wars. *Variety: Strictly Business*. [podcast] 30 December. Available at: https://open.spotify.com/episode/45Jqs4m kCDOx1PnNgph1v1?si=12ddb42f1d0841ff&nd=1 [Accessed 25 August 2022].

Whitenack, D. (2021) Episode 150: From notebooks to Netflix scale with Metaflow. *Practical AI*. [podcast] 21 September. Available at: https://changelog.com/practicalai/150 [Accessed 25 August 2022].

Winslow, G. (2021) Pluto TV hits 100 Spanish channels in LatAm. *TVtech*. [online] Available at: www.tvtechnology.com/news/pluto-tv-hits-100-spanish-channels-in-latam [Accessed 25 August 2022].

CHAPTER 8

Broadcasters

Existentially threatened, pivoting to video-on-demand and fighting back

....

THE VALUE CREATION MODEL

In business, the phrase 'burning platform' is taken to mean any company or industry whose business model is under existential threat. Nowhere has that been more true – perceptually at least – than in broadcast television. For two decades it has been relentlessly challenged by both online advertising and streamers.

- Inflation-adjusted spend on content by UK terrestrial broadcasters fell between 2006–20 by 39%, to £2.07 billion (OFCOM, 2021b).

Yet in 2021, television (pay TV and advertising-funded) was also a $219 billion industry (PWC, 2021), expected to grow to $267 billion in 2022 (Business Research Company report, 2022). For all the industry *angst* about a consumer shift to streaming, in revenue terms TV remains approximately six times bigger than the whole subscription streaming sector ($60 billion).

So how does any TV channel business succeed? And how is that business model changing as broadcast channels follow their customers online?

"Television delivers people to an advertiser ... It is the consumer who is consumed," said commentator Richard Serra in 1973 (Wu, 2017). That was true of TV advertising at the time, and is even more true now of digital advertising now – directly addressable to the user, and targeted based on their own data.

Categories of TV channel

We will explore how the relationship between the content, consumer and commercial model works in TV.

DOI: 10.4324/9781003213611-10

There are four principle categories of television channel, and each business model is in flux, as commercial broadcast advertising is challenged by more precisely targeted digital advertising, and broadcast viewing of all types faces competition for eyeballs from streaming and other forms of online video, such as *TikTok* or *YouTube*.

- State-owned broadcaster (like the vast *China Central Television*, itself owning 50 channels).
- Publicly funded TV, but at arm's length from the state via some kind of licence fee arrangement (like the UK's BBC).
- Commercial advertising-funded channel, like US network *NBC* or Brazil's *Globo*.
- Subscription driven TV, like *beIN Sports* in Saudi Arabia (the Middle East is the world's fastest-growing TV market) or *Sky* in the UK.

Unlike media productions – a TV programme, film, video game, song or book – a TV channel is never delivered or complete. It is perennial work in progress. A channel must continually flex its content, positioning, audience segmentation, technology, design, communications, revenue model and customer acquisition strategies.

- Bob Iger, CEO from 2005–20 of Walt Disney, which owns TV channels *ABC* and *ESPN*, likened running a channel to the quest of Jiro Ono, a perfectionist *Michelin* three-star Tokyo sushi chef. "He's in his late eighties and still trying to perfect his art … the living embodiment of the Japanese word *shokunin*, which is 'the endless pursuit of perfection for some greater good' " (Iger, 2019).

Pursuit of perfection in the TV channels business requires the sustaining of commercial brand advertising revenues, combined with development of individually addressable technologies. These are the stock-in-trade of both the streaming and search advertising models, the sector's main challengers. But TV channels were slow in the period 2007–20 to embrace recommendation engines, and their online interfaces (UX) remain generally weak compared to streaming disruptor *Netflix*. Their programmatic advertising and ability to target users contextually, relevantly and individually remained, in the early 2020s, behind those of Meta sites *Instagram* and *Facebook*, and Google site *YouTube* (see below).

But channel owners have commercial advantages, too. They have great content – say, the *Super Bowl* – and through decades of production experience, know-how to make more of it. They have viewers. They have technical tools to go head-to-head with digital competitors, and a revenue mix (TV and streaming) more flexible than pure-subscription streamers. We will discuss the transformation that led to this point.

Meanwhile, there are complimentary strategies to build a channel business. We will look at the UK's *ITV*, as it reduces dependence on cyclical adverting revenue by leveraging IP ownership globally as a production business. We will examine pan-African broadcaster TRACE TV. And we will analyse AI at the BBC.

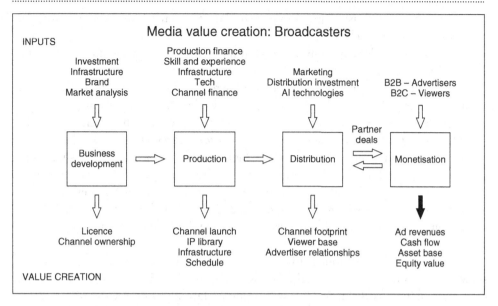

FIGURE 8.1 Broadcasters succeed or fail according to the clarity of their brand, quality of their programming, and depth of their distribution partner relationships

Business development

The development phase of value build in the TV channels business is about proposition design, and content. Good programming is a *sine qua non* – a prerequisite. From a marketing standpoint, the clearer the product-market fit, the better.

The channel business' principle inputs are a rigorous market analysis to specify the niche which the channel will occupy (e.g., 18–35 year olds) combined with a clear market positioning (e.g., comedy). Significant investment is needed into content, the organisation's brand and infrastructure, marketing, staff and other costs. These commitments are expensive compared to pure-play production businesses, which can remain fleet-footed on cost, using third parties to fund their development, in return for giving away rights in the projects produced. Outputs at the development phase for a channel are a licence to broadcast (usually awarded by governments and/or regulators), ownership of a channel and slots on distribution platforms (usually owned by commercial operators).

For channels, as for streamers in the previous chapter, content is blended from five main sources:

(1) In-house production: this offers the benefits of vertical integration, with full IP ownership. It brings high fixed costs, but is high margin when it works.
(2) Direct commissioning from production companies: this brings high marginal costs and cash flow challenges (the producers are substantially paid upfront), but it also brings diminished risk, through lower fixed costs. External production can be scaled up and down with relative flexibility relative to in-house.

(3) 'Acquisitions' of finished programmes on the open market: this is lower cost, but also lower profile. The best shows are likely to have been snapped up at inception stage by rivals, leaving only more commoditised or second-window programming available.
(4) Bought-in rights, like sports: these expensive to buy, but high return and customer loyalty derive from the best sports rights, like the *NFL* for Fox in the US, the *Premier League* for Sky in the UK or *Suning* for soccer in China (LI, 2017). The value of major sports rights (soccer, baseball, *Indian Premier League* cricket) in customer retention over time are the single biggest driver of their globally rising value.
(5) Channel branding assets: these are the content assets (e.g., channel idents, or branded news bulletins, on-screen continuity announcers, even breakfast programmes) which define the brand and personality for a channel. Some channels even have people's names to humanise them, like *Dave* in the UK.

Channels are usually positioned either as mass market or niche. *Dave* is a niche male-skewed UK comedy channel. At the opposite extreme, a quintessential mass market broadcast channel is Britain's *ITV*, with populist fare like *I'm A Celebrity, Get Me Out of Here*. Both strategies can work, provided the positioning is clear, and the content sufficiently strong to deliver a desirable audience cohort to advertisers.

Production

In the production phase of the media value creation process for a TV channel, key inputs are production/programme acquisition finance, the skills, infrastructure and experience of the channel-owner, technologies deployed in content creation for competitive advantage, and further overall enterprise financing. Outputs are the channel launch, its IP/rights library, infrastructure and the programme schedule.

Production is about how, and how well, the content is made, licensed and positioned for the audience. This has two dimensions: commercial value and public value.

Commercial value

Commercial TV channels maximise traction by showing programmes which bring in strong and commercially logical audiences, giving advertisers acceptable return on their investment. Well-known networks in Asia are South Korea's *SBS* or Hong Kong's *TVB*. In the US, key networks are *ABC*, *CBS*, *NBC* and *Fox*. In Germany, major channels are *RTL* with 7.2% of total viewing, *Sat 1* with 5.2% and *Vox* with 4.5% (2021).

The value generated by channels is in viewing numbers, and a qualitative assessment of the commercial value of those 'eyeballs.'

The UK's ITV half-year 2021 financial results and presentation (ITV, 2021) shows that for that channel, mass market reach and traction is key, and its content is positioned accordingly.

- Whilst ITV has a 90,000-hour catalogue, its main channel, *ITV1*, shows new shows. (Meanwhile *ITV4*, a niche channel within its portfolio, plays old series, to a small audience.)
- *ITV*'s own productions include the world's longest-running TV soap opera *Coronation Street*, dating reality show *Love Island* and game show *Walk the Line*. Part of the channel's commercial value is as on-air testing and proving ground for entertainment formats and tapes which it will then sell globally at high margin, via its tape and formats distribution operation (see Chapter 11).
- ITV also plays a role as producer, making shows for other channels too. Its production operation makes internationally scaleable formats like talent show *The Voice*, for UK rival channel *BBC One*. It makes scripted titles that it does not itself broadcast as well, such Italian gangster series *Gomorrah* (shown on UK rival *SKY*) hit detective series *Line of Duty* and submarine thriller *Vigil* (both again sold to *BBC One*). ITV earns margin on these sales, and retains as many international rights as it can, to then exploit titles for international sale. It makes commercial sense for ITV to not broadcast its own shows when they do not map to the demographics of its advertisers' audience aspirations, or when the profit from rights sales justifies it.

In the case of a niche commercial network, the challenge is different – to maximise traction with a very specific audience that is attractive to niche advertisers (e.g., young, female fashion fans). The niche channel business model is to capture enough dedicated fans in a coherent demographic or behavioural cohort in aggregate across wide geographies to sell targeted ads, subscriptions or cable TV carriage fees (see below). That means the content has to be food for the fanatics, a double-down value creation principle via audience segmentation applicable to any sports or music channel. It is how *MTV* was built.

Disney was one of the first companies to spot the business opportunity in niche. In their case it was sports: "the human drama of athletic competition" (Iger, 2019) which they still pursue via their cable channel ESPN, a key driver of both their broadcast TV and streaming operations, and profit in an era (May 2022) when their streaming service was losing $887 million per quarter, as it was built up.

Niche sports can also work well in a hybrid of channel transmission and global content syndication. Human drama is the thesis behind *World Wrestling Entertainment Inc*, whose *WWE* brand is iterated across TV channels and online platforms globally. The *WWE* has a formula for making money: "Travelling to cities across the country and televising acrobatic wrestling matches between spandex-clad athletes" (Broughton, 2021). As entertainment, it could have worked in 1925 as well as it does in 2025, and that enduring appeal of the format drives value.

Public role

The second dimension of broadcast channels is the public good.

A TV channel is more than just a logo and the programmes and adverts it shows. Requiring a state-authorised licence, it occupies visible, socio-political real estate, a point of shared national experience and a public service. This applies when the channel is publicly licensed but commercially funded, like ITV. And it applies for the publicly owned and funded BBC, with its £1.4 billion TV budget in 2021; or, at a smaller scale, Guatemala's equivalent, *Guatevision*.

Public service channels – the BBC, or Brazil's Empress Brasil de Comunicacao which runs *TV Brasil*, or Canada's *CBC* – are funded by variants of annual licence fees, government funds, advertising and (in the case of America's *PBS*) donations. But they largely retain (in some democracies) editorial independence.

Because of their public role, usually written into their licence are environmental, social and governance priorities (ESG), even for a commercial channel like the UK's *ITV*. In its 2021 results, ITV showcased diversity initiatives, two mental health *Britain Get Talking* campaigns and a children's diet-focused *Eat Them to Defeat Them* project (ITV, 2021).

Some channel go further for public value. ITV's commercially funded (though publicly owned) UK rival Channel 4, claimed a focus on the country's nations and regions delivered about £1 billion value to the UK economy every year. (In 2022, the UK government nonetheless announced a provisional plan to sell it.)

Whether the audience is incentivised by these civic communication efforts is questionable. In one UK survey, 51% were unaware even which channels were advertiser-funded (OFCOM, 2021a). The audience that matters on ESG is not viewers, so much as the politicians and regulators who award broadcast licences.

In the US, channels translate ESG through brand promises. In a study (Förster, 2011), NBC was shown to give a (diversity-focused) brand promise in the phrase "More colorful." ABC used the "emotionally loaded" slogan "Your favorite shows live here," to connect with female audiences by addressing closeness to social good, in neighbourhood and family. Programmes may then match the branding with public value content, but they may also tend more to the commercial mainstream. There, ABC went for women with *Desperate Housewives* and *Grey's Anatomy*. CBS targeted males with crime series like *CSI* and *Criminal Minds* (Förster, 2011).

Distribution and digital technology

Distribution in the media business is about how firms deliver their content to the audience. For TV channels, distribution combines broadcast licences, carriage deals and online platforms, including potentially short-form versions of content on social media.

At the distribution phase of media value creation in broadcast TV, key inputs required are marketing distribution and transmission investment, plus any technologies deployed for customer centric, competitive advantage (e.g., customisation). Outputs are the channel's footprint, viewers and advertisers. A feedback loop between the distribution and monetisation phases of the value creation chain sees additional platform distribution outlets (cable and satellite, or overseas territories) create additional financial returns, that in turn can cycle back to fund more programme investment and expansion.

Measuring success

Broadcast TV had one huge legacy advantage over digital distribution: advertisers believed the eyeballs.

Streamers have been opaque with their numbers (though that may need to change as *Netflix* and *Disney+* add advertiser-funded options to their streaming offer). Digital advertising has been beset by scandals around inflation of view counts (known as 'ad fraud') and content moderation issues.

TV, meanwhile, has long been independently benchmarked, by third party firms such as Nielsen (US) or BARB (UK) providing independent measures of viewership. This credible transparency has given pricing power to broadcasters, since media buyers accept, for the most part, the information they are being offered.

However, that disparity is changing. Third party agencies are starting to measure streams as well as TV views. Nielsen itself entered the market in December 2020 to create the US ratings standard by 2024, in competition with Comscore and start-ups like TVision. "This is fundamentally the future of the business," said an analyst (Maurer, 2021). Credible benchmarking of viewing figures across both broadcast and streaming platforms will underpin the competitive offer of TV advertising as a whole against pure-play digital advertising options such as search.

AVOD: an online alternative to broadcast

Channels have mitigated the vulnerability of their distribution to global shifts toward streaming, by adding their own free, ad supported streaming TV services. These are known by the acronyms FAST (free ad-supported streaming TV) or AVOD (advertising video-on-demand).

Examples of such channels are specialist offers *Roku*, *Xumo*, *Tubi*, *Vudu*, Amazon's *IMDb TV*, *Pluto TV* (see analysis below), plus the AVOD version of any given broadcast channel in most countries.

- Global AVOD revenues were forecast to rise by 144% from 2020 and 2026, to $66 billion (Whittingham, 2021) with the US market alone reaching $31.4 billion, and China $10.6 billion.
- ITV, in 2021, pursued twin-track distribution strategies, indicative of the 2020s channels industry – with a set of broadcast and niche TV channels as the legacy distribution option, plus the AVOD platform, *ITV Hub*, and 2022 announcement of a new, younger-skewed streaming service *ITVX*.
- Adding advertising-funded on-demand hedges bets for broadcast TV businesses in a contemporary advertising economy: a mass-market branded advertising core business, plus the option value of a hyper-segmented online layer.

- To enhance the digital, targeted offer, channels have added 'adtech' solutions. ITV's product is sold by its own start-up business, Planet V, marketed to advertisers as a new approach reminiscent of the advertising buying process of Meta or Google. "Now, you're in total control over the way you buy, track, and optimise your TV video campaigns – always in a brand safe, premium, automated environment" (PlanetV, 2022). These words might equally have been found in *Facebook* or *YouTube*'s ad-buying tools.
- ITV is part of a global AVOD trend. UK rival Channel 4 aimed in 2021 to double programme views on its AVOD channel, *All4*, from 1 billion in 2019 to 2 billion by 2025, as "Britain's biggest free streaming service," also doubling the percentage of revenue in online advertising from 15% to 30% in the process.
- Paramount Global described three ways they can generate business as a 'super funnel' (Lafayette, 2021) of broadcast/cable channels, AVOD and social media businesses
- *Discovery+* (now part of conglomerate Warner Bros. Discovery) evolved its offer from US-centric cable TV to global streaming platforms. Its CEO said: "The North Star that has been the focus for over three decades has been following the consumer … This incredible content that we're producing and stories are universal, and we can tell, not just to great American audiences but we can tell them to audiences around the world" (Littleton, 2021).

Programmatic advertising

Not only is the style of advertising being shown changing to digital, but so also is how it is sold. Programmatic advertising is an arcane, acronym-rich, near-universal system whereby incoming page views are digitally auctioned to potential advertisers in a fraction of a second, on the basis of the known and perceived profile and value of the individual customer. That approach has reached TV.

A leading cable TV executive said:

> You've probably heard of SSPs [supply side platforms] and DSPs [demand side platforms] and all the sort of matching of audiences and inventory through programmatic automatically. That's also beginning to become more homogenized, so it's easier again for the campaign managers to place their ads very quickly. We think the next big [programmatic] push is going to be in VOD.

VOD is video-on-demand.

- Programmatic is gaining pace on TV as channels migrate to more data-intensive online distribution. In 2021, the UK's Channel 4 launched the *All 4 Private Marketplace*, to sell advertising around its 14,500 hours of content (Channel 4, 2021).
- Even hardware is getting in on the act: "TV makers are suddenly going all show business" (Hough, 2021). They sell display ads through the TV operating system, keeping track of how many times a viewer has seen an ad on one service, so that

that ad doesn't keep running on another. In 2021, set maker *Vizio* secured $100 million in advertising commitments for this product – a "tsunami of ad dollars" as one stock market analyst described it (Hough, 2021).

Data

Advertisers can now export their own, valuable, anonymised customer data to channels, reaching 'lookalike' audiences of similar viewers programmatically through their digital platforms. This ad-tech approach is standard to buyers of *Facebook* advertising, but new ground in TV.

- ITV said, in 2021: "We are piloting data match campaigns through InfoSum, which allows advertisers to use their own first party data in campaigns" (ITV, 2021).

Pace of change

As distribution evolves for TV channels, broadcasters are flexing into "multi-product, multi-platform media companies" (Oliver, 2014).

- Brazil's major broadcaster has evolved to become a 'media tech' company by doing a deal with Google Cloud in 2021, using Google's data management, AI and machine learning to "accelerate the main pillars of our transformation, such as focus on the public, data management, partnership for innovation and new business models," said CEO Jorge Nóbrega (Fuente, 2021).
- Flexing the model tracks the urgency of the commercial challenge in any given country. In Germany, public service broadcasters are powerful (*ARD* and *ZDF* have 25% market share) so the commercial sector needs competitive energy, explaining the pace of change at commercial channel owners RTL and ProSiebenSat1 (Förster, 2011). But in Russia, even before the 2022 Ukraine war sanctions, state control resulted in "deceleration of the technological development," and hampered tech progress in TV (Vartanova et al., 2021).
- Digital migration can be overstated. In the mixed ecology of global distribution, when territories evolve at different paces. In March 2022, Disney, despite investing substantially in its global *Disney+* streaming platform, and despite having undertaken to shut down over 100 linear networks by the end of 2021, actually renewed TV channel carriage deals in Spain (Easton, 2022). As potential recession loomed in 2022, a diversified revenue strategy appeared credible, compared to reliance on streaming subscriptions that can be easily cancelled.

Monetisation

At the monetisation stage of media value creation the key inputs are advertisers and viewers. Key outputs are ad revenues, cash, growth in assets (which may include IP ownership and brand equity) and equity value.

There are six key ways to make money out of channel ownership:

TV ADVERTISING

This remains the dominant revenue source. ITV's 2021 results presentation shows over 70% of its advertising revenue still came from TV. Channels which charge premium prices for their advertising slots need premium content to generate the eyeballs to justify them. That is why, in 2014, US network *Fox* signed an eight-year, $4.2 billion for the broadcast rights to *Major League Baseball*, more than double what it had previously paid, then re-signed again just four years later, for another ten years.

AVOD

Revenues from advertising slots sold on the streaming of broadcast channel content are growing their share of total TV revenues. At ITV, digital ads were up 55% in 2021, targeted to double again by 2026.

When NBC Universal launched its *Peacock* advertising-funded video-on-demand service, Jeff Shell, CEO of NBC Universal, said: "We have very strong demand on Peacock; we could sell any spot we had." NBCU launched *Peacock* with 10 initial advertisers – like *Capital One*, *L'Oreal* and *Subaru* (Friedman, 2020). Time will tell whether that level of AVOD advertising sales is sustainable – analysts did not consider *Peacock* as a top-tier streamer – or whether the new advertising inventory opened up will be partially unsold.

Some broadcasters (including Britain's *ITV* and *Channel 4*) use excess ad inventory to barter for equity in start-ups that can't afford the cash price of advertising slots, thereby building a venture capital style equity portfolio. In 2022, *ITV* also used advertising inventory for the purpose of driving diversity within business as well, giving space for free to some of the 40 start-ups within Google's *Black Founders Fund*.

Where specific pieces of content can drive monetisable niche audiences, channels can deploy them. Niche channel *WWE* pivoted radically in 2021, not just to a third party channel to find new audiences and monetise them – but to an exclusive streaming deal with NBCUniversal's *Peacock* streaming service (Broughton, 2021) expanding reach among younger consumers, and giving up on US TV altogether. *WWE Network* had 1.5 million paid subscribers at December 2020.

CARRIAGE FEES

Also on a subscription model, cable television aggregates services into a single, wired box in the home. Major global players include Comcast and Liberty Global. Satellite TV offers similar channel packages and consumption models, but by a different delivery means – the relay of programmes via dishes on the side of user's houses. Satellite has over 100 million users in Asia, with players like *Measat*, *Intelsat*, *Singtel* and *Thaicom*.

Premium channels (such as, in news, *CNN* or *Fox News*) then attract fees from these cable and satellite broadcasters (Insider, 2022). Such fees can cause tension between cable operators and channels, because as the fees are rising, cable subscribers are falling. That process is known as 'cord-cutting,' where customers switch to broadband only, prioritising streaming services like *Netflix*. Generation Z cohorts, who may never subscribe to cable, are known as 'cord nevers.'

- Nonetheless, where carriage fees work, in the US, monthly affiliate revenue per average subscriber can be substantial. Disney-owned sports channel *ESPN* earned $7.64 per subscriber from such fees in 2020. Many of the subscribers are thought to not even watch *ESPN*, because they buy it as part of a wider bundle.
- Even broadcast networks, which are otherwise available to watch for free, can extract revenue for cable carriage: like CBS ($1.59) and Fox $1.39 (Bridge, 2020).
- The economics are not always matched by usage statistics. Research agency Wizer found only 12.1% of people who were paying for *Fox Sports 1* channel via their cable subscription were actually even watching it. If only actual ESPN viewers paid for it, the cost would need to be $34.13. This not a sustainable cognitive dissonance in the market, so as cable subscriptions drop, carriage fees are likely also to drop, damaging broadcaster revenues, and potentially putting high prestige but low-viewership, high cost operations such as news channels in medium term funding jeopardy.

PROGRAMME SALES

As discussed above, ITV not only buys and commissions programmes, but also makes and sells them.

Of its total 2021 revenue of £3.45 billion, 50% came from *ITV Studios*, its production arm. Revenue is often generated through sophisticated 'windowing' of different rights to the distribution of titles. In 2017, its World Productions subsidiary made the political thriller *Bodyguard* for *BBC One*, and in 2018, prior to the show going on air, *ITV*'s in-house distributor Global Entertainment sold the streaming rights package to the programme to *Netflix*. The show was a hit, and by 2021 the *Netflix* window had closed, rights reverted to *ITV*, and it sold them again – to linear broadcasters in 55 countries. (A more detailed discussion of format rights exploitation is found in Chapter 11.)

PUBLIC FUNDING

Public funding for TV comes from various forms of licence fee or direct state funding. It is challenged worldwide, as younger viewers choose streaming services, and politicians question the logic of what is arguably a universal tax for non-universal consumption. For the UK's BBC, some politicians challenge the licence fee model on the grounds that diverse competition online provides diverse viewing quality without the need for state intervention to mandate licence fee payment by every home owning a television set. "Earlier this year the BBC issued a report claiming its services would cost £450 in the open market ... Even by framing the argument in these terms, the BBC risks inviting a toe-to-toe comparison with *Amazon* and others" (Cumming, 2021). Many take the opposite view – of the BBC as a national treasure. A similar argument is played out in some other countries.

E-COMMERCE

TV can be used to sell direct – via click-through advertising on AVOD. ITV emphasises its merchandising revenues from its own shows. *Amazon Prime Video* allows content on its site to feature commercials, but does not sell advertisements on its own service yet (Palomba, 2020). That might change. "You have to understand that Amazon's video app is not a free content player or even a premium video service along the lines of *Netflix*. It is a store. Amazon always wants to sell you stuff" (Downey, 2020). Technology companies such as London-based Wirewax offer clickable video solutions whereby programming can be directly shoppable.

Class discussion questions

- Why are broadcast TV channels starting, and prioritising, AVOD services?
- Why are sports rights important to broadcast TV channels? If you ran a TV channel, what factors would you consider in valuing a given set of sports rights?
- Access online and read the most recent results statement of ITV PLC in the UK. Taking the role of an analyst, give your detailed views on how well they are (a) growing broadcast TV advertising revenue (b) growing AVOD revenue and (c) growing international formats/tape sales. Are these categories of revenue at ITV optimally balanced?

Analysis: global niche broadcasting at TRACE TV

Background

Global Afro Urban Media Group *TRACE* is bringing a niche product to an international audience (BusinessWire, 2018). The third most distributed French channel in the world (Schmitt, 2013), it has 60 million PayTV subscribers and 200 million users in 162 countries, through specialising in Afro-Urban entertainment. The business for TRACE opportunity is substantial: there are 840 million people in Africa yet to connect to the internet (Kemp, 2022). But how can it maximise its opportunity?

Founded in 1998 as *MCM Africa* by French conglomerate Lagardere, the original business was sold in 2002 to France/Martinique entrepreneur Olivier Laouchez, who had previously run a successful French hip hop label (Strategies, 2003). He relaunched the channel as *TRACE TV*, modelled on US channel *BET* (which stands for *Black Entertainment*

Television) aiming to build the biggest French urban television network (Amawhe, 2018). France has a large African diaspora, of a little over 6 million people.

- *TRACE* won a 2006 award for best global music television channel (Key4biz, 2006), launching in the US in 2009 (Otterson, 2017) with US shareholders and advisors including musician Wyclef Jean. (Lieberman, 2017). Expansion was rapid.
- In 2013–14, *TRACE* added personalised content recommendation on its website, and launched the *TRACE Urban Music Awards* plus the *TRACE Music Star* event, seeking Africa's next urban talent. The first winner was mentored by Senegalese/American singer Akon, the second by RnB star Keri Hilson (CapitalFMKenya, 2016).
- In 2017, a distribution division, TCD, launched, with African entertainment like *Wives on Strike*, *Before 30*, and *The Gang of the French Caribbean*, music shows *Guest Stars* and *The Year Of*, and documentaries like *Afrobeats – From Nigeria to the World*.
- In 2018, digital player TRACE Play allowed global users all its live channels and on-demand content. (Amawhe, 2018). Now TRACE had UK-based music channels (Lora-Mungai, 2018) plus Afro-Urban and Latin content on *Sky TV* (DTVE, 2019). TRACE encourages new artists by paying then for video plays rather than (as is common practice in African media) charging them (AgBana, 2018).
- *TRACE TV* now runs 24 pay TV channels, 70 radio stations and mobile platforms (TBB, 2019), the world-leading Afro Urban media brand – especially strong in Sub-Saharan Africa, Europe, the Caribbean and Indian Ocean. Other ventures include music festival *TRACE Made in Africa*, and creator training app *TRACE Academia*.
- Content creation arm TRACE Studios makes shows in South Africa for TRACE and other broadcasters (Trace Studios, 2022). In 2022, they signed a global distribution deal for their formats, like South African reality show *2 Weddings & A Superstar* and *The Ultimate Braai Master*. CEO Sivan Pillay said the goal was to "create more opportunities for African based IP" (Franks, 2022).

Questions for class discussion

- What lessons can you draw from *TRACE*'s expansion for other broadcasters?
- TRACE's philosophy is to be "glocal." How achievable is 'glocalisation' in the media business?
- If you ran TRACE, what would be your strategic priorities this year?

Technology analysis: AI and machine learning at the BBC

The British Broadcasting Corporation, founded as a radio provider in the 1920s, was by the beginning of the twenty-first century a leader in video streaming, launching the *iPlayer* in 2007.

With a long history as a technical innovator in broadcasting, the BBC also pioneered series stacking (2008), high definition streaming (2009), downloads (2013) and other innovations. Individually tailored recommendation engines has been a technical priority, achieved through a dashboard offering people different ways of cutting their data, called *My PDS* (Sharp, 2021).

The BBC has continued to innovate in AI and Machine Learning, used in five keys ways at the corporation as part of an overall strategy to "harness the power of responsible AI/ML to modernise the BBC and delight our audiences."

Personalisation

- The BBC aims to mimic within its recommendation engines the organisation's wider editorial policies on ethics and bias – making them more privacy-friendly than alternative sources of streaming.
- Within *iPlayer*, there is a unique kind of recommendation system, focused on promotion of categories like education and information content that other streamers might not priorities. A public service, the BBC is optimising not for engagement (as might be found on *YouTube* or *Facebook*) but for breadth of experience. This is closest to a 'knowledge-based' recommendation algorithm approach, to follow the methodology outlined in the *Netflix* section in Chapter 7 (Hinkle, 2021).

Exploration and enrichment

- Because the BBC prioritises a broad range of viewing and viewers as much as the length of engagement of any given user, the BBC's policy for user content exploration is called 'five five two for.'
- The target is for the BBC to be consumed by each user for *five hours* a week, and on *five days* a week, on at least *two services* – like *BBC Sounds* or *iPlayer*, or *News* or *Radio*. The 'for' is 'for me,' as in content relevant to the user.

Provenance verification

- The BBC uses machine learning to tackle disinformation. Most BBC content is predominantly consumed on its owned and controlled services, so it control the information on its own sites. But where BBC content appears on social media and external websites, it can be misused or misrepresented, as part of wider global disinformation efforts by individuals, groups or governments.
- One of the solutions for the BBC (and other responsible media outlets) may be to use blockchain technologies in provenance verification.

Operational efficiencies

- Every piece of content that the BBC produces appears in different ways. For example, the edit of *Killing Eve* in the UK may have slight variation to what is published on *Netflix*. These versions were hitherto produced manually, through additional time spent in edit suites by producers. The BBC is moving towards creating versions in a more automated work flow.
- The BBC produces content, particularly news, in 42 different languages. Machine Learning can translate into eight languages so far, and is being scaled up for more languages and UK regional dialects. The BBC has machine learning models which can convert speech to text with 85% accuracy, at low cost.

Content Creation

- The BBC uses image recognition in the Bristol-based *Natural History* programmes unit, which pioneered computer vision applications for image classification at scale from multiple in-the-field camera rushes. Producers of its live-broadcast *Springwatch* and *Autumnwatch* shows now have faster access to video edits of the best moments in the field (see Chapter 12).
- Machine Learning is also used to clean up the audio component of video streams with lots of background noise.

Discussion questions

- Why – and how – are the technologies of Artificial Intelligence useful to the national broadcaster in your country?

CHAPTER SUMMARY

TABLE 8.1 Key themes in this chapter

Broadcaster	Development	Production	Distribution	Monetisation
Business model	Heavy investment required to define the transmission, regulatory permission, programming, target market and other brand of the channel.	Heavy investment required to obtain programming – whether self-produced commissioned, acquired or based on third party rights.	Conventionally by broadcast TV, and carried on cable/satellite/digital channels. But now also by advertising video-on-demand streaming sites.	Advertising sales on TV. More targeted and programmatic ad sales on AVOD. Plus e-commerce, merchandising, carriage, programme formats.

(continued)

TABLE 8.1 Cont.

Broadcaster	Development	Production	Distribution	Monetisation
Uses of AI	Low use – almost no visible innovation with AI at creative stage of broadcast channels.	Edit, studio and camera technologies.	Increasing use of AI-powered ad-tech tools in distribution, advertising, and other revenue maximising approaches.	Broadcasters slow to embrace personalisation and subscription in VOD platforms, but catching up. Integration of ad tech to monetise customer data.
Value Creation	Strong potential value creation if channel is successful, though heavy investment risks relatively low ROI.	Direct monetisation of programming success via advertising sales uplift. Extra value created from broadcast platform to develop formats and tapes and resell globally.	Widening of distribution footprint creates additional ad sales and data. Scaleability of successful content de-risks business to advertising cycle and globalises revenue.	Advertising sales creates profitable business traded at equity multiple, but subject to long-term sectoral changes. Other streams – e-commerce and programme sales – offer higher multiples.

BIBLIOGRAPHY

AgBana, R. (2018) We don't collect money to air music videos – Trace TV Boss. *Vanguard*. [online] Available at: www.vanguardngr.com/2018/01/dont-collect-money-air-music-videos-trace-tv-boss/ [Accessed 26 August 2022].

Amawhe, O. (2018) Trace Group represents a cultural bridge between different regions – Laouchez. *Vanguard*. [online] Available at: www.vanguardngr.com/2018/08/trace-group-represents-a-cultural-bridge-between-different-regions-laouchez/ [Accessed 26 August 2022].

Bridge, G. (2020, 27 October 2020) The true cost to consumers of pay TV's top channels. *Variety*. [online] Available at: https://variety.com/vip/pay-tv-true-cost-free-1234810682/ [Accessed 26 August 2022].

Broughton, K. (2021) How Covid-19 upended WWE; World Wrestling Entertainment's CFO outlines how the pandemic has altered the company's live-event business model. *Wall Street Journal*. [online] Available at: www.proquest.com/newspapers/how-covid-19-upended-wwe-world-wrestling/docview/2490764051/se-2?accountid=13042 [Accessed 26 August 2022].

BusinessWire. (2018) TPG growth to acquire TRACE, Africa's Leading music and entertainment company. *BusinessWire*. [online] Available at: www.businesswire.com/news/home/20180118006551/en/TPG-Growth-to-Acquire-TRACE-Africa%E2%80%99s-Leading-Music-and-Entertainment-Company [Accessed 26 August 2022].

CapitalFMKenya. (2016) Airtel Trace Music Star launches in Kenya, Keri Hilson to mentor winner. *Capital Lifestyle*. [online] Available at: www.capitalfm.co.ke/lifestyle/2016/04/08/airtel-trace-music-star-launches-keri-hilson-to-mentor-winner-kenya-africa/ [Accessed 26 August 2022].

Channel 4. (2021) Channel 4 launches real-time bidding on All 4 in UK broadcast industry first. *Channel 4*. [online] Available at: www.channel4.com/press/news/channel-4-launches-real-time-bidding-all-4-uk-broadcast-industry-first [Accessed 26 August 2022].

Cumming, E. (2021) Goodbye to the golden era of cheap TV. *Financial Times*, 30 April.

Downey, R. (2020) Why am I getting ads in Amazon Prime? *The Streaming Advisor*. [online] Available at: www.thestreamingadvisor.com/why-am-i-getting-ads-in-amazon-prime/ [Accessed 26 August 2022].

DTVE. (2019) Trace launches three new channels in the UK. *Digital TV*. [online] Available at: www.digitaltveurope.com/2019/10/18/trace-launches-three-new-channels-in-the-uk/ [Accessed 26 August 2022].

Easton, J. (2022) Disney is not giving up on linear … yet. *Digital TV Europe*. [online] Available at: www.digitaltveurope.com/comment/disney-is-not-giving-up-on-linear-yet/ [Accessed 26 August 2022].

Förster, K. (2011) Key Success factors of TV brand management: an international case study analysis. *Journal of Media Business Studies*, 8(4), 1–22. doi.org/10.1080/16522354.2011.11073528

Franks, N. (2022) South Africa's Trace Studios saddles up with Media Ranch to grow formats reach. *C21 Media*. [online] Available at: www.c21media.net/news/south-africas-trace-studios-saddles-up-with-media-ranch-to-grow-formats-reach/ [Accessed 26 August 2022].

Friedman, W. (2020) NBCU's Peacock at 8 Months hits 26 million subscribers, sees strong advertising. *MediaPost – Television News Daily*. [online] Available at: www.mediapost.com/publications/article/358502/nbcus-peacock-at-8-months-has-26-million-subscrib.html [Accessed 26 August 2022].

de la Fuente, A. M. (2021) Brazil's Globo pacts with Google Cloud in bid to become a mediatech company. *Variety*. [online] Available at: https://variety.com/2021/digital/global/globo-google-cloud-mediatech-company-1234945642/ [Accessed 26 August 2022].

Hinkle, D. (2021) How streaming services use algorithms. *Arts Management & Technology Laboratory*. [online] Available at: https://amt-lab.org/blog/2021/8/algorithms-in-streaming-services [Accessed 26 August 2022].

Hough, J. (2021) The dongle is dead. *Barron's streetwise with Jack Hough*. [podcast] 25 September. Available at: www.barrons.com/podcasts/streetwise/the-dongle-is-dead/a941bcd7-953e-4773-9aab-3152de1e4159?page=1 [Accessed 26 August 2022].

Iger, R. (2019) The ride of a lifetime: lessons in creative leadership from 15 years as CEO of the Walt Disney Company. London: Transworld Digital.

Insider, L. (2022) Carriage Fee. *Law Insider*. [online] Available at: www.lawinsider.com/dictionary/carriage-fee [Accessed 26 August 2022].

ITV. (2021) Half year results for the six months ended 30th June 2021. *ITV plc*. [online] Available at: www.itvplc.com/~/media/Files/I/ITV-PLC/documents/reports-and-results/ITV%20Plc%202021%20Half-Year%20Results%20Presentation.pdf [Accessed 25 August 2022].

Kemp, S. (2022) Digital 2022: global overview report. *Datareportal*. [online] Available at: https://datareportal.com/reports/digital-2022-global-overview-report [Accessed 26 August 2022].

Key4biz. (2006) Hot Bird TV Awards 2006: premio ai migliori canali tematici via satellite. *Key4biz*. [online] Available at: www.key4biz.it/News-2006-09-29-Contenuti-Hot-Bird-Tv-Awards-2006-177587/55381/ [Accessed 26 August 2022].

Lafayette, J. (2021) Tom Ryan on ViacomCBS's streaming 'super funnel.' *Next|TV*. [online] Available at: www.nexttv.com/news/tom-ryan-on-viacomcbss-streaming-super-funnel [Accessed 26 August 2022].

Li, P. and Jourdan, A. (2017) Game on: Suning leads China's $2 billion soccer rights frenzy. *Reuters*. [online] Available at: www.reuters.com/article/us-china-sports-broadcast-idUSKB N1AA0OC [Accessed 26 August 2022].

Lieberman, D. (2017) Afro-urban media company Trace Plans US streaming music & video service. *Deadline*. [online] Available at: https://deadline.com/2017/06/afro-urban-media-company-trace-plans-us-streaming-music-video-service-1202109279/ [Accessed 26 August 2022].

Littleton, C. (2021) Think global, act local: discovery international chief on how to win in global streaming. *Variety: Strictly Business*. [podcast] 18 August. Available at: https://variety.com/2021/tv/news/discovery-international-jb-perrette-streaming-1235043503/ [Accessed 25 August 2022].

Lora-Mungai, M. (2018) TRACE acquires four UK music channels from Sony Pictures Television. *TRACE*. [press release] 13 December. Available at: https://trace.company/wp-content/uploads/2019/01/PR-TRACE-Acquires-Four-UK-Music-Channels-from-Sony-Pictu res-Television.pdf [Accessed 26 August 2022].

Maurer, M. (2021) Nielsen Invests in new tv ratings platform after selling $2.4 billion unit. *Wall Street Journal*.[online] Available at: www.wsj.com/articles/nielsen-invests-in-new-tv-ratings-platform-after-selling-2-4-billion-unit-11621857600 [Accessed 26 August 2022].

OFCOM. (2021a) *Adults' media use and attitudes report 2020/21*. [online] Available at: www.ofcom.org.uk/__data/assets/pdf_file/0025/217834/adults-media-use-and-attitudes-report-2020-21.pdf [Accessed 26 August 2022].

OFCOM. (2021b) Media nations report. *OFCOM*. [online] Available at: www.ofcom.org.uk/__data/assets/pdf_file/0023/222890/media-nations-report-2021.pdf [Accessed 26 August 2022].

Oliver, J. (2014) Dynamic capabilities and superior firm performance in the UK media industry. *Journal of Media Business Studies*, 11(2), 57–78. doi.org/10.1080/16522354.2014.11073580

Otterson, J. (2017) Urban media company TRACE enters US market with new streaming service. *Variety*. [online] Available at: https://variety.com/2017/tv/news/trace-usa-trace-play-streaming-service-1202457747/ [Accessed 26 August 2022].

Palomba, A. (2020) Do SVOD product attribute trade-offs predict SVOD subscriptions and SVOD account access? Using utility constant sums to predict SVOD subscriptions and SVOD account access. *International Journal on Media Management*, 22(3–4), 168–90. doi. org/10.1080/14241277.2021.1920023

PlanetV. (2022) Your advertising in your hands. [online] Available at: www.planet-v.co.uk [Accessed 26 August 2022].

PWC. (2021) *Global entertainment and media outlook 2021–2025*. [online] Available at: www.pwc.com/gx/en/industries/tmt/media/outlook.html [Accessed 25 August 2022].

Schmitt, F. (2013) Trace TV, le petit français qui mise sur l'international. *LesEchos*. [online] Available at: www.lesechos.fr/2013/02/trace-tv-le-petit-francais-qui-mise-sur-linternatio nal-317331 [Accessed 26 August 2022].

Sharp, E. (2021) Personal data stores: building and trialling trusted data services. *BBC Research & Development*. [blog] 14 October. Available at: www.bbc.co.uk/rd/blog/2021-09-perso nal-data-store-research [Accessed 26 August 2022].

Strategies. (2003) MCM Africa vendue à Alliance Trade Media. *Stratégies*. [online] Available at: www.strategies.fr/actualites/medias/r74141W/mcm-africa-vendue-a-alliance-trade-media.html [Accessed 26 August 2022].

TBB. (2019) Leading brand and media group, TRACE, is launching three new Sky TV Channels in the UK. *TheBritishBlacklist*. [online] Available at: https://thebritishblacklist. co.uk/leading-brand-and-media-group-trace-is-launching-three-new-sky-tv-channels-in-the-uk/ [Accessed 26 August 2022].

Trace Studios. (2022) @*CampaignCards*. [online] Available at: https://trace.wishpondpages. com/trace-studios/reference [Accessed 26 August 2022].

Vartanova, E., Vyrkovsky, A. and Vyugina, D. (2021) Online strategies of the largest broadcasters in the times of uncertainty. the case of Russia. *International Journal on Media Management*, 1–25. doi.org/10.1080/14241277.2021.2002868

Whittingham, C. (2021) C21's 2021 news review: the biggest stories in factual TV this year. *C21 Media*. [online] Available at: www.c21media.net/news/c21s-2021-news-review-the-biggest-stories-in-factual-tv-this-year/ [Accessed 26 August 2022].

Wu, T. (2017) *The attention merchants: the epic struggle to get inside our heads*. London: Atlantic Books.

CHAPTER 9

Digital publishers

News sites and social channels now share revenue models and AI technologies

....

INTRODUCTION TO THE SECTOR

"A newspaper should have no friends," said nineteenth-century US newspaper owner Joseph Pulitzer. Commercially, that almost came true in the early twenty-first century, as the business models of news were all but decimated by the internet.

- In the USA, 78% of the adult population read a daily paper in 1970. That number dropped to 51.6% by 2005, 33.7% by 2014, and just 28% in 2016, raising "worldwide alarms about the future viability of newspapers" (Noam, 2019). In 2022, Amazon's ad revenue matched that of the global newspaper industry.
- In print specifically, the UK *Daily Mirror*'s circulation dropped from 2.27 million in 2000 to 0.33 million in 2022 (Tobitt, 2022). Few businesses in any industry can sustain an 86% collapse in consumption.
- Digital competition damaged advertising revenue – down 62% in the US from $37.8 billion in 2008 to $14.3 billion in 2018 (Grieco, 2020). The short classified advertisement at the back of newspapers, which had been the plankton at the bottom of the journalism-funding food chain since the nineteenth century, was wiped out by *Google* search. PWC's Media Outlook report 2020–24 forecast a decline in total global newspaper advertising from $49 billion in 2019 to $36 billion in 2024, with subscriber revenue also falling from $58.7 billion to $50.4 billion (Mayhew, 2020).

Migration of legacy titles to digital models became a rout in the twenty-first century. Owners that failed to move simply expired – like the McClatchy Group which went

DOI: 10.4324/9781003213611-11

bankrupt in July 2020, owner of US titles *Kansas City Star*, *Miami Herald*, *Charlotte Observer* and *Fort Worth Star-Telegram* (Grieco, 2020).

But after a forest fire, the ecology restarts with new vigour. Digital publishing today has strong winners and new titles. New creative tools (many AI-driven) are powering production, distribution and monetisation. Publications – *The New York Times* or *Financial Times* – which made a successful digital switchover, thrived and grew. Innovation was "driven by new entrants and start-ups emerging in the news media ecosystem" (Kosterich and Weber, 2018). Successive generations of agile, new digital publishers have entered the market, from *Huffington Post* to *LADbible* to *Puck News*.

This re-segmentation of media disrupts historic constructs of publishing, newsprint and magazines. Since *Mail Online*, *Buzzfeed* or *Bloomberg* all populate the consumer's same browser window, they all occupy a single vertical: digital publishing. Even storied magazine publisher Condé Nast (*Vogue*, *Vanity Fair*) pivoted in 2022 to a subscription model, "digital and global," combining titles, experience and events, under CEO Roger Lynch (Arlidge, 2022).

After all this change, the specifically digital publishing market now has $65.31 billion revenue, annual growth forecast at 13%, and steeper 41% growth in the emerging Asia-Pacific. Companies in this market re-modelling include what would look like an exotic mix in a twentieth-century construct. It is a sector publishing components of software companies *Adobe* and *Apple*, financial information companies *Bloomberg*, *Dow Jones* and *RELX*, magazine group *Conde Nast*, newspapers like *Guardian*, *New York Times*, *The Washington Post* and newswire *Thomson Reuters Corporation* (Technavio, 2021).

With a reshaped industry, new entrants and new revenue sources, we can set out the 2020s business model of digital publishing.

THE VALUE CREATION MODEL

The value creation process of (business) development, production, distribution and monetisation is applied.

Revenue derives from subscription, branded content and programmatic advertising. AI informs commercial activity, journalism and creativity. Publications which have upgraded with social marketing, dynamic content optimisation, predictive analytics, e-commerce and programmatic advertising have advanced. All these tools are analysed below.

Business development

At the business development stage of a digital publishing business, the requirements are a market analysis, crystal clear positioning (vital in a complex market), a technical plan (including AI tools) and high-quality editorial product.

The twentieth-century model of news publishing was that publishers produced the content, and passive consumers read it, apart from occasional "letters to the editor"

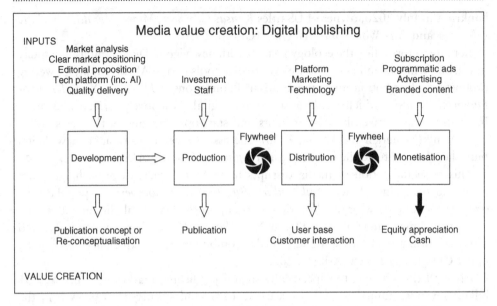

FIGURE 9.1 If marketing costs are controlled digital publishers have low marginal distribution costs, and therefore high marginal returns, as they access additional customers

(Hess, 2014). That model has evolved. Through social media, consumers now co-create and distribute content in alliance with digitally published titles. They are as likely to interact with a title through its podcast as by buying it at the supermarket. Newer titles (such as *Puck News*) introduce innovations such as elite subscriber clubs and paid-for one-to-one Zoom calls with key journalists. This evolution has consequences for the business model both of legacy titles going digital, and natively digital market entrants.

Legacy titles

With competition for advertising and eyeballs from social platforms like *YouTube* and *Facebook*, traditional publications retooled their models to survive (Gundlach and Hofmann, 2021).

As a study of news publishers in the UK, Switzerland and Finland found (Lischka, 2019), there are two steps in their digital journey; first, digitise the news product, second, diversify into other digital spaces. When publications diversified, the study found, they made money doing so.

• Major newspapers performed better after the transition to digital as a whole. In the UK. *The Times* pivoted from loss to profit as it went digital (Edge, 2019). But for smaller titles, the picture was tougher. Regional newspaper groups didn't pick up global online user bases like the scaleable, globally appealing titles did. Papers were "struggling with constraints, such as lack of financial and human resources and general organisational anaemia" (Villi et al., 2020). Migrating a legacy business to digital requires the kind of investment to which smaller, older groups may not have access. A 2018 study of venture capital funding examined relationships between "legacy news media firms and new entrants, vying for scarce investment resources amid rapid change." Older firms struggled to grow in digital news' ecosystem (Kosterich and Weber, 2018).

Migration to new models is not just happening in the West.

- In Japan, print sales of newspapers declined by 7% in 2020 alone.
- But innovation offers solutions. The digital *SlowNews* site publishes long form investigations and local journalism, for around $15 per month. Leading newspaper, *Asahi Shinbun*, has 320,000 paid digital subscribers and has innovated with newsletters (Sawa, 2021).

China is innovating too.

- Journalism professor Fang Kecheng at the Chinese University of Hong Kong said: "The common perception in the West is that we have this kind of very mono-lithic media system in China, where they're just very few party-owned outlets … But if you look at it from the inside, we see that there is quite a bit of diversity" (Kecheng, 2021).
- A study of Chinese media 2014–17 found whilst politics constrained major media firms' growth, niche companies could "pioneer the process of media convergence and innovation" (Li et al., 2020).

New titles – ad-funded

If legacy titles have struggled, digital start-ups have had huge investment – possibly too much. Venture capital in the news business has created potentially unreasonable growth expectations, focussing on 'platform businesses' with network effect and 'hockey stick growth.' Early, growth-oriented journalism companies, like *BuzzFeed*, saw themselves as tech and "created outsized or unrealistic expectations for the industry" (Shields, 2021) which would later be under-achieved.

Jonah Peretti founded *Huffington Post* and then, in 2006, *BuzzFeed*. The company grew 50% compound annually, and hired political blogger Ben Smith to build an investigative journalism function, attracting venture investment, and $400 million from *NBC Universal* in 2015–16. (Disney and Time Warner also made digital publishing investments) (Mullin, 2021). This inflated expectations. When *BuzzFeed* later listed in New York, in 2021 (see below), it claimed growth across digital sources – e-commerce, video and advertising – plus brand-safe digital content at scale. "Data-driven business model enables massive audience reach and establishes *BuzzFeed* as a premier destination for advertisers" (Buzzfeed, 2021). But the reality was not a big return on NBC's investment. The financial ambition had outstripped consumer and advertiser demand for the product.

BuzzFeed was not alone. Ready capital meant other publishers were too ambitious. Many chased the goal of large user counts large in *Facebook* clicks, with short-form video, but found it hard to then monetise them usefully (Shields, 2021). A whole industry was built on testing the *Facebook* algorithms for accelerating traffic. *Upworthy*, *ViraNova* and *Distractify* built millions of followers and clicks, but only modest brand equity. Many used analytics service *Crowdtangle* to see trending topics on *Facebook* and other viral channels, which had the surprise effect of the publications all seeing the same data, and covering the same topics. This lead to diminishing returns. (*Facebook* bought *CrowdTangle* in 2016) (Shields, 2021).

Digital businesses that succeeded often used more conventional value creation.

- A study of German-language media professionals found four routes to success in twenty-first-century digital publishing: distribution, market orientation, design and HR (Verhoeven et al., 2018).
- When the profitable *LADbible* group successfully listed itself on London's Alternative Investment market in 2021, it described how it made money. It published to a specific and clear 18–34 demographic, with 262 million global followers and 28 billion content views in 2020.
- "The creative content, such as videos uploaded by LBG Media to the social platforms, provides the necessary advertising space and digital impressions (i.e., views) to promote the brand owner's adverts" (LBGMediaPLC, 2021).

Production

At the production stage of value creation, key ingredients are investment and staff – the right creative people for a business which for all its mechanised content production, depends on editorial flair for value generation.

- A Finnish study found that journalism, ostensibly a fact-based trade, actually needed to be creative to succeed. "Idea generation mostly takes place outside of formal meetings. Many meetings are limited to discussing what other news media have already covered" (Nylund, 2013).

The metric that matters in digital publishing is not clicks, but engagement, which drives the propensity of a user to subscribe (and pay). "The critical element in that is actually entertainment" (Riskos et al., 2021).

- The team matters. A study of digital media start-ups in Spanish markets found sites with women in the team had more diversified sources of income and offered "more deliberate and reflective information" (Caro-González et al., 2021).
- Curation matters, and volume of output may be less important than quality. Apple CEO Tim Cook said, without curation: "you wind up with this firehose of things that I would not want to put into an amplifier" (T. Cook, 2021).

Distribution

At the distribution phase of value creation, key drivers are the platform, marketing (including social media) and technology (see below.) In digital publishing a 'flywheel' effect between production and distribution sees better marketing and technology drive smarter editorial decisions, better user-targeting, more successful and clickable content, and in turn creates better distribution metrics.

Digital publishers need to be smart not just about what is on their site, but also about what they do beyond it; off-platform social media distribution. Marketing of media is as much about the network effect as direct customer interactions.

- A study of the traffic of top 50 news organisations and their 230,000 *Tumblr* posts showed that pictures in posts drove engagement exponentially. Having a link to news websites in posts did not increase engagement (Kim and Desai, 2021).
- A study of how China's *WeChat* platform interacted with 35 other media services in "showed that media outlets could mobilise audiences and exhibit identity through news flow networks" (Sun, 2020) – meaning social network interactions.

Digital publishers tend to do better by managing their social distribution themselves rather than handing it over to (say) *Facebook*, not least because of the imperfect user data they would get back.

- A study of four media companies found that going through *Facebook* trapped publishers in the "attention economy." Meanwhile, leaving *Facebook* would cost news companies traffic, but not actual money. In the companies studied, revenue from social media traffic made less than 0.2% of their total (Myllylahti, 2018).

Digital publishing has the significant advantage over print publishing that it liberates titles to go global, unconstrained by the logistics of print delivery. This partly explains strong subscriber growth at the *Financial Times* and *New York Times*, since they went digital. When France's *Le Monde* opened its English-language digital edition (April 2022) it created a similar opportunity.

Monetisation

The final stage of the value creation process in digital publishing requires a clear means of revenue generation; these principally are subscription, programmatic advertising, display advertising or branded content – all of which also depend on the value of first-party, customer usage data. A flywheel between the distribution and monetisation phases turns higher revenue generation back into further distribution, via better user data allowing more precision targeting, and the financial resource for digital marketing and social promotion.

- The digital publishing market is a quintessential, innovation 'skunkworks' (a term originating in the 1940s US aviation industry, for an off-site experimental facility to reinvent solutions from scratch) for new monetisation models.
- Not everything works. Models based on free content funded by advertising alone floundered in the digital environment, often not even covering costs. Different models for paid content were created to refinance content production and distribution (Goyanes and Dürrenberg, 2014) not all of which worked. But by the time *Buzzfeed* listed on the stock exchange in 2021, the models had clarified somewhat: its revenues were 50% advertising, 32% branded content and 18% commerce (Spangler, 2021).

The evolution of revenue models towards effective funding mechanisms has been positive and has settled down to seven broad alternatives.

Subscription model (blogs)

In 2021 (prior to the 2022 attempt on his life at a book reading), author Salman Rushdie chose to release his next novel the same way Charles Dickens had launched *The Pickwick Papers* almost 200 years earlier – in instalments, and for cash.

Rushdie's platform was *Substack*, a blog site that offers paid subscriptions. It allows writers to monetise their work directly, by disintermediating the newspaper and publishing groups which have consolidated power globally, often to claims of lack of democratic access. (Two thirds of the UK newspaper market is controlled by two groups, DMGT and News UK.) *Substack* is a digital newsletter platform, with writers from civil liberties advocate Glenn Greenwald to campaigning journalist Bari Weiss, forming part of a wider, evolving picture of subscription-driven business models in digital publishing.

- Writers create an email newsletter. The minimum monthly subscription is $5, so an author with 1,000 regular readers can earn some $60,000 annually (Larman, 2022) with minimal production, and zero additional distribution cost. (They may choose to develop their audience with some paid social marketing.)
- The top ten writers on *Substack* are making a combined $20 million a year – more than they would earn in salary at newspapers (Nicolau, 2021).
- *Substack* also entered the local news business with a $1 million investment, recoupable against revenue shares. Co-founder Chris Best said: "We want to make *Substack* a vehicle that can get every other barrier out of your way ... We're going to take 10%" (Best, 2021).

Substack is not alone in the test kitchen of digital publishing models.

- *The Mill* in Manchester, UK was founded June 2020 by journalist Joshi Hermann. In 2021, it had 14,000 readers paying £7 a month for quality writing about local issues – delivered by email. "We believe in the power of proper reporting and good writing rather than chasing clicks." It had three staff journalists plus free-lance contributors (Herrmann, 2021).

• Niche publications *The Information* (providing tech news, for $400 a year) and *Puck News*, costing $100 a year for "the details and plot that only the true insiders know" about Hollywood, Silicon Valley, Washington and Wall Street, are gaining profile in the US, albeit at small absolute levels as yet (Nicolau, 2021). Jessica Lessin, ex-Wall Street Journal, launched self-funded *The Information* with a staff of about 40. On customer growth she said: "My advice is … get the email, get the email, get the email … And you just see a sort of hockey stick when, even if they're not yet a subscriber you're capturing … the permission to keep communicating with them" (Lessin, 2020).

• There are many others. *Air Mail* was started by ex-*Vanity Fair* editor Graydon Carter. *Capital B* is a news site for minority communities founded by former Vox editor in chief Lauren Williams. Washington News sites *Punchbowl News* (with 100,000 subscribers paying $300 a year) and *Axios* (see below) are growing (Robertson, 2022).

Subscription model (newspaper paywalls)

After a turn-of-the-century period of business turmoil not dissimilar to the music industry's travails at the hands of file sharing networks (see Chapter 15) the newspaper industry finally arrived at a viable model for online subscription when in 2010, the *New York Times* landed on the "metered" paywall. This maximised both advertising and subscription revenue online by allowing readers limited free articles per month, but driving frequent readers to subscribe (Goyanes and Dürrenberg, 2014). Such hybrid solutions have proved optimal for newspapers.

• By 2018, the *New York Times* had over 2.6 million digital subscribers, and reader revenue above US$1 billion a year, accounting for 60% of its sales (Edge, 2019). In November 2021, that number had risen to 8.4 million subscriptions, of which 7.6 million were digital (Tracy, 2021).

• Paywalls are rationalised in the consumer's eyes by product quality: "exclusivity and quality journalism," found a 2018 Norwegian academic study. Subscription-driven content was perceived as "unique" at *Drammens Tidende*. "We can lock a lot of content and tempt readers in new ways, and they will think there is so much they're missing out on that they decide to sign up" (Olsen and Solvoll, 2018).

• Subscription has been embraced by newspapers worldwide. "Not only are newspapers profitable on an operating basis, most are more than just marginally so" (Edge, 2019).

• That transition to a subscription model can still be risky. When *The Times* of London became the first newspaper in the UK to put in a paywall, traffic dropped by 90%. Imagine the business impact on your local supermarket of only a tenth of its normal customers walking the aisles.

- Newspapers have weathered the downturn in their revenues by cutting their costs, too. Britain's *The Daily Telegraph* did so early, weathering the 2008–9 recession with annual profits of around 10% as a result, and then returned to even higher levels of profitability.

Advertising

Advertising has long driven publishing revenue. But how advertising is implemented has fundamentally changed with the internet: and again, many models are being tested in the wild.

- The UK's *Lad Bible Group* described its multichannel advertising-driven business model in its 2021 listing document: "*Facebook*, *Snapchat* and *YouTube* are currently the only social media platforms which facilitate the monetisation of its users through adverts. *Facebook* introduced this functionality in 2018 and, as a result, LBG Media saw an increase in social video revenue from £0.9 million in FY18 to £4.2 million in FY19" (LBGMediaPLC, 2021).
- US news site *The Grid*'s innovation is a start-up without a paywall. Co-founder Mark Bauman said it would monetise through advertising its 'unique' 360-degree story format (Robertson, 2022).

Yet web publishers are still struggling with advertising alone, despite digital ad spending surpassing traditional media spend.

- According to *eMarketer*, global digital advertising spend for 2021 was set to reach $455 billion, reaching $645 billion by 2024 (Cramer-Flood, 2021).
- But major brands prefer the scale and perceived accuracy of performance measurement on *Google* and *Facebook*, which obtain some 85% of digital media spend, and their scale-driven efficiency in selling programmatic advertising (Shields, 2021).

Branded content

Attempting to disguise advertising as journalism is old news, and sometimes even fake news.

- In 1915, Theodore MacManus advertised for General Motors in a *Saturday Evening Post* essay titled The Penalty of Leadership.
- But a 2019 study found "camouflaging advertising as journalistic content" doesn't work. Consumers actually prefer banner ads to adverts masquerading as stories (Harms et al., 2019).
- Branded content in journalistic contexts is sometimes called 'native advertising.' A study found reputable news organisations can risk reputational damage by using it (Bachmann et al., 2019).

- However, in China, the line between legitimate news and promotion is all but erased. "Promotional articles," produced by the commercial departments to promote e-commerce look like lifestyle journalism – but are really about bringing readers to the promotion (Meo, 2019).

E-commerce

Digital publications are aware of the opportunity in direct consumer sales. *BuzzFeed*'s 2021 listing presentation document discusses e-commerce. "*BuzzFeed*'s commerce revenue stream is enabled by its ability to deliver content to high-value audiences. This revenue stream drove $500M in attributable transactions in 2020, up 60% year-on-year" (Buzzfeed, 2021). UK magazine publisher Future PLC reported that in the first half of 2021 it saw e-commerce affiliate revenue, whereby it was driving business directly to e-commerce partners, of £85.2 million.

But digital publishers are only rarely succeeding with their own "direct to consumer" models. They are slow to match fleet-footed of consumer brands like optician Warby Parker (Shields, 2021), they're not shops, and they lack the supply chain to become them.

Public sector funding

In some countries, the public sector funds digital journalism: for instance, in the UK – via the licence fee – the tax system in effect funds substantial BBC news websites. In fact, 32% of people in Ireland, and 51% of people in India, think the government should fund news media (Fletcher, 2021).

Long-term equity value creation/company sale

As with games producers (see Chapter 5), one of the best ways of monetising media output can be to simply sell the company that produces it. In the right market, this can yield high returns.

- *Buzzfeed* went public in 2021 via Special Purpose Acquisition Vehicle, with a valuation dramatically at odds with its profits, buying the *Verizon* and *Hearst*-owned youth-targeted platform *Complex Networks* at the same time, for $300 million. *Buzzfeed* was a "Leading 'Media 2.0' platform for the next generation of Internet," which had "globally recognized digital brands with massive, engaged audience" (Buzzfeed, 2021), targeting $521 million in 2021 revenue including the *Complex* deal (Spangler, 2021). The valuation, $1.5 billion, was a huge multiple of *Buzzfeed*'s 2020 EBITDA (earnings before interest, depreciation and amortisation) of just $17 million, and Complex had made a loss of $14 million). It proved too high and by October 2022, *BuzzFeed*'s valuation had dropped to $238 million.
- The *New York Times* bought *The Athletic* for $550 million in 2022. The San Francisco-based sports news website was founded in 2016, with estimated 2021

revenue of $77 million, putting the valuation at 7 times revenue (Anna Nicolau, 2022). This was a high valuation, since normal metrics are applied on multiples of profit. The secret may have resided in the lift to *New York Times*' overall subscriber that *The Athletic* facilitated. It added 1.2 million digital subscribers (gross – there may of course have been some overlap) to the *Times*, helping the newspaper towards its 2025 goal of 10 million. With subscribers, the customer lifetime value, thanks to recurring revenue, is higher (see Chapter 3). They also bought product review website *Wirecutter* in 2016, for a reported $30 million, and, in 2020, podcast company *Serial* for a reported $25 million (Anna Nicolau, 2022).

- Germany-based media company *Axel Springer* bought US-based website *Politico* for about $1 billion in 2021, five times revenue. In a fundraising round, the news website *Axios* was valued at $430 million – again, five times its annual revenue. It was then sold to Cox Enterprises for $525 million in August 2022, earning substantial returns for its journalist founders and staff.

These high multiples paid are high. And there have been notable valuation mistakes in digital publishing.

- The entertainment and tech news site *Mashable* built audience in the mid 2000s, raising $32 million in 2015–16, reaching $250 million valuation. But its value dropped, and it sold in 2017 for under $50 million.
- In October 2019, *Vice* bought female-targeted news site *Refinery29* for some $400 million (around 4 times revenue), valuing the combined publishers at around $4 billion, in a deal described in the *New York Post* as "misogyny meets feminism." By May 2021 *Vice*'s market value had reportedly dropped 25%, to $3 billion.

AI technologies in digital publishing

Artificial intelligence technologies are changing digital publishing at all phases of value creation - in business development, production, distribution and monetisation.

A 2018 study measured use of AI tools by news media. Content recommendations were used by 59% of publishers, workflow automation by 39%, commercial optimization by 39% and AI to help reporters find stories 35%. It warned that when integrating AI, publishers needed to bear in mind the perils of human/AI interactions (e.g., proliferating the inherent bias in a dataset) and to keep focussing on customers (Chan-Olmsted, 2019).

Analytics and subscription

John Ridding, CEO of the *Financial Times* (*FT*) from 2008, described in an interview the pivot newspapers made to drive subscription and a globalised user base.

We score each of our readers in terms of their engagement with the *FT*. So we've really driven something called the Engagement Model. Every reader has a measure based on the frequency they come to the *FT*, the recency that they've come and how much they read when they come there.

The *FT* built predictive models in reader behaviour and subscription propensity.

We can focus our marketing on readers with a higher propensity to subscribe, and it's obviously much more efficient. Given that we have a very limited marketing budget, that makes sense. It's one of the reasons why we've managed to grow our subscriber base and manage the retention and churn.

AI's computational efficiency facilitates the subscription flywheel. "The more subscribers you have, the more data you have, and the more data you have, the more powerful the analytics and the opportunity for AI."

"One of the things we've learnt from AI is that the software sees patterns in the data that we don't see. So I think there are lots of opportunities to bring a lot of that insight through the analytics, through AI to create a more efficient organisation" (Ridding, 2020).

Practitioner story discovery/workflows

In journalism and publishing, AI is being used for content creation.

- AI can find breaking news stories, which otherwise can be a time consuming task for journalists (Underwood, 2019). *News Tracer* from Reuters (introduced 2017) claims to have spotted and validated stories in real time.
- AI can detect 'anomalous' events through data analysis, or elucidate existing ones. Conspiracy theories promoted by the mysterious *QAnon* in the US 2019–21 drove radicalisation leading to the Capitol Riot of January 2021. AI identified that there was not one *QAnon*, but actually two. Q1 is on *4chan*, Q2 on *8chan*, based on analysis of forum posts, according to Orphan Analytics (Manfield, 2021).

There are also AI workflow tools.

- *The New York Times* uses NLP for *Switchboard*, clustering 35,000 reader questions to find fast expert answers. The model was built with a pared-down iteration of the Google BERT language model, and tuned on question pairs to find similarities. It also uses 'zero-shot' models, which associate observed and non-observed classes of data through auxiliary information. "We don't know what the news will be about next week … so it's difficult to source training data and pre-train topic-specific models" (Cook, 2021). *The Times* is also using machine translation to publish more of its content in Spanish – an otherwise cost-inefficient, by-hand translation task.
- *The New York Times* also used NLP to make its 160-year content archive available and searchable through *TimesMachine*, using OCR (Optical Character Recognition) image classification and entity extraction to convert it into searchable

text. Similarly, AI (deep learning) can recover or enhance damaged historical images (OFCOM, 2019).

- The BBC's *Juicer* helps journalists streamline workflows – an aggregation and content extraction API which semantically tags 850 global news RSS feeds, as organisations, locations, people or things.
- *INJECT* from London's Bayes Business School helps journalists and editors find new angles for stories. Computational NLP allows journalists to search in multiple languages, so a search begun in English can add Dutch and Norwegian. It reads 400 titles in six languages.
- *Newswhip* is an Associated Press media monitoring tool to predict topics that will go viral, and even the number of interactions they will have. It is used by journalists and communications teams to get ahead on trending stories.
- AI can help readers too, pointing them to content as a recommendation engine. News aggregator *Recent News* uses machine learning to study users' reading habits and recommend stories (Godwin, 2020).
- Financial journalists use NLP to analyse CEO word usage in stock market earnings calls for sentiment analysis – not just looking for obvious words like 'costs,' but also finding subliminal connections between seemingly random word choices (like 'box') and later poor corporate performance. Tools assist hedge funds in doing this too – such as Sentieo, Factset's Thematic Sentiment and Textual Data Analytics from S&P Global. In a circular process, danger words flagged by NLP analysis are then passed back to CEOs by PR advisers, as things they should not say (Thornhill, 2021).

Some AI tools that play a tangential role in news media are controversial. The US *ShotSpotter* system aims to detect gunshots in cities via 20 microphones per square mile, and can integrate with predictive policing AI models to "forecast when and where crimes are likely to emerge," according to *Shotspotter*'s 2020 SEC Form 10k. *Shotspotter* evidence has been associated with controversial incidents. Michael Williams spent a year in jail on murder charges before charges were dismissed (Burke, 2021). News sites may find themselves both using AI tools to generate stories, and generating stories about the problems those same tools can create.

Automated journalism

Automated journalism goes further than just assisting news gathering. Now the articles are written by AI.

- *Forbes* magazine uses NLP tool *Bertie* to save editors time by writing the first draft of articles.
- *Washington Post* tool *Heliograf* writes bulletins based on structured data, like financial or sports news, as does Reuters' *Lynx* service.(Willens, 2019). The *Quill* from *Narrative Science* turns raw data into intelligent stories for dashboards (Underwood, 2019).

- *Automated Insights* tool *Wordsmith* uses NLP to transform fantasy football data into stylistically credible, sports reporter accounts of matches, for fantasy team owners. The AI was trained in "a particularly snarky tone" (Underwood, 2019).
- There are many examples of journalists testing AI systems like Open AI's *GPT-3* on newswriting of all kinds. *The Guardian* said: "A robot wrote this entire article. Are you scared yet, human?." AI academics were unconvinced: "Some argued it was misleading and a case of poor journalism. We tend to agree" (Floridi and Chiriatti, 2020).
- AI blogger Janelle Shane trained a neural network on 2020 headlines to devise new ones. It's machine-created journalism was psychedelic, as well as entirely untrue: "Fears rise of new dwarf hippo public relations disaster after rise in sightings." "Mysterious Origin of Monster Deep-sea Toads Solved" (Shane, 2020).

Comment moderation

Engagement is key to digital publishing. But so are other key drivers: content moderation, legal and regulatory risk.

- *The New York Times* used the *Perspective API* from Jigsaw to expand the ability of its 14 content moderation staff to review 11,000 incoming comments each day. Previously they only managed to look at 10% of them (Underwood, 2019).
- On *Facebook*, the percentage 'success rate' for intervention in content grew through the use of AI tools. Ninety per cent of hate speech was flagged by AI before it was even reported, rising to 99.5% for child nudity.

Disinformation detection

George Orwell, author of the quintessentially dystopian novel, *1984*, said: "the most effective way to destroy people is to deny and obliterate their own understanding of their history." The centrality of AI in disinformation was exemplified by the 2022 Ukraine war, where between them the combatants deployed a combination of legitimate and false news, social media, bloggers, commentators, bots and deepfakes to amplify their message. This was a fully fledged 'information battlespace' which would have fully resonated with Orwell as he wrote his novel on the remote, off-grid, Scottish island of Jura, 73 years earlier, in 1949.

Misinformation is widespread. A 2021 Oxford Internet Institute study found campaigns in 82 countries. "Early on in our work, the bulk of these countries were authoritarian regimes … Now it's a fairly normal part of the communications toolkit," said co-author, Professor Phil Howard. In authoritarian countries: "it's about creating fake accounts, citizens who aren't actually real" (Howard, 2021). Misinformation is often about the deployment of fake citizens to promote fake news in service of real events.

AI philosopher Stuart Russell observed in his 2021 *BBC Reith Lectures:* "AI is a force both for malign actors and those seeking to prevent malign action." That reflects Francis

Bacon's observation from *The Wisdom of the Ancients* (1609): " 'The mechanical arts may be turned either way, and serve as well for the cure as for the hurt.' The hurt with AI includes racial and gender bias, misinformation, deepfakes, and cybercrime" (Russell, 2021). Just 3% of people believe everything online is true, but 30% think most of it is (OFCOM, 2021) – creating a substantial window of opportunity for AI-driven misinformation.

Author Niall Ferguson said in his book *Doom: The Politics of Catastrophe*: "A networked society needs to have well-designed circuit breakers that can swiftly reduce the connectivity of the network in a crisis, without atomizing and paralyzing society completely" (Ferguson, 2021). To function at sufficient speed and scale, these circuit-breakers need to themselves be turbocharged by AI.

- Dutch AI-powered voice-scanner *Voyc* identifies questionable statements in two seconds (Higgins, 2018). (It is otherwise used in bank call centre security.)
- *ClaimBuster* from California Polytechnic State University performs "automated live fact checking" by scanning stories against databases. *WIRED* magazine described this as "A Heroic AI" which in pursuit of democratic transparency "will let you spy on your lawmaker's every word." One of the researchers on the project, Chengkai Li, said: "Algorithms don't have an intrinsic feature to identify facts; humans must provide them. We do this by building what I'll call truth databases" (Borel, 2018).
- *Crowdtangle* (owned by *Meta*) offers verification tools during major news events. MIT project *Truth Goggles* aimed to provide fact-checking information at the point of consumption. (But it was scaled down in 2021 as a standalone product.)
- *Decodex* (owned by leading French newspaper *Le Monde*) offers a searchable database to appraise websites' reliability (Maruti Techlabs, 2021).
- *Veracity.ai* has identified 1,200 fake news sites and 400,000 fake posts (Borel, 2018).
- *Hoaxy* spots fake news sites and provides a network graph of any subject or assertion, colour-coding how 'bot-like' or 'human-like' those interacting with the subject are, as it spreads across the network graph of social media (Hoaxy.ai).

Sentiment detection

Sensing the public mood is a challenge for marketing technology (martech), intelligence and news organisations. It is probably one of the biggest fields of innovation in both marketing and journalism in the 2020s.

Signal AI uses AI to analyse over 5 million documents a day from global media, blogs, social and regulatory sources. Amongst other capabilities it can conduct textual analysis at scale in real time, to provide that sentiment analysis; rather than just discovering what topics people are talking about, it aims to map the direction of the conversation.

In an interview, CEO David Benigson said:

We wanted to build this platform that could essentially aggregate the world's information, that would sit outside of an organisation to be ambivalent about media type and structure and language and modality and format, and bring all of that disparate data into a single platform that could then apply machine learning and AI to that data. The AI could be trained by experts from within these large organisations and thereby unlock a set of insights that would help business leaders essentially make better decisions.

(David Benigson, 2021)

- Taking, for instance, the 2020 Coronavirus story, the *Signal AI Media Report* identified some 152 million articles globally about coronavirus. As Covid-19 cases rose and global lockdowns loomed, use of the word "fear" in news headlines spiked. By March 2021, however, the tracking changed as there was a first glimmer of "hope." This gave advance notice of a change both in the public mood and potentially even in the medicine itself. Any advance knowledge of shifts in societal sentiment is valuable to governments, journalists, marketers and hedge funds.
- *Signal AI* runs a net sentiment calculation akin to the net promoter score formula in marketing. It is based simply on a formula: Sum of Positive Articles – Sum of Negative Articles = Net Sentiment.
- Benigson demonstrated the huge increase in the volume of coverage for *Black Lives Matter* after the killing of George Floyd: and also the inherent potential bias of the three major outlets [CNN, Fox News and MSNBC]. "Fox News proved the least likely to mention either police brutality or racism … and was approximately three times more likely to mention riots and approximately twice as likely to talk about looting."

Deepfake detection

AI creates 'deepfake' videos using deep learning and generative adversarial networks – like the one of Ukraine's President Zelensky in March 2022, ascribed to Russian propaganda. Poacher and gamekeeper as in so many fields, AI is also being used to spot deepfakes.

- *Adverif.ai* uses machine learning, looking for minuscule movements that represent breathing or a pulse, which would indicate a real video (Gershgorn, 2018).
- Michigan State University researcher Vishal Asnani uses deep learning to identify the architectural traits of unknown models or hyperparameters (Vincent, 2021).
- *Facebook* held a 2020 deepfake detection challenge (DFDC) event with 2000 participants testing models against real world examples (MetaAI, 2020).
- The winning algorithm was able to detect just 65% of AI-manipulated videos (Vincent, 2021). So there remains work to do.
- Experts in the field report that it is hard to spot fake content created by AI systems whose signature is not known. A fear of intelligence agencies is that the adversary will have an NLP system which they do not know about.

Class discussion questions

- Why and how did *The New York Times* and *Financial Times* succeed in pivoting their businesses to subscription models when so many other newspapers failed?
- Identify a market niche for a digital publishing start-up. Specify your proposition, and its editorial and business model.
- What are the most useful AI tools for audience growth in digital publishing?
- What is semantic analysis? Which AI-driven products are available in the market to deliver it, and which customers would be most interested in using it?

CHAPTER SUMMARY

TABLE 9.1 Key themes in this chapter

Digital Publishing	Business Development	Production	Distribution	Monetisation
Business model	Modest investment in content proposition creation and calibration to market.	Significant investment in staff and content creation, but calibrated to scale of platform.	Investment required for platform, digital marketing and technology.	Four key methods – programmatic ads, subscription, advertising and branded content.
Uses of AI	AI used in multiple ways for content creation.	AI used in multiple ways for research, production and content creation.	High AI usage in marketing, distribution, customer interface.	AI use in optimisation of returns.
Value Creation	Low value creation pre-launch or (of legacy title) re-launch.	Low value creation at the production phase until audience traction is achieved.	Value created rises with audience engagement.	Exceptional value creation for successful business turnaround to digital, or business creation. High exit multiples.

BIBLIOGRAPHY

Arlidge, J. (2022) *Condé Nast* chief Roger Lynch: how I'll rescue *Vogue* and *Vanity Fair*. *The Sunday Times*, 2 April.

Bachmann, P., Hunziker, S. and Rüedy, T. (2019) Selling their souls to the advertisers? How native advertising degrades the quality of prestige media outlets. *Journal of Media Business Studies*, 16(2), 95–109. doi.org/10.1080/16522354.2019.1596723

Best, C. (2021) Recode Media In *Substack's Next Target: Local News*, 15 April.

Borel, B. (2018) Can AI solve the internet's fake news problem? A fact-checker investigates. *Popular Science*, 20 March.

Burke, G. (2021) How AI Powered Tech Landed a Man in Jail with Scant Evidence. *AP*, 20 August.

Buzzfeed. (2021) *Buzzfeed Inc, Investor Presentation, December 2021*. [online] Available at: www.bzfd.com/static-files/13d20068-d21b-456d-910d-4796060cd352 [Accessed 29 August 2022].

Caro-González, F. J., Sánchez-Torné, I. and Pérez-Suárez, M. (2021) Female entrepreneurs in digital journalism. *Journal of Media Business Studies*, 1–19. doi.org/10.1080/16522354.2021.1918434

Chan-Olmsted, S. M. (2019) A Review of Artificial Intelligence Adoptions in the Media Industry. *International Journal on Media Management*, 21(3–4), 193–215. doi.org/10.1080/14241277.2019.1695619

Cook, J. (2021) Streamlining reader Q&A with Zero-Shot Learning. *New York Times R&D*. [online] Available at: https://rd.nytimes.com/projects/streamlining-reader-qa-with-zero-shot-learning [Accessed 25 August 2022].

Cramer-Flood, E. (2021) Worldwide digital ad spending 2021. *eMarketer*. [online] Available at: www.emarketer.com/content/worldwide-digital-ad-spending-2021 [Accessed 25 August 2022].

David Benigson, S. A. (2021) *Interview*. Oxford University.

Edge, M. (2019) Are UK newspapers really dying? A financial analysis of newspaper publishing companies. *Journal of Media Business Studies*, 16(1), 19–39. doi.org/10.1080/16522354.2018.1555686

Ferguson, N. (2021) Doom: the politics of catastrophe. London: Penguin.

Fletcher, R. (2021) How do people think about the financing of the commercial news media? *Reuters Institute for the Study of Journalism*. [online] Available at: https://reutersinstitute.politics.ox.ac.uk/digital-news-report/2021/how-do-people-think-about-financing-commercial-news-media [Accessed 25 August 2022].

Floridi, L. and Chiriatti, M. (2020) *GPT-3*: its nature, scope, limits, and consequences. *Minds and Machines: Journal for Artificial Intelligence, Philosophy and Cognitive Science*, 30(4), 681. doi.org/10.1007/s11023-020-09548-1

Gershgorn, D. (2018) The hottest trend in AI is perfect for creating fake media. *Quartz*. [online] Available at: https://qz.com/1230470/the-hottest-trend-in-ai-is-perfect-for-creating-fake-media/ [Accessed 23 August 2022].

Godwin, J. O. (2020) *Artificial intelligence: a modern approach and machine learning*. Independently Published.

Goyanes, M. and Dürrenberg, C. (2014) A taxonomy of newspapers based on multi-platform and paid content strategies: evidences from Spain. *International Journal on Media Management*, 16(1), 27–45. doi.org/10.1080/14241277.2014.900498

Grieco, E. (2020) Fast facts about the newspaper industry's financial struggles as McClatchy files for bankruptcy. *Pew Research Center*. [online] Available at: www.pewresearch.org/fact-tank/2020/02/14/fast-facts-about-the-newspaper-industrys-financial-struggles/ [Accessed 23 August 2022].

Gundlach, H. and Hofmann, U. (2021) Information search, behavioural economics, and relevance decisions in the online media industry: how strongly do the algorithms of intermediaries influence the relevance evaluation of information? *Journal of Media Business Studies*, 18(3), 179–98. doi.org/10.1080/16522354.2020.1854602

Harms, B., Bijmolt, T. H. A. and Hoekstra, J. C. (2019) You don't fool me! Consumer perceptions of digital native advertising and banner advertising. *Journal of Media Business Studies*, 16(4), 275–94. doi.org/10.1080/16522354.2019.1640517

Herrmann, J. (2021) The Mill is Greater Manchester's new quality newspaper – delivered by email. *The Mill*. [online] Available at: https://manchestermill.co.uk/about?utm_source=menu-dropdown&sort=about [Accessed 23 August 2022].

Hess, T. (2014) What is a media company? A Reconceptualization for the online world. *International Journal on Media Management*, 16(1), 3–8. doi.org/10.1080/14241277.2014.906993

Higgins, L. (2018) Behind an effort to fact-check live news with speed and accuracy. *Wall Street Journal*, 23 November.

Howard, P. P. (2021) Interview at Said Business School, University of Oxford for Diploma in Artificial Intelligence for Business.

Kecheng, F. (2021) Chinese whispers: what is is like to be a journalist in China In *Chinese Whispers*. [online] Available at: www.spectator.co.uk/podcast/journalism-in-china-what-can-and-can-t-you-say- [Accessed 23 August 2022].

Kim, D. H. and Desai, M. (2021) Are social media worth it for news media?: Explaining news engagement on *Tumblr* and digital traffic of news websites. *International Journal on Media Management*, 23(1–2), 2–28. doi.org/10.1080/14241277.2021.1958820

Kosterich, A. and Weber, M. S. (2018) Starting up the news: the impact of venture capital on the digital news media ecosystem. *International Journal on Media Management*, 20(4), 239–62. doi.org/10.1080/14241277.2018.1563547

Larman, A. (2022) Stacking up *Substack*. *The Spectator*, 3 January.

LBGMediaPLC. (2021) Admission document. [online] Available at: https://lbgmedia.co.uk/docs/ladbiblelibraries/archive/company-docs/admission-document.pdf [Accessed 23 August 2022].

Lessin, J. (2020) How Jessica Lessin built a digital media business by covering digital media. *Variety: Strictly Business*. [podcast] Available at: https://variety.com/2020/tv/news/jessica-lessin-information-digital-media-1234874369/ [Accessed 16 August 2022].

Li, X., Gong, X. and Mou, R. (2020) Pioneering the media convergence: lifestyle media production in the digital age in China. *Journal of Media Business Studies*, 1–17. doi.org/10.1080/16522354.2020.1853467

Lischka, J. A. (2019) Strategic renewal during technology change: Tracking the digital journey of legacy news companies. *Journal of Media Business Studies*, 16(3), 182–201. doi.org/10.1080/16522354.2019.1635349

Manfield, J. (2021) *Content moderation – a strategic priority*. Presentation to Diploma in AI for Business, Said Business School, University of Oxford.

Mayhew, F. (2020) Report predicts five years of steep global decline for newspaper industry revenue (print and online). *Press Gazette*. [online] Available at: https://pressgazette.co.uk/report-predicts-five-years-of-steep-global-decline-for-newspaper-industry-revenu-print-and-online/ [Accessed 16 August 2022].

Maruti Techlabs. (2021) Is artificial intelligence the key to combat fake news?

Meo, G. (2019) Transformation of Chinese newspaper companies: management, production and administration. *International Journal on Media Management*, 21(2), 159–60. doi.org/10.1080/14241277.2019.1639253

MetaAI. (2020) *Deepfake Detection challenge results: an open initiative to advance AI*. [online] Available at: https://ai.facebook.com/blog/deepfake-detection-challenge-results-an-open-initiative-to-advance-ai/ [Accessed 16 August 2022].

Mullin, B. (2021) The fight over BuzzFeed's move to go public. *The Journal*. [podcast] 20 August. Available at: www.wsj.com/podcasts/the-journal/the-fight-over-buzzfeed-move-to-go-public/8fe74b08-7630-4c13-8503-b1893fb510c6 [Accessed 25 August 2022]

Myllylahti, M. (2018) An attention economy trap? An empirical investigation into four news companies' *Facebook* traffic and social media revenue. *Journal of Media Business Studies*, 15(4), 237–53. doi.org/10.1080/16522354.2018.1527521

Nicolau, A. (2021) Growth of *The Information* is good news for media business. *Financial Times*. [online] Available at: www.ft.com/content/0b34cbd7-041a-40c7-a1c7-6dd3b9958 570 [Accessed 23 August 2022].

Nicolau, A., Germano, S. and Fontanella-Khan, J. (2022) *New York Times* agrees $550m deal for *The Athletic*. *Financial Times*, 6 January.

Noam, E. M. (2019) *Media and digital management*. London: Palgrave Macmillan.

Nylund, M. (2013) Toward creativity management: idea generation and newsroom meetings. *International Journal on Media Management*, 15(4), 197–210. doi.org/10.1080/14241277.2013.773332

OFCOM. (2019) *Use of AI in online content moderation*. [online] Available at: www.ofcom.org.uk/__data/assets/pdf_file/0028/157249/cambridge-consultants-ai-content-moderation.pdf [Accessed 16 August 2022].

Olsen, R. K. and Solvoll, M. K. (2018) Bouncing off the paywall: understanding misalignments between local newspaper value propositions and audience responses. *International Journal on Media Management*, 20(3), 174–92. doi.org/10.1080/14241277.2018.1529672

Ridding, J. (2020) Interview with John Ridding, CEO Financial Times, conducted at Oxford University, 20 July.

Riskos, K., Hatzithomas, L., Dekoulou, P. and Tsourvakas, G. (2021) The influence of entertainment, utility and pass time on consumer brand engagement for news media brands: a mediation model. *Journal of Media Business Studies*, 1–28. doi.org/10.1080/16522354.2021.1887439

Robertson, K. (2022) *Grid*, a 'fuller picture' news site, goes live. *The New York Times*, 12 January.

Russell, S. (2021) BBC Reith Lectures 2021 – Living with Artificial Intelligence. *BBC*. [online] Available at: www.bbc.co.uk/programmes/articles/1N0w5NcK27Tt041LPVLZ51k/reith-lectures-2021-living-with-artificial-intelligence [Accessed 29 August 2022].

Sawa, Y. (2021) *2021 Digital News Report*. [online] Available at: https://reutersinstitute.politics.ox.ac.uk/digital-news-report/2021/japan [Accessed 23 August 2022].

Shane, J. (2020) When killer orchids attack: how the deadly Corpse Orchid is turning up in US backyards. *AI Weirdness*. [online] Available at: https://aiweirdness.com [Accessed 29 August 2022].

Shields, M. (2021) Pivot to peril. Variety, 25 March.

Spangler, T. (2021) BuzzFeed valued at $1.5 billion in SPAC deal to go public, will acquire complex networks for $300 million. *Variety*. [online] Available at: https://variety.com/2021/digital/news/buzzfeed-public-spac-merger-complex-1235004331/ [Accessed 29 August 2022].

Sun, J. (2020) China's media organisations' adoption of the *WeChat* public platform: news flow network, exploitation and exploration. *Journal of Media Business Studies*, 1–18. doi.org/10.1080/16522354.2020.1840711

Technavio. (2021) Global digital publishing market by type and geography – forecast and analysis 2021–25. [online] Available at: www.technavio.com/report/digital-publishing-market-industry-analysis?utm_source=prnewswire&utm_medium=pressrelease&utm_campaign=tnv2_autov6_rep1_wk3_2022_007&utm_content=IRTNTR40619&nowebp [Accessed 29 August 2022].

Thornhill, J. (2021) FT Tech Tonic In *You Can't Always Get What You Quant*. [online] Available at: www.ft.com/content/51f3053a-1d2f-44af-bce1-2777604886a5 [Accessed 23 August 2022].

Tobitt, C. (2022) National press ABCs: *Daily Mail* falls below 900k but stays top of pack with *Metro. Press Gazette*, 23 March.

Tracy, M. (2021) New York Times Adds 455,000 Subscriptions in Third Quarter. *The New York Times*, 3 November.

Underwood, C. (2019) Automated Journalism – AI Applications at New York Times, Reuters, and Other Media Giants. Emerj.com. https://emerj.com/ai-sector-overviews/automated-journalism-applications/

Verhoeven, M., von Rimscha, M. B., Krebs, I., Siegert, G. and Sommer, C. (2018) Identifying paths to audience success of media products: the media decision-makers' perspective. *International Journal on Media Management*, 20(1), 51–77. doi.org/10.1080/14241277.2017.1402019

Villi, M., Grönlund, M., Linden, C.-G., Lehtisaari, K., Mierzejewska, B., Picard, R. G. and Roepnack, A. (2020) 'They're a little bit squeezed in the middle': Strategic challenges for innovation in US Metropolitan newspaper organisations. *Journal of Media Business Studies*, 17(1), 33–50. doi.org/10.1080/16522354.2019.1630099

Vincent, J. (2021) Facebook develops new method to reverse-engineer deepfakes and track their source. *The Verge*. [online] Available at: www.theverge.com/2021/6/16/22534690/facebook-deepfake-detection-reverse-engineer-ai-model-hyperparameters [Accessed 23 August 2022].

Willens, M. (2019) Forbes is building more AI tools for its reporters. *Digiday*. [online] Available at: https://digiday.com/media/forbes-built-a-robot-to-pre-write-articles-for-its-contributors/ [Accessed 23 August 2022].

SECTION C
Producers

Content creation at scale – and
the transformative impact of AI

CHAPTER 10

Scripted

Digital-driven change in production and distribution models

....

INTRODUCTION TO THE SECTOR

Vladimir Ilyich Ulyanov – Lenin – lead the 1917 Russian Revolution, a critical moment in the twentieth century. Aside from geopolitics he knew the vital importance of another sector: entertainment. Lenin said: "Charlie Chaplin is the only man in the world I would like to meet." And over a hundred years later, in the 2020s, TV and film still hold both vast cultural power and economic opportunity.

Demand and income from the scripted genre have changed its size and shape in the twenty-first century. Delivery has been revolutionised by the addition of a new category which sits between cinema and TV: streaming. The viewer now combines the majority of their film, TV and streamer-produced drama on a single big screen at home, or their phone. So unlike in twentieth-century textbooks we combine all three categories in to a single chapter: scripted.

For those who succeed, scripted confers profit and kudos. But the core business problem in scripted content is a simple one: most projects fail. Most film scripts don't get made, and most ideas for TV shows don't get produced.

This chapter therefore surveys principles for media business value generation in the scripted market segment. Then it examines AI and other digital tools impacting production, and considers their implications.

First, some basic facts about the industry.

- The 2021 global cinema and home entertainment market was £328 billion (MPA figure). (Source: KFTV, June 2021)
- Whereas in 2010, 216 scripted original series were produced in the US, by 2022, that number was 559 series.

DOI: 10.4324/9781003213611-13

- Scripted dominates the output of major streamers: in 2020, *Netflix* had 1833 TV shows available in the US, of which 1,456 were scripted (77%) and *Amazon Prime* was 66% scripted.
- Even smaller services like *BritBox* are heavily scripted-based (82%). "TV executives have long wondered whether we would one day hit a point of saturation, dubbed 'Peak TV.' The new data suggests we aren't there yet" (Fischer, 2022).
- Scripted has also been globalised. Staple English-language producer Disney commissioned its first Dutch crime thriller, the eight-part *Nemesis*, in March 2022, as part of a much wider movement to access new audiences. In 2022, Amazon Studios produced a major German drama, *The Gryphon*, an adaptation of author Wolfgang Hohlbein's cult novel.
- In a sign of the times, the world's highest grossing movie – for the first time – was produced outside Hollywood: Chinese film *The Eight Hundred*. China now produces over 1,000 films a year.
- India produces some 2,500 films, a quarter of the global total, and the streamers are driving expansion of the industry. *Netflix* spent $405 million on original and licensed Indian content in 2019–2020 (Gupta, 2022).
- The US produced 814 movies in 2019 – but higher budgetary value.
- "The top three producer countries accounted for 48.2% of all movies produced in the world in 2019." Western Europe is a big producer too. And amongst the smaller regions – Latin America stands out. Middle Eastern film production is low, but growing (Hancock, 2021).

Distribution of film has migrated towards TV and the streamers, but there remains a significant, traditional, film exhibition industry globally, and its demise may have been called too early (see below on cinemas). At $25 billion revenue, cinemas remain a bigger media sector than music.

THE VALUE CREATION MODEL

Development

At the development stage in the value creation process in scripted, market analysis is vital for the producer. They must understand demand amongst a limited number of buyers, on the basis of required genre and style of programming. The firm must position itself carefully, such that its choice of product directly matches its credibility and perceived ability to deliver. There is no point in a horror production company pitching investors with romantic comedies or TV soap operas. From there, the key inputs are script investment and the brand of the producer, writer and production company. Outputs at this stage are IP, and a potential sale to a broadcast, streamer or distributor client.

Scripted content begins with a script. A writer must have sufficient reputation to be credible to investors, and an idea must have a market-relevant emotional or

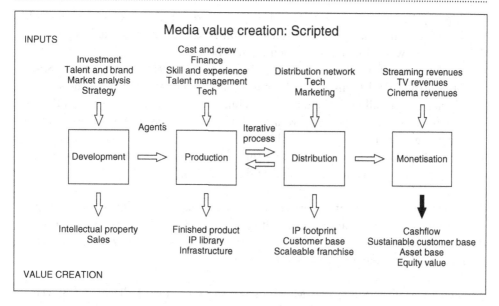

FIGURE 10.1 In scripted, production quality can generate distribution success, leading to further production, and franchise development: a *Game of Thrones* or *Star Wars*

intellectual hook. Comedian Steve Martin said: "All of life's riddles are answered in the movies."

Selection of ideas

The first value-creation challenge in scripted is therefore to pick and back the *right* ideas from a vast field. In the ocean of would-be screenwriters, there is constrained supply of top names trusted to deliver hit content.

For every Julian Fellowes (*Downton Abbey*) there are 1,000 people who cannot sell their ideas; an enormous filtration. "Since inevitably most projects will be rejected, any selection mechanism will be unpopular with the artistic community" (Noam, 2019). Scripts are often provided free at the development stage, or via option agreements, in which a low fee is paid, against a future fee if the option is taken up. Very occasionally, scripts from substantial writers whose involvement guarantees a green light for the project (Stephen King) are commissioned for hundreds of thousands of dollars.

Scripts may require not only value as standalone stories, but also as potential sources of long-running future IP. US channel AMC Networks CEO Josh Sapan told podcast *Strictly Business* in August 2022 that in commissioning dramas based on the Anne Rice vampire novels, they had conceived an entire, decade-long 'Metaverse' of mutually complementary future series.

- The entertainment industry, and systems of agencies such as CAA, WME and UTA have evolved to find and pre-filter talent.

- Many projects sit in a hinterland between interest and firm commission; 1920s Hollywood producer Sam Goldwyn famously said of his green lighting decision making power: "I'll give you a definite maybe."
- In the data-informed era of 2021, buyer instinct still matters. Scott Stuber, Head of Original Films at *Netflix* has a modern day assessment of the selection challenge: "It's all gut. The data stuff is hugely overstated. At the end of the day, you have to ask: Do you believe in it? Do you have passion for it? Do you think it's going to work?" (Lang, 2021b).
- Some AI start-ups would argue that they do now have forensic script assessment tools (see the AI section at the end of this chapter).

Producers cover the risk of any given script, by buying many. One major European production company is said to write off as much as $25 million per year on scripts that it has invested in but will not pursue. An example from the 1990s demonstrates the scattergun approach of slate development:

> Guys like Oliver Stone and Martin Scorsese and Sidney Pollack and Steven Spielberg buy scripts like you or I buy toilet paper, thinking that maybe one day they'll wake up and want to direct them. It took Redford eight years before he finally made *A River Runs Through It*, and by that time the guy who wrote the book was worm food.
>
> *(Hamsher, 1997)*

Flow of good scripts can be enhanced by alliances between scripted producers and publishers, such as the 2019 deal between HarperCollins and Sony Pictures Entertainment: "Our close collaborations with authors and their material gives us a tremendous advantage because the development process begins with a terrific story and great characters, and even more so after publication, with the added bonus of audience pre-awareness" (HarperCollins, 2019).

An individual network may build a relationship with a particular writer to ensure script flow: for instance, the five-year *Netflix* deal with Harlan Coben, for shows including *Safe*, *The Stranger* and *The Woods* (Baxter-Wright, 2022) or its deal with writer/producer Shonda Rhimes (*Bridgerton*).

Importance of track record

One answer to the risk of buying brand new stories is to buy sequels to old ones. This explains the wave of Hollywood re-makes and franchises – *Star Wars* and *Marvel* universes, for instance.

- In 2022 alone, sequels included *Avatar 2*, *Top Gun 2*, new titles from *Halloween* and *Spiderman*, *Minions*, *Thor*, *Jurassic Park*, *Doctor Strange*, *Downton Abbey*, *Scream* and *Ice Age*.

- Academics analysed TV spin-offs from different genres. Success factors for spin-offs were found to be the parent show's fan base ... and consistency in plot and "character constellation" (Kilian and Schwarz, 2013).
- If the intellectual property is familiar, creativity in the name can help. Academic research shows sequels with novel titles generate a higher box office gross than sequels without, and not just on the opening weekend when familiarity might be a marketing shortcut (Kim, 2021). In that vein, a series that started as *Spiderman* has ended up with more complex titles, such as *Spider-Man: Across the Spiderverse (Part Two)* (2023).

Studios and streamers back one asset even above a script: talent with track record. When, in 2021, *Netflix* contracted with Steven Spielberg's hitherto cinema-focused company Amblin Partners, it was for big names. "The partnership grew stronger after *Netflix* signed on for Bradley Cooper's *Maestro*," a biopic of [conductor] Leonard Bernstein. Explaining his switch to streaming from cinema, Spielberg said: "I want people to find their entertainment in any form or fashion that suits them." *Netflix*'s head of original films Scott Stuber said: "I would love him to make movies like *Goonies* or *Indiana Jones* for us." Their ambition was to hire the most bankable of directors, and the reference point was potential franchise movies (Lang, 2021b).

Top franchises in scripted

As a result of all this, franchises in the Top 50 North America box office have mushroomed.

- 56% of Top 50 movies in 2019, and 71% of their revenue, were franchises.
- Disney lead with $3.1 billion across eight franchise titles, including the $858 million that *Avengers: Endgame* earned its home market. They also had animated younger titles (*Lion King, Frozen 2, Aladdin, Toy Story 4*), Marvel (*Avengers, Captain Marvel*) and *Star Wars* (Hancock, 2021). The Marvel Universe cost Disney $4 billion in 2009, but by 2022 had generated over $18 billion in box office.
- Franchises can come from tangential sources too: the 2022 TV drama series *Bel-Air* was created by filmmaker Morgan Cooper as a reimagining of the light 1990s sitcom *Fresh Prince of Bel-Air* (and was sold through a viral trailer for a show that did not yet exist).
- But of course there is a paradox. *Star Wars* was itself once (in 1977) an original idea, not a franchise. From a low budget it achieved a high return on investment, its producer Lucasfilm eventually selling to Disney for $4.05 billion in 2012, which now is generally seen as a bargain (Beattie, 2021) based on the massive subsequent exploitation of the titles.

However, without franchises to rely on, enhanced creativity can result – for instance, with new streamers who do not have legacy IP. "We didn't have anything," *Netflix*'s

Scott Stuber was quoted as saying (2021.) "We didn't have a library. We couldn't remake *Nutty Professor*. For me it was important to define ourselves, and the way to do that was by working with great filmmakers. Original storytelling was our super-power" (Lang, 2021b). Because *Netflix* didn't own *Marvel* or *Star Wars*, it was actually able to take bigger risks on original movies. But not all those originals were critically successful: 2022 release *The Gray Man*, which cost a reported $200 million to make, starred Ryan Gosling and Chris Evans – but scored only 46% amongst critics on review aggregator *Rotten Tomatoes*. By its third week on *Netflix* it was not the top-rated film.

Stars

So the maths is not simple when hiring star talent. The idea that price and value are equated in a star name – like the $29 million paid to Arnold Schwarzenegger for *Terminator 3* in 2003 – is incorrect.

> Statistical studies show that stars (and big production budgets) create higher revenues but not higher profits. A study of 600 movie stars and 500 movies concluded the effect of a star on theatrical revenue was, on average, $3 million and did not increase the market value of the firm distributing or producing the film.
>
> *(Noam, 2019)*

Why? It may be the movie that makes the star look good, but not the other way around. "Movies with stars are successful not because of the star, but because the star chooses projects that people tend to like," found a USC academic. Keanu Reeves was the face of *The Matrix*, but not the reason for its success, which was multifaceted (Fabrikant, 2006).

In one University of Calgary study of 2,000 movies between 1985 and 1996, only seven actors – including Tom Hanks and Sandra Bullock – actually had a positive impact on the box office. The most profitable arrangement for a producer is to find a "rising star," who will work at relatively low pay yet break out (Noam, 2019). Glenn Close broke through in the 1987 thriller *Fatal Attraction*, despite being so despised by test audiences for the script is rewritten for her character to be shot dead (Bay, 1988).

Production

In 2019, there were 31,600 shows on TV, a landscape so crowded that differentiation was a major challenge, and demanding quality delivery, which costs money (Schneider, 2019). To go into scripted production therefore requires commitment of upfront funding. Only the rarest productions work on a shoestring budget. The most famous, *Paranormal Activity*, earned a reputed 434,000% return on its initial investment (before factoring in additional post-production and marketing costs.) But it was the exception. Box office receipts are often confused with return on investment (ROI), but they are not the same. ROI matters to investors. Box office gross matters to stars, because that's the driver of renumeration and future jobs.

Cash flow requirement is a major constraint on scripted value generation, and that is important to emphasise, because other segments of the media business have evolved ways of avoiding this constraint. *YouTube* (with $8.6 billion of quarterly revenue in 2021) does not require production cash flow to produce content. Major media industries such as music recording, audio/podcasts, digital publishing and social/creator content have all been existentially disrupted by bedroom production, the toolkit of digital transformation. Scripted has failed to do that. *YouTube* gave up on scripted production in 2020 (Jarvey, 2018).

Average prices for scripted content have shot up. "It's an explosion," said a 2019 industry study of the then $15 million per hour cost of ultra high-end scripted TV (Schneider, 2019).

Production funding options

So who is financing scripted content?

Specialist banks (like the UK's Coutts) and gap financiers bridge cash flow gaps. But all films need either equity investors, or paying trade customers, segmented into seven categories: broadcasters, streamers, studios, brands, distributors, investors and states. (Crowdfunders like *Slated*, *Seed&Spark*, *Indiegogo* and *Junction* often get enthusiastic mention for lower budget indie films. But the funds raised are not comparable.)   •

- Broadcast TV channels buy scripted as a function of their overall budgets – which are challenged by funding changes and a shift of advertising to digital. "The global crisis of public service television will make independent companies even more inclined to redirect their strategies and to go increasingly beyond broadcast" (Nylund and Mildén, 2012). Major terrestrial networks, especially US, have lost their first call on talent to better-funded streamers. *Succession* (HBO Max) pays Brian Cox alone $4 million per season, a price unthinkable on broadcast TV in his native Scotland (Burgos, 2021) and around double the entire budget for a normal hour's drama on a UK television channel.
- Streamers *Apple TV+*, *Netflix* and *Amazon* have impacted the economy of scripted. "In four short years, *Netflix* has done more to reshape the way that movies are made, distributed and consumed than perhaps any other single company in the history of the film business" (Lang, 2021b). On the artistic end, *Netflix* made Alfonso Cuarón's *Roma* and Paolo Sorrentino's *The Hand of God*. In action films they made *Extraction* with Chris Hemsworth and *The Harder They Fall* with *Idris Elba* (Lang, 2021b). Amazon reportedly committed over $450 million to five episodes of its *Lord of the Rings* series. In the event of a successful acquisition, storied *James Bond*-producing studio MGM may start to "make an impact with Amazon's weight behind it" (Kafka, 2021). Amazon Studios has seen growing international perspective amongst its producers: "It's

not like we have a remit of you have to make your shows travel but I think producers generally across Europe are becoming so much more sophisticated in wanting their shows to travel" (Brown, 2022). *Paramount Plus* made the huge hit *Yellowstone* with multiple spin-off series, such as *1883*.

- Studios – the 'big five' of Universal, Paramount, Warner Bros, Walt Disney Pictures and Sony Pictures – traditionally used their own equity to finance projects, against the cash flow from long-term rights ownership. Streaming can confound that model, because of the streamers' emphasis on powerful rights ownership positions. Where the studios own the streaming sites that are an eventual destination for the titles (*Disney+*, or *HBO Max* in the case of Warner Bros. Discovery) this is less of an issue.

- Brands put cash into productions against product integrations (see Chapter 13). *James Bond* film, *Tomorrow Never Dies*, raised over $100 million from Smirnoff, Heineken, Avis, Ericsson, Gateway, BMW, Brioni, Omega, and Visa. But academic research shows comedy is the best performer: with 23.48% of the product placement market share. The answer "may lie in the fact that humour brings attention to a brand and boosts liking of the brand" (Cha, 2016).

- Distributors determined the historic economics of scripted by phasing different transmissions between different platforms, called 'windowing.' That has been replaced by viewers finding the shows they want on their first run. "This is the inherent challenge with developing contemporary windowing strategies, as the introduction of online streaming video has exacerbated existing audience fragmentation to such a high degree, that a growing critical mass of buyers has the accessibility necessary to go to any medium in search of their preferred entertainment experiences." (Shay, 2015).

- Investors can provide capital and take positions in content, or the companies that produce it. Sometimes this is for tax mitigation. Increasingly private equity are taking direct stakes in production companies, attracted by perceived cash flow from streamer demand. "Investment firms have been on a spending spree, snapping up stakes in production entities, or financing new vehicles" (Weprin, 2022). US deals identified by *The Hollywood Reporter* in 2022 included Candle (backed by private equity firm Blackstone) adding *Fauna* producer Faraway Road to earlier purchase of Reese Witherspoon's production company (see below); Centricus buying a majority stake in Imagine Entertainment; and athlete LeBron James selling a stake in his SpringHill entertainment company to RedBird Capital.

- States and governments play a huge role in content production through tax rebates and other incentives. Australia, Canada and China all incentivise production. Germany offers 20% cash for the production expenses. French regional funds will go to 100% for the right project (Law, 2022). Britain gives 30% tax rebates to producers filming on location, rising to 40% if they post-produce as well. Combined with strong local expertise, the industrial effect is spectacular. Around London alone, in 2022 Leavesden studios was location for *Mission: Impossible 7*, *The Batman* with Robert Pattinson and the *Game of Thrones* prequel, *House of the Dragon*. Pinewood studios had a new *Indiana Jones* and two *Star Wars* series. Shepperton, *Netflix*'s UK base from 2019, had *Knives Out 2*, and Neil Gaiman's *The Sandman*; and Longcross had new *Doctor Strange* and *Captain Marvel* films plus a new series of *Band of Brothers* (Potton, 2021). Tax-based co-funding of scripted content is a subject so complex that it can only be briefly touched upon here; but any would-be producer should study it carefully.

Production execution

Once the financing is in place, the scripted project has to be shot. There is low opportunity for profit at the production stage, and every opportunity to lose money by going over budget. The more pre-planned the shoot, the more likely it is to be efficient. "If I have to go on set, I feel I've failed," Tim Bevan, at Working Title, has said, producer of titles like *Four Weddings and a Funeral* and *Bridget Jones' Diary*.

Chaotic sets are financially and ethically challenging. Consider this from the set of the 1976 Vietnam war film *Apocalypse Now*. "The Kurtz compound was finally ready. It was strewn with corpses, many of which were real, recalls Frederickson. "It turned out that the guy procuring the dead bodies who said he was getting them from a medical research lab, had actually been robbing graves." (Biskind, 1998).

The disaster on the set of the 2021 independent movie *Rust*, in which cinematographer Halyna Hutchins was tragically shot by a prop gun which should have only included blanks, is a benchmark of what can go wrong on a poorly-run set.

Distribution and monetisation

Implicit in the funding of films is a distribution and monetisation solution, which sets up an iterative relationship between the distribution channels. As one distribution partner or financier is added, the production changes to suit their needs, a process that can occur up to a dozen times whilst the full financing and international footprint of a film is created. Separate chapters on streamers and broadcasters explore this.

Scripted content as a category has been a remarkably consistent earner. In fact: "in the Great Depression, Louis Mayer, the head of MGM, was the world's highest-paid manager. Of the world's next 25 highest-paid executives, 19 were Hollywood studio officials" (Noam, 2019).

Producers, actors, investors and other participants monetise their efforts in three ways: upfront payment, backend payment or sale of equity.

Upfront payment

The safest return in scripted production is from fees from the budget, cash-flowed across the production itself and guaranteed, plus potentially a margin for successful delivery. Often the guarantee of upfront fees has a concomitant downstream effect of lowering the rights retained by a participant, but not always.

In streaming, the payment to the production company will amount to all production costs plus a fee on the total budget (negotiable but typically 5%) and a possible premium (up to 30% in exceptional cases, depending on negotiating advantage) beyond the budget, as a rights buyout. None of this is fixed: "Thanks to today's abundance of streaming options, TV has become a chaotic free-for-all that seems to get more expensive every year" (Cumming, 2021). Agents play a key role in the calibration of what deals are possible in the scripted economy, as information conduits between players, because they have transparency into all facets of deals across the media economy.

Backend payment

It is hard to accurately predict the success of a piece of scripted entertainment, because of unexpected upside and downside risk. As scriptwriter William Goldman said: "In Hollywood, nobody knows anything ... Every time out it's a guess, and if you're lucky, an educated one" (Goldman, 1983). The key to success is to balance the security of upfront payment against the unknowable upside of profit participation.

- "Occasionally, if you have a very hot property for which many of the studios are competing, you can force one of them – they hate doing it – into an uncrossed deal. This gives you the best of both worlds: the type of back-end terms that you would get from the independents and the worldwide distribution that you can get only from a major studio" (Eberts and Ilott, 1990).
- In 1983, *Paramount* was releasing a small movie which had cost $7 million to make, called *Flashdance*. "To show you just how much Paramount believed in the movie," reported one executive, Dawn Steel: "they sold off 25 percent of it to a private investment firm as a hedge against losses-a few weeks before it opened. They wanted to cover themselves in case it bombed." When it came out, critics hated it – but the public loved it. At the *Village Theater* in Westwood. "We paced all day and all evening watching this movie over and over again ... The manager ... saw we were nervous and he kept bringing us popcorn and soda ... The moment I'll always remember-is standing in back of the theater when, in the middle of the movie, an audience full of young girls stood up and began dancing in the aisles. I knew then that the movie worked, and that I'd participated." The movie ended up earning $90 million at the domestic box office (Steel, 1993).

Sale of equity, business or rights

Perhaps the best way to monetise a scripted production company is to simply sell it. (That is also true of other media sectors, particularly podcast makers and games makers.)

There was a boom in sale of UK production companies in the first decade of the twenty-first century after a regulatory intervention gave independent producers better rights. "Their principals were rewarded with large financial windfalls" (Paterson, 2021). Companies like Shine, Endemol, All3Media, TwoFour productions and many others were sold, some of them more than once, and often for tens of millions of pounds.

In the US, the windfalls were larger. Actor Reese Witherspoon's company Hello Sunshine sold to private equity in 2021 for a reported $900 million. Investors were attracted by her strong production slate (*Big Little Lies* and *The Morning Show*) and her *Bookjoy* book club; a bet that Reese Witherspoon could become the next Oprah or Martha Stewart, a personality around which media businesses can be launched.

But there is a problem with the model. The main customers for production businesses are streamers, who do not leave production companies with comprehensive residual rights in their output. The premium of up to 30% that they pay on production costs (see above) has a downside, which is that it cuts long-term equity value for the production company. "Unless they significantly amp up their their deal making they're not going to get ownership of these shows, and so you're not getting that long-term value" (Belloni, 2021).

Class discussion questions

- Why have streamers been successful in the Scripted content space?
- Imagine you had packaged a strong proposal for a TV drama series, and had interest from both a major streaming platform *and* a major cornerstone broadcaster. How would you approach each negotiation?
- As a scripted production company, you were able to option the rights to some best-selling Italian detective books. How would you turn that into a commercial proposition for global TV distribution?
- Lenin was mentioned at the start of this chapter. His successor, Stalin, learned that 90% of the films made in the previous year lost money, but 10% were hits. Stalin's answer was simple; next year only make the 10%. Is there any value to his strategy?

Cinema distribution: decline or reinvention?

Cinema was for 100 years the default distribution and monetisation channel for film, the leading content form within scripted. Now streamers have both challenged and surpassed it.

So is the cinema dying, or is it in the process of reinvention? We will look at the case for decline, the case for growth, and a middle ground where cinema is reinvented.

The case that cinema is in long-term decline

Cinema has lost the pivotal position it once had in the entertainment economy. It has failed to reinvent its business model and product offer in the era of digital, compared to radical solutions discovered by TV (streaming), music (streaming), newspapers (digital) and games (multiplayer).

Cinema attendance numbers have declining since 1948, when 1.4 billion cinema tickets were sold in the UK alone – as a result of first TV (1950s) and then digital distribution (2000s). Before the 2020–21 coronavirus pandemic, cinema admissions had already dropped in the US by about 6% in the prior decade.

- In February 2022, Italian exhibitors alone decried the closure of around 500 of the country's 3,600 screens (Vivarelli, 2022).
- Analysts predicted in 2022 that the US cinema footprint would shrink to some third of its then size, to 15,000 screens, on the back of box office that was 60% down from 2019 (Nicolau, 2022). In September 2022, cinema chain Cineworld reported that it was filing for bankruptcy.
- In 2021, major movies such as *Dune* and *Halloween* were released simultaneously on streamers such as *HBO Max* or *Peacock* – a move unthinkable even a couple of years earlier.
- Straight to TV/streaming movies, once thought of as low quality, can now be as big in size and talent as a theatrical blockbuster. As some kind of evidence of that, *Netflix* has been accepted as a member of the Motion Picture Association of America (MPAA) (Hancock, 2021).

The case that cinema will survive

Yet cinema remains globally powerful. It has scale, and its footprint is shifting. In Asia it is actually growing fast. And the cinema is still by far the best place to make serious money from a major movie.

Global box office in 2019 was $42.2 billion, of which U.S./Canada was $11.4 billion (Motion Picture Association 2020). There are 203,000 cinema screens worldwide. Cinema advertising is seen as premium, with high engagement, a mark of quality to advertisers.

Whilst in some countries cinema has contracted, in other countries cinema exhibition has grown.

- In China screens grew at a double-digit annual percentage rate every year from 2006–20, to over 82,000 screens, around 40% of the world's total (Statista, 2022). Other growth countries include Mexico, Brazil, Russia, Colombia, Indonesia and Turkey.
- Film production is going more global. India made 26.9% of global films in 2019, China now makes up 11.4%. Other production players are Japan (3.7% of global box office) UK (3.5%), South Korea (2.1%) and France (2.1%). The US made 9.1% of

global film production in 2019, but still takes 65.4% of box office takings (Hancock, 2021). If that revenue disparity starts to shift, so the balance of global revenues back to cinema may shift too, given cinema's higher growth in Asia.

- Even in Europe, cinema attendances actually grew by 34% between 2000 and 2019 across the 38 territories represented by the cinema trade body, the *Union Internationale des Cinémas* (UNIC, 2021).

Whilst the pandemic of 2020–21 pivoted distribution to streamers, when cinemas reopened, they did so with a title so big that it reminded studios and producers of the attractions of cinema itself. *Spider-Man: No Way Home* took over $800 million at the US box office alone, and $1.8 billion globally. It could not have generated those revenues without cinema, since the maximum that streamers will pay for a film is in the low hundreds of million of dollars. Therefore the biggest movies will still be incentivised to launch in the cinema.

- "The latest Spidey movie isn't merely a *deus ex machina*, something that swings in like a gift from the heavens to boosts ticket sales and popcorn purchases," said the editor of Hollywood trade newspaper *Variety*. "It's also a welcome reminder, after a brutal 22 months, that movie theaters can still create a kind of grand cultural happening that simply can't be replicated on *Netflix*" (Lang, 2021a).

The middle ground: a mixed entertainment ecology

In the debate around whether cinema will die or grow, the most likely outcome is: neither.

Cinema will survive, but with a shorter exclusive release window for films, smaller films moving to streaming, and cinema itself continuing becoming more global.

- In 2021, Warner Bros moved to put titles straight to its streaming service without first going on cinema screens in 2021 (partially driven by coronavirus). This created a backlash in the creative community, on which studios depend for their output.
- "Some of our industry's biggest filmmakers and most important movie stars went to bed the night before, thinking they were working for the greatest movie studio, and woke up to find out they were working for the worst streaming service," filmmaker Christopher Nolan, whose relationship with Warners dates back to *Insomnia* in 2002, said in a statement to *The Hollywood Reporter* (Masters, 2020).
- To some extent, Warner backtracked, as a *Variety* correspondent observed: "Warner's, as we know, spent the early part of 2021 writing big fat checks to everybody, and much of the rest of the year saying 'we're really committed to theatrical in the future, and we didn't really mean it'" (Masters, 2021). (Warner was later that year merged with Discovery to form entertainment conglomerate Warner Bros. Discovery. The new board cancelled a $90 million *Batgirl* movie late in post-production in August 2022.)

Distribution options in future

In the new reality of cinema, some movies will go to cinema and streamers simultaneously. (That is known in the industry as 'day and date.') There is "a changing relationship with a new type of consumer … the opportunity to explore new business models" (Kehoe and Mateer, 2015). The change will be to a more freestyle system where "studios are going to do whatever the heck they want to do with these movies" (Masters, 2021).

The evolution of the category was summed up by one leading industry analyst like this: "The truth most likely lies in a complex economy going forward: an adjustment to the 'windowing' strategy for movies, so that the release exclusivity in cinemas is shorter, and smaller films go straight to streaming" (Hancock, 2021).

Studios will decide how their content will be released. Exhibitors will seek to retain their slice of distribution, "an exclusive theatrical window … to preserve the cinematic experience and 'event' of theatregoing." The streamers will want content as soon as possible: "*Netflix* is no longer an auxiliary revenue source, but an original content powerhouse in its own right" (Henschel, 2020).

Even the shape of what is produced will be in flux as platforms change: director James Cameron announced in 2021 that he wanted make different versions of his future films – such as the *Avatar* sequence – for streaming and theatrical release.

Class discussion questions

- If you were releasing a mid-budget comedy movie, would you sell it to a streamer for a reliable fee, or would you take the risk of releasing it into the cinema for unknown box office returns? Why?
- Where you live, is cinema growing or shrinking? Discuss the statistical evidence.

AI technologies in scripted

AI has long been a staple of dystopian fiction, whether the murderous intent of *The Terminator* (1984) and *Ex Machina* (2014), the superior intelligence in *Her*, running hundreds of simultaneous affairs with besotted humans, or the impetus-sapping technology in *WALL-E* (2008). AI philosopher Stuart Russell identified that movie as emblematic of the risk that "humans become increasingly dependent on the Machine, but they understand less and less about how it works" (Russell, 2021).

Behind the camera, AI now has traction in scripted production at every stage of the value creation process; script selection, interactive storytelling, scriptwriting, virtual actors, virtual studio, post-production tools and special effects.

Some of the AI techniques that are on the edges of the industry in the early 2020s will go mainstream.

Voice application *Respeecher* claims to change a singing voice from male to female. And Israel technology *Deepdub* is able to simultaneously translate an actor's actual voice into another language – without need for a dubbing artist. "So the actor could be speaking Spanish, but it will look and sound like he's speaking English. And if you know that actor's voice, it will actually sound like that actor" (Gamerman, 2021).

Script selection

Tools use NLP (see Chapter 4) driven by neural networks to analyse the language and structure of scripts.

- *Cinelytic* offers a script review service (Cinelytic, 2021). The idea of such a process arrived in 2013 with the Worldwide Motion Picture Group, a $20,000-per-script evaluation service using the data of past performance of movie tropes to inform investment decisions – a form of training data. "Demons in horror movies can target people or be summoned ... If it's a targeting demon, you are likely to have much higher opening-weekend sales than if it's summoned. So get rid of that Ouija Board scene" (Barnes, 2013).
- *Scriptbook* analyses scripts in six minutes for its structure, assigning more than 400 parameters. "Most people believe that cast is everything, but we've learned that the story has the highest predictive value" the company says (supporting the academic research cited above on star power.) It claims selection success rates of 83% against human success (it says) at 27%. Back-testing against a historic data set of Sony titles from 2015–17, it said it successfully spotted 22 out of the 33 releases that would go on to lose money (Scriptbook, 2021).
- *RivetAI* uses deep learning/NLP to automatically generate storyboards and shot lists based on an uploaded script (RivetAI, 2022).
- Disney reportedly has *Deep Story AI*, its own in-house storytelling tech product (Cook, 2020).

Flexible/interactive storytelling

Interactive storytelling is a creatively high-profile segment, but economically niche.

- The TV series *Black Mirror's Bandersnatch* episode reportedly gave millions of story options to the viewer, who could take 40 minutes to complete the show if they got them right, or 90 if they didn't. Writer Charlie Brooker followed up with the animated show *Cat Burglar* (2022), an interactive game in which the viewer answers quiz questions to help the criminal *Rowdy Cat* rob a painting from a museum (Jeffries, 2022).

- The BBC has *StoryFormer*, a "flexible storytelling tool," allowing "content creators to string audio-visual sequences together in a way that allows the work to respond to audience interventions." It was used on the branching first person narrative *Philip 21*, tracking a man's experience of microaggressions ("Philip 21," 2021).
- AI philosophers are following the interactive movement. Of the robot bees from the *Black Mirror* episode, *Hated in the Nation*: "They aren't conscious. They don't hate people. They are precisely programmed by one person to hunt 387,036 specific humans, burrow into their brains, and kill them" (Russell, 2021).

Scriptwriting

Whilst produced scripted content projects have not been substantively written by AI yet, that is coming.

GPT-3, an Open AI autoregressive language model that uses deep learning, was used to continue the opening of Jane Austen's uncompleted 1817 novel, *Sanditon*. *GPT-3* provides text that is a statistically good fit, given the starting text – without supervision, or training. The original book has a couple travelling from Tunbridge towards the coast when their coach crashes. The language model wrote: "The gentleman was very little hurt, but the lady had two of her ribs broken, and sustained some other injuries, from which she did not recover for several months. She never saw her husband again." It's not what Jane Austen wrote, but it feels like it (Floridi and Chiriatti, 2020). NLP could be trained to replicate the style of any screen writer.

Virtual actors

Alongside fully synthetic metahumans, a practical iteration of AI could revolutionise actors' performances and economics, via voice. It can change both the language stars speak, and the lifespan over which they can speak it.

- If an actor were to not wish to turn up on set, they could now licence their synthesised voice instead. "Morgan Freeman would at least have revenue share and have control and licensing power … he could just type out what he wants to say … just say, 'Yep, put me in there, have me in there.' … And then the final cherry on top is with machine translation" (Harris, 2021).
- For that translation, Hollywood AI company Flawless digitally edits an actor's face so that they seem to be speaking any language into which they are dubbed. British director Scott Mann started the firm after being disappointed by dubbed versions of Robert De Niro in his 2015 thriller *Heist*. The system studies variations in head, neck and mouth movement, then re-calculates it in a new language (Knowles, 2021). This could create "individual actors who are far more empowered than they have ever been before" (Harris, 2021).

Virtual studio

Major scripted shows no longer have to shoot location scenes actually on location.

- With a virtual studio – a technology that uses platforms like the *Unreal Engine* from Epic Games – they can build them in pre production, with more realism in lighting, camera movement and foreground/background integration than the previous, Hitchcockian 'green screen' technology.
- An early adopter was Disney's *Star Wars* spinoff *The Mandalorian*, shot by Industrial Light & Magic on its LED StageCraft volume set in Los Angeles. Now it has a similar set at Pinewood Studios in the UK.
- Virtual studio shortens productions, with much less post-production and huge scale (Debbagh, 2021).
- But it is expensive: productions can reach $20 million or more per episode. In the UK *House of the Dragon*, HBO's prequel to *Game Of Thrones*, used a virtual production stage at Warner Bros, Studios, Leavesden. "Advocates insist that virtual studios not only allow more creative possibilities, but also save money, speed up workflows and make production more sustainable by reducing long-distance travel" (Dams, 2021).

Post-production tools

The editing process is an enormous consumer of time, money, data and other resources in scripted production.

A wide range of tools are coming on stream to help solve that.

- *Otter.ai* is a simple transcriber (of rushes, for instance) with timecode. Adobe's industry-standard *Premiere Pro* now has speech-to-text built in. *Descript* is an intuitive, all in one audio and video editing tool (Descript, 2021).
- *Simonsays* adds other tools and (it says) a five-fold increase in editing speed (SImonSays, 2021). "They all leverage AWS or Google or MS web services in the back end, so are cheap and efficient compared to the old way of doing transcriptions," says a specialist manager of large edit facilities. "We'll soon be assembling the edits like we would a Word document, but using even more AI tools to hone in on the elements that make up the story. Users could even train an AI in various storytelling methods, environments and camera setups to enable the fine tuning of the editing and shot selection based around these conventions."
- *Da Vinci Resolve 18* is the industry-default colour-grading tool. It has built AI applications into its workflow from the previous version: face refinement (like sharpening the actor's eyes, even on a moving camera), and scene cut identification (so the editor can edit the right set of images).

- In the *Magic Mask* tool, a convolutional neural network (CNN) is trained to follow a given subject through a clip, using pertained inference AI, and automating foreground and background adjustments (Bowdach, 2021).
- Video-matting models deploy a self-supervised generative adversarial network, using frames extracted from real unlabelled videos, to put participants from one video into a completely different one with complete realism. Combining that with Virtual Reality, producers could create radical leaps in interactivity.

Special effects

"So there's there's always this kind of race in being able to do something that no one else can" says an engineer at an effects company. "AI offers benefits primarily in two key areas: efficiency and effectiveness."

Rendering software and hardware from the real-time calculations required in the games industry will make special effects in movies much faster. A lot of the 3D assets that an effects team create for a major movie need to be rendered, which used to demand substantial compute. "Now there's Real-Time Rendering, using a game engine. That shift is going to move towards AI," says one specialist at a key London studio.

For all the technology, however, the key remains to make what you create relatable. AI systems designed purely as interfaces to appear in cutting-edge movies have actually been borrowed for real-world industrial design.

David Sheldon-Hicks has worked on movies from *The Batman*, *Dune*, *Bond*, *Ex Machina* to *Blade Runner 2049*. "Directors want to connect with the audience and their understanding of use of technology in aid of the world-building. And that's the mind shift that we as a studio have to make all the time. We'll have creatives that are on a feature film, and then they'll drop onto an automotive in-car experience that has to be extremely functional because it's all about human safety" (Sheldon-Hicks, 2021).

Class discussion questions

- Does AI represent a threat to the VFX industry through wider democratisation of production tools, or a business opportunity through increased high-end capabilities?
- Once the edit of a film has been 'locked,' how might it still continue to interact with AI technologies during its continuing distribution and monetisation?
- What is the business opportunity in the creation of virtual humans?
- At the production stage, what are the best AI tools available to the film producer?

CHAPTER SUMMARY

TABLE 10.1 Scripted producers have limited financial exposure, assuming that they offset the financial risk – to investors, distributors, broadcasters, streamers or studios – at the production stage

Scripted	Development	Production	Distribution	Monetisation
Business model	Significant investment in scripts.	Funded by customer (broadcaster, streamer) distributor (which may be the studio itself) or financial investor.	Broadcaster, streamer, cinema exhibitor or any 'windowed' combination – determined by financing.	Pre-determined by financing arrangement. Participants need to balance their upfront and backend participation.
Uses of AI	Script analysis.	Edit systems of all kinds, post-production and colourisation tools, audio effects, virtual humans, synthetic voices.	Heavy AI usage by streaming platforms in research, marketing, distribution optimisation.	Suppliers at present, plus optimisation of subscription revenues by streamers.
Value Creation	Strong script drives value into the financing and production phase.	Some value will be released in the production phase in return for services, but not outsized profit upside.	Where project sold outright to streamers, limited upside, but costs covered. Where upside opportunity retained, lower guarantee, but equity value uplift possible.	Function of ownership position and rights retention, monetisation can be long-term, including through equity sales.

BIBLIOGRAPHY

Barnes, B. (2013) Solving equation of a hit film script, with data. *New York Times*. [online] Available at: www.nytimes.com/2013/05/06/business/media/solving-equation-of-a-hit-film-script-with-data.html [Accessed 23 August 2022].

Baxter-Wright, D. (2022) Harlan Coben's Netflix shows. *Cosmopolitan*, 13 January.

Bay, W. (1988) What if E.T. died? Test audiences have profound effect on movies. *CNN*. [online] Available at: http://edition.cnn.com/SHOWBIZ/Movies/9809/28/screen.test/ [Accessed 23 August 2022].

Beattie, A. (2021) Why is the Star Wars franchise so valuable? *Investopedia*. [online] Available at: www.investopedia.com/articles/investing/102215/why-star-wars-franchise-so-valuable.asp [Accessed 23 August 2022].

Belloni, M. (2021) In Recode Media with Peter Kafka on Puck, sale of Hello Sunshine. [online] Available at: https://open.spotify.com/episode/3KuXKPJszGFPn2NB2LGefh?si=54186 2d4df5a4d66 [Accessed 23 August 2022].

Biskind, P. (1998) *Easy riders, raging bulls: how the sex-drugs-and-rock-'n'-roll generation saved Hollywood*. London: Simon & Schuster.

Bowdach, J. (2021) The 5 most powerful AI Tools in DaVinci Resolve (and when to use them). *Frame.io Insider*. [online] Available at: https://blog.frame.io/2021/09/27/davinci-resolve-ai-tools/ [Accessed 23 August 2022].

Brown, G. (2022) Conference interview onstage at Edinburgh TV Festival August 2022 by Georgia Brown, Head of Originals at Amazon Studio.

Burgos, J. (2021) The highest-paid *Succession* actor is exactly who you'd expect. *Yahoo*. [online] Available at: www.yahoo.com/lifestyle/highest-paid-succession-actor-exactly-000055657.html [Accessed 23 August 2022].

Cha, J. (2016) Product placement in movies: perspectives from motion picture firms. *Journal of Media Business Studies*, 13(2), 95–116. doi.org/10.1080/16522354.2016.1159802

Cinelytic. (2021) Cinelytic. [online] Available at: www.cinelytic.com [Accessed 23 August 2022].

Cook, G. (2020) AI's fairytale ending: the future of Disney storytelling. *Medium*. [online] Available at: https://medium.com/swlh/when-ai-meets-the-fairytale-ending-the-future-of-storytelling-is-disney-deep-story-325608a69cd8 [Accessed 23 August 2022].

Cumming, E. (2021) Goodbye to the golden era of cheap TV. *Financial Times*, 30 April.

Dams, T. (2021) Virtual studios: future of production takes shape. *Broadcast*. [online] Available at: www.broadcastnow.co.uk/tech/virtual-studios-future-of-production-takes-shape/5166 186.article [Accessed 23 August 2022].

Debbagh, A. (2021) Interview by Dr Alex Connock at National Film and Television School, 13 December.

Descript. (2021) *Descript*. [online] Available at: www.descript.com [Accessed 23 August 2022].

Eberts, J. and Ilott, T. (1990) *My indecision is final: the spectacular rise and fall of Goldcrest Films, the independent studio that challenged Hollywood*. New York: Atlantic Monthly Press.

Fischer, S. (2022) New scripted series hit record high following pandemic dip. *Axios*. [online] Available at: www.axios.com/2022/01/17/scripted-series-streaming-pandemic [Accessed 23 August 2022].

Floridi, L. and Chiriatti, M. (2020) *GPT-3*: its nature, scope, limits, and consequences. *Minds and Machines: Journal for Artificial Intelligence, Philosophy and Cognitive Science*, 30(4), 681. doi.org/10.1007/s11023-020-09548-1

Gamerman, E. (2021) Wall Street Journal Tech News Briefing In *AI May Be Voicing the Next Foreign Film You Watch*. [podcast] 8 October. Available at: www.wsj.com/podcasts/tech-news-briefing/ai-may-be-voicing-the-next-foreign-film-you-watch/420b5532-618c-4c79-89cd-510a8aa535a7 [Accessed 23 August 2022].

Goldman, W. (1983) Adventures in the screen trade: a personal view of Hollywood and screenwriting. New York: Warner Books.

Gupta, P. (2022) Streaming is driving a 'golden age' for Indian drama. *BBC News*. [online] Available at: www.bbc.co.uk/news/business-60873073 [Accessed 23 August 2022].

Hamsher, J. (1997) *Killer instinct: how two young producers took on Hollywood and made the most controversial film of the decade*. New York: Broadway Books.

Hancock, D. (2021) *Movie content tracker 2020*. London: OMDIA.

HarperCollins. (2019) www.harpercollins.com/blogs/press-releases/sony-pictures-entertainm ent-and-harpercollins-publishers-join-forces-with-elizabeth-gabler-and-entire-fox-2000-team-in-unprecedented-partnership

Harris, J. (2021) Towards Data Science In 2021: A Year in AI (so far) – Reviewing the biggest stories of 2021. Towards Data Science podcast 21 July 2021. Podcast https://open.spotify.com/episode/0mgLGLqeMtYcr5CBJINmOn?si=7f430decaf874e2d

Henschel, S (2020) Movie windows: adapting for the future. London: OMDIA.

Jarvey, N. (2018) YouTube to Pull Back on Scripted in 2020 Amid Ad-Supported Push (Exclusive). *The Hollywood Reporter.* www.hollywoodreporter.com/tv/tv-news/youtube-pull-back-scripted-programming-ad-supported-push-1164256/

Jeffries, S. (2022) Cat Burglar review – Charlie Brooker's note-perfect nostalgia trip for cartoon fetishists. *The Guardian*, 22 February. www.theguardian.com/tv-and-radio/2022/feb/22/the-cat-burglar-review-netflix-charlie-brooker

Kafka, P. (2021, 26 May 2021) In Why is Amazon Buying MGM? Recode Media. Podcast www.vox.com/recode/22451787/amazon-mgm-james-bond-streaming-netflix-analysis

Kehoe, K., and Mateer, J. (2015) The Impact of Digital Technology on the Distribution Value Chain Model of Independent Feature Films in the UK. *International Journal on Media Management*, 17(2), 93–108. doi.org/10.1080/14241277.2015.1055533

Kilian, T. and Schwarz, T. (2013) Spinning the Wheel: What Makes TV Series-Spin-Offs Successful? *Journal of Media Business Studies*, 10(2), 39–61. doi.org/10.1080/16522354.2013.11073563

Kim, D. H. (2021) What types of films are successful at the box office? Predicting opening weekend and non-opening gross earnings of films. *Journal of Media Business Studies*, 18(3), 214–34. doi.org/10.1080/16522354.2021.1887438

Knowles, T. (2021) AI steps in when dubbed words fail. *The Times*, 8 May.

Lang, B. (2021a, 30/12/2021) How Movie Theaters Fought to Survive (Another) Year of Turbulence and Change. *Variety.*

Lang, B. (2021b, July 2021) Netflix's Film Chief Scott Stuber Is Shaking Up Hollywood: 'The Movie Business Is in a Revolution.' *Variety.*

Law, R. (2022) Countries With The Best Film Incentives.

Masters, K. (2020, 7 December 2020) Christopher Nolan Rips HBO Max as "Worst Streaming Service," Denounces Warner Bros.' Plan. *The Hollywood Reporter.*

Masters, K. (2021, 24 December 2021) The Business In *Megabanter 2021: Streaming Wars get Real.*

Nicolau, A. (2022) Spider-Man a hit for cinemas but the web is still the future. *Financial Times*, 5 January.

Noam, E. M. (2019) *Media and digital management.* London: Palgrave Macmillan.

Nylund, M. and Mildén, P. (2012) New Strategies in Finnish Independent Television Production. *Journal of Media Business Studies*, 9(1), 85–99. doi.org/10.1080/16522354.2012.11073538

Paterson, R. (2021) Handmaidens of consolidation in the UK television production sector. *Journal of Media Business Studies*, 1–17. doi.org/10.1080/16522354.2021.1952037

Philip 21. (2021) www.bbc.co.uk/taster/pilots/philip-21

Porter, E. and Fabrikant, G. (2006) A Big Star May Not a Profitable Movie Make. *New York Times.* www.nytimes.com/2006/08/28/business/media/28cast.html

Potton, E. (2021) The death of Hollywood: why no one shoots movies in LA any more. *The Times*, 19 August.

RivetAI. (2022) *RivetAI.* www.rivetai.com

Russell, S. (2021) BBC Reith Lectures 2021 – Living with Artificial Intelligence. *BBC.* [online] Available at: www.bbc.co.uk/programmes/articles/1N0w5NcK27Tt041LPVLZ51k/reith-lectures-2021-living-with-artificial-intelligence [Accessed 29 August 2022].

Schneider, M. (2019, 23 October 2019) 'It's an Explosion': Inside the Rising Costs of Making a Scripted TV Series. *Variety.* https://variety.com/2019/tv/features/cost-of-tv-scripted-series-rises-1203378894/

Scriptbook. (2021) *Scriptbook*. www.scriptbook.io/#!/

Shay, R. (2015) Windowed Distribution Strategies for Substitutive Television Content: An Audience-Centric Typology. *International Journal on Media Management*, 17(3), 175–93. doi.org/10.1080/14241277.2015.1099526

Sheldon-Hicks, D. (2021, 16 October 2021) *Interview* [Interview].

SImonSays. (2021) Simon Says. www.simonsays.ai

Statista. (2022) Annual growth of the number of cinema screens in China from 2006 to 2019 with an estimate for 2020. www.statista.com/statistics/260293/number-of-cinema-screen-growth-in-china/

Steel, D. (1993) *They can kill you but they can't eat you* [sound recording]. Simon & Schuster AudioWorks.

UNIC. (2021) *Annual Report 2021*. https://unic-cinemas.org/fileadmin/user_upload/Publications/2021/UNIC_annual_report_2021.pdf

Vivarelli, N. (2022, 21 February 2022) Italian Exhibitors Decry Death of 500 Screens as Box Office Fails to Reignite. *Variety*.

Weprin, A. (2022) Why Hollywood Is Private Equity's New Money Machine. *The Hollywood Reporter*. www.hollywoodreporter.com/business/business-news/private-equity-hollywood-1235076358/

CHAPTER 11

Entertainment

A rapidly globalised content footprint

....

INTRODUCTION TO THE SECTOR

Entertainment TV is a mass market media product invented in the 1950s with the classic game show *The Price is Right*, which has survived and thrived into the 2020s.

Even in the era of streaming, digital media, crypto, micropayments, gamification and content personalisation, entertainment TV remains both commercially powerful and culturally relevant.

An academic survey in Spain showed that in TV "entertainment is the characteristic that the audience most consistently associates with the concept of quality" (Bayo-Moriones et al., 2018).

Programmes can become a society-wide provider of relatable 'water cooler' moments. Liu Wei played the piano with his feet to win *China's Got Talent* in 2010. Homeless orphan Sunbong Choi was runner-up on *Korea's Got Talent* in 2011, by revealing an extraordinary voice for Italian opera.

Global programme formats – *Who Wants to be a Millionaire (*licensed to 102 territories*)*, *The Voice (*originating in the Netherlands, 70 territories*)*, and *The Great Bake Off* (with over 40 local versions including Japan and Kenya) – can become an emotional and visual *lingua franca* around the world. They bring people together both on a national and sometimes global level, through shared experience.

Range of entertainment TV

The entertainment genre spans a wide spectrum, from studio-based 'shiny floor' shows like *Dancing with the Stars* to quiz shows like *The Weakest Link* (49 territories). It stretches from game shows like *Family Feud* (in the US, Nigeria and 66 other countries) to factual entertainment like *MasterChef* (65 versions). It covers physical game

DOI: 10.4324/9781003213611-14

shows like *Ninja Warrior* or *Total Wipeout* and reality shows like *Big Brother*, *Love Island* and *Married at First Sight* (31 countries). When shows work, they work really well: "Every single night at 9pm on ITV2 is this show for eight weeks, that more people watch than they watch anything else," ITV Managing Director, Kevin Lygo, told the Edinburgh TV Festival in August 2022. "We should all take great joy that if you get the right show, they will watch it."

It is a market of globally transferrable IP; "a market for intangibles such as programming concepts and production expertise, which today cross borders as much as finished programmes" (Chalaby, 2012).

Entertainment TV properties, often long-running formats iterated in multiple countries, are a recognisable feature in the $219 billion (PWC, 2021) creative economy of broadcast TV and (to a lesser degree, since major players focus on drama and documentary) streaming. Entertainment formats are therefore a globally scaleable and distinct business model.

THE VALUE CREATION MODEL

A good global format has universal themes (dating: *The Bachelor*) and strong visual identity (the boardroom in *The Apprentice*).

There is a distinction between paper ideas, productions, sellable tape and sellable formats, which maps to the media value creation construct used in this book.

- In development, TV ideas are created 'on paper' (like *Undercover Boss*, where the title says it all).
- Production starts when a channel or streamer funds the project.
- Distribution occurs when that provider puts it on air.
- Monetisation occurs at the moment of production, but becomes more scaleable when the show displays either an ability to sell around the world as a tape of the original production, or as a recognisable structure and brand DNA capable of being replicated and sold as a format, for local production in multiple territories.

Most programmes do not become transportable tapes or formats, and therefore lack international scaleability – because their content is too country-specific, for instance, named after a particular host.

A show can also be suitable for tape export but not format – like the syndicated *The Oprah Winfrey Show* which depends on her involvement. Or a show might not be exportable because it is just not very good.

But when formatting works – business success follows. Studio-based *Dancing with the Stars*, has been licensed by the BBC in 60 countries and is still on air in 40% of those countries, despite being nearly 20 years old. *Dancing with the Stars in* Mongolia is as recognisable as the UK original version, with the same format, glitter ball, ballroom and judges holding scoring paddles. The same brand recognition is true of *The Masked Singer* or *American Idol*.

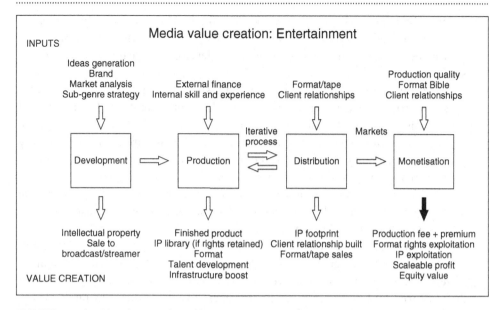

FIGURE 11.1 In entertainment, the critical moment of value generation is when distribution success generates further production, or further production territories, at high margin

Development

In TV production companies, intellectual property and value are created in the development process.

Everything starts with analysis (or at least awareness of) the market for ideas. A strategy develops around which sub-genre within the market will be targeted – game show (*Deal or No Deal*), factual entertainment (*Farmer Wants A Wife*), cookery (Spain's *My Mom Cooks Better Than Yours*), property (Denmark's *Buying Blind*), quiz shows (*Are You Smarter Than...?*), physical game show (*Fort Boyard*).

Modest investment may be required. The brand equity of the producer and production company (say, Fremantle) will be absolutely critical to the credibility of the ideas and the likelihood of a sale. The exact same idea, pitched by a novice producer versus an experienced show runner, will have dramatically different chances of success.

The key output at this phase of the media value creation process is intellectual property (like the simple conceit behind the long-running daytime cookery format *Come Dine With Me*, in which four individuals competitively invite each other for dinner).

Development slates may contain dozens of ideas, out of which a low percentage (as low as 1%) of ideas emerge as saleable. The process by which an idea from a slate is sold is not algebraically predictable. To the frequent dismay of investors new to the space, there is no reliable equation translating investment into TV development into projected return.

- A format can have a single creator (like *Big Brother*, from Jon de Mol) or many. It can be derived at no cost through simple inspiration, or the subject of significant investment, usually through hiring of a development team, and creation of sizzle tapes.
- Anyone, anywhere can have the idea for a TV show, but their achievement is illusory. The true sales determinant is not the idea, but reputation. The number of individuals trusted by broadcasters to deploy the investment needed to produce an idea and turn the paper idea into valuable reality, is barely 50 people in any given country. Thus a paradox of value creation in TV formats is that the industry is open to all, yet also one of the most exclusive and elitist clubs in the business world. (A pitch from showrunner Mark Burnett, who produced *Survivor*, *The Voice*, *Shark Tank* and *The Apprentice*, will be taken more seriously than the exact same ideas pitched by anyone else, which might not sell at all.)
- Production company size offers development advantage and disadvantage. Small boutiques can be more creatively nimble, but international production companies have a history of successful delivery – like Fremantle delivering *Got Talent* in 26 territories and access to more broadcasters to whom they can pitch shows. "Large companies can create development funds to push formats internationally. For instance, once *Pointless* had become an established game show on BBC2, [production company] Endemol funded the pilot for France Télévision's [version] using the old BBC set" (Chalaby, 2012).
- A successful creative team will require a combination of talents – some veteran, some early career, as seen on the long running US network NBC's show *Saturday Night Live*, first made in 1975. "What you learn from Lorne [Michaels, the show's executive producer] … is that by design the show has ups and downs, mostly because it's impossible to constantly be rolling out. So you have people who are veterans, people who are new … that just means that in a year or two, you'll have a great many people who are completely coming into their own" (Miller and Shales, 2014).

Nature of TV formats

At inception, a TV format can be as short as a single line, often a question.

- How will amateur celebrities fare in a ballroom dancing competition if paired with a professional? (The BBC format *Strictly Come Dancing* or – internationally – *Dancing with the Stars*.)
- What will happen if people are left to fend for themselves on a desert island and face daunting challenges? (The *Survivor* format, created by UK producer Charlie Parsons, first produced in Sweden, but most known for US and Australian iterations amongst 58 territories.)
- Can you recognise the celebrities behind the elaborate costumes in a live singing competition? (South Korea-originated *The Masked Singer*, now a global hit, see below.)
- Could a marriage sealed the very moment people first met ever succeed? (*Married at First Sight*, 26 territories so far.)

- What would happen if you turned the cameras around and watched ordinary people at home watching TV? (*Gogglebox*, 39 countries).
- Can I pitch my business idea and get instant investment? (Originated as *The Tigers of Money* (Japan) before being localised as *Dragons' Den* (UK) and *Shark Tank* (US). It is now in 43 territories.)

Details of formats

Entertainment TV formats are both simple conceits that can be summed up in a single sentence, as above, and complex style guides whose replication is governed by detailed factors – from colour palette, design and music, to the detailed rules and the balance of live action and recorded packages. (These are called the 'Bible' of a show.)

The Great British Bake-Off, devised by the UK's Love Productions, now owned by Sky, was first on BBC Television. It then moved to Channel 4, though remains distributed globally as a format by BBC Studios. It is, at first glance, a simple amateur baking competition. But each format point is brand-critical. The judges are tough (Paul Hollywood and Pro Leith in the UK) but the presenting team (Matt Lucas and Noel Fielding) are about comedy and empathy. Design (bunting, a tent) points to a non-specific moment of rustic nostalgia. Music (light orchestral), the collaborative spirit of the competitors, and the fact that everyone is eating cakes, all point to family viewing. Focus is on use of natural ingredients rather than pre-mixed ones (there are no shortcut brands like *Nutella* on set) and they are spoken of in prescribed language including *Signature Challenge*, *Showstopper* and *Star Baker*.

Creative sequencing of a TV format is multifaceted.

- Origination: it begins with either spark of originality, or twist on an established format genre: Dutch format *The Voice* was a singing competition like *X Factor* or *Pop Idol*, but with judges who could not see the contestants until they committed by turning their chair around. From that initial idea is born a complete creative world, including format points as discussed above.
- Specification: format points exemplify precision. *The Weakest Link*, for instance (distributed by BBC Studios in 46 countries), has strong similarity between each version, down to studio design (amphitheatre-style and the 'tunnel of shame') gameplay (banking, cash and voting off 'the weakest link') and even the way the host host signs off each show with a wink.
- Adaptation: formats can be flexible: *MasterChef* (distributed by French company Banijay) varies between its US, Australian and UK versions, in design, style, duration and even key plot beats.

Business model of development

The key costs prior to the idea being written and pitched are usually salary to development staff.

Once an idea is codified in a document, it can be traded, but it has little value as a theoretical document. Standard practice is for TV entertainment show ideas to make money only when actually produced, and for entertainment formats when they have been a proven ratings success somewhere. However, there are exceptions: 2022 quiz show *The 1% Club* sold in three territories (France, Israel and Netherlands) before airing in its originating territory, the UK.

- Territories where producers are protected by legislation (in the UK since the *2003 Broadcasting Act*) to maintain rights in negotiation with broadcasters, are favoured for format launches. This enables production companies to retain transportable, protected IP. Countries exporting the most formats in 2020 were UK (42.1%), Netherlands (10.3%) and South Korea and US (each 10.1%) (K7, 2021).
- As in other branches of entertainment, shows which can bring the pedigree of being part of a franchise can gain an early advantage. *The Voice Kids* sold in 42 territories. *Beat the Chasers*, from the UK's ITV Studios, sold in four territories in 2020, outperforming its original parent show, *The Chase* (K7, 2021).

Production

At the production phase of value creation, the key inputs are production finance and the skill and credibility of the producer. Key outputs are finished product (a show or a series), IP, potentially scaleable formats, talent development, ancillary revenue opportunity and a potential infrastructure boost to the wider firm.

Production of TV formats requires broadcaster or streamer funding, whether in the studio (as with most 'shiny floor' shows such as *The Masked Singer, Idol*) at a fixed external location (reality formats like *I'm a Celebrity Get Me Out of Here* or *Love Island*) or at multiple locations (factual entertainment *The Apprentice, The Amazing Race* or *Undercover Boss*). For the format creator, value creation occurs when the core idea is translated by a producer (or 'show runner') into a first iteration, and broadcast.

- Having production and broadcast in-house was a factor behind producer Jon de Mol (major shareholder in production companies Endemol and Talpa) and his success using the Netherlands as a creative platform.
- Production skill is the *sine qua non* of long-term success: UK/US group Argonon has proven effectiveness, which enabled it to licence and iterate *The Masked Singer* format for ITV in the UK, even though it had not originated the format.

Major buyers of TV formats fall into four categories.

- State-run, state-owned channels (like China Central Television, or CCTV, in China).
- National (but non-state) public service broadcasters such as Britain's BBC, Germany's ZDF, Italy's RAI or Japan's NHK.
- Commercial TV networks, such as *ITV* in the UK, *Globo* in Brazil, *Televisa* in Mexico, or *SBS* in Korea (Noam, 2019).

- Streamers, such as *Netflix, Roku, Disney+/Hulu, HBO Max, Peacock* and *Amazon Prime Video*.

Production issues

Shows are cash-flowed by the client channel or streamer, topped up with advances from distributors of either the tape or the format for potential reiteration.

- When it comes to the production of live programming, live interaction can create challenges. Providing a 'return path' gives producers real-time audience data, but creates IP challenges if the return path material is used in the show.
- There was a dispute between rights holder *ITV* and *YouTube* over revenues generated by views of the *Britain's Got Talent* contestant Susan Boyle in 2009. Other disputes have involved integration of social media content into a show. "In 2009, basketball team owner Mark Cuban complained that *ESPN* had collected and published a selection of his personal tweets without permission and questioned whether that use constituted copyright infringement" (Green and Erickson, 2014).

Entertainment TV has been slower than film, music and games to embrace AI tools in the creation process. But their use is coming. Deepfake technology (which uses generative adversarial networks, or GANs) was deployed in 2020 by *South Park* creators Trey Parker and Matt Stone in their satirical show *Sassy Justice*, including a deepfaked Donald Trump interviewing other fake characters such as Jared Kushner, or former vice president Al Gore (Heaven, 2020).

Distribution

At the distribution phase of the value creation process, the key inputs are the tape and formats of shows. Key outputs are a footprint for the firm's IP, client relationships and sales.

Independent production companies strive to multiply the number of broadcasters, streamers, genres and territories with which they trade. This requires that they build their network across geographically disparate customers. There are two effective approaches to this reputation-building marketing challenge.

- First: merge indies into international entities – 'Super Indies' – with local production in multiple genres and territories; for instance, the UK-based All3Media.
- Second: work with distributors.

Distribution is the engine of super-indie growth. Distributors (whether owned directly by the super indie, or independent) market shows to TV channels in return for licence fees. The world's largest distributors in 2020 by sales volume were Fremantle (23.8%, with four of the top ten best-selling formats, including *Game of Talents*) and BBC Studios (12.7%.) The *Indian Idol* format iteration of the *American Idol/ Pop Idol franchise* has nine different iterations in local languages in a single country.

Components of distribution

Of the two elements to distribution of an entertainment show – the tape and the format – format bears the most value. (In fiction, by contrast, it is tape – see Chapter 10.) To reiterate: the tape is the finished version of a show, whilst the format is the recipe for how to make a new version of it.

Distributors tailor content to market needs.

- From an academic viewpoint: "Psychographic labels are … applied using the dominant characteristic of each audience type and then matched to a specific windowed distribution strategy" (Shay, 2015).
- From a content makers' viewpoint: the priorities are the level of upfront distributor advance, and their ability to control the iteration of their format in global versions, via 'flying producers.'
- A format's preponderance to sell internationally depends on ratings in its home market, plus the footprint of the network the original show is on. A bigger launch (especially the US, but also UK, Holland, South Korea, Australia and other key territories) creates a bigger global splash. As one producer said: "It's like we're on a rocket ship" (Zakarian, 2021). Australian format *You Can't Ask That* went to 47 territories in a short time span.

Making IP travel is the way super-groups transform local shows into super-formats.

- Endemol turned *Das Hairdresser* into *The Salon* and *Now*, and *Neverland* into *Fear Factor*. Shine transformed *MasterChef* and BBC Worldwide powered up *Dancing With the Stars* (Chalaby, 2012).
- Some territories are strong consumers of overseas formats. In 2020, for the third year on the run, Vietnam was the biggest formats buyer in Asia – particularly of game shows, with 25 formats bought. One factor driving format imports in the country was the proliferation of both private channels, like *VieChannel*, and production companies, such as *Dong Tay* (K7, 2021).

Monetisation

At the monetisation phase, the key input is tangible success of the production: "Only if a TV show can meet the interest of the viewer can further revenue be achieved from the advertising market" (Lis and Post, 2013). "People are starting to actively look for a TV show that is independent of the network brand itself."

The main outputs are production fee/margin, plus format rights for future exploitation (unlikely in the case of streaming sales) and enhanced equity value for the firm.

Format monetisation

Formats are like Silicon Valley start-ups. Only a small percentage ever receive funding, and the vast majority fail – but, like hit start-ups, a successful format is transformatively profitable. (Another similarity is that both are funded externally to those who create them: start-ups by venture capital, TV formats by broadcasters.)

The TV formats business model is akin to betting on a set of start-ups with low odds of success, but high returns if they do succeed. In venture capital, the business model is based on a few of the financial bets placed having sufficient returns to pay for all the rest. This philosophy necessarily means that the projects invested in have to be scaleable paradigm shifts, in order that the winners do produce sufficiently high-powered returns (Mallaby, 2022). The same logic applies in TV development: the really big wins tend to be from formats that are a paradigm shift – like *Big Brother*.

A production budget pays a production fee or margin to the production company of around 10%. This is a different entity (or at least division, in the case of in-house production, like ITV Studios at ITV) from the broadcaster or streamer, or a division of the same entity.

Once a show has gone into production, the format creator or owner will make profit, irrespective of its first series success, via three routes.

- Service provision as show runner or on-screen talent, like Simon Cowell on *Pop Idol* and *American Idol*, on a per-show or per-series basis. Cowell's onscreen judging defined the format itself: "Last year, I described someone as being the worst singer in America. I think you're possibly the worst singer in the world."
- Ownership of the production company, which generates profit from overhead budget lines, post-production or licence fees.
- Production fee margin on a cost-plus basis on the budget as a whole, varying from 5% to 15%.

Budget principles

Budgets per hour vary by territory, genre and show. A major shiny-floor show in the US market costs more than $2 million per produced episode, sometimes significantly more. In major European markets, a figure of $1,000,000 per episode is more typical. In smaller markets; the cost is as low as $100,000.

There are additional potential profit lines from shows.

- Recharges of budgeted edit facilities, office overhead, graphics teams, and other staff who are already sunk costs elsewhere. Producers can extract (say) another 10% of profit to the production. Ownership of the titles music and other repeatable assets adds profit.
- Brand integration revenues, substantial in some territories (e.g., Latin America) accrue to the broadcast platform and do not generally profit the producer.
- Merchandising opportunities (e.g., e-commerce from online distribution) can make money for the channel.

- Long-term monetisation and value generation derive from international scale-ability of the format. The UK commercial broadcaster ITV Plc's production arm, ITV Studios, in 2021 reported "strong growth" and 58% of its revenues from outside the UK. "Globalising our formats: 7 formats in three or more countries, up from 6 in 2020, including *The Voice* sold in over 70 countries, *Love Island* sold in 21 countries and *The Chase* format sold in 17 countries." Those formats were entertainment/shiny floor (*The Voice*), reality (*Love Island*) and game show. Pipeline development included *The Void*, *Rat in the Kitchen*, *Moneyball*, *Ready to Mingle*, *Bling* and *Sitting on a Fortune*. Margin improvement came from cost savings and "high margin license deals" (ITV, 2021).

The best-selling genres in formats in 2020 were Game Show/Quiz (12.1%), Reality Competition/Studio (9%) and Game Show/Challenge (8.4%) (K7, 2021).

Tape sales and 'windowing'

The other principle way to monetise TV shows is by selling the tape.

This is done by networks and distributors through 'windowing,' where release periods for finished content (a tape, not a format) are bought by channels or streamers. A show might start on a network, move to a secondary channel, sell internationally, then end up on channels in off-peak slots, or on a streamer as an 'acquisition' (see Chapter 7).

- A big show – like *Friends* (a comedy rather than an entertainment show) can be sold repeatedly, entering 'syndication nirvana.' Through massive repeat transmission in non-premium slots, it reportedly earned its three creators alone – David Crane and Marta Kaufman, and co-executive producer, Kevin Bright – at least $550 million (Chmielewski, 2021). Warner Brothers Television also profited.
- Ideally a producer sells both format and tape simultaneously in each territory. Dating series *Married At First Sight Australia* originated in Denmark, was supersized as a format by Endemol Shine for Australia's *Channel Nine*, and then sold in 2021 to *A+E Networks* for Japan and Korea (Layton, 2021). Even the taped *Married At First Sight Australia* was one of the best-performing shows on UK's *E4*; and in 2021 the newly produced UK version became the channel's highest-rated series launch ever.

Tape windowing and format permit a complex ecology of revenue-maximising sales from core IP. How to balance windows is a complex art: "The decision of whether to window the release of substitutive television programming, and if so how long the delay should be, is a complex one with a multitude of variables … and an incredibly high-risk threshold" (Shay, 2015).

Class discussion questions

- If you were a finance director looking to evaluate performance in a TV development team, how would you do that?
- What are the arguments for and against selling the tape of an entertainment show from your home territory to a global streamer?
- What are the strengths and weaknesses of the entertainment-focused super indie business model in the age of globalised, streamed content?
- Devise a TV entertainment format which might be capable of scaling to multiple series, involving the use of a centre-of-town food market as a location. Be ready to pitch the show to a potential broadcaster client with a set of 6–8 slides.

Analysis: *The Masked Singer* (South Korea)

In 2021, *The Masked Singer* was the world's best-selling format. How did that happen?

The King of Mask Singer format was created, and first produced, by the entertainment division of Munhwa Broadcasting Corporation (MBC) the South Korean production and broadcast company. In 2020, South Korea was the third-placed country in the world for format exports – on the same level as the United States (K7, 2021). Previous hits had included *I Can See Your Voice* and *Grandpa's Over Flowers*.

In the format, mystery celebrities wearing fantasy costumes perform to a studio audience, whilst a panel of judges attempt to identify them from their voice and other clues, through choreographed rounds, each providing 'reveals' (to the chanted catch phrase "take it off"). There is an eventual celebrity winner, but the real joy is in taking part at all.

- Some 90% of MBC's entertainment shows are produced in-house. The show went on Korean TV in 2015 as a pilot with Kim Sung-too presenting, and then as a series, on air every Sunday since.
- As soon as the format was on air, MBC sold it to China, where MBC had succeeded with other formats such as *Where Are We Going, Dad?* But shortly afterwards, the Chinese regulators cut the number of foreign formats permitted, in favour of local originations. A local lookalike show competed with the official version, stopping progress for the title in China. But it was bought in Thailand, where it added higher production values, and became *The Masked Singer*.
- A major breakthrough came when Rob Wade, then running *Fox TV* in the US, bought the show. It became a major hit. The first series was hosted by Nick Cannon, and produced by indie Endemol Shine. Series 2 it moved to Fox's in-house studio, Fox Alternative Entertainment. Panellists included singers Nicole Scherzinger and Robin Thicke. Stars included Mickey Rourke and – improbably– Rudy Giuliani, Donald Trump's former lawyer. The *Masked Singer* achieved the highest Nielsen ratings for any non-sports show, in its first year.

- Optioned in over 50 countries, the show also prospered in Mexico, Australia, France, Germany, Colombia, Estonia, Bulgaria, Portugal and the UK, described by trade press as: "a perfect fit for today's audiences who want the sizzle of a well-produced music show and the opportunity to join in live debate during the broadcast, on the sofa or on social media" (K7, 2021).

Class discussion questions

- *The Masked Singer* format owners did not control the format's implementation worldwide as closely as some other titles are policed – instead allowing the format to flex significantly in international markets. Was MBC right to be flexible or did that approach jeopardise long-term value?
- What conditions in the South Korean market accelerate format and other creative innovation?

CHAPTER SUMMARY

TABLE 11.1 Key themes in this chapter

	Development	Production	Distribution	Monetisation
Entertainment				
Business model	Low investment. High chance of failure.	Cash flow by broadcast/ stream client, production margin available.	Sales agents.	Format sales generate consultancy fees and licence fees.
Uses of AI	Low involvement as yet. Future possibility for avatars informed by machine learning.	Virtual studio, sophisticated edit technologies.	Low AI usage. Format sales are an in-person B2B sale offering few automation gains.	Rights management (music and artist contributions) may be manageable with data science.
Value Creation	Potential for high return to equity owner, low probability of delivery.	Production margin accrues to production company and revenue to channel.	Scale economy yields outsize profits if achieved, but in highly competitive market space.	High profitability at the format sales stage with low marginal cost generates strong value.

BIBLIOGRAPHY

Bayo-Moriones, A., Etayo, C. and Sánchez-Tabernero, A. (2018) Revisiting Quality Television: Audience Perceptions. *International Journal on Media Management*, 20(3), 193–215. doi.org/10.1080/14241277.2018.1538146

Chalaby, J. K. (2012) Producing TV Content in a Globalized Intellectual Property Market: The Emergence Of The International Production Model. *Journal of Media Business Studies*, 9(3), 19–39. doi.org/10.1080/16522354.2012.11073550

Chmielewski, D. (2021, 28 May 2021, 04) How 'Friends' Generated More Than $1.4 Billion For Its Stars And Creators. *Forbes*. www.forbes.com/sites/dawnchmielewski/2021/05/28/how-friends-generated-more-than-14-billion-for-its-stars-and-creators/

Green, T. and Erickson, K. (2014) For Those Playing along at Home: Four Perspectives on Shared Intellectual Property in Television Production. *Journal of Media Business Studies*, 11(2), 1–23. doi.org/10.1080/16522354.2014.11073578

Heaven, K. H. W. D. (2020) *The year deepfakes went mainstream*. www.technologyreview.com/2020/12/24/1015380/best-ai-deepfakes-of-2020/

ITV. (2021, 28 July 2021) ITV Plc 2021 Half Year Results Presentation. www.itvplc.com/~/media/Files/I/ITV-PLC/documents/reports-and-results/ITV%20Plc%202021%20Half-Year%20Results%20Presentation.pdf

K7. (2021). Tracking the Giants: The Top 100 Travelling Unscripted TV Formats 2020–2021. https://k7.media/wp-content/uploads/2021/04/K7-Special-Report-Tracking-the-Giants-2020-2021-1.pdf

Layton, M. (2021) 'Married At First Sight' lands in Japan and Korea as Red Arrow strikes global sales for dating show. *Television Business International*. https://tbivision.com/2021/03/16/married-at-first-sight-lands-in-japan-korea-as-red-arrow-strikes-global-tape-sales-recommissions-and-format-option-for-dating-show/

Lis, B. and Post, M. (2013) What's on TV? The Impact of Brand Image and Celebrity Credibility on Television Consumption from an Ingredient Branding Perspective. *International Journal on Media Management*, 15(4), 229–44. doi.org/10.1080/14241277.2013.863099

Mallaby, S. (2022). The power law: venture capital and the making of the new future. London: Penguin.

Miller, J. A. and Shales, T. (2014) Live from New York: the complete, uncensored history of Saturday Night Live, as told by the stars, writers, and guests (Revised edition. ed.). New York: Little, Brown and Company.

Noam, E. M. (2019) *Media and digital management*. London: Palgrave Macmillan.

PWC. (2021) The PwC Global Entertainment & Media Outlook 2021–25. www.pwc.com/gx/en/industries/tmt/media/outlook.html

Shay, R. (2015) Windowed Distribution Strategies for Substitutive Television Content: An Audience-Centric Typology. *International Journal on Media Management*, 17(3), 175–93. doi.org/10.1080/14241277.2015.1099526

Zakarian, G. (2021). Variety Strictly Business podcast. https://open.spotify.com/episode/7uaUoAs1ztk9mAo7ujTdMd?si=b9a345163f524cdd

CHAPTER 12

Factual

Merged distribution channels have changed a traditional industry

....

INTRODUCTION TO THE SECTOR

Factual is a fast-moving and high volume presence in the global media landscape.

- Apple reportedly paid $25 million for the documentary *Billie Eilish: The World's a Little Blurry* (Vourlias, 2022) in what *The Hollywood Reporter* called a "massive payday."
- When streamer *Discovery+* launched in 2021, it signed up 15 million paying subscribers in the first quarter alone – the fruits of what its CEO David Zaslav called a "shock and awe" global rollout strategy (Whittingham, 2021) to challenge the scripted streamers with the power of unscripted TV.
- Discovery generated $2.4 billion of free cash flow in the year 2021. Its factual networks constitute a huge portfolio – *Discovery Plus, Discovery Channel, HGTV, Food Network, TLC, Investigation Discovery, Travel Channel, Turbo/ Velocity, Animal Planet, Science Channel* and *OWN* (*Oprah Winfrey Network*) – merged as of 2022 with WarnerMedia's factual portfolio including *CNN* and *TruTV* to form Warner Bros Discovery (Mass, 2022).
- And of the UK's £1.48 billion television content exports in 2019–20, 48% was from sales of factual programming, such as natural history show *Seven Worlds, One Planet* or science series *The Planets* (Morgan, 2020). There was strong sales to streamers too, nearly 44% of the UK's TV revenues.
- Georgia Brown, Head of European Originals at Amazon Studios, told the Edinburgh TV Festival in August 2022 that when she started in the role: "Everyone was very obsessed with drama and the golden age of drama. And so I thought, actually the bigger opportunity for us in that white space was absolutely

DOI: 10.4324/9781003213611-15

moving quickly into unscripted." (A 'white space' in business is a market segment with low competition.)

But take the reductive approach that "the social responsibility of business is to maximise its profits" (economist Milton Friedman in the *New York Times Magazine*, 1970) and an inconvenient truth emerges. Unlike in entertainment TV – factual production rarely builds fortunes for producers.

A bespoke, B2B production model, it rarely achieves scale economy where production is a sunk cost, making marginal sales equal marginal profit, as games or music do. A 2021 *International Documentary Association* survey found that 75% of documentary makers have a second job to make a living (Vourlias, 2022).

There is also more supply than demand. With over 41,000 attendees, more documentary makers may have attended the (hybrid) 2021 Sheffield Documentary Festival (DocFest, 2021) than actually have full time work in the UK industry.

Social good

But factual has another vital function – social good and democratic transparency. In an era of disinformation and democratic challenge, factual changes minds. Some companies build a 'dual bottom line' of profit and social change into their business model, like documentary company Participant Media (*Flee*, *A Most Violent Year*, *American Factory*, *The First Wave*) founded in 2004 by social entrepreneur Jeff Skoll "with a commitment to producing entertainment with socially relevant themes."

In 2022, political scientists at UC Berkeley and Yale paid 304 *Fox News* viewers to watch seven hours per week of *CNN* for a month. By the end, their views were not as right-wing – ten percentage points less likely to believe that President Joe Biden was 'happy' when police officers were shot (Gabbatt, 2022).

Factual programmes and films drive democratic transparency and other environmental and scrutiny objectives. *Seaspiracy* (2021) exposed the damage done by the fishing industry. *Collective* (2021) exposed healthcare fraud through the investigative work of Romanian newspaper *Gazeta Sporturilor*. *Crip Camp: A Disability Revolution* told the empowering story of a Summer camp for teenagers with disabilities. Chilean documentary, *The Mole Agent*, was based on undercover reporting at a retirement home on suspected 'elder abuse.'

- Factual can provide new perspectives, like *Netflix*'s 2020 inspiring film *My Octopus Friend* asking about humans' perceptions of sea creatures. Or it can show extraordinary exploits, like *Free Solo* (2018) with Alex Honnold climbing 1,000 metre rock faces in *Yosemite*, without ropes. Or it can take a populist approach to enhance understanding; Fremantle's UK production company Naked-produced 2022 show *Planet Sex* for *BBC Three* and *Hulu*, presented by actor Cara Delevingne to explore topical issues in sexuality; *Netflix*'s *Down to Earth with Zac Efron* travelled the world with a wellness expert finding sustainable living solutions (Barraclough, 2021).

- Factual tells more diverse stories than regular TV or other media, like Waad Al-Kateab's *For Sama* (2019), about the female experience of the Syrian war. The *Apple TV+* series *They Call Me Magic* told the story of Magic Johnson's (initially difficult) relationship with his gay son, to a mainstream sports audience (Hailu, 2022).
- Factual can viscerally alert the world to climate change. Ex US vice-president Al Gore made ground-breaking environment documentary *An Inconvenient Truth* in 2006. Germany's Fremantle-owned production company UFA made a documentary series *Arctic Drift* tracking a climate research expedition. (Whittingham, 2021) Silverback Films made *Earthshot: How to Save our World*, with a Prince William prize for projects to repair the planet (Barraclough, 2021).
- Factual can introduce viewers to culture. "The BBC's commitment to premium factual, arts and classical music programming is unique in the UK and central to our public service mission" (Holland, 2021).

Like many media sectors, factual combines both intensely fashion-driven stylistic trends, and timeliness universality.

Putting that succinctly, US documentary maker Ken Burns, known for archive-based TV series *The Vietnam War* (2017), *The National Parks: America's Best Idea* (2009) and *The Civil War* (1990), said: "Storytelling is the future of storytelling" (Swisher, 2021).

Sector in evolution

Before streaming, factual TV production and documentary features did not belong together in a textbook chapter. One shot film for TV sets, the other for cinema seats. The streamers changed that.

- On terrestrial TV in the UK, inflation-adjusted spend on factual programmes dropped by 21% between 2006 and 2020, to £483 millio. (OFCOM, 2021). But over the same period demand for first-run programming from international buyers (mostly streamers) more than doubled.
- Streamer demand for populist, feature-length documentaries like *The Great Hack* (2019) or *The Rescue* (2021), and substantial factual series like *Netflix*'s *The Tinder Swindler* (2022), pulled producers on both sides towards what a well-funded, combined genre in the middle.
- Success with streamers brings risk of over-commercialisation of factual, with insatiable demand for populist fare like *Netflix* crime series *Tiger King*, or an entire genre of drug barons programmes; *Cocaine, The Legend of Cocaine Island* or *Cocaine Cowboys* (all also *Netflix*) and many more. Fremantle's global head of documentaries Mandy Chang argued in April 2022 that it was important for filmmakers to have creative freedom with their subject choice, and not to default to high-budget, commercial projects (Vourlias, 2022).

Scale of factual industry

Factual programming features on channels from major broadcasters (the UK's BBC, CBS in the US with its long running *60 Minutes* series, Japan's NHK, Germany's ARD, Australia's ABC) to niche providers like *Smithsonian* or *History*, as well as subscription streamers like *Paramount+* and now broadcasters like the UK's *All4*.

- Factual creates robust international titles like *Top Gear* (BBC) or *Duck Dynasty* (2012–17), and is especially strong in key sub-genres like natural history programming, like *Seven Worlds, One Planet* (BBC). (The genre borderline between factual and entertainment, a genre known as factual entertainment, is ill-defined at both edges in entertaining but factual formats like *MasterChef*).
- Broadcasters with so-called FAST/AVOD channels (see Chapter 8) seek content in volume to fill airtime cost-effectively. Cheaper than entertainment or scripted, demand for factual is growing. It can also travel as tape (as opposed to format, see Entertainment section in Chapter 11) which makes costs lower and delivery faster.
- Factual is a business delivered by small production units, often combined into wider at-scale international businesses like broadcasters (such as Discovery or the BBC) or super indies. There is almost no such thing as a factual 'set' to visit in the way way as there are scripted sets. A factual crew is sometimes just a person with a camera phone, but they are not 'creators,' because their monetisation and distribution model is entirely different from *YouTube or Instagram*.
- France-based super indie Banijay owns 20 production companies in the UK alone, of which many make factual content, including Tiger Aspect (*The Home Show*), Workerbee (*Idris Elba's Fight School*), Dragonfly (*One Born Every Minute*), IWC (*Location, Location, Location*), RDF (*My New Greek Life*), Remarkable (*Your Garden Made Perfect*) and Shine TV (*Rick Stein's Cornwall*). Banijay's COO Peter Langenberg told a December 2021 conference that they planned acquisitions of still more – adding Natural History output too: "there is a demand for it from broadcasters and streamers."
- Major European producer/distributor Fremantle bought 12 Nordic factual production companies in a single 2021 deal. This focus on small, cellular production units, even when within larger corporations, gives the genre its dazzling intellectual eclecticism. Fremantle's 2021 slate spanned Chiwetel Ejiofor-hosted water-scarcity documentary *Day Zero*, Samuel L. Jackson project *Enslaved – How it Feels to be Free*, and jazz film *Oscar Peterson: Black & White* (Whittingham, 2021).

Factual is a solid, sustainable and relatively simple business to understand. Compared to the more granular, project-based scripted film distribution, factual series can be commoditised for channels with large schedules.

- In a single deal, UK distributor *All3Media* sold 50 hours of factual programming to a single Thai cable/satellite operator, *TrueVisions* (Blichert, 2018).

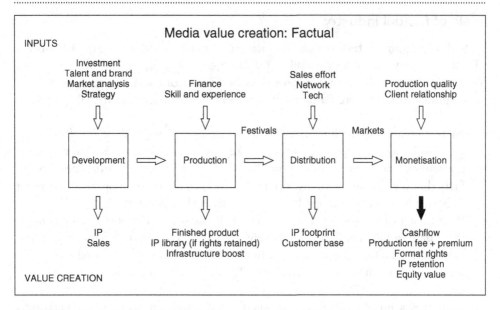

Media value creation: Factual

INPUTS

Investment
Talent and brand
Market analysis   Finance   Sales effort   Production quality
Strategy   Skill and experience   Network   Client relationship
                                                                  Tech

⇩   ⇩   Festivals   ⇩   Markets   ⇩

| Development | ⟹ | Production | ⟹ | Distribution | ⟹ | Monetisation |

⇩   ⇩   ⇩   ⬇

IP   Finished product   IP footprint   Cashflow
Sales   IP library (if rights retained)   Customer base   Production fee + premium
                     Infrastructure boost   Format rights
                                                                                    IP retention
VALUE CREATION   Equity value

FIGURE 12.1 Factual titles are generally low volume. They can scale as tape sales, but at lower prices than scripted. They are less likely to scale as formats than entertainment shows

THE VALUE CREATION MODEL

Development

The first priority for a factual production company or producer is understanding of the market in which they aim to participate. Who is buying or funding projects, and what are their project selection considerations? (Those are sometimes couched vaguely by commissioners, to the frustration of producers, with platitudes like "surprise us," "we want edgy content" and so forth.)

From that market analysis will be born a positioning strategy: what content does this production company have the credibility, and the market, to sell? A factual company without journalistic credentials will not be able to sell a current affairs documentary to a significant channel, because of the legal and delivery risk.

From there, the principal source of factual content and ideas generation is journalistic storytelling combined with creative spin. (*Tiger King* was a factual story told like an entertaining thriller. *RuPaul's Drag Race* – now on Season 14 – is borderline factual and entertainment.)

- Whether a programme is about fishing in Alaska (*Deadliest Catch*, 2005, 15 seasons), lorry driving in Canada (*Ice Road Truckers*, 11 seasons) or notorious disappearances (*Unsolved Mysteries*, *Netflix* 2020) the determinant factor in factual is that underlying story material is real.
- Documentary maker Ken Burns observed: "*Ecclesiastes* says, 'What has been will be again, what has been done will be done again, there's nothing new under the

sun,' which means human nature doesn't change. So any time you tell a story in the past, you've actually activated the best teacher I know to understand the present" (Swisher, 2021).

Key outputs at this stage are IP in the form of worked-up ideas (a development slate) and actual sale of those ideas to broadcast, streamer or foundation/funder clients.

Selling factual programme production is a B2B marketing challenge, dependent on personal connections and knowledge of often arcane and non-transparent commissioning systems. Broadcasters and foundations nonetheless have a 'job to be done' (Christensen, 2016) in terms of audience and any regulatory requirements or social performance objectives on their network or foundation, and it is the documentary maker's goal to be market-led, and provide a project which credibly satisfies those needs.

From a marketing perspective, there are numerous sub-genres within factual. A non-exhaustive set of examples includes:

- *Specialist Factual*: "the genre that explores and explains the world and makes us think about it differently," as the UK's Channel 4 describes it, with shows like *Things We Won't Say About Race* or *SAS: Who Dares Wins* (Channel 4, 2011).
- *Natural History programmes*: covering the natural world, with demand high from effective syndicates of major channels, large budgets and production periods up to four years in length: for instance, six hours of *Frozen Planet II* (2022), eight hours of *Planet Earth III* (2023) from the BBC.
- *Polemic documentaries*: these can make an impact in cinema, streaming and TV: Michael Moore's *Roger and Me* (1989) or *Fahrenheit 9/11* (2018); or *Inside Job (2010)* about the 2008 financial meltdown (which won a 2011 *Academy Award*).
- *Music documentaries*: which drive global viewing on streamers through their wide appeal. Kanye West's three-part documentary *Jeen-yuhs* broke on *Netflix* in February 2022, continuing a long tradition. Classics of the genre include *Metallica*'s *Some Kind of Monster* (2004) with a heavy metal band going into therapy, or director Asif Kapadia's *Amy* about Amy Winehouse (2015), or Beyonce's *Homecoming* (2019) (Grierson, 2021). In the international market, celebrity itself is a sales tool: like Idris Elba's *Mandela, My Dad and Me* (2015).
- *Docudramas*: these are factual projects but with heavy components of drama, often where there is no possibility of access. The documentary *Gun No. 6* traced a single weapon which had been used in 11 shootings and three murders in the UK (BBC, 2018). The filmmakers worked with convicted criminals to reconstruct the shootings. Other good examples from the BBC are *Armada: 12 Days to Save England* and *House of Saddam*, about Saddam Hussein. Because of the drama component, docudramas can be more expensive than normal factual TV.
- *Purpose-led documentaries*: for instance, countries have private or public funds allocated to serving specific social or linguistic groups. Scotland has *BBC Alba* for the purpose of keeping the Gaelic language alive. It has made factual projects like *An t-Uisge/Rain Stories*, or *An Cuan Sgith (The Minch)* with low absolute

viewing numbers, but valuable alternative rationale. In 2021, *lorram*, the first theatrical documentary shot entirely in Scots Gaelic, set in a fishing community in the Outer Hebrides, was supported by *Screen Scotland* and *BBC Alba* (OurCreativeVoice, 2021). Also in 2021, Canada launched its second channel in an indigenous language. *Uvagut TV* broadcasts in Inuktut, which has 35,000 speakers across the country (Warner, 2021).

Production

Whatever the strength of their idea, the factual producer needs cash upfront to go into production. Key inputs at the Production stages of the value creation process are therefore external production finance, and the internal skill and experience to deliver the project effectively. Key outputs are the finished product (a programme, series or documentary film), a contribution to the firm's IP library and a potential infrastructure boost to the firm via allocation of production expenses towards central costs and equipment. (For instance, the firm may buy edit suites or cameras for a production, and then retain them afterwards as a sunk cost, for use, effectively for free, on other productions.)

- Production takes place in very small units, typically five or fewer people on set (and often just a solo filmmaker) plus a modest support staff in the production unit, if they are even well resourced enough for that.
- The resources available to the documentary maker – money – are directly related to the nature of the end distribution client. The bigger the channel, the more money there is, in broad terms.
- Whilst it is possible to start filming a documentary production without broadcast/streamer funding, it is usually a bad idea tactically. Lack of interest at the start of a project rarely translates into interest on delivery, and a finished project is an 'acquisition' to a buyer, which they would expect for a fraction of the cost of a pre-production commission.
- The exception to this rule is where extraordinary access is achieved during production, and strong editorial value is demonstrated with actual tape. For instance, 2022 documentaries from Kanye West (*Jeen-yuhs: A Kanye Trilogy, Netflix*) and *Janet Jackson (A&E)* were each shot for some four years before a major distribution deal was then announced.
- With a budget in place, the production company covers costs through recharge of lines on a production budget: staff, travel, office overhead related to the project, hire or purchase of shooting equipment, edit equipment, time, insurance (a significant cost) and other lines. The producer's objective is to not be out of pocket for the period of production, but this is not always achieved.
- Producers then typically earn a production fee margin on the budget, of around 10%. Ostensibly their profit, in reality this is used at least in part to offset central costs, including overheads and staff costs for unfunded development

periods. This model applies to the thousands of small production companies (the UK's *PACT*, *Producers Alliance for Cinema and Television*, has 500 members alone).

Production budgets per hour vary very significantly in factual.

- Basic documentary production for a European broadcaster or major international channel (like *Discovery* of *Nat Geo*) is in the approximate range of $120,000 to $350,000 per hour.
- Feature documentaries can be far higher, because of high archive or talent costs, often related to the buyout of footage and music for global usage on streaming platforms.

Distribution and monetisation

In the distribution and monetisation phases of the media value creation process in factual, key inputs are client relationships and production quality. Key outputs are IP, building client relationships, production fee, format rights and a potential enhancement to equity value.

- Rights matter. The value creation opportunity in the factual business model is to deliver the show to the core territory or customer, making the production margin, whilst retaining enough IP ownership to scale the property internationally at a profit through further sales.

The challenge is that the core funder also sees potential international and secondary window sales as an opportunity to recoup their original investment, and having taken the cash flow risk, will drive a hard bargain on rights of their own.

- A streamer, or major international network like *Discovery* or *A&E Network* is likely to seek a rights buyout. Loss of bargaining position in this zero sum game further squeezes the producer's profit opportunity.

Funding and monetisation are inextricably tied to the distribution channel(s), which have five main types: mainstream broadcaster/streamer, foundation/sponsor, commercial sponsor (see also Chapter 13 on content marketing production), distribution investor or self-investing directly monetised specialist website. We examine each in turn below.

Broadcaster/streamer

The closer the broadcaster is to paying the full cost of the production, the more rights they take, up to and including full buyout. The advantage of full buyout for them is that they can play the show unlimited times on their networks with zero or (if there are residual rights holders, e.g., music performance rights) low marginal cost.

Diversified and constantly evolving programming strategies are the norm in the industry, as audiences tire of a given sub-genre of content.

- The Hearst Corporation owns channels *A&E*, *History* and *Lifetime*, amongst other media assets; "experimenting, placing bets, taking risks, and failing fast are necessary in any strategy mix, pushing the boundaries for not only a corporation, but also the marketplace itself (and emerging ones, too)" (Palomba, 2018).
- Niche streamers can be more eclectic in their factual tastes than conventional broadcasters. Teremoana Seguin, MD of Hong Kong's Harbour Rights told a trade publication: "Overall, traditional broadcasters seem to play it safe and acquire the same genre as they always do, in any given territories, while platforms are generally more open and often consider history and science. It's really the niche VOD services focusing on documentary and factual only which drove the demand, regardless of genre or type of programs" (Layton, 2021).

Foundations

In the world view of the production company, foundations are a better bet from a rights perspective, but of limited financial utility.

- Typically – such as the *Ford Foundation*'s *Just Films* – they put funding into a project against wider ESG or other societal objectives that they are looking to achieve, rather than a profit motive. "We support independent, documentary film, video, and emerging media projects that explore timely social justice issues" (Ford, 2022).
- Foundations may not drive as hard a bargain as broadcasters on rights, not least out of awareness that they may not be fully funding the project and will need to leave rights on the table to entice broadcast or distribution investment clients to enter the project as part of a syndicate of funders.
- Some examples of such funding options include the *Miller/Packan Documentary Film Fund*, which gives $200,000 per year to between 6 and 12 projects. *Points North* offers six documentary makers a mentoring programme. *Film Independent Los Angeles* invites up to five factual projects to join an intensive funding market every November. The *Pare Lorentz Documentary Fund* backs feature length films. The *IDA Enterprise Documentary Fund* backs contemporary stories with cash and support. There are many more, but the aggregate is still piecemeal in effect, and the size of grants small compared to the commercial sector.

Commercial sponsor

Many corporations back factual branded content projects to further their wider brand management objectives.

- Austrian drinks company *Red Bull* funds its own production company, which gives it the scale and right ownership to run its own online channels. It produces content like *Markus Eder's The Ultimate Run – The Most Insane Ski Run Ever Imagined*, launched in November 2021 (see Chapter 13).
- Filmmaker Ken Burns works closely with US public broadcaster PBS (Public Broadcasting Service), which is funded by donations and corporate sponsors and balances its lack of resources with artistic freedom to its contributors. Burns has had films funded by sponsors such as (until 2009) General Motors, whilst retaining artistic freedom.
- Burns has said: "With my track record, I could go to a streaming service or a premium cable thing and say, I'm making a film on the Vietnam War, I need $30 million, and I'd walk out of it with $30 million that day. There's just no question about it. But they wouldn't give me 10-and-a-half years, which is what it took us to make it. And so what I've said about PBS for years is that it has one foot, tentatively, in the marketplace and the other proudly out. And that part that's proudly out permits it, over the course of its decades, to be actually disproportionately committed to underserved communities and listening to voices that aren't usually heard in the mainstream, until the mainstream is shamed by events" (Swisher, 2021).
- The PBS network was, however, criticised in 2021 by 140 factual filmmakers for alleged insufficient of diversity in its commissioned projects, on which the network, in response, vowed to improve (Wicker, 2021).

Distribution investor

Professional investors back projects upfront which they think will sell in the (usually) international markets, as tape. They take a slice of rights which they think are marketable, often as top-up for the international dimensions of projects which have been core-funded by a first tier of broadcast clients.

- Sometimes for a major factual or natural history project there can be an effective syndicate of 4–5 major international clients (*BBC, NHK, TF1* and so on) backed by a distribution investor which plans to aggregate the rest of global demand once the show is made, and takes a commission on sales as well as preferentially recouping its advance.
- That investor could be the distribution arm of one of the broadcasters (e.g., in the case of BBC natural history programming, BBC Studios). Or it could be a fully independent investor, for instance, British documentary investor *Dogwoof*.
- Distributors of factual TV stay close to shifting market demands. During the global covid pandemic of 2020, Canada's Blue Ant International noticed a spike in demand for "factual programming that provides escapist content, DIY and cooking themes, travel series and high-impact documentaries." In a year of lockdown, nature documentary, *A Wild Year On Earth*, was therefore a big seller (Layton, 2021).

Directly monetised specialist website.

A relatively new category of investor in factual content is that of businesses built on the creation of their own end-to-end value chain, without going through external distribution or channels at all.

A good example is the *Masterclass* brand, founded in 2015:

- With over $225 million funding for short courses from global celebrities, it advertises heavily on *Facebook*, and self-distributes on a niche streaming model.
- Celebrities recruited include sports star Serena Williams, chef Gordon Ramsay, Disney's ex-CEO Bob Iger, directors Jodie Foster, Spike Lee, Ron Howard, and Judd Apatow, actors Samuel L. Jackson and Helen Mirren, writers David Mamet and James Patterson.
- *MasterClass* has claimed growth of up to 1,000% per year for its innovative model. True to the ESG priorities of the wider factual sector, it has given away socially beneficial programming for free, for instance, around *Black History Month*, with leaders like Kimberle Williams Crenshaw and John McWhorter (BOTWC, 2022).
- The project is a bridge between the factual content industry and the fast-growth EdTech (education technology) market.
- Founder David Rogier said: "A lot of it was thinking about how do you bring the joy back to learning," and "If you talk to most people about did they like school, the answer is 'No.' If you ask people if they like learning, the answer is, 'Of course' " (Rogier, 2021).

Sale of the company

Like in games and podcast creation elsewhere in this book, possibly the best way to monetise factual TV is to sell the company making it.

- UK channel ITV bought *The Garden* for a reported $27 million plus earnout in 2013, and TwoFour productions in 2015.
- Germany's ZDF Enterprises bought Dutch factual distributor Off the Fence in 2019, for its production skills, and catalogue of more than 6,500 hours of programming across wildlife, science, history, travel and lifestyle. (They did not state the price.)
- Again, factual is not the most lucrative sphere. In animated scripted content, for instance, UK-based eOne was acquired by toy company Hasbro for $4.6 billion, on the back of its Peppa Pig and PJ Masks children's franchises – an order of magnitude higher than any factual deal (Westcott, 2021).

AI technologies in factual

In 2021, documentary filmmaker Ken Burns said of digital transformation:

> I didn't move to computer editing for 10 years after my colleagues had. I didn't leave film until 10 years after that, although most of my colleagues had abandoned it for digital. Because I did not want the technological tail to wag the dog. That's the problem just with my own dynamic.
>
> (Swisher, 2021)

He is indeed in a minority. AI is one of the staple subjects of documentary features and, like all of video production, is starting to play a role in the creative process.

- *Netflix's Coded Bias* (2020) exposed the data privacy infringements of AI training models for a wide population, as well as the civil rights dimension of racially biased facial recognition systems – topics collectively characterised as 'algorithmic justice'(Kantayya, 2020).
- *Unseen Skies* (2022) explored the AI tools that are changing everyday lives (Fuente, 2022).
- *Netflix's The Social Dilemma* (2020) examined the power of algorithmic recommendation in influencing negative behaviours.

AI technologies are chipping away at both the workflow and the output assets of factual TV.

- The BBC is working with universities on 'object based media,' with fragmented assets capable of being viewed in any combination by viewers to create individualised storytelling, "as large as the audio or video or as small as an individual frame" (Miller, 2021).
- In Scotland's River Ness, an AI system was used underwater by the BBC's *Springwatch* and *Autumnwatch* team to spot salmon as they swam upstream. "An 'Anomaly Detector' generated feature vectors from each recording, driving evaluation of whether the recording fits the general trend of those previously seen from a particular camera or whether it is an 'anomaly,' and therefore more likely to be of interest" (Judge, 2021).
- With terns, the anomaly detector picked out clips such as the birds turning an egg over. Later iterations used external cloud-based infrastructure (Computing and Networks at Scale or CANS) to increase analytical, video and sound quality (see Chapter 8 for more examples of BBC AI technology).
- In documentary production, machine learning has been used to clean up sound on 50-year-old archive footage in the 2021 *The Beatles* documentary, *Get Back*, made by *Lord of the Rings* director Peter Jackson: "We developed a machine learning system that we taught what a guitar sounds like, what a bass sounds like, what a voice sounds like. In fact we taught the computer what John sounds like and what Paul sounds like. So we can take these mono tracks and split up all the instruments [so] we can just hear the vocals, the guitars … That that allows us to remix it really cleanly" (Woerner, 2021).

- Elsewhere, on a chimpanzee conversation research project, for decades, video has been captured, offering "immense potential for answering biological questions that requires longitudinal data." But the cost of manual labelling is too high. So by combining facial recognition with face tracking using convolutional neural networks Oxford researchers were able to build a social network graph for a group of chimpanzees over time. They could also do automated audiovisual behaviour recognition in wild primates, using body detection, tracking and behaviour recognition (Bain, 2022).

Class discussion questions

- What kind of factual TV formats do you think would be most internationally scaleable? What examples can you find of global scaled formats, and what are their key format points?
- Conversely, what kind of factual TV shows sell internationally as finished tape? If you were developing factual TV for international sale, which sub-genres would you focus on?
- What is the threat to the veracity and credibility of factual TV from Artificial Intelligence technologies? How can the industry mitigate that threat?
- Devise an idea for a new, factual TV format which uses Natural Language Processing and/or Computer Vision as a format point.

Analysis: *Noma Projects*

Who has the right to make factual TV? What strategies enable market entry into factual production? And is it best to enter as a generalist, or a specialist producer? This is fascinating case around how a business can leverage a pre-existing reputation in a different field, to enter the factual market with a specific offer.

Noma is a three-star *Michelin* restaurant in Copenhagen, Denmark, led by founder and head chef René Redzepi, that in 2021 was recognised, for the fifth time, as the number one restaurant on the planet. "One of the most coveted restaurants on the planet, Noma and its founder, Redzepi, are known for creating New Nordic Cuisine and inspiring an entire generation of chefs the world over" (The World's 50 Best Restaurants, 2021).

Noma has been careful with brand extensions so as to not dilute its purpose or equity through franchise or other subordinate operations. It has not followed the path of "traditional" celebrity chefs and restaurants. Instead, *Noma* has made an adjacent move – into the creation of high-end factual TV.

Interviewed at Oxford in 2021, then Chief Operating Officer Ben Liebmann said:

Noma is a restaurant whose influence is far greater than the 75 people that it serves five days a week. Going well beyond the four walls of the restaurant, television allows us to share the purpose and values that have underpinned the work and success of Noma over the last twenty years. One of the similarities between hospitality and entertainment is that it is heavily dependent upon human capital, and upon the human experience as guests.

(Ben Liebmann, 2021)

Going into TV

"Two years ago Rene Redzepi and I decided to establish a media company ... We decided to go about this to create – or to ask the question of *could* we create – premium original content that was platform-agnostic."

They were looking to produce documentary content of a particular kind, and on a particular business model, content that Liebmann said was "more than *Noma*, more than entertainment, that was entertainment with purpose and impact at the core."

They started the media and rights business in January 2020. Liebmann outlined how the production would begin.

It's the beginning of a journey, for us to leverage the platform that we have, the soapbox that we have been afforded, to try to still to tell stories that would at the same time entertain as they would inspire and create hope and change. Because we believe, like companies like Participant Media out of the US, that that is going to be a key part of where entertainment goes.

It has produced socially issues-informed projects, such as *Contagion*, *An Inconvenient Truth* (with Al Gore) and *American Factory* (Participant, 2022). Participant describes 'double bottom-line filmmaking': "doing well by doing good."

Liebmann continues:

After a year of kind of finding our feet and deciding who we wanted to work with, we wanted to build this business in partnership, rather than take it on board ourselves. We formed a partnership with Endeavor Content [a Los Angeles-based production company created by a major talent agency] and we began building a development slate – our portfolio of ideas.

Up and running

- In February 2022, *Apple TV+* announced the order of an 8-part docuseries from Redzepi and the filmmaker Cary Joji Fukunaga [director of *Beast of No Nation*, *True Detective* and *No Time to Die*].
- Narrated by Redzepi and called *Omnivore*, the series would tell "the story of humanity and the planet through eight defining ingredients" (Otterson, 2022) and "look at the world through the lens of food, and explore how food binds and defines us, powers politics, shapes our beliefs, explains our past, and forecasts our future" (Middleton, 2022).

- The series was to be produced by Film 45, Noma Projects, Parliament of Owls and Endeavor Content.

Class discussion questions

- Do you agree it was an effective brand extension for Noma to launch a TV company? Look up the work they have done, watch it if you can, and evaluate how it fits with the brand of *Noma*.
- Discuss whether in your view a Participant Media-style model of factual producer with a 'dual bottom-line' in both profitability and social good is (a) achievable and (b) a sensible business strategy in general.
- Identify another situation where a brand of any kind has entered the production of factual TV content by leveraging its reputation external to the industry, in the same way that *Red Bull* (action sports) and *Noma* (food) have done. What leverage did they bring to bear? What was their operating model? Have they been successful?

CHAPTER SUMMARY

TABLE 12.1 Key themes in this chapter

Factual	Development	Production	Distribution	Monetisation
Business model	Low investment in ideas generation, possibly some spend on sizzle tapes or demo shooting of subject	Cash flow by broadcast/streamer client, production margin available	Channels streamers, in-house or third party sales agents	Tape sales for producers if back-end retained. Long-term exploitation of titles if rights bought out.
Uses of AI	Some AI tools starting to be used in research and data analysis.	Significant AI tools in mechanics of. production and post-production	Low AI usage, except by streamers and broadcast video-on-demand platforms for marketing	Little use as yet
Value Creation	Potential for return on equity if sale is made	Production margin accrues to production company.	Library ownership accrues equity value to either production company or channel/streamer	Modest long-term value from ownership of factual titles relative to other media genres

BIBLIOGRAPHY

Bain, M. (2022, 16 February 2022) *Automated Video Understanding* [Interview].

Barraclough, L. (2021) Broadcasters turn to documentary series and factual shows to inform, inspire and entertain. *Variety*, 11 April.

BBC. (2018) How dramatic reconstruction transformed the documentary. *BBC Arts*. [online] Available at: www.bbc.co.uk/programmes/articles/hTpnDmGXV219Wd5MWGXw1p/how-dramatic-reconstruction-transformed-the-documentary [Accessed 27 August 2022].

Ben Liebmann, C., Noma. (2021, July 2021) *Interview, Oxford* [Interview].

Blichert, F. (2018) Extra: sales updates for All3Media International, looking glass. *RealScreen*, 7 November.

BOTWC. (2022) Masterclass releases more than 50 free lessons in honor of Black History Month. *Because of Them We Can*. [online] Available at: www.becauseofthemwecan.com/blogs/culture/masterclass-releases-more-than-50-free-lessons-in-honor-of-black-history-month [Accessed 27 August 2022].

Channel 4. (2011) Specialist factual. *Channel 4*. [online] Available at: www.channel4.com/press/news/specialist-factual [Accessed 27 August 2022].

Christensen, C. M. (2016) *Know your customers' "Jobs to be Done."* Harvard Business Review. [online] Available at: https://hbr.org/2016/09/know-your-customers-jobs-to-be-done [Accessed 27 August 2022].

DocFest. (2021) Sheffield DocFest 2021: Festival Report. *Issuu*. [online] Available at: https://issuu.com/sheffielddocfest/docs/sdf_report_spreads [Accessed 27 August 2022].

Ford. (2022) Our grants: just films. *Ford Foundation*. [online] Available at: www.fordfoundation.org/work/our-grants/justfilms/ [Accessed 27 August 2022].

de la Fuente, A. M. (2022) Utopia snaps up distribution rights to participant's Yaara Bou Melhem doc *Unseen Skies*. *Variety*, 21 January.

Gabbatt, A. (2022) What happens when a group of Fox News viewers watch CNN for a month? *The Guardian*, 11 April.

Grierson, T. *et al.* (2021) 70 Greatest Music Documentaries of All Time. *Rolling Stone*. [online] Available at: www.rollingstone.com/movies/movie-lists/70-best-music-documentaries-24757/ [Accessed 27 August 2022].

Hailu, S. (2022) Magic Johnson on learning to accept his gay son EJ: 'He Changed Me.' *Variety*, 6 April.

Holland, P. (2021) BBC unveils new factual, arts, music orders. *Televisual*. [online] Available at: www.televisual.com/news/bbc-unveils-new-factual-arts-music-orders/ [Accessed 27 August 2022].

Judge, M. (2021) AI on Winterwatch: an automated eye for watching the wildlife. [blog] 14 April. Available at: www.bbc.co.uk/rd/blog/2021-04-winterwatch-artificial-intelligence-automated-monitoring [Accessed 27 August 2022].

Kantayya, S. (2020) Coded bias. *AJL*. [online] Available at: www.ajl.org/spotlight-documentary-coded-bias [Accessed 27 August 2022].

Layton, M. (2021) What is driving the factual boom? *Television Business International*. [online] Available at: https://tbivision.com/2021/01/26/what-is-driving-the-factual-boom/ [Accessed 27 August 2022].

Mass, J. (2022) Discovery closes acquisition of AT&T's WarnerMedia. *Variety*, 11 April.

Middleton, R. (2022) Apple TV+ orders food docuseries from Cary Joji Fukunaga, René Redzepi and Endeavor Content. *Television Business International*, 14 February.

Miller, M. (2021) BBC R&D partners with unis for personalisation research. *Broadcast*. [online] Available at: www.broadcastnow.co.uk/tech/bbc-randd-partners-with-unis-for-personalisation-research/5158728.article [Accessed 27 August 2022].

Morgan, J. (2020) UK TV exports reach US$1.97b, factual programming revenue rises: pact report. *RealScreen*, 23 November.

OFCOM. (2021) Media nations: UK 2021. *OFCOM.* [online] Available at: www.ofcom.org.uk/__data/assets/pdf_file/0023/222890/media-nations-report-2021.pdf [Accessed 27 August 2022].

Otterson, J. (2022) Cary Joji Fukunaga, chef René Redzepi set docuseries *Omnivore* at Apple. *Variety*, 11 February.

OurCreativeVoice. (2021) Iorram: uncovering Scotland's forgotten Gaelic sound archive www.ourcreativevoice.scot/iorram

Palomba, A. (2018) Managing Media Businesses: A Game Plan to Navigate Disruption and Uncertainty. *International Journal on Media Management*, 20(2), 153–5. doi.org/10.1080/14241277.2018.1484624

Participant. (2022) *About Us.* https://participant.com/about-us

Rogier, D. (2021). Variety Strictly Business In How MasterClass CEO David Rogier Brought Star Power to Online Learning.

Swisher, K. (2021) Sway in is Ken Burns taking up too much space? He doesn't think so. *New York Times*. [online] Available at: www.nytimes.com/2021/08/02/opinion/sway-kara-swisher-ken-burns.html [Accessed 27 August 2022].

Vourlias, C. (2022, 1 April 2022) Fremantle's Mandy Chang Warns Against a 'Corporate Age' of Documentary as Streamers Fuel Docmaking Boom. *Variety*. https://variety.com/2022/film/global/fremantle-mandy-chang-documentary-streamers-cphdox-1235220861/

Warner, A. (2021, 26 January 2021) Canada Launches First Indigenous-Language TV Channel. *Language Magazine*. www.languagemagazine.com/2021/01/26/canadas-launches-first-indigenous-language-tv-channel/

Westcott, T. (2021, 22 February 2021) TBI Tech & Analysis: Charting the path of M&A in TV. *TBI Vision*. https://tbivision.com/2021/02/22/tbi-tech-analysis-charting-the-path-of-ma-in-tv/

Whittingham, C. (2021, 22 December 2021) C21's 2021 News Review: The biggest stories in factual TV this year. *C21 Media*. www.c21media.net/news/c21s-2021-news-review-the-biggest-stories-in-factual-tv-this-year/

Wicker, J. (2021) Film-makers condemn PBS over lack of diversity and dependence on Ken Burns. *The Guardian*. www.theguardian.com/media/2021/mar/31/pbs-diversity-letter-ken-burns

Woerner, M. (2021, 3 December 2021) Peter Jackson Details How 'Get Back' Used Machine Learning to Restore the Beatles' Sound and Footage. *Variety*.

The World's 50 Best Restaurants. (2021) www.theworlds50best.com/the-list/1-10/Noma.html

CHAPTER 13

Marketing content

Video content is now used in marketing at unprecedented scale and range

....

INTRODUCTION TO THE SECTOR

The *Mad Men* era was an imaginary, if not entirely unrealistic, universe of New York advertising in the 1960s.

The long-running *AMC Network* series (first aired from 2007) described a period in the media business when commercial storytelling was based around one simple filmed asset: the 30-second TV commercial. The whole industry at that time was known by the street where the agencies mostly were headquartered: Madison Avenue.

In the twenty-first century, Madison Avenue retains some power – but it has neither geographical nor sectoral exclusivity.

TV commercials are now just one element in a diverse ecology of commercial video content and producers. This video 'big bang' has had profound impact on the marketing industry. As one commentator said, "the *Mad Men* lost the plot" with the arrival of digital and social media advertising (Leslie, 2015). Geoff Northcott, Global Chief Experience Officer at the major agency AKQA, described the change as: "a smashing of boundaries."

- US consumers watched 12.2 billion minutes of video in 2020 (Daniel, 2021).

TV spots still remain effective for brands willing to spend big to get noticed fast – either to access new audiences at scale (think about new digital brands) or to defend a 'moat' around their product (think *Coca Cola*).

- *Super Bowl* TV ads are "a chance for brands to reach new customers and promote themselves like no other" – accessing a 112 million-person audience, and costing $6.5 million each to make in 2022 (Paton, 2022).

DOI: 10.4324/9781003213611-16

But TV is now only part of a marketing industry where traditional silos have been demolished. Now a huge range of video content assets are produced, and by myriad creators, not just advertising agencies. All businesses now produce media – to sell products, or even to fund themselves.

- A study of 652 crowdfunding projects using image recognition found video performed strongly in generating investment (Ma and Palacios, 2021).

Irving Berlin wrote the famous song in a 1954 Marilyn Monroe movie: *There's No Business Like Show Business* (IMDB). In many ways, with millions of companies making video for platforms from *TikTok* to *LinkedIn*, it could be more accurate to say that there is now no business *unlike* showbusiness.

Diversification of marketing content

Video content is today produced by TV channels, advertising agencies, internal marketing departments, PR agencies, design agencies, production companies, social agencies, creators, broadcasters, social channels, brands, companies, sports teams, charities, intelligence agencies, armies, e-commerce brands, retailers and governments.

- In 2021, the global premium branded digital content market was estimated at $20 billion (Statista, 2021), part of the global $336 billion internet advertising industry (PWC, 2021). (Estimates of advertising industry size are always subjective, because it depends on what assets one includes.)
- *Facebook* alone claimed over 7 million advertisers in 2022, all creating content assets – from a photo and tagline to long videos to further their marketing objectives (Meta, 2022).
- Today, "millions of people and brands have more *Instagram* followers than the *New York Times* has subscribers" (Frier, 2020).
- *Instagram* had 1.48 billion audience reach in January 2022, the most of any social network (Kemp, 2022).
- 61% of firms have a budget for marketing content (Geyser, 2022).
- Even conventional advertising has been reinvented for a viral era. A 2022 *Super Bowl* advert with simply a bouncing QR code lifted *Coinbase* from 186th position in the App Store to 2nd (Harley-McKeown, 2022) and was voted best advert of the night by many (Hein, 2022).

Diversification of production

Pursuing this theme of expansion, every food brand is now also a content company. *Oreo's* 'won' the 2013 US *Super Bowl* by being fast and savvy enough to tweet 'You can still dunk in the dark' during a power outage (Drum, 2016). The Danish three-star restaurant *Noma* is also a TV production brand (see Chapter 12.) In 2020, Unilever, owner of brands from *Ben and Jerry's* to *Marmite*, has no fewer than 38 in-house content studios, all *U-Studio*-branded (Gwynn, 2020).

Not only are companies content producers – but also governments. From education to police, public sector organisations worldwide make video at scale for education and communication.

- Australia has 5.2 million followers on its successful *Tourism Australia Instagram* page alone (February 2022).

Every airline, religious institution and national park is also a content company, as is every sports competition.

- The *Premier League* is a major video producer. Through its 2019 deal with agency IMG it co-operates *Premier League Productions*, making "more than 40 hours of unique live content and more than 40 hours of magazine shows each week" (PremierLeague, 2019).
- The *UFC Ultimate Fighting Championship* has circa 9 million followers across *Weibo*, *WeChat* and *Douyin* in China, showing fight clips.

Every educational institution is a content producer.

- According to a Courses Online 2021 survey, Oxford University has over 6.9 million total social followers, to whom it distributes video, news, profiles and marketing (Bhardwa, 2017).
- In education delivery, the 'edtech' market is expected to reach $282 billion by 2027 (Grand View Research) through content creation companies working with universities – like *Coursera*, *2U*, *Kahoot!* and *Udemy* (Shahid, 2021).

This transformation of industries into content producers is a consequence of the digital transformation and democratisation of media.

Categories of marketing content

Whatever the producer, the purpose of integrating a brand's message into video content, whether a TV commercial or branded content, is to drive marketing objectives. These could be in sales, brand positioning with investors, customers, voters, regulators or other groups.

Whilst platforms and media change, the objectives of direct advertising (say, TV commercials) or more indirect brand integration, are perennial. Current categories of video marketing content are:

- TV commercials, which are shown in the advertising breaks on commercial networks. Commercial TV had advertising from its 1 July 1941 US start (hence the title), and advertising is still the principal way TV is funded globally (see Chapter 8).
- Brand integration, where the brand is more tangential, was a revenue driver in US commercial TV in the 1950s. *The Flintstones* cartoon was used to market

Winston cigarettes in the 1960s (*Flintstones*, 1961). The category has loosely defined descriptive names like branded entertainment, native advertising, advertorial, brand journalism, brand integration and engagement marketing (Connock, 2018). Today, Brazil's *Globo TV* runs brand integration campaigns with Unilever for its nearly 100 million daily viewers (Ariens, 2017).

- Product placements (Tom Cruise's *Ray-Ban Aviator* sunglasses in *Top Gun: Maverick*, amongst many) and prop placements (James Bond's *Aston Martin*) which co-fund some scripted content. Academic studies of India's film industry found rising brand integrations in films from 1995, to over 12 minutes and 10 brand appearances in the average film in 2015, since marketers found it effective (Natarajan et al., 2018).
- Influencer/creator marketing videos (see Chapter 14), which are funded by product integration, with influencer credibility in the market segment determining the price charged (Xiao et al., 2018) along with the size of their audience.
- Brand integrations appearing in online video at scale, like education technology companies using *YouTube* to access India's 325 million users (Swami, 2021).

Companies produce marketing content direct, or they commission it through agencies. Key production players include:

- Global advertising groups *WPP*, *Publicis* and *Interpublic*, each of which owns dozens of subsidiary agencies. WPP alone has 104,000 staff (Spanier, 2021).
- Major traditional advertisers, such as the Coca-Cola Company (which spent $2.77 billion on advertising in 2020, a pandemic year) (Goodfellow, 2021) or Procter & Gamble.
- Influencer-driven consumer brands, such as *Fenty Beauty*, using founder Rihanna's 126 million *Instagram* followers plus *YouTube* channels and influencers like British *YouTuber* Patricia Bright with 2.88 million followers, to bypass traditional advertising (Harker, 2020).
- Social platforms, such as *Meta* (owner of *Facebook* and *Instagram*), *YouTube*, *We Chat*, and China's *Sina Weibo* and *Youku/Tudou* (see Chapter 6).
- Social channel owners such as *Buzzfeed* and countless others (see Chapter 9).

This chapter examines the spectrum of marketing content, and how new technologies, including AI, are shaping evolution of marketing content production, and we do that through the mechanism of the four-step media value creation model.

THE VALUE CREATION MODEL

Development

At the development phase in marketing content, producers start with analysis of the market they wish to enter, and a positioning plan. Key inputs are the ideas the producer, has plus their own brand and client relationships. Investment is low, or zero.

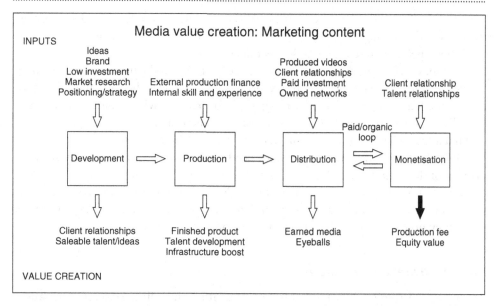

FIGURE 13.1 Marketing content is often launched and promoted with paid media, in the hope that it achieves additional distribution value (earned media) through viral sharing

Key outputs at this stage are client relationships (advertisers and sponsors), talent and ideas.

TV commercials (destined for ad breaks) and branded content (destined for the main feed or show) are made differently.

TV commercials

Adverts destined for TV are produced in a clear sequence. Brands commission agencies to research, plan and design their campaigns. They are hired with fixed renumeration components, plus (increasingly) a performance-based element – based on metrics ranging from engagement to actual sales. Agencies often (but decreasingly) subcontract the making of commercials to external production companies, which are usually based around individual director talents – who deliver the work, signing a full rights buyout with the brand. No brand would want a third party to retain significant rights in an advertising asset, as this could constrain their ability to deploy it. The director is paid a fee (often substantial: $20,000 or much more) and the agency is paid a profit margin (10%–20%) on the production budget. Actors and other talent are paid either a complete buyout for their services, or a tiered deal which pays them residually per use of the commercial (or other metrics). Commercials are placed on broadcast networks in the ad breaks by the brand's media agency.

Branded content

For branded content, the genesis of a production is similar, but the ecology is different. Brands are more likely to produce branded content in-house (not least for cost reasons) though they may contract agencies, who then either produce content themselves (increasingly) or subcontract to production companies. By whichever of these three parties, the content is then produced.

In branded content, the content funders (e.g., the brand's finance director) may perceive value in greater levels of brand prominence, not least because they will have been schooled in the metrics of performance advertising, where there is direct and (usually) positive correlation between investment and outcome.

That approach is often wrong. Branded content is most successful when it does *not* put the brand front and centre, and does not feature the brand for a significant proportion of the output. This may map to classic marketing theories around stimulating customers' use of their peripheral faculties (Petty et al., 1983). Or customers may simply prefer not to watch a lot of branding and respond more positively to brands when they do not feel they are being too vigorously targeted.

How much brand to integrate

Analysis has determined the level of brand integration an audience tolerates, or causes the audience to stop watching – the 'cliff edge' over which the advertiser would not want to tumble (Kevill, 2013).

Inserting too little brand in content will create marketing underperformance. But excessive brand presence will have the same effect, plus customer alienation. Calibrating the content exactly right to determine these levels is the challenge.

For a branded TV show where increasing levels of brand integration were continually added, a 'cliff edge' at which marginal additional branding had a negative effect was shown to be the point at which the manufacturer was given a say (or final say) in the programme's editorial content. This cliff edge point showed a drop of 16% from those previously willing to watch the show in the UK, or of 17% for the US audience (from 81% to 64%). There is therefore a non-linear function with respect to the level of branding (Connock, 2018). So marketing effectiveness was optimised by calibrating brand integration to the level that was acceptable to the audience before the marginal effect of extra branding insertion turned negative. Finding that optimal point will require case-by-case sensitivity and testing by the producer.

How much of each type of content to make: hero/hub/hygiene

No brand can produce a new TV commercial every day – and no customer wants to watch one. So producers and brands make different types of content to maintain both the impact of special content, and the affinity of regular content. This is the Hero/Hub/Hygiene model. Each of three content forms has its own production cost, cadence (how often it appears) and objectives.

- Hero content is a TV commercial or film with high production values, perhaps made once every six months, and with long shelf-life.

- Hub content is useful but basic content, like how-to films or company information videos, available long-term, but not high-cost to produce.
- Hygiene content might appear on *Instagram* or *TikTok* a couple of times per day, and disappear fast. It is cheap and fast to produce, and may have many versions. It is increasingly subject to dynamic customisation to small customer groups or individuals according to their known or perceived tastes, and AI tools are heavily engaged in this form of creative optimisation, at pace and at scale. Most of the video adverts on *Instagram*, for instance, are hygiene content. Rob Pierre, CEO of Jellyfish, said: "What we're seeing is that it's just so complex. That you need hundreds of thousands of different formats in order to have a conversation or to engage with your target audience. In the good old days, in the *Mad Men* days, it was a billboard poster, a magazine advert or a 30-second TV slot. That's all you had to do. Now it's ludicrous how much you need to reformat your messaging in order to reach your audience" (Rob Pierre, 2021).

Production

At the production phase in marketing content, key inputs are production finance (most obviously, from a brand), internal skills and experience. Key outputs are finished product, talent development for the production unit, and infrastructure boost. There is weak IP generation for a producer/agency, because commercial customers take substantial rights (if not all).

The production process for branded video content maps closely to the delivery genre where it will be placed (factual TV, drama, entertainment, social) and style required (hero, hub etc).

Production without a clear distribution strategy is a waste of money. Smart producers are also smart distributors. So distribution intention is rigorously built in at the production stage.

- Brand integrations take as many forms as there are distribution products in TV, social media and other video channels; pre-roll or mid-roll video, product placement (which is where a brand pays to have its product in shot), prop placement (where a brand provides the goods, such as a car, for free), verbal mention, incidental video appearance and live shopping.
- Brand integrations can be made for any purpose in the 'funnel,' a traditional (potentially outmoded) textbook construct where customers pass through a sequence of gates from awareness, through consideration, to activation (purchase). Some videos might be aimed to elicit a direct response (liked donating to charity), which would be 'lower-funnel;' others might be to simply position that charity positively in the eyes of consumers, which would be 'upper funnel.'
- Academic thought now sees customer engagement as a less linear, and often circular process than the funnel, especially when marketers know how to respond to digital signals consumers are sending out as they interact with a brand over time (Schweidel et al., 2022), and throughout their ownership of a product.

- So content can be designed to retain customer engagement post purchase (e.g., with how-to videos) and cycle customers back towards either loyalty or purchase. Consider how *Apple*, *Amazon* or *Samsung* market their products in a continuous cycle of customer engagement, through a mutually reenforcing ecosystem.

Brand integration success factors

The effectiveness of brand integration can be driven by up to eight factors (Baetzgen and Tropp, 2015) but "content-centric factors such as content quality and the non-advertising character of brand-owned media are most important for creating relevant content and for achieving media success in terms of reach and frequency."

- In e-commerce, a study was run by the author of this book with market research company Ipsos MORI in 2017 to ascertain the optimal style of brand integration was in a video.
- The study analysed the style of video delivery most likely to result in customers clicking to buy, presenting nine comparable but editorially varied presentation options, from a sales-driven approach to a user review and branded content video – all around a London-based e-commerce jewellery brand.
- Of the content types tested, branded content rated highest out of all of the videos, with 44% saying they would watch the whole video, and 20% would click to buy.
- In this study, just 38% of users would take action after the customer review video, compared to 58% for the product only (mute) videos, and 52% for branded content.
- The *Instagram*-style product-only mute advert also performed well on recognition, with 96% of people able to identify the product.
- The most poorly performing content types were those with hard sell. Less brand integration is potentially more powerful.

Finally, co-creation techniques – where the audience and the brand work together to create content – can be effective.

- Academic studies show brands that balance their identity with that of the audience work out new approaches "that stimulate and motivate brand co-creation all the while preserving the brand's essence" (Bange et al., 2020).
- Successful co-creations include *made.com* asking users to upload pictures of their furniture in their homes, *Lego* asking users to design their *Lego League* trophies (out of *Lego*), and *BMW*'s *Co-Creation Lab* (Gilliland, 2018).

Distribution

At the distribution phase of value creation, key inputs are produced videos, and client relationships. Very often the brand clients fund paid distribution as a way to promote content to new audiences who have not hitherto engaged with the brand. Key outputs include client relationships and talent franchises. Note, as above, IP is not a key output for producers or agencies. They are likely to not own any.

Branded content is distributed in three types of channels: paid, owned and earned media.

Paid media

A brand may pay to distribute via third party channels – known as 'paid media,' or just advertising. The advantage is that it enables brands to reach new customers, targeted in useful potential customer cohorts defined on geographic, demographic, behavioural or (within ethical boundaries) psychographic lines. They may even be targeted down to individuals – via tracking data.

The disadvantage of paid media is simple but important: it costs money. It is harder to achieve a positive return on investment with a piece of content if it costs money to distribute it, since the investment is by definition higher than organically viewed content. Additionally, the brand may not have access to first-party data about the consumers reached through paid media, which makes it much harder to re-target them efficiently.

Advertising space can be bought by human – or computer. Machine buying is called 'programmatic' advertising.

- Digital publisher the *LADbible* group described how that works. They sell advertising space "through an auction process via several automated ad exchanges, including AdX Google, Rubicon, AppNexus, and Pubmatic. Under these models, advertisers typically pay a set price per 1,000 views of their advert (known as CPM). Bidders (brand owners) do not have sight over the space they are bidding for, only the audience size and demographics" (LBGMediaPLC, 2021).
- Rob Pierre, CEO of global digital agency Jellyfish describes the process experienced by a site visitor: "Okay, you're a BMW driver, you live in the Southeast, you've got affluent friend network and you're now looking at *Autotrader*. All of that information is made available through a cookie, allowing the advertiser [who might be Mercedes] in real time to ask the question: 'Do I want to bid for this person, based on all that information? The answer's is likely to be, yes" (Rob Pierre, 2021). "Programmatic advertising is where a decision is being made on the appropriateness of the ad, based on information at the point of the auction."

Owned media

A brand may create content for its own website or *Facebook* channel – known as 'owned media,' because the brand controls content on the channel, if not the channel itself. (Think of Manchester United's *YouTube* channel.) The advantage is that these channels are fully controlled by the brand, and in effect free. (Of course, running a website has fixed costs, but these don't change the logic of the owned media approach.)

The disadvantage of owned media is that it does not extend the brand's network graph. Owned channels only reach people who have previously engaged with the brand – and not new people.

Where producers of branded content also have relevant distribution channels, they achieve a close match between the consumer 'reach' aspiration of the brand, and the footprint delivered.

- For instance the fashion brand *Pretty Little Thing*, based in Manchester, UK, has 17.9 million followers on its *Instagram* alone – a sizeable owned channel to sell its product, and a valuable source of first-party data.
- Also Manchester-based, the LADbible Group explained the role of its internal agency and owned channels in its 2021 stock market listing document: "*Joyride* helps brands and other partners navigate the competitive digital content space by tapping into LBG Media's huge community of over 250 million followers across the Group's social channels. This community gives the Group unfiltered insights into what content best connects" (LBGMediaPLC, 2021).

Earned media

The brand may see its content distributed when other people talk about it – 'earned media.' The advantage of earned media is that it is free. When a piece of content goes viral, the brand is achieving reach to new consumers without paying for it. A good example is a response to a Kanye West tweet in which he said, on November 4, 2018, "*McDonalds* is my favourite restaurant." *Burger King UK* tweeted, via their agency, Coolr: "Explains a lot." Their tweet achieved massive global traction, and an estimated $6 million in media value.

The disadvantage of earned media is that it is uncontrollable. Discussion about the brand might go in a detrimental direction, and cause negative perception about the brand.

Most marketing content in which a brand becomes engaged will involve a combination of these three channels – paid, owned and earned media.

A particularly striking TV commercial gets talked about by users on social media: paid media, then earned media. A brand produces a short film and puts it on *Instagram*, then pays for some additional promotion to reach new users; owned media, then paid. That content then goes viral: now it's owned, paid and earned.

Monetisation

At the monetisation phase of the value creation process, key inputs are the quality and traction of the production, combined with client relationships. Key outputs are the production fee profit, and equity build for the production company and producer.

Once again, IP may not be a powerful output in this category of media, because clients take rights.

There is a feedback loop (a possible 'flywheel') where increased investment by the commercial client in paid media promotion drives further organic views too (since more people are accessed, some of whom repost the material). That generates additional revenue, capable of reinvestment into more paid media.

Value of brand integration

Brand integration campaigns drive sales performance for companies – from a start-up fashion brand trying to access the market (like Malaysia's *MKLZ Collection* (MKLZ, 2022) to a major e-commerce firm.

- *Pepsi* brand logos were on-screen for as much as 9 of the 12 minutes of the *Super Bowl* 2022 half-time show with Snoop Doog, Dr Dre and other stars, earning a major part of the circa $170 million in-content (i.e., not advertising slots) brand exposure for the match (Young, 2022). This was paid media. As users then reposted the material, additional value was created. This was earned media.
- E-commerce is growing rapidly, and 58.4% of adult internet users buy online each week (Kemp, 2022).
- Brand integrations in both product and featured videos appear on e-commerce sites such as the $51.58 billion market-capitalised Latin American giant *Mercadolibre* (MercadoLibre, 2022) the UK's £1.19 billion *BooHoo* (BooHoo, 2022) or the global giants *Alibaba* ($338 billion) or *Amazon* ($1.58 trillion) (Values at 17 February 2022).
- Beauty company *Shiseido* used online video to promote a new product on China's *BiliBili* network in 2020 and claimed over 1.23 billion views, only 15% short of one for each citizen of the world's most populous country (Pabari, 2021).

How the vast volume of newly produced brand-integrated content is created, distributed, viewed and perceived by customers can then affect the overall financial performance of brands. Some have been almost entirely built using powerful content marketing.

- UK-founded *Gymshark* achieved a £1 billion valuation (Jahshan, 2020) driven in substantial part by its effective social video marketing (with 5.6 million *Instagram* followers in February 2022).

Class discussion questions

- Find examples from your own country of brands using different combinations of paid, owned and earned media. In each case, show what content assets the brand is using.
- Describe, with examples plus posting frequencies and any reach/effectiveness data, the branded video output of a major brand in your country in terms of the hero/hub/hygiene model.

- Evaluate the Brazilian branded content market. Consider regulatory permissiveness around brand integrations on commercial TV, and contrast cost-effectiveness of that environment with *YouTube* to access younger viewers.
- Identify a public sector body that uses video content marketing. Explain what it is doing, what its metrics are, and evaluate the effectiveness of its offer.
- Consider the case of a specific charity in your home country. Write a strategy for their video content marketing for next year, including proposed spend, channels, content types and risk mitigation strategies.

Welsh Protein Organics: practical exercise in social video marketing

You are newly hired CMO (Chief Marketing Officer) at this UK healthy food brand, in the fast-growing 'athleisure'/nutrition niche. The core customer base are people who would go to the gym for a workout, then spend £20 on well-sourced protein in reception or online. Now the brand is going mainstream. *Welsh* has been marketed so far in an unstructured way – word of mouth online, promotional deals with specialist outlets.

- Some 15% of *Welsh* sales are online, though the e-commerce site does not have visual content. The board want this 15% number to climb steeply to at least 50%. The brand will not advertise on TV for cost reasons.
- The social feed is thin, apart from occasional pictures of the charismatic founders Jolyon and Clare.

Your job is to design and build an instant social content strategy. You don't have an advertising agency, so you have to plan this in-house. You do have a small external video/photo production company, who will make the content you need.

You have a £60,000 budget to spend with them for three months' worth of social/website content. Prices per unit of different content types are below. You have to present tomorrow morning. Here's what you need to produce by then.

Style guide for the content production team

Show in a single page or a few PowerPoint slides the video and photography style you want, combined with a reasoning as to why. If you like, you can use influencers, who bring with them category followings of at least 50,000 followers each, but they cost £10,000 each. Look at relevant real-world brands for inspiration.

Organic distribution plan

Allocate how much of each level of content you want to make – in Hero/Hub/Hygiene. Each has a different production quality and length, and therefore price. Invest wisely, making sure you spend across the whole 3 months.

- Remember: hero videos are agenda-setting 'commercial'-type films which showcase brand, costing £25,000.

- Hub videos are how-to material which might sit on your website for a year– for instance, where the protein is sourced. These cost £2000.
- Hygiene videos are short, shareable content perhaps 8–10 seconds long, in front of mind for the customer for a day each in the feed, like *Instagram*. They cost £200 each. Hygiene photos cost £5000 for 50.

So how are you going to spend your £60,000 budget? (If you pay an influencer £10,000 for a video, you can assume that the video production price is included.)

Now show which *channels* you will be prioritising across the three months.

Once you have done that, you will be ready to present to the board. In class, people who are not presenting can play the role of the board, and ask the difficult questions.

CONTENT PRODUCTION	Number of items commissioned	Money spent
HERO (£25k)		
HUB (£2k)		
HYGIENE video (£200)		
HYGIENE photo (£5000 for 50)		
INFLUENCER (£10,000)		
TOTAL (no more than £60,000)		

FIGURE 13.2 Allocating your production budget

CONTENT DISTRIBUTION	Number of videos posted over the three months
YouTube	
Facebook	
Instagram	
TikTok	
Other channels	
Website	

FIGURE 13.3 Planning the frequency of your content distribution in each channel

AI in advertising: global cases

AI is used throughout the marketing content, and specifically advertising, industry – to customise and personalise in real time.

- The West's leading e-commerce company *Amazon* uses of AI in marketing content. "At *Amazon*, technology is the key driver to everything it does. Consider that for the development and upgrading of its magic genie, *Alexa*, which runs on AI voice software, the company as of 2019 had deployed some ten thousand workers, the lion's share of which were data scientists, engineers, and programmers" (Levinson, 2020).

Some of the issues around AI in advertising are counter-intuitive:

- "Results from six experiments show that lay people adhere *more* to advice when they think it comes from an algorithm than from a person" (Moore, 2018).
- Acting unions are becoming increasingly concerned about the use of AI instead of 'real' actors. In April 2022, performing arts workers union Equity launched a campaign titled "Stop AI Stealing the Show" (Vallance, 2022). One Canadian voice-over artist, Bev Standing, sued *TikTok* over what she said was use of her voice in text-to-speech content implementations beyond what she had agreed. *TikTok* settled the lawsuit.

But there are many positive use-cases, such as those below from around the world.

Driving digital commerce for pets (Brazil)

Problem: What can AI do to help creatives produce digital commerce content?
AI Solution: Use AI in the creative process itself, including writing style and narrative.

Agencies Ogilvy and Hogarth created a 2019 digital experience for Brazilian pets chain *Petz*, "to put shopping decisions in the paws of dogs," using facial recognition and other tools trained on dog faces, that enabled the reading of different emotions when images were shown to them. (Hogarth, 2020).

- Convolutional neural networks (CNN) were employed, with image recognition on ImageNet.
- The dog faces dataset used had 8300 images from 130 breeds. There is a fascinating technical guide to how the dog facial recognition was done in this reference (Bagheri, 2019).

TV commercial in the style of a deceased film director (Italy)

Problem: Accurately replicate the visual and verbal style of a famous film director.
AI Solution: Use AI to analyse his methodology.

Drinks brand *Campari* brought the cinematic approach of celebrated film director Federico Fellini back to life on the 100th anniversary of his birth.

- The agency team said: "Fellini didn't usually shoot commercials, but in 1984 he made an advertisement for *Campari*," and Campari were intrigued by the idea of another one (Marongiu, 2022).
- AI was used to analyse Fellini films for data on his script, plus technical choices like camera moves, duration and types of shots.
- A scriptwriting tool used natural language processing to mimic Fellini's writing style. Creative Marc D'Souza said: "When writing with the AI you're basically riffing off each other."
- A pre-visualisation tool allowed the creatives to visualise the commercial, using Fellini's cinematic language – scenes, cuts and camera moves.
- Then the final product was validated by experts. The commercial premiered at the Venice Film Festival and was shown on *Amazon Prime*.

Individualising an advert (USA)

Problem: Make a different version of a commercial to suit each user.
AI Solution: Dynamic Content Optimisation.

Teams look to optimise the ingredients of an advert uniquely for each individual viewer, can use machine learning and AI to mass-produce social content.

Sir Martin Sorrell is CEO and founder of advertising group S4 Capital, tech-driven advertising agencies such as Media Monks.

- In a podcast interview, he gave the case of a campaign for the launch of *Netflix* drama *Narcos*.
- The agency created versions of trailers for different times of the day and different customer tastes.
- Sorrell said that there were more than 50,000 versions of the *Narcos* ad in that campaign. "If you were a *Facebook*-using petrolhead who generally sat down to watch TV dramas at 8pm, you might have seen a clip of a *Narcos* car chase on your feed shortly beforehand" (Armitage, 2021).

Engaging with young children (China)

Problem: How does a brand create engaging content for the under 5's?
AI Solution: Voice to text recognition.

The app *Voice Doodler* allows children to create beautiful story illustrations simply by talking to it, using speech recognition and machine learning.

- It was built for infant nutrition brand Wyeth Illuma, and launched in China for *WeChat*.
- The product was a *WeChat* Microsite with WebGL and Voice Recognition. The front end included a user interface and 3D content. The back end used voice command,

and the fitting of the tool for likely responses around story surrounding, object creation or weather conditions. Voice to text recognition enabled users to create their story by issuing voice commands (Cameron, 2020).

Gaining global earned media through AI deployment in 'art'

Problem: How to encapsulate a client's commitment to arts and culture?
AI Solution: Create a new painting by Rembrandt, using AI.

In 2016, Bas Korsten, Global Creative Lead for advertising agency Wunderman Thompson and his team, were looking for a new project for ING, the Dutch bank.

- To signify the bank's ten-year commitments to the arts, they alighted on creating a new Rembrandt painting, using AI.
- Which subject matter was the right one? "We looked at landscape, Biblical scenes, but what he painted most, was men, and within that sub group was men with hats and white collars. So through statistical analysis we got to a rough idea of what Rembrandt would look at."
- Over 160,000 fragments from 346 Rembrandt paintings were analysed, upscaled by deep learning algorithm.
- Using a height map to mimic his brush strokes, the detail was then fed to a 3D printer with 13 layers of ink.
- The result was a 'painting' which "looks exactly like a Rembrandt, it's mind boggling" wrote the *Wall Street Journal*. Korsten said: "If you go up to the painting, it looks as if there is a soul behind the eyes."

From the agency perspective, Korsten said: "one of the important goals that ING had was to get young people involved. In any sponsorship, the number of times the brand gets mentioned is under 10%. In this case it was over 60%."

- The work also became a show on *Netflix*. Going forward, Korsten said: "There is still more that we can do to bring AI into the creative process."

Multiversioning an advert (India)

Problem: Make a TV advert with a star in thousands of local versions.
AI Solution: Use machine learning to replicate, and reversion the star's voice.

Agency WPP has a strong share of India's $10 billion media-buying market, working with most of the country's top 50 advertisers.

- The group created a 2021 *Cadburys* Diwali activation, through its agencies Ogilvy and Wavemaker, titled *Not just a Cadbury Ad*.
- The campaign was all about helping local retailers – 85% of Indian retail – using a brand ambassador, major Bollywood star Shah Rukh Khan.

- He could not appear in every commercial, so the agency used machine learning to recreate his face and voice, reiterating it in thousands of different versions, each targeted to the zip code of the viewer.
- The campaign drove 35 million total impressions of #NotJustACadburyAd, with 9.4 million video views, 20% sales increase, 14.4% uplift in ad recall and 5.9% uplift in consideration (WPP, 2022).

This was not WPP's only use of AI in advertising in India.

- Effectiveness of a *YouTube* campaign for *Burger King* was algorithmically optimised, to move budget between multiple strategies, resulting in a 9% decrease in cost per thousand against the plan.

CHAPTER SUMMARY

TABLE 13.1 Key themes in this chapter

Content Marketing	Development	Production	Distribution	Monetisation
Business model	Modest investment required to generate content ideas.	Investment required to produce the content, usually externally funded.	Usually done via client resources.	Percentage of client funding.
Uses of AI	Increasing use of AI tools in content, avatar and other asset generation.	AI tools in production becoming increasingly common.	Hi AI usage in distribution technologies.	Low AI usage at this stage.
Value Creation	Potential for high return to equity owner via scale up.	Production margin to production company.	Scale economy on success .	Multiple channels of value, including exit on high multiple.

BIBLIOGRAPHY

Ariens, C. (2017, 1 September 2017). How Brazil's Globo TV Uses Its Massive Reach to Snag Partnerships With Brands Like Unilever and Vivo. *AdWeek*. www.adweek.com/convergent-tv/how-brazils-globo-tv-uses-its-massive-reach-to-snag-partnerships-with-brands-like-unilever-and-vivo/

Armitage, J. (2021, 12 September 2021). Sir Martin Sorrell's wild ride from Mad Men to Silicon Valley. *Sunday Times*. www.thetimes.co.uk/article/sir-martin-sorrell-wild-ride-mad-men-silicon-valley-xz53f22sr

Baetzgen, A., and Tropp, J. (2015). How Can Brand-Owned Media Be Managed? Exploring the Managerial Success Factors of the New Interrelation Between Brands and Media. *International Journal on Media Management*, 17(3), 135–55. doi.org/10.1080/14241277.2015.1088017

Bagheri, R. (2019). Deep Learning: How to build a dog detector and breed classifier using CNN?! *Towards Data Science*. https://towardsdatascience.com/deep-learning-build-a-dog-detector-and-breed-classifier-using-cnn-f6ea2e5d954a

Bange, S., Moisander, J., and Järventie-Thesleff, R. (2020). Brand co-creation in multichannel media environments: a narrative approach. *Journal of Media Business Studies*, 17(1), 69–86. https://doi.org/10.1080/16522354.2019.159672

Bhardwa, S. (2017, 21 November 2017). UK university social media league table 2017. *Times Higher Education*. www.timeshighereducation.com/student/news/uk-university-social-media-league-table-2017

BooHoo. (2022). www.boohoo.com

Cameron, R. (2020, 27 May 2020). Voice Doodler Allows Children to Transform Their Stories into Animations in Real-Time. *Branding in Asia*. www.brandinginasia.com/voice-doodler/

Connock, A. (2018). Optimising Video for eCommerce: A Critical Commentary on Works Published 2013–18 by the Author: University of Salford].

Daniel, K. (2021). The State of Content Marketing in 2021 [Stats & Trends to Watch]. *Hubspot*. https://blog.hubspot.com/marketing/state-of-content-marketing-infographic

Drum. (2016, 31 March 2016). 2013: Oreo wins the Super Bowl with 'dunk in the dark' tweet. www.thedrum.com/news/2016/07/10/marketing-moment-101-oreo-wins-super-bowl-dunk-dark-tweet

Frier, S. (2020). No filter: the inside story of *Instagram*. Simon & Schuster.

Geyser, W. (2022). *The State of Influencer Marketing 2022: Benchmark Report*. https://influencermarketinghub.com/influencer-marketing-benchmark-report/

Gilliland, N. (2018). *Lego to BMW: How brands have used co-creation to earn consumer trust*. https://econsultancy.com/lego-to-bmw-how-brands-have-used-co-creation-to-earn-consumer-trust/

Goodfellow, J. (2021, 22 July 2021). Coca-Cola says it has doubled marketing spend year-on-year. *Campaign*. www.campaignlive.co.uk/article/coca-cola-says-doubled-marketing-spend-year-year/1722853

Gwynn, S. (2020, 10 March 2020). Unilever upped marketing spend to €7.27bn in 2019. *Campaign*. www.campaignlive.co.uk/article/unilever-upped-marketing-spend-€727bn-2019/1676543

Harker, L. (2020, 29 October 2020). How Fenty Beauty Has Built Brand Awareness – and Wo. *Latana*. https://latana.com/post/build-brand-awareness-fenty/

Harley-McKeown, L. (2022). Crypto apps soar in popularity after Super Bowl splurge. www.theblockcrypto.com/linked/134101/crypto-apps-soar-in-popularity-after-super-bowl-splurge

Hein, K. (2022, 13 February 2022). Watch adland's favorite Super Bowl LVI commercials as Coinbase & Uber Eats steal the show. *The Drum*. www.thedrum.com/news/2022/02/13/coinbase-s-qr-code-uber-eats-score-super-bowl-lvi

Hogarth. (2020). *Petz*. Retrieved 22 February 2022 from www.hogarth.com/case-study/pet-commerce-award-winning-digital-first

Jahshan, E. (2020, 14 August 2020). Gymshark hits £1bn valuation after securing major investor. *Retail Gazette*. www.retailgazette.co.uk/blog/2020/08/gymshark-hits-1bn-valuation-after-securing-major-investor/

Kemp, S. (2022). *DIGITAL 2022: GLOBAL OVERVIEW REPORT*. https://datareportal.com/reports/digital-2022-global-overview-report

Kevill, S. and Connock, A. (2013). Ask the Audience: Evaluating New Ways to Fund TV Content. Reuters Institute, Oxford University. https://reutersinstitute.politics.ox.ac.uk/news/ask-audience-evaluating-new-ways-fund-tv-content

LBG Media PLC. (2021). *Admission* to Trading on AIM https://lbgmedia.co.uk/docs/ladbibleli braries/archive/company-docs/admission-document.pdf to Trading on AIM https://lbgme dia.co.uk/docs/ladbiblelibraries/archive/company-docs/admission-document.pdf

Leslie, I. (2015). How the Mad Men lost the plot. *Financial Times.* November 6, 2015

Levinson, M. (2020). 'Bezonomics' Review: Spinning the Flywheel. *Wall Street Journal – Online Edition* www.wsj.com/articles/bezonomics-review-spinning-the-flywheel-11589139434

Logg, J., Minson, J. and Moore, D. (2018). Algorithm Appreciation: People Prefer Algorithmic To Human Judgment. *Working Paper 17-086.* www.sciencedirect.com/science/article/pii/S0749597818303388

Ma, Z. and Palacios, S. (2021). Image-mining: exploring the impact of video content on the success of crowdfunding. *Journal of Marketing Analytics*, 9(4), 265–85. doi.org/http://dx.doi.org/10.1057/s41270-021-00133-8

Marongiu, L. B. D. (2022, 31 March 2022). Interview about Wunderman Thompson work for Campari [Interviewed by Dr Alex Connock, Said Business School, Oxford University].

MercadoLibre. (2022). *Website.* https://mercadolibre.com

Meta. (2022). *Insights to Go.* www.facebook.com/iq/insights-to-go/6m-there-are-more-than-6-million-active-advertisers-on-facebook

Natarajan, T., Balasubramaniam, S. A., Stephen, G. and Inbaraj, J. D. (2018). Brand placements: prevalence and characteristics in Bollywood movies, 1995–2015. *Journal of Media Business Studies*, 15(1), 57–88. doi.org/10.1080/16522354.2018.1460051

Pabari, M. (2021). Everything you need to know about Bilibili. *Pattern.* www.practicology.com/insights/blog/everything-you-need-know-about-bilibili

Paton, J. (2022, 18 February 2022). Super Bowl ads 2022: what they can tell us about marketing in the future? *Dotdigital.* https://dotdigital.com/blog/super-bowl-ads-2022-what-they-can-tell-us-about-marketing-in-the-future/

Petty, R. E., Cacioppo, J. T., and Schumann, D. (1983). Central and Peripheral Routes to Advertising Effectiveness: The Moderating Role of Involvement. *The Journal of consumer research*, 10(2), 135–46. https://doi.org/10.1086/208954

PremierLeague. (2019, 20 May 2019). *Premier League extends deal with PLP* www.premierlea gue.com/news/1223547

PWC. (2021). The PwC Global Entertainment & Media Outlook 2021–25. www.pwc.com/gx/en/industries/tmt/media/outlook.html

Rob Pierre, J. (2021, June 2020). *Interview on Jellyfish* [Interview by Dr Alex Connock, Oxford University, Said Business School, MBA module The Business of Arts, Culture and Entertainment].

Schweidel, D. A., Bart, Y., Inman, J. J., Stephen, A. T., Libai, B., Andrews, M., Rosario, A. B., Chae, I., Chen, Z., Kupor, D., Longoni, C., and Thomaz, F. (2022). How consumer digital signals are reshaping the customer journey. *Journal of the Academy of Marketing Science.* doi.org/10.1007/s11747-022-00839-w

Shahid, M. (2021). 15 Largest EdTech Companies in the World. *Yahoo Finance.* https://fina nce.yahoo.com/news/15-largest-edtech-companies-world-155126885.html

Spanier, G. (2021, 5 August 2021). WPP hikes staff bonuses after 'stand-out performer' Group M fuels H1 growth. *Campaign.* www.campaignlive.co.uk/article/wpp-hikes-staff-bonuses-stand-out-performer-group-m-fuels-h1-growth/1724049

Statista. (2021). *Revenue generated from premium branded digital content worldwide in 2017 and 2021.* Retrieved 22 Dec 2021 from www.statista.com/statistics/714673/premium-bran ded-digital-content-revenue-worldwide/

Swami, A. (2021, October 2021). *How India's leading EdTech brands unlocked the power of YouTube video marketing for growth*. www.thinkwithgoogle.com/intl/en-apac/marketing-strategies/video/edtech-youtube-video-marketing-india/

Vallance, C. (2022). Actors launch campaign against AI 'show stealers.' *BBC News*. www.bbc.co.uk/news/technology-61166272

Winston Cigarette Commercial (1961). Featuring The Flintstones. www.youtube.com/watch?v=BVRO6GAfvzA

WPP. (2022). Agency figures.

Xiao, M., Wang, R., and Chan-Olmsted, S. (2018). Factors affecting YouTube influencer marketing credibility: a heuristic-systematic model. *Journal of Media Business Studies*, 15(3), 188–213. https://doi.org/10.1080/16522354.2018.1501146

Young, J. (2022). NFL sponsors Nike, Pepsi dominate non-traditional media exposure during Super Bowl. *CNBC*. www.cnbc.com/2022/02/14/nfl-sponsors-nike-pepsi-dominate-2022-super-bowl-exposure.html

CHAPTER 14

Creators

A new, global and democratic model of media ownership

....

INTRODUCTION TO THE SECTOR

Chapter 6 described the social media universe from the top down – the perspective of the platforms. This chapter takes the opposite point of view – that of the content creators.

Of all the media production sectors in this book, creator is perhaps the most universal. Over 50 million people globally view themselves as content creators, and the true number could be argued to be over 3 billion – the number of people who use a smartphone.

Either way, audiences share their enthusiasm.

- An academic study of *YouTube* influencers found they were more popular among US teens than mainstream celebrities (Xiao et al., 2018).
- *Streampunks*, a key book on the sector, described it like this: "If attention is the currency of the digital age, every company should be after the biggest source of people's attention: watching video ... There are only two things we spend more time doing: working and sleeping" (Kyncl and Peyvan, 2017).

The global creator economy is a significant media segment in its own right, but is also integrated into content marketing (see Chapter 13) and social networks (see Chapter 6). It feeds music (see Chapter 15,) podcasting (see Chapter 16), games (see Chapter 5), digital publishers (see Chapter 9) and much else across the media. It includes influencer marketing – a subset because creators can also monetise their work directly rather than for sponsors, for instance, via subscription.

DOI: 10.4324/9781003213611-17

Value-creation in the creator economy is substantial and global, from *YouTube* to *TikTok*, *Cameo*, *Clubhouse*, *OnlyFans* and publisher-monetising site *Substack* (see Chapter 9). Every facet of this new digital media economy is intrinsically linked to several others.

The global creators media market segment was estimated by an industry report to be worth $104 billion revenue in 2022 (Geyser, 2022).

- A report (albeit self-serving) that *YouTube* commissioned, calculated its total contribution to the US economy's creative ecosystem at $20.5 billion in 2020, supporting the equivalent of 394,000 full-time jobs, partly through over 38,000 channels with 100,000 subscribers (Goodwin, 2020).
- Influencer marketing-related software firms, which optimise production and distribution for creators, raised $800 million in venture capital investment in 2021, implying a thriving ecology (Geyser, 2022). And it is global.
- In Kenya, the number of *YouTube* channels making seven-figure earnings in shillings (that's roughly $8,000+ annually) is growing fast, increasing in 2021 by 60%, to 400. Seven channels – such as *Churchill Show* and singer *Otile Brown* – had over 1 million subscribers. One had over 1 billion views.
- In Brazil, 122,000 full time equivalent jobs resulted from the *YouTube* economy in 2020 (Goodwin, 2020).
- Sectorally, Fashion & Beauty is the largest space, accounting for 15% of creators, followed by Health & Fitness (13%), Travel & Lifestyle (12%), Gaming (11%), Family/Home (%) and Sports (4%) (Geyser, 2022).

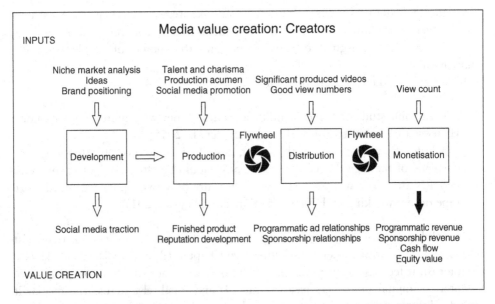

FIGURE 14.1 Creators have minimal development and production cost. When audiences like the content, distribution success and monetisation positively impact each other, driving revenues back to the creator for further production

- Yet creators are still dwarfed by their audience. *YouTube*'s 31 million creators represent only 1.2% of its 2 billion monthly user base (Lai, 2022).

THE VALUE CREATION MODEL

The Creator business model is simple and global. This is how it works.

Individuals conceive and produce videos, often of themselves, at extremely low cost compared to 'professional' production, using the readily available self-shooting tools of the smartphone era. They distribute the videos (for free) using massively scaled social platforms (see Chapter 6).

Most fail.

Whilst *OnlyFans* has paid over $2 billion to creators, and singer/model Bella Thorne earned $1 million in her first 24 hours on the (mainly adult) site – most creators make less than $145 per month (Geyser, 2022). Those that do succeed grow audiences that are either exceptionally large (Kylie Jenner had 305 million followers in March 2022, roughly the population of Western Europe) or usefully niche (so-called micro-influencers). Either is attractive to advertisers

Creators monetise their work through one of eight methods: programmatic advertising, affiliate advertising, a platform's creator fund, sponsorship/product placement, e-commerce, direct follower subscription (and donations), NFTs and back-catalogue monetisation. We take each in turn in the Monetisation section below.

Within that framework is variety and nuance. The near-universal footprint of influencers, rate of change, ceaseless impact of new technology, integration of e-commerce, crypto, NFTs and other monetisation tools all combine to make it the quintessential modern media sector.

Development

At the development phase of the media value creation model for creators, informal market analysis, or market awareness, matters. An influencer needs to know what trending topics will have market appeal, around which a basic brand positioning can be created – even one as simple as 'snowboarding influencer.'

Key business inputs are ideas, a producer/presenter brand, and social media skills. No significant financial investment is required – which is the heart of the democracy of the space. The output is social media traction – an audience. Unique to influencer content amongst media sectors is mass market, global traction without the commissioning mediation or funding of any third party. That upends traditional models.

> Try placing yourself in the seat of a network studio head. If someone came to you and said they wanted to film a show of themselves nailing trick shots, braiding his or her daughter's hair, or filming cool things with a 4K high-speed camera in super slow motion, would you give that person the green light? Probably not.
>
> *(Kyncl and Peyvan, 2017)*

Yet of course, each of those is a hit YouTube channel – *Cute Girls Hairstyles* and *Slo-Mo Guys*.

Celebrity creators fall into three simple categories: self-grown, celebrities from other fields, and virtual celebrities.

Self-grown stars

This ability to innovate without external finance is why creators, despite their global fame and substantial economic success, often sit well outside the perceptive and economic mainstream of media. Their fame is extensive but niche, often not translating to other platforms. Most creators are media brands eponymously created on the platform where they are distributed. "Most people visit *YouTube* to watch something they can't find anywhere else: a generation of auteurs and entertainers who have built their success on the platform, inspired by the challenge to share their creativity with the world" (Kyncl and Peyvan, 2017).

- In 2022, the leading *YouTube* creators were video gamer *PewDiePie* (Felix Kjellberg) with 109 million subscribers, toys reviewer *Kids Diana Show* (75 million subscribers), kids toys and amusement parks vlogger *Like Nastya* (real name Anastasia Radzinskaya) (70 million) and toys/adventures bloggers *Vlad and Niki* (63 million).
- Even including the rest of the top ten – *Mr Beast, Badabun, JuegaGerman,* and Brazilians *Whinderson Nunes* and *Felipe Neto* – none of the leading *YouTube* creators was famous before coming to the platform, and most have done little on TV.
- Bigger channels exist on *YouTube*, like *SET India*, with 128 million subscribers. But these are not primarily creator-driven (SocialBlade, 2022).

Influencer content is not *ersatz* entertainment on the existing TV model: it chases a different paradigm. "Engagement through social media content marketing is highly contextual and platform dependent" (Wang and Chan-Olmsted, 2020). 'Outsider' status means that early in the value creation stage, influencers are not investable. That keeps content self-shot and low-cost – and those values actually affirm its authenticity. Brands imitating influencer content often mistakenly increase the production values, and thereby diminish the effectiveness of the work.

- "Even the more successful creators struggle when it comes to raising lump sums to get started," Neil Mohan, Chief Product Officer of *YouTube* said. "That was the kind of the key product insight or sort of genesis, if you will, of *YouTube Shorts*" (a short-form on-ramp for the network in general).
- *Instagram* has a similar product (*Reels*).
- Both mimic *TikTok*'s main product offer. *TikTok*'s advertising reach grew by 60 million adult users (7.3%) in the last quarter of 2021 to 885 million (Kemp, 2022).

Despite the global nature of the platforms, where a creator starts is important. German academic research showed creators in talent 'clusters' performed better.

- Researchers found that professional *YouTube*, *Facebook*, *Instagram* and *Twitch* content producers in Germany benefitted from presence in urban centres like Berlin, Cologne and Hamburg. Advantages they cited included broadband speed and quality of life, as well as proximity of creative staff, advertisers and even political supporters (Zabel et al., 2020).

Celebrities from other fields

Of course, there are TV and sports stars iterating creator business models too. On *Instagram*, the biggest influencers are all stars from other fields – in 2022 footballers Ronaldo (409 million followers) and Messi (310 million), actors Dwayne "The Rock" Johnson (302 million) and Selena Gomez (301 million) and TV star Kylie Jenner (316 million).

- The *Kardashians* command respect as business women – "a golden age of celebrity branding … Today you can wear Kim Kardashian shapewear under Nicole Richie sleepwear on a Rita Ora duvet tossed with an Ellen DeGeneres pillow" (Hess, 2021).
- Tropes of celebrity coverage – exclusive paparazzo photos – are both valued and devalued by mass reproduction. A photographer complains: "It's happened to me a million times over – fans screen grab the image [and] post it on socials, with no copyright" (Taylor, 2021). But clever stars embrace erosion of copyright by allowing their content to be virally spread, and monetise the downstream earned media (see Chapter 14).

Virtual influencers

As well as being made famous by computers, influencers are also now being created on them, using (amongst other AI tools) deep learning.

- There is a computer-generated supermodel, *Shudu*, created by London photographer Cameron-James Wilson. Rihanna used her for the *Fenty Beauty* makeup line.
- *UneeQ Creator* has a platform that allows businesses to build their own digital human.
- Tencent used metahumans to work with a broader variety of models with different skin tones, heights and weights.
- Other leading virtual influencers include *Lil Miquela*, *Lu do Magalu*, *Guggimon*, *Knox Frost*, *Thalasya* and *Janky*. (See Chapters 2, 10 and 18 for more on AI-created synthetic people, a growing phenomenon.)

Production

At the Production phase of media value creation, key inputs are the individual skill and production acumen of the creator, and their social media promotion abilities. Key outputs are finished product and reputation development (i.e., brand). Again, little if any financing is required. With resulting lack of filtration, creator content has dazzling eclecticism and virtuosity, and zero quality control

- At one point in December 2020, the creator-subscription site *OnlyFans* was signing up 500,000 new users per day (Geyser, 2022).
- On 18 February 2022, in the UK 144,848 viewers tuned in live for a live stream from *Big Jet TV* during Storm Eunice in the UK to watch commentary on planes landing at Heathrow. As well as live feed, they also heard host Jerry Dyer's negotiations about TV appearances, as old-media channels dialled into his success (BigJetTV, 2022). The project is a full time operation, supported by financial contributions from members who pay for extra streams (Waterson, 2022).
- In Kenya, creator content export is strong enough for 45% of the content to be consumed by a global audience.
- Nigeria has 300 channels with over 100,000 subscribers, each with up to 75% of its content consumed globally.
- South Africa's content attracts 65% of viewers from across the world (Ngugi, 2022).

In production, creators have tools, even on smartphones, with edit and graphics capabilities barely available to professionals even a decade earlier.

- *Adobe Creative Suite* has AI baked-in, via the *Adobe Sensei* brand.
- Adobe seeks to "help its customers unleash the artist inside themselves," through what it's CEO Shantanu Narayen calls the notion of "creativity for all" (Yeomans, 2022).
- These are supplemented by new technologies such as *VSCO* (photo-editing app), now valued at $550 million, or *Splice* (audio-editing platform), valued at $500 million (Geyser, 2022).
- As a software and hardware suite, smartphones are the most dramatic democratisation of any media tool in history, on a level of importance akin to the fifteenth century Johannes Gutenberg 'invention' of the printing press.

Distribution

At the distribution phase of value creation, key inputs are produced videos at critical mass, and material numbers of views. Key outputs are nascent commercial relationships – through passing the view-count threshold on platforms for programmatic advertising, and reaching sufficient sector-specific followers that sponsors take interest.

There is a 'flywheel' between production and distribution, where more traction with audiences and high view numbers drive demand for creator posts and more content.

A second flywheel between distribution, monetisation, and production sees greater view numbers drive additional revenue, in turn funding creation and distribution of more content. This is the virtuous circle to which creators aspire.

Mastering the platform algorithm

Creators do not own, control or even pay to access distribution platforms that make them rich. Therefore their ecology is vulnerable to platform changes. They have no leverage with the platforms, and live in thrall to the algorithm, "the mysterious, all-seeing recommendation engine that powers the platform" (O'Brien, 2021). Algorithm changes – a tweak to *YouTube* recommendations – profoundly impact livelihoods of creators.

In 2012, *YouTube* algorithmically prioritised longer videos, not least because it had invested $100 million to work with outside media brands (a project soon shut down). Creators started making longer videos too – but alienated viewers. "The creators who have found the most success playing into the platform's algorithms have all demonstrated profound errors in judgment, turning themselves into cultural villains instead of *YouTube*'s most cherished assets" (Alexander, 2019).

Successful US car-review creator Doug DeMuro said: "It's a proprietary algorithm, they don't want you to know what it is. But I've always found it a little bit strange. If they told us a little bit more about the algorithm, we would probably be able to create content that better served it, but they don't do that" (Patel, 2021). To DeMuro, a key creator attribute is to simply time devoted to the algorithm. "They give you so much data that you can peruse."

The same vulnerability applies to rules. When, in August 2021, subscription-driven creator platform *OnlyFans* changed policies to prohibit adult content, it dealt a major shock to the adult entertainment industry, a substantial user of the subscription-driven platform. (The policy was reversed almost immediately.)

Monetisation

In the Monetisation phase of value creation for creators, the key input is view count, and key outputs are programmatic and other revenues, cash flow and the resulting equity value increase, either in a firm or an individual. (An individual's equity value is virtual, but with tangible utility, e.g., in raising rates for in-video product placements.)

In October 2021, a data leak revealed earnings of top *Twitch* creators. *The Wall Street Journal* said: "It confirmed the suspicion that the top streamers make a really large amount of money." And "the ones with the most eyeballs are making the most money."

- In September of that year, viewers spent 1.7 billion hours watching *Twitch*. (Needleman, 2021).
- According to *Dot Esports*, *Twitch* streamer *CriticalRole* made $9,626,712 between August 2019 and 21 October, followed by streamers *xQcOW*, *summit1g* and *True*. The top 25 all earned over $1 million per year (Miceli, 2021).
- Given the minimal investment required on production, the ROI for successful content creators is stellar.

The business model can be life-changing on other platforms too.

- *YouTuber* April Wilkerson gives tips on home repairs, with 1.45 million subscribers in March 2022. "YouTube took me from a hobbyist to a full-time maker with three wildly successful businesses, seven full-time employees, and a TV show!" (Goodwin, 2021).
- Chinese influencer *Viya*, age 34, real name Huang Wei, is reportedly a dollar billionaire through e-commerce live-streaming (Hilotin, 2021).

Across the industry, there are now eight means of monetising creator output: programmatic advertising, affiliate advertising, a platform's creator fund, sponsorship/product placement, e-commerce, direct follower subscription (and donations), NFTs and back-catalogue monetisation. We will take each in turn, then look at combinations.

Programmatic advertising

This model pays a CPM (cost per thousand views) rate to the creator, which therefore tallies their overall click count to how much money they can make on a given platform. It is the staple revenue stream for creators. This is covered in Chapter 13.

Affiliate programmes

Companies of all kinds, including e-commerce businesses, pay commission for referrals of customers from creators as one of their primary marketing tools. (The process is known as 'creator codes.') Indeed, 45% of companies said when surveyed that they keep track of sales using referral links (Geyser, 2022). This can be a significant source of revenue to creators – provided that they have the viewer numbers to deliver volume. Many automated affiliate networks are available online for creators to join, such as *ShareASale*, *AWIN* and *ClickBank* (from a list compiled by e-commerce platform *Shopify*).

Creator funding

Sometimes, there is direct payment or access to funds provided by the platform. *TikTok* has a specific Creator Fund for over-18-year-old creators with more than 10,000 followers, which it characterises as "not a grant or ad revenue sharing programme," in 2022 representing a global figure of £231 million over three years. Creators receive funds from their videos, and "will know that performance on *TikTok* is dynamic – it changes naturally – so your funds will ebb and flow in the same way" (TikTok, 2021).

That is an elegant way of describing the fact that the fund does not rise as the number of creators rises, which could mean the creator fund is actually de-optimised for the site's growth from the creator's perspective. The better *TikTok* does overall, the worse any given creator does, since the total payment does not grow in line with total site usage. Creator Hank Green said: "When *TikTok* becomes more successful, TikTokers become less successful … What?" He claimed his earnings had halved from 5 cents to 2.5 cents per 1,000 views on *TikTok*. (Both the model and the global sum frequently change, of course.)

E-commerce

Direct e-commerce is growing fast. *Instagram* is, "for all intents and purposes, Millennial QVC" (Hess, 2021). QVC was a successful 1990s TV shopping channel. Social e-commerce is expanding, and 1 billion *Facebook* users access its *Marketplace* service each month, where ads reach 560 monthly users (Kemp, 2022).

- 54% of firms that work with influencers run e-commerce stores. And 42.3% of brands measure a campaign's effectiveness directly by the ultimate performance marketing measure of conversions/sales that result (Geyser, 2022).
- Some creators go further and use their marketing platform to directly launch a significantly off-line business – like singer Rihanna with her *Fenty* brand, or *YouTuber MrBeast* launching an instant, nationwide burger chain.

Sponsorship/product placement

The creator can sell a product integration directly or via an agency or platform to a brand (see Chapter 13). For instance, *TikTok* has 'In-Feed Ads,' which are embedded in a creator's feed.

Issues include the need to modulate the demands of the brand vs the readiness of consumers to watch branded content and brand integrations. Demands of the platforms – who will de-prioritise or even take down content where the brand integrations are particularly visible and/or the platform has not been involved in creating the sale to the brand – come into play.

Regulatory interventions are important. In the USA the FTC (Federal Trade Commission) sent over 700 Notice of Penalty Offences letters in 21 October about misleading endorsements by creators, including for some major brands like Apple, Amazon and Ford. In the UK, the Advertising Standards Authority reported that an analysis of 24,000 creator posts showed low compliance with a requirement that they made clear where they were being funded by brands. Sixty-one per cent of complaints they received in 2020 were about ad disclosure on *Instagram* in particular (Geyser, 2022).

Direct subscription

Creators with committed following can directly monetise that relationship by using a subscription service. We will look at two models: *Patreon* and *OnlyFans*.

Patreon is a membership platform for creators to monetise their work. It has over 84.7 million monthly visits (March 2022) growing fast, with an average of nearly three minutes on the site. *Patreon* reached 192,000 creators in June 2020 (Statista). Members offer a service for someone and their supporters (or 'patrons' – hence the title) use the platform to pay them. This can be done in any combination of the these models: community, pay-to-view content, donation. "On *Patreon*," says the site, "you can let your fans become active participants in the work they love by offering them a monthly membership" (Patreon, 2022).

OnlyFans lets creators to put content behind a paywall, allowing access for a monthly fee. In January 2022, it had 248 million site visits. *OnlyFans* takes a 20% cut of creators' subscription revenue. Founded in 2016 by British entrepreneur Timothy Stokely, the site has a reputation for adult content (though it also has a somewhat wider editorial footprint) with over 1 million registered users and 1 million content creators.

True to the wider picture of unequal spoils in Creator content, it is likely that only a small percentage of users of the site make money. The minimum subscription price is $4.99 per month and the maximum subscription price is $49.99 per month. Creators can also set up tips or paid private messages starting at a minimum of $5. *Blac China* reportedly has 16.1 million followers on the site and has earned $20 million in 2021. Bella Thorne reportedly earned $2 million in her first week on the site (Mehrotra, 2021). (Figures are hard to verify.)

Alternative and hybrid monetisation tools

There are many alternatives to the market leaders, each with a unique selling proposition. *FanCentro* only takes a 10% revenue share (as opposed to *OnlyFans* 20%). *AVN Stars* pays a lifetime royalty of 5% to a user for the earnings from anyone they refer to the site. *LoyalFans* and *ManyVids* offer live-streaming, video store e-commerce sales and referrals.

As a further example, the (mostly) video game live stream platform *Twitch* offers five ways for creators to make money, each across two tiers, from a beginner programme and then a partner programme bringing added marketing tools (e.g., chatbots) and editorial tools (e.g., chat rooms). This is the mix of revenue sources listed by the channel.

- Subscriptions: 50% of revenue from subscribers to the channel.
- *Twitch Bits* (which are a virtual good used by the platform): $1 per 100 bits the channel gets.
- Video game sales: 5% share when the purchase comes from the Twitch channel.

- Donations: 100%
- Ad revenue.

But creators can equally add monetisation options beyond *Twitch* as well – bringing in sponsors, using third party apps to drive donations, creating e-commerce stores for merchandise and setting up affiliate links – where creators are paid a percentage of the sale from any monetised traffic they bring to a third party site (Johnson, 2021).

In some cases live games streamers have allegedly made more money from programmatic advertising on their 'let's play' videos than the actual game developer. Developer Ryan Green claimed this was the case with his game *That Dragon, Cancer* (Matulef, 2016).

New technologies such as NFTs

Non Fungible Tokens may become a valuable additional revenue stream for creators. Creators may use NFTs to sell directly to fans while innovating on the kinds of additional value they can attach to the asset. Video games companies will potentially continue use NFTs of virtual goods in 'play-to-earn' games (Deloitte, 2022).

Long-term catalogue sales

In the music business, artists' back catalogues have been bought up by companies like Hipgnosis, the listed music fund, and aggregated as reliable cash flows (see Chapter 15). These then form assets with reliable income streams not correlated with the stock market, therefore attractive to investors as a risk-diversifier.

The same movement is starting to occur on *YouTube*. One creator signed up to a fund is *MrBeast* – real name Jimmy Donaldson. He ran an audience participation event inspired by the South Korean *Netflix* show *Squid Game* with a $456,000 prize, and did a deal with the fund Spotter to crystallise some of the future income from his videos (Shah, 2022).

Class discussion questions

- What are the opportunities to brands from using influencers, and what are the risks?
- Create a list of all the ways in which a typical influencer marketing campaign deploys and interacts with AI technologies.
- If you owned a popular creator channel with 2 million social followers on a major platform, how would you take control of your own data, brand, customers and ad revenue?

Analysis: *Roblox* influencer

Challenge

Thousands of *YouTube* creators are looking for the fame and fortune of an 'influencer career.' For those that succeed, the first reality check is that posting frequently and regularly is a full time job. It needs perseverance and consistency to find and grow your audience online.

Megan Letter has build her influencer work into a multimillion dollar business through daily content on her *YouTube* channels to keep her fanbase engaged and growing. This drives value, but also risk for the business: everything depends on her personal brand. How can she change that?

Background

Megan Letter, previously known by her maiden name Leeds, started on *YouTube* in 2014 at university, posting videos of herself playing the life-simulation game *The Sims*. She earned around $400 a month, her *YouTube* success was modest and she wasn't earning enough to support herself full time (Zabasajja and Kharif, 2021).

But by 2022, she was best known for her online name *MeganPlays*, a pink-purple-haired personality she created for role-playing on *Roblox*, the fastest-growing gaming platform for user-created games.

In Spring 2022, Roblox had 202 million monthly active users, having added 80 million new users in 2020 alone. (Dean, 2022) The switch to *Roblox* solidified Megan's Influencer status as a superstar to *Roblox*-playing kids. Her main *YouTube* account has over 3.3 million subscribers, and she has over 1.4 million followers on *Roblox* itself.

In six years, earnings grew from $400 a month to a seven-figure influencer business, diversifying her *YouTube* channels, revenue streams and a venture into game design. She went from 240,000 subscribers (September 2018) to 1 million subscribers (September 2019) in just a year. She achieves some 40 million monthly views on her *Roblox* gaming channel alone (Stubbs, 2021).

Diversification

In 2019, Letter diversified, launching other *YouTube* channels (*Honey the Unicorn*, *Perry the Panda*, a real-life channel, a live-streaming channel and a *Roblox* funny moments channel titled *BFF Squad*) and a merchandising line, *Stay Peachy*. She worked with several brands for paid promotion on her content. *YouTube* channels alone have paid out seven figure sums through programmatic advertising, plus merchandise revenues (Stubbs, 2021).

Mid-2020, Megan and her husband launched *Wonder Works Studio* and their first *Roblox* game, to leverage Megan's audience within *Roblox*. They also invested $120,000 to design a *Roblox* game, *Overlook Bay*, which made $350,000 in revenue in beta, and

$1,500,000 in its first four months. The game is free to play and makes $150,000 to $300,000 a month via in-game monetisation. Then in late 2020, *Wonder Works Studios* launched a second game, *Traitor!*, again with strong growth, 2 million players, and some $2,000 per day (Stubbs, 2021). Her game development studio now has about 14 staff (Konstantinovic and De Luce, 2021).

Besides diversifying and investing more in creating *Roblox* games, Megan has also built channels outside her personal brand. *VTubers* are virtual characters that act as hosts for their *YouTube* channels like any other influencer would.

Audience

MeganPlays has a 90% female viewership, aged between 7–14 years. Most viewers are aged 9–10. Her content therefore matches the main demographic of *Roblox* (Sidhwani, 2021) and Letter has mastered the art of online fan engagement.

The workload is high. She manages channels, creates and uploads up to three videos per day, streams on *Twitch* and interacts with her community online (Konstantinovic and De Luce, 2021).

Case discussion questions:

- Is Megan Rocks principally a creator, celebrity or business? Why is she successful?
- Does the multichannel distribution strategy make sense to you or not?
- What is the business model and opportunity in virtual influencers?
- What other specific creators impress you with their business acumen, and why?
- Choose a successful creator on any platform, and dissect their business.

Creators' legal scenarios: exercise

As described in the chapter, creators do not generally have the security of a larger company backing their output. It is therefore important to them that they manage their financial, production and legal risks. This is an exercise in working out what those risks might be, based on a fictional case.

- A loose collective of creators – Joe, Andy, Nihar, Deepa and Adaku – have between them amassed over a billion *YouTube* views, making brands interested in working with them.
- They also have calls from Hollywood agents, broadcasters and streamers. This is the moment to take their business mainstream, adding mainstream production to their portfolio. To meet the market demand they are on their way to LA.

There are five new projects on the slate. The problem is that lurking within the projects are legal and production risks not fully discovered. Have a look at the list of legal terms at the end and see if you can work out which might relate to each project. Which projects could be made viable with mitigation of the risks, and how? And which are non-starters?

Airbnb'd

Joe has a drone and has got some big viewing numbers already on *YouTube* for his witty, alternative property show. Now he wants to go big with it on TV. In each episode he flies his drone over the most incredible properties in the US, filming in beautiful 4k video, with music and commentary, a pastiche promotional video for anyone who would want to *Airbnb* them – if only they could. "Check out the amazing infinity pool. Look at those Ferraris. This must be one of the best homes in Miami. And who are those celebrities that we can spot on the sun deck? We're putting a price on that of an incredible $80,000 for the weekend." The show has every chance of being a huge hit for TV.

Blocked

A really socially valuable show that helps young people who've been bullied at school to feel better. All you have to do to get on this TV show is send Deepa's team social media posts where you've been bullied, plus the names and account details of the people who sent them. We'll show those posts on the show, then start a campaign to shame those bullies into reconciliation and apology. Or if they're not up for that – we'll get the bullies *blocked*, not only on the victim's social media channels too – but in the whole town's too. Justice is served – in Blocked.

You've Got Mall

Nihar's been doing well on *TikTok* with popup dance-offs in the street, and has persuaded a big e-commerce brand to let him take that idea nationwide – they'll sponsor the show, for TV. In each episode Nihar turns up by surprise at a different shopping mall or town centre with a massive sound system, along with a small but well-lit dance floor, on the back of a truck. With no warning – the party gets started. Once the music starts (he's going to play major artists' current tracks, using his *Spotify* subscription) anyone in the street can get up on stage and dance for the prize.

Our journey

Adaku is doing a scripted drama series with a difference – the incredible story of everyone in the collective, a really moving account of five peoples' journeys from obscurity and hard times to success. She's known them for years and she's the perfect person to tell it. The drama is in five parts, each telling the story of one individual. They've always been friends, and there is no need to write a deal down as they've always been fair to each other, and they've agreed that they will split the money from the show five ways, plus an extra fee to Adaku for writing it. The idea actually came from Nihar's friend Emma, but everyone agreed it would be much better if one of the collective wrote it themselves. They're hoping *Netflix* could be really interested.

Deliverance

Remember the movie? Well this show has nothing in common with that – apart from the great title. Instead, this is a TV show about the best takeouts in America. From a studio, hosts Joe, Andy and Adaku will check out and read out the best and worst reviews on sites like *Trip Advisor* for restaurants that deliver. Then they'll order some food from the best – and the worst – and give it to their own panel of food critics (a football team one week, a dance studio the next) to taste and enjoy. At the end of the series, *MasterChef* style, they'll give a prize for the best – and the worst – takeout in America!

Legal and production terms to consider

Intellectual property rights
Chain of title
Defamatory content/libel
Obscene or offensive content
Copyright
User privacy and confidential information
Duty of care
Infringement of platform rules
Data collection/privacy
Production cost control
Music copyright owner – composition
Music copyright owner – performance
Music copyright owner – recording
Public performance licence
Trademark rights
Passing off and endorsements
Guild rights
Child actors
Health and safety
Filming permissions
Contractual arrangements

CHAPTER SUMMARY

TABLE 14.1 Key themes in this chapter

Creator	Development	Production	Distribution	Monetisation
Business model	Low or zero investment (apart from time) in content creation.	Low investment in producing content.	Zero investment in distribution (except when using paid promotion strategies).	Programmatic ads, affiliate ads, sponsorship, e-commerce, subscription, NFTs and back-catalogue monetisation.
Uses of AI	Low AI usage.	Production tools and custom software integrate AI.	High AI usage by platforms for personalisation, audience segmentation.	Use of AI in advertising optimisation to maximise returns for platform and creator.
Value Creation	Most creators do not succeed economically.	Low value creation at the production phase until audience traction achieved. Content release cadence important: regular and frequent.	Combined with audience numbers. response rates directly inform both visibility on the platform, viral spread and ultimately revenue.	Exceptional value for successful creators via direct monetisation. Low value for resale of creator ideas. Library purchase starting to happen.

BIBLIOGRAPHY

Alexander, J. (2019, 5 April 2019) The Golden Age of YouTube is over. *The Verge*. www.theve rge.com/2019/4/5/18287318/youtube-logan-paul-pewdiepie-demonetization-adpocalypse-premium-influencers-creators

BigJetTV. (2022) www.youtube.com/watch?app=desktop&v=vPQh1FrbOc0&feature=youtu.be

Dean, B. (2022) Roblox User and Growth Stats 2022. https://backlinko.com/roblox-users

Deloitte. (2022) 2022 media and entertainment industry outlook. *Deloitte*. [online] Available at: www2.deloitte.com/us/en/pages/technology-media-and-telecommunications/articles/media-and-entertainment-industry-outlook-trends.html [Accessed 23 August 2022].

Geyser, W. (2022) *The State of Influencer Marketing 2022: Benchmark Report*. https://influen cermarketinghub.com/influencer-marketing-benchmark-report/

Goodwin, A. (2020) *From opportunity to impact: assessing the economic, societal and cultural benefits of YouTube in Brazil.* www.oxfordeconomics.com/recent-releases/From-Opportunity-to-Impact-Assessing-the-Economic-Societal-and-Cultural-Benefits-of-YouTube-in-Brazil Published by Oxford Economics

Goodwin, A. (2021) The State of the Creator Economy. Published by Oxford Economics. www.oxfordeconomics.com/resource/youtube-us/

Hilotin, J. (2021, 12 November 2021) Meet Viya, China's billionaire retail 'queen of live-streaming.' *Gulf News.* https://gulfnews.com/photos/business/meet-viya-chinas-billionaire-retail-queen-of-live-streaming-1.1636651634365

Johnson, J. (2021) Twitch Monetization. www.uscreen.tv/blog/twitch-monetization/

Kemp, S. (2022) *DIGITAL 2022: GLOBAL OVERVIEW REPORT.* https://datareportal.com/reports/digital-2022-global-overview-report

Konstantinovic, D., and De Luce, I. (2021, 2021-04-29) *Exclusive: How YouTuber MeganPlays turned Roblox videos into a million-dollar business* [Interview]. www.businessofbusiness.com/videos/meganplays-interview-megan-letter-roblox-youtube/

Kyncl, R., and Peyvan, M. (2017) Streampunks: YouTube and the rebels remaking media. Published by Harper Business.

Lai, J. (2022) Meet me in the metaverse. *andreesen horowitz.* [online] Available at: https://a16z.com/2020/12/07/social-strikes-back-metaverse/ [Accessed 23 August 2022].

Matulef, J. (2016) That Dragon, Cancer 'has not yet seen a single dollar from sales.' *Eurogamer.* www.eurogamer.net/that-dragon-cancer-has-not-yet-seen-a-single-dollar-from-sales

Mehrotra, V. (2021) OnlyFans Top 10 Earners And Creators List 2022. *TSG. The Sports Grail.* https://thesportsgrail.com/onlyfans-top-10-earners-and-creators-list-2022-know-which-is-the-highest-earning-account/

Miceli, M. (2021) Full list of all Twitch payouts (Twitch leaks). *Dot Esports.* https://dotesports.com/streaming/news/full-list-of-all-twitch-payouts-twitch-leaks

Needleman, S. (2021, 10 November 2021) WSJ Tech News Briefing In *Twitch Hack Revealing Streamers' Earnings Isn't the Full Picture.* www.wsj.com/podcasts/tech-news-briefing/twitch-hack-revealing-streamers-earnings-isnt-the-full-picture/e94ae0a0-e043-4626-93c6-27c38b15ca96

Ngugi, N. (2022) Kenyan YouTube Channels With Over 1 Million Subscribers. *Citizen Digital.* www.citizen.digital/news/kenyan-youtube-channels-with-over-1-million-subscribers-n293185

O'Brien, J. (2021, 7 October 2021) Welcome to the TikTok Economy. *Fortune.* https://fortune.com/longform/tiktok-economy-monetization-business-social-media-platforms-creators/

Patel, N. (2021, 24 August 2021) The Verge In The Quirks and Features of YouTube car reviews with Doug DeMuro. www.theverge.com/22637871/doug-demuro-car-reviews-youtube-decoder-interview

Patreon. Retrieved 22 December 2021 from www.patreon.com/en-GB

Shah, O. (2022) How start-up Spotter is making a mint from YouTubers like MrBeast with ex-BBC man Danny Cohen. *Sunday Times.* www.thetimes.co.uk/article/how-ex-bbc-man-danny-cohen-is-making-a-mint-from-youtubers-like-mrbeast-with-start-up-spotter-mbk2whnwl

Sidhwani, P. (2021) Roblox Queen MeganPlays Is Making Millions – TechStory. Retrieved 2021-05-20, from https://techstory.in/roblox-queen-meganplays-is-making-millions/

SocialBlade. (2022) *Top 100 Subscribed YouTube Channels.* Retrieved 6 March 2022 from https://socialblade.com/youtube/top/100/mostsubscribed

Stubbs, M. (2021) How 'Roblox' Star MeganPlays Diversified Her Business To Bring In Millions. www.forbes.com/sites/mikestubbs/2021/01/27/how-roblox-star-meganplays-diversified-her-business-to-bring-in-millions/

Taylor, A. (2021) Bennifer 2.0: How Jennifer Lopez and Ben Affleck got us talking again. www.bbc.co.uk/news/entertainment-arts-58030649

TikTok. (2021) *TikTok Creator Fund*. Retrieved 6 March 2022 from https://newsroom.tiktok.com/en-gb/tiktok-creator-fund-your-questions-answered

Wang, R., and Chan-Olmsted, S. (2020) Content marketing strategy of branded YouTube channels. *Journal of Media Business Studies*, 17(3–4), 294–316. https://doi.org/10.1080/16522354.2020.1783130

Waterson, J. (2022) Big Jet TV: live-streaming of planes landing during Storm Eunice goes viral. *The Guardian*. www.theguardian.com/uk-news/2022/feb/18/livestreaming-of-planes-landing-during-storm-eunice-goes-viral-bigjettv

Xiao, M., Wang, R., and Chan-Olmsted, S. (2018) Factors affecting YouTube influencer marketing credibility: a heuristic-systematic model. *Journal of Media Business Studies*, 15(3), 188–213. https://doi.org/10.1080/16522354.2018.1501146

Yeomans, J. (2022, 20 March 2022) Adobe boss Shantanu Narayen seeks to conquer the metaverse. *The Sunday Times*. www.thetimes.co.uk/article/adobe-boss-shantanu-narayen-seeks-to-conquer-the-metaverse-8n2hntmm2

Zabasajja, J., and Kharif, O. (2021) Roblox Queen MeganPlays Is Making Millions With a Blocky Digital Empire. www.bloomberg.com/news/articles/2021-04-27/how-meganplays-built-a-multimillion-dollar-roblox-rblx-gaming-empire

Zabel, C., Pagel, S., Telkmann, V., and Rossner, A. (2020) Coming to town. Importance of agglomeration factors for media cluster development in the German online video industry. *Journal of Media Business Studies*, 17(2), 148–71. doi.org/10.1080/16522354.2019.1699325

CHAPTER 15

Music

A business model transformed by technology, from creation to monetisation

....

INTRODUCTION TO THE SECTOR

The music business faced an existential crisis in the early twenty-first century, losing over half its revenue through illegal downloads and the collapse of CD sales (Robinson, 2021b). But now it is back on song – with revenues up 18% to $26 billion in 2021, a seventh consecutive year of growth.

- Successful artists have staying power. Global leaders going into 2022 were *Justin Bieber*, *Ed Sheeran*, *Drake*, *Bad Bunny*, *The Weeknd*, *Eminem*, *BTS* (see analysis below), *Rihanna*, *Ariana Grande* and *Taylor Swift*.
- Led by AI-driven Swedish company *Spotify*, streaming now accounts for 65% of revenues, with paid subscribers also up 18%, to 523 million.
- Sales of CDs, vinyl and cassettes constituted 19% of revenue, downloads 4% and 11% royalties and licensing (Savage, 2022). That was in a pandemic year.
- Long-term, concerts and festivals are growing performance revenues too (Simon, 2019). In the UK alone, live music was worth over £1 billion in 2019, according to industry body UK Music.

Some two-thirds of global music industry revenues are earned by just three major record labels: Universal, Sony and Warner – the 'majors.' Universal has 3 million songs in its catalogue, from *The Beatles* to *Lady Gaga*, and had a 17.4% profit margin (earnings before interest, depreciation and amortisation) in 2021.

But many artists today don't see the need a record company, earning revenue direct from streamers and live performance (Economist, 2021b) or working with an independent, music company like *Kobalt*, *Hawk* or *Nagaswara*. The industry is partially

DOI: 10.4324/9781003213611-18

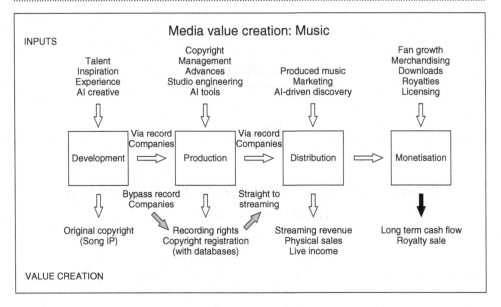

FIGURE 15.1 Music producers have a distinct choice of working with or without record companies. Service providers can offer key functions instead

pivoting to the creator model (see Chapter 14) with some shared revenue sources (notably, *YouTube*).

This is, therefore, like many creative sectors in the age of digital, an industry at an inflection point. What will be its future business model? And what effect does new AI technology over each stage of value creation?

THE VALUE CREATION MODEL

Development

The key input in the development phase of the music value chain is the talent and inspiration of the artist – but that is not simple to quantify.

Chris Martin, lead singer of *Coldplay*, has said: "Nobody really knows where songs come from." There is no known algorithmic relationship between inputs and outputs in music industry value creation. Robert Plant, lead singer of quintessential 1970s rock band *Led Zeppelin*, referred to "the huge mind bomb that was the creativity of the group" (Plant, 2022).

An academic study of entrepreneurs found psychological drivers familiar in star creators: "a positive self-illusion, such as self-aggrandisement" (Schreiber and Rieple, 2021). A longitudinal academic study in Cuba following *Reggaeton* artists concluded of the creative process: "The artists leveraged their ingenuity, collaboratively developed digital literacy practices, and produced multimodal texts to create new possibilities" (Butler et al., 2021). All this only partially describes any band's mysterious alchemy.

Though there is no equation for a hit song, a seasoned listener, like the CEO of Sony Music can use their industry knowledge to spot quality: "Someone being artistically gifted … being an amazing songwriter … cuts through generations" (Stringer, 2021). But not always.

Even when a hit song is delivered there is no certain way to predict whether it will be successful. EMI executives disliked the 1975 *Bohemian Rhapsody* when they first heard it. But there is now AI software to help predict success, based on datasets of past hits (see below).

There is a legal construct that engages from the moment a song is created, through its full copyright of up to 120 years (or 70 years from the death of the author). When a musician sings, there are three sets of rights are created: the song, the recording, and the performance. The principal output of the development phase of the value chain is therefore the potentially valuable original copyright in a song:

- *Ed Sheeran*'s *Shape of You* had by April 2021 earned over $13.3 million, *Post Malone*'s *Rockstar* $10.4 million.
- *Happy Birthday To You*, created in 1893 and owned by Warner Chappell, has topped $50 million in its lifespan, and can cost $25,000 to use in a TV show. Irving Berlin's *White Christmas* has earned over $36 million.

AI technologies are impacting music IP development (see below). The future may be AI-assisted composition, and seamlessly integrated synthetic music or elements.

Production

The production phase of the media value creation process in music is the point at which the IP (the song, for instance) is performed and recorded. Here the key inputs are the IP itself, combined with management skills. Artist managers typically take 20% of their gross earnings in return for providing strategy, creative guidance and deal-making, or some combination thereof.

There is also potential involvement of a record company, providing a cash advance for studio production and marketing recoupable against future sales of all kinds. Record companies play a capital allocation role. They aim to earn returns through their ability to select which talent and material to invest in, and bring that to market, based on their long-term understanding of both demand, and talent. The CEO of Sony Music Entertainment said: "talent, and the way the artist interprets those ideas, is prevalent across decades and decades" (Stringer, 2021).

Professional studio engineers and other technical experts can be involved in production of music. Storied studios such as Abbey Road (London) or Capitol Studios (Los Angeles) continue to prosper. But much is also now made entirely on laptops far from the legacy centres of power.

At this point, the output is valuable additional rights, generated and registered in recorded songs/compositions.

Technologies of AI in music production

- A transformer AI model, trained on 1.2 million songs was used by Open AI to compose and perform a *Frank Sinatra* song ('It's hot tub time') from scratch, as well as *faux* material from *Katy Perry*, *Elvis*, *2Pac* and others. (Robertson, 2020).

- A new *Nirvana* song was created 27 years after Kurt Cobain's death as part of the *Lost Tapes of the 27 Club*, that included 'new' tracks from *Jimi Hendrix*, *Jim Morrison* and *Amy Winehouse*, all created with generative audio (Harris, 2021).

- AI producers *Dadabots* launched a non-stop *YouTube* channel in 2019, playing real-time, AI-generated death metal music 24 hours a day, created by a neural network trained on the songs of Canadian band Archspire. They also did this with *John Coltrane*-inspired Free Jazz, under the brand *Outerhelios* (Freeman).

- *Flow Machines* performs 'augmented creativity with AI,' using machine learning. It can create a custom melody to a user-inputted chord progression, and aims to create music autonomously (Freeman). The music video *Magic Man* on *YouTube* is an example.

- *Musenet* from OpenAI uses unsupervised learning (the same approach as the natural language processor *GPT-3* in many examples elsewhere in this book, e.g., writing in the style of Jane Austen) on hundreds of thousands of MIDI files. It then create compositions with up to 10 instruments, in styles "from country to Mozart." It trains itself to predict harmonies and the next notes in a given musical sequence.

- Amazon Web Services produced the *Amazon Deep Composer* keyboard, using cloud AI processing and generative adversarial networks (the same technology used in video deepfakes) to instantly turn a user's melody into a fully mixed track in styles from rock to jazz. (Wood).

- *Lifescore* uses an AI to generate soundtracks that adapt to listener inputs through 'Cellular Composition.'

- *Google Magenta*, which uses deep learning and reinforcement learning, can generate songs. Experimental *AI Duet* uses neural networks to let the user perform in real-time with a computer. (Mann) Using deep learning, rather than backing tracks, the computer can be creatively sensitive to user performance. "It picks up things such as key and rhythm, even though I never programmed in key and rhythm," said coder Yotam Mann.

- Once a song is finished, *Hitlab*'s DNA (Digital Nuance Analysis) is an AI recommendation engine aiming to predict the success potential of a new song in a given market category, based on analysis of millions of songs (a similar approach to *Cinelytic* and *Scriptbook* in film).

For content marketing and video games needing licensed music, tools also abound.

- Cloud-based *Ampermusic* (from photo library *Shutterstock*) creates instant library music to fit a user's precise video edit. This flexibility is not unique: in House House's *Untitled Goose Game*, an adaptive soundtrack of Debussy's *Preludes* has so many variables that no game player will ever have the same performance (Lee, 2019).

- Adaptive music generator *Melodrive* uses AI to compose music directly integrating user-assigned emotions – like a live silent movie pianist in 1920s cinema.
- *Brain FM* uses AI to compose music that it says will improve brain function. And *Endel* automatically takes inputs like the user's heart rate for personalised soundscapes.

Ethical challenges of AI in music

These changes to music production will create many ethical and IP challenges.

Music created by AI algorithms where the training dataset is unknown has uncertain ownership. If a system is trained (without permission) on (say) the output of *Eminem* and *Dr Dre*, which artist will own the copyright in the new song it creates? "Our legal systems are going to be confronted with some messy questions regarding authorship … This is a total legal cluster****" (Deahl, 2019).

A UK music industry executive says:

This is a really interesting challenge, which mirrors many of the issues grappled with in the recent *Ed Sheeran* case [a 2022 case, which he won, around the copyright of his song, "Shape of You."] All new music is the result of digestion and regurgitation of existing compositions – with new creativity overlayed, which is what justifies it being deemed "new IP"; artists have always been able to draw inspiration from myriad sources. If the total universe that AI draws from comprises existing copyrights algorithmically blended, does this meet the threshold to be deemed new IP?

Distribution

At the distribution phase of the media value creation process, recorded songs are made available to global audiences through channels such as streamers, radio stations, live concerts and (less so) physical product.

The key inputs are the music itself, marketing effort (social media, PR, digital marketing, concert promotion), finance and the AI-driven recommendation tools that augment music discovery. Outputs are streams (the number of times the song is heard for at least 30 seconds), royalties, sales and live revenue.

As each player enters the value chain of a piece of music, rights ownership is made more complex. Debates around rights create tensions between artists/publishers and distributors (Simon, 2019).

The twentieth-century default delivery mode for music was vinyl – which is enjoying a well-publicised but minor renaissance. Artists like Taylor Swift and Ed Sheeran have added vinyl to recent releases, taking sales to 1999 levels, and booking factory capacity 12 months in advance (Economist, 2021a). But the numbers are small. Radio distribution and live performance also matter (see below).

But the main distribution engine in music is streaming. (AI technologies are highlighted throughout.)

Introduction to music streaming

Streaming is "the greatest record store ever," said David Joseph, CEO of Universal Music UK, and it provides nearly half the label's revenues. But it is an odd kind of record store. Neither the artists, customers nor store owners are clear about the price for anything, and the buyers never get to own any of the product (Colbjørnsen et al., 2021).

- *Spotify* is the streaming heavyweight, with 31% of global revenue, and 162.4 million subscribers in Q2 of 2021.
- Other players include *Apple Music* (15%) *Amazon Music* (13%), *Tencent Music* (13%), *YouTube* (8%) and small players such as *Netease* (6%), *Deezer* (2%) and *Yandex* (2%) (Porter, 2022).

It is hard to ascertain the value to an artist of a stream of their song.

- On any given stream, 55% of royalty goes to the labels, of which 13% goes to artists, 30% to PRS, the royalty collection agency for performers, and another 15% to other royalty payments, collected by MCPS for copies of songs (Savage, 2021).
- An approximate net figure in 2022 to artists was between $3 and £5 per 1,000 streams, or 0.3 cents per stream.
- Payment depends on which rights the artist has in the song (copyright, performance), whether a record company was involved in funding or distributing it, and whether that deal explicitly covered streaming or not (many classic songs were contracted before streaming was invented, creating legal grey areas.) The per-stream figure is neither universal, transparent nor reliable. And that is a source of endemic tension between artists, labels and streamers.

Spotify's growth

An academic study found that people will be influenced by peers to sign up for a music streamer – but whether they will stay is driven by the performance of the service itself (Chen et al., 2018). Service is where *Spotify* excels, and part of the resulting customer loyalty is AI-derived.

- *Spotify*'s free, advertising-supported tier earns little for the platform (9% of 2020 revenue, and less than 1% of gross profit) (Robinson, 2021b). But it is a nursery slope, driving subscription overall (182 million paid subscribers in 2022, and 406 million users overall).
- *Spotify Canvas* echoes the video creator economy (see Chapter 14), letting artists upload eight-second video loops alongside songs – and making users 20% more likely to playlist the song (Robinson, 2021a).

Controversies of the streaming business model

Major record companies combine share of the artist royalty with shareholdings in *Spotify* itself (reportedly Sony Music had 3%, Warner 2% and University 3.5% in 2021) (Ingham, 2021). This puts them on both sides of the net profit calculation, and open to accusations from some artists and politicians of low transparency and high profits.

- A 2021 UK parliamentary committee report described musicians' alleged 16% returns from the UK's £736.5 million overall streaming revenue as "pitiful."
- Tom Gray, from the band *Gomez*, ran the #brokenrecord campaign to address the rules of the UK streaming economy, noting that *Drake*, the most streamed artist in the world, earns just 33% of his income from streaming.
- The committee chair said: "Only a complete reset of streaming, that enshrines in law their rights to a fair share of the earnings, will do."
- *Spotify* allows brands to sponsor *Discover Weekly*, its AI-driven user-specific playlist (Tiffany, 2019). This is controversial with artists, since it commercially associates their music to brands without payment or permission. "The very idea of what it means to be an 'independent artist' has been eroded" by the corporate-branded playlists (Pelly, 2017).
- *Spotify* uses 'collaborative filtering' (an AI tool) to collate data user listening and matches to other data via comparative analysis. It can determine a user's real-time mood from their song choice. As in other social media fields of social media, users assert data privacy, and are prepared to pay more for it (Weinberger and Bouhnik, 2021).
- Algorithmic music distribution risks market balkanisation, whereby discovery of new entrants or eclectic choices is de-prioritised in streaming services. "This shows the importance of a radio station like *BBC Radio 1/1 Extra*, whose stated role is to champion new music, a quintessentially human task which may be incapable of replacement with technology" (Ross, 2022).

The diverse streaming ecosystem

Streamers are not homogenous. They have different models, shaping the market in different ways. As early as 1995, US legislation described a 'celestial jukebox' (ie streaming.)

- *Amazon Music*, a relatively small division of a global e-commerce company whose priority is drive customer lifetime value and retention (see Chapter 3) for its *Prime* service, may have a lower profit motive on song transactions than competitors.
- *YouTube*, a major streamer, earns programmatic advertising revenue which positions musicians as creators and incentivises view counts (see Chapter 14).
- *TikTok* royalties are calculated idiosyncratically as a share of a total allocated royalty pot. This paradoxically means artists earn less the more people use the site. Artists have complained that whilst *TikTok* has promotional value, that is at

the expense of creative control. Songs – like the *TikTok* hit *Dance Monkey* – are applied to third party users' video, without artist mediation. But some genres – such as West Africa-inspired *Afrobeats* – used *TikTok* for expansion of artists' commercial footprints.

- *Tencent Music Entertainment* (TME) is China's main streamer. It has five brands – *QQ Music*, *WeSing*, *Ultimate Music*, *KuGou* and *Kuwo* – 800 million monthly active users, of whom 23.3 million are paid, $1.3 billion in revenue (2018) and 75% market share. Its strength over competitors *NetEase Cloud Music* and *Xiami Music* is integration into the dominant *WeChat* messaging app (Simon, 2019). Tencent Music Entertainment in 2017 swapped shares with *Spotify*, around 7–9% of each company, further complicating streaming transparency.
- Niche players include Lebanon's *Anghami*, France's *Deezer*, founded before *Spotify*, in 2006, and now in 180 countries with $400 million revenue, diversified up the value chain into content production and artist recruitment (so-called A&R) (Simon, 2019).

AI in streaming distribution

Like *Netflix* in video streaming, the defining characteristic of audio streaming category champion, *Spotify*, is its use of AI – specifically its recommendation engine. This is seen across the streaming ecology, because they are optimised to drive retention, of users and advertisers. (The converse is that, as with all algorithmic recommendation engines, they may mitigate against users experiencing unconventional, non-linear musical journeys and therefore expanding usage.)

- Of its *Discovery Weekly* service, Sidney Madison Prescott, global head of intelligent automation at *Spotify* said: "there is a heavy amount of data mining/ machine learning that's being used … to create almost this visualization, if you will, of what your listening landscape has been" (Prescott, 2022).
- *Amazon Music* combines 'hand curation' ('50 hottest R'n'B tracks') with algorithm-driven recommendation (say, top Beyonce tracks, *plus* tracks Beyonce fans listen to), in service of retention.
- Nielsen-owned data provider *Gracenote* uses the *Sonic Styles* neural network-powered tool to analyse the world's music catalogues, creating a tight analysis of the styles of 90 million songs, based on 450 descriptor values. However, without supervision it may focus on irrelevant audio artefacts (Roettgers, 2018).
- Musicians and bands can use Non Fungible Tokens (NFTs) (not AI, but often comprising AI technologies) to offer exclusive collectibles or VIP treatment to fans.
- NFTs can carry usage rights to songs that will automatically pay artists and labels if, for instance, the song is used in a game. Fans can also become investors – buying a share of royalties via an NFT version of songs (Deloitte, 2022). At present, NFTs are high in the hype cycle, but low amongst proven sources of artist royalties.

Distribution: touring and festivals

A primary revenue driver for artists is live performance. Paradoxically, in the era of globalised digital platforms making all music universally available via streaming, performance is more lucrative than ever. "Whereas in the past, the tour promoted the album, now the music releases' primary function is to promote the tour," says one music executive. In six months of 2014, *Katy Perry* earned $18 million from touring, compared to just $1.7 million from recorded music sales (Simon, 2019).

Like any business, a tour's success is a function of revenue, minus costs. *Ed Sheeran* grossed $776.2 million from his 2017–19 tour, reaching 8.7 million fans. *U2* took $736.4 million gross in their 2009–11 *U2 360* tour. Because Sheeran's tour was a single man on stage, whereas *U2* has four band members and complex staging, he would earn more profit – he paid himself £21 million in dividends in 2021) (Leyfield, 2021).

Smaller bands deal with more prosaic economics. A night in a 600-person venue on tour with $10 tickets, could earn a modest profit on $6,000 gross revenue. But such are the fixed costs of live performance and touring (transport, technicians, equipment) that underselling the venue by even 20% would take the net profit negative.

Touring is typically a narrow margin business of all the of the stakeholders other than the Artists, and is only reliably profitable of established artists. Hence the necessity (and utility) of labels financially supporting touring activity on a recoupable basis during the important but unprofitable early stages, through "Tour Support."

(Ross, 2022)

To support the touring effort, promoters *Live Nation* (part-owned by Saudi Arabia's sovereign wealth fund), AEG and OCESA/CIE offer upfront tour funding and tour execution (Simon, 2019). Academic research showed bands that tour win enhanced festival bookings too (Hiller, 2016), which makes intuitive sense, as demand generation.

Artists and promoters continually innovate touring models to maximise returns.

- Customer segmentation: *Taylor Swift*'s 2018 *Reputation* tour gave preferential access to fans who had bought official merchandise.
- Price maximisation: *Bruce Springsteen* played $500-a-seat theatres (rather than concert halls) as a price maximisation strategy, in an environment where ticket prices had already risen by 100% ahead of the inflation rate over the previous decade (Economist, 2019).
- Demand maximisation: *Garth Brooks* adds dates until demand is exhausted.
- Unethical practices: Some innovations are disreputable. Industry magazine *Billboard* exposed a 2017 scandal where some promoters and bands re-routed tickets from venues to resellers, to sell them above face-value.

How tours are organised

Tour plans are made around two years ahead, by a band's artist management. (Venues sometimes overbook ten acts for the same night, confident most will drop out.)

- Artist earnings will be a nightly performance fee, plus around 80% of the tour's net profit.
- Booking agents mediate the band and venues, specifying date, concert duration and fee, and equalising demand and supply by calibrating venue sizes. Their fee is a revenue share.
- Promoters fund considerable upfront logistic and rehearsal costs, then hire venues or hand that to local promoters. Their fee is a net profits share: tour revenue o minus costs and agent's share. A promoter like *Live Nation* improves margin by vertically integrating the entire tour value chain. "The fact that it is a narrow margin business with a lot of risk for promoters has contributed to the consolidation in this sector" (Ross, 2022).
- Tour managers run logistics on the road, including technical crews. Festivals – *Glastonbury*, *Coachella* – offer limited fees, but marketing to wider audience segments than the band's core fans. This incentivises record companies and publishers to see tours as promotion for music streams and sales (Pastukhov, 2019). Some see them as more important even than that. "Pre-internet, the equation was for tours to augment a record campaign and drive sales by being in-market; post internet where the value of music in reals terms has reduced, while live revenue increased, this equation has been reversed for established artists, with touring plans being the foundation and the driver, with records augmenting tickets sales" (Ross, 2022).
- Major artists can also raise money from live performances simply by doing direct gigs for wealthy individuals or brands; seven-figure fees normal. In 2016, *U2* entertained a *Salesforce* event (Cross, 2018).
- Prototypical Metaverse technology, AI-driven, empowers live, digital fan engagement. A Tai Verdes show was viewed by 10 million fans in *Roblox*. Other artists to perform in *Fortnite* and elsewhere include *Marshmello*, *Travis Scott*, *Ariana Grande*, *21 pilots*, *Lil Nas X* and *The Weeknd* (Knutson, 2021).

Distribution: radio

In the twentieth century, radio was the quintessential music marketing platform. Radio play made careers, and the lack of it killed them. The weekly playlist meeting at major radio stations such as Britain's *BBC Radio 1* could have pivotal significance for artist careers. With social media and streaming, radio is still useful, but unquestionably more marginal.

- "Older generations are dying and the traditional radio is fading away with them. The new generations see things differently: they have grown with a computer on the table and a mobile phone in their pocket" (Kemppainen, 2012).

- In-car radio listening, once dominating music consumption, fell from 43% in 2016 to 29% in 2019 in millennial and Gen Z segments while daily music streaming on smart-phone grew from 33% to 41% (Robinson, 2021b).

Radio still has financial attractions.

- UK radio plays create royalties – performance (PRS) for lyrics and melody and broad-cast (PPL) for recording.
- This is good income for musicians, especially compared to streaming. A *BBC Radio 1* play was in 2016 worth £14.91 per minute for PRS and £37.76 per song for PPL, and £.22 and £.92 respectively for a city commercial station (Sentric, 2016). Some other countries have similar arrangements.

In music radio, every station is primarily a marketing insight. Station branding combines network brand (say, *Heart*) and demographic (say, 70s) or genre (Rock). Radio networks curate playlists of as few as 30 songs to maintain marketing positioning. Broadcast licences are necessary for any AM or FM transmission, but not for online stations.

Radio is declining in Europe, but satellite subscription services have prospered in the US, like $25.9 billion market-capitalised (March 2022), NASDAQ-listed *SiriusXM*. Radio is growing in parts of the southern hemisphere. "Radio stations have mushroomed in Africa" (Spurk and Dingerkus, 2017).

AI in radio

In radio there are many AI production and adtech tools.

- US network *iHeartMedia* uses AI to drive customised song transitions and volume, like a live DJ (Reigart, 2020).
- When radio politics reporter James Dupree lost his voice due to medical issues, Scottish tech company CereProc used *Balabolka*, text-to-speech software based on SAPI, Microsoft's native speech API, to synthetically voice his scripts.
- Cloud-processed AI transcription gives advertisers live contextual analysis of how their promotions are playing out on air (Cramer, 2017), which can drive timing of other activities (like purchase of search terms).

Monetisation

At the final phase of the value creation process in music, key inputs are fan base and its exploitation (e.g., with live gigs), merchandising channels and products, and streams achieved. Outputs are cash flow, artists' commercial relationships (i.e., with brands) and opportunity to turn the royalty stream into equity value, by sale of the copyright to an aggregator.

Cash generation channels

- Licensing opportunities (referred to as 'synch') are created as sales to film and TV projects, commercials or video games – either the original recording, or simply a licence of the IP in the song for re-recording. In (say) the Brazil market, the licence to a TV advert of a global commercial track could easily command $200,000.
- Much of the playbook of the creator economy (see Chapter 14) applies equally to music. The use of *Patreon* and other membership/subscription sites can be replicated for bands who choose to go independent and eschew record companies.
- *Pearl Jam* have had their own membership service, offering exclusive benefits, *Ten Club*, since 1990. Other independent and music-centric membership platforms include *Ampled* and *Currents*.
- US band *Imagine Dragons* have built a substantial following through fan curation and membership features.
- Artists like Dua Lipa and Rita Ora have used their musical success to leverage strong commercial success beyond their music.
- Live-streaming models also can be applied – for instance, *Twitch* (and its virtual currency 'bits') or *YouTube* (with its own subscription features) (Nguyen, 2019).
- Concerts and events are already working in the Metaverse. Travis Scott's *Fortnite* appearance in April 2020 not only had in-game engagement from 28 million players attending the game 46 million times, but also 16.2 million live hours watched on *YouTube* and *Twitch* (Mudrick, 2021). Scott himself picked up 1.4 million new social followers and had 81.9 million *Spotify* streams.

Equity value realisation

As with podcast businesses and scripted production companies, the best way to make money can be to sell the whole business.

- Warner Music bought *David Bowie*'s 26 studio albums for circa $250 million. *Bruce Springsteen*'s catalogue was sold to *Sony* for circa $550 million. In 2021, *Stevie Nicks* and *Bob Dylan* sold song writing catalogues for nine-figure sums (Nicolau, 2022).
- UK-listed vehicle *Hipgnosis Songs Fund*, buys catalogues, with market capitalisation of £1.43 billion (March 2022).
- Major private equity companies like KKR have entered the field, attracted by the lack of correlation to cyclical indices, and the enduring value of proven, established catalogues.

Class discussion questions

- Other than superstardom, what is the best position in the value creation chain in music?
- What legal and business issues will arise if AI is used for music composition?
- How could streamers stop users going down a 'rabbit hole' of algorithmic recommendation, and offer them diverse music?
- Structure a digital marketing campaign for a Latin America tour by a French artist.
- What is the business case for a major artist of Las Vegas residency versus a US tour?

Analysis: *BTS* and the challenges of *K-POP*

South-Korean boy band *BTS* are the first to sell out Wembley Stadium in London, which they did in June 2019 in 90 minutes (Savage, 2019).

- To an academic audience, meanwhile, they are "a counter-hegemonic cultural formation" offering new models of "peripheral societies and subjects in the globally networked cultural sphere" (Kim, 2021).
- For the artists themselves, K-POP is just tough. Record labels run 360 management in which they have monopoly over every aspect of the artist's life and career.

So, how can *BTS* maintain momentum and keep engaging with their fans through music, content and tours? Can *BTS'* success be replicated for other boy bands, or is this a unique success story?

K-POP industry

Fusing fashion with highly produced singing and dance, K-POP "idols" first emerged in the 1990s. A handful of companies dominate the market – vertically integrated and employing producers, composers and choreographers.

- The "idols" can have onerous contracts and lifestyle (Zaugg, 2018), discovered at age 13–15 amid 20,000 annual applications, with about 30 contracted as trainees and coached for three years at a cost to the company of up to $100,000 per year; millions of dollars in investment (Hong, 2016), which music companies need to recoup.
- They do that through concerts, touring, merchandising, endorsements and paid appearances for the minimum seven years of an artist's contract, after which a K-POP career is generally over.
- Artists can profit-share only after recoupment of historic costs – hard to achieve – hence the accusations of 'slave contracts.' Some artists even have strict no-dating clauses, any breach leaving them liable to pay back their development (Fulara, 2021).

Success

BTS Big Hit Entertainment, set up by music producer Bang Si-Hyuk, discovered Namjoon Kim – stage name RM – from a 2011 demo tape. The now 25-year-old megastar became fulcrum of a group debuted in 2013. *BTS* is short for *Bangtan Sonyeondan* ("bulletproof boy scouts"), seven men in their twenties: RM, rapper Suga, underground dancer j-hope, plus vocalists and dancers Jin, Jimin, Jungkook and V (Abramovitch, 2019).

- Their 2013 debut album *2 COOL 4 SKUL*, flopped. Just 19,000 units sold in a month. It peaked at No. 10 in the charts, and the follow up did little better.
- But their 2014 mini album, *Skool Luv Affair*, had momentum, driven by a tour, and the first Japanese-language album, *Wake Up* (KpopBehind, 2018).
- By 2015, *BTS* were superstars in South Korea, and in the US. 2016 album *Wings* reached 26 in the *Billboard 200* (SBSPopAsia, 2016).
- Success was sealed by a 12-country tour, the *Top Social Artist* award at the *US Billboard Music Awards*, their 2018 US No. 1 *Love Yourself: Tear* plus *Love Yourself: Answer*, the first album to sell 2 million copies in South Korea (Herman, 2018; McIntyre, 2019).
- In October 2018, *BTS* renegotiated their contract with Big Hit for another seven years (Abramovitch, 2019).
- The 62-date world tour, *BTS World Tour: Love Yourself* grossed $200 million overall (Herman, 2019). Their 2020 album, *Map of The Soul: 7*, sold over 400,000 units in the US in the first week, sold over 4 million in South Korea, and reached number one from Australia to Ireland (McIntyre, 2021).
- In January 2020, *BTS* was the first Korean act to perform at the *Grammys*, coming back to perform their hit "Dynamite" in 2021 during the worldwide pandemic from a Seoul rooftop (Martoccio, 2021).

Marketing

BTS used *YouTube* as a fan building resource, releasing short-form video series like *Bangtan Bomb* and encouraging fan videos. (*Dynamite* had 1.4 billion *YouTube* views alone).

- Western platforms like *Instagram* and *Twitter* were fan-driven rather than band-organised.
- Brand endorsements included *Hyundai*, *FILA*, *Lane Friends*, *VT Cosmetics*, *Mediheal* and *Mattel*.
- The fans-first approach focused on offering the "ARMY" fan base (Adorable Representative M.C. for Youth) new, unique experiences, rather than just products (Chia-Ming Liu, 2020).

Their contribution to South Korea's GDP has been $4,9 billion. Up to 800,000 people were visiting South Korea annually because of the band (Vanek Smith, 2021).

Discussion questions

- Why are *BTS* successful?
- Where in the value creation process is the major driver in the K-POP business model as a whole – development, production, distribution or monetisation?
- If you were *Big Hit Entertainment* how you would break the standard K-POP seven-year cycle, and stay relevant?

CHAPTER SUMMARY

TABLE 15.1 Key themes in this chapter

Music	Development	Production	Distribution	Monetisation
Business model	Low investment apart from talent.	Investment potentially required from a record company to produce (but not always).	Streaming, physical sales, licensing, radio and live performance.	Royalties, cash payments from touring. Potential equity sale of catalogue.
Uses of AI	AI tools being used in song creation.	Substantial suite of AI tools in production which are changing processes and creating legal challenges.	AI the defining factor in the success of the biggest players in streaming.	AI plays a role in money collection.
Value Creation	Potential for high return to equity owner, low probability of delivery.	Value is created if a quality product is created in the 'studio' process, but the odds are low.	High value creation from success at the distribution phase.	Very high value creation if catalogue acquires value and longevity.

BIBLIOGRAPHY

Abramovitch, S. (2019). *BTS* Is Back: Music's Billion-Dollar Boy Band Takes the Next Step. www.hollywoodreporter.com/movies/movie-features/bts-is-back-musics-billion-dollar-boy-band-takes-next-step-1244580/

Butler, E. D., Flint, T. K., and da Silva Iddings, A. C. (2021). The liberatory potentials of multimodality: Collaborative Reggaeton music video production in Habana, Cuba. *Media, Culture & Society*, 43(5), 842–59. doi.org/10.1177/0163443720987747

Chen, C. C., Leon, S., and Nakayama, M. (2018). Converting music streaming free users to paid subscribers: social influence or hedonic performance. *International Journal of Electronic Business*, 14(2), 128–45. doi.org/http://dx.doi.org/10.1504/IJEB.2018.094870

Chia-Ming Liu, M. (2020). The branding genius of K-POP band *BTS*. Retrieved 2020-01-30, from www.washingtonpost.com/business/2020/01/30/bts-kpop-bighitentertainment/

Colbjørnsen, T., Hui, A. and Solstad, B. (2021). What do you pay for all you can eat? Pricing practices and strategies in streaming media services. *Journal of Media Business Studies*, 1–21. doi.org/10.1080/16522354.2021.1949568

Cramer, P. (2017, 19 April 2017). Radio – The Next Frontier For Artificial Intelligence. *Radioink*. https://radioink.com/2017/04/19/radio-next-frontier-artificial-intelligence/

Cross, A. (2018, 7 October 2018). Playing private, corporate gigs – no longer music's biggest taboo. *Global News*. https://globalnews.ca/news/4515034/private-corporate-gigs-music-artists-alan-cross/

Deahl, D. (2019, 17 April 2019). We've been warned about AI and music for over 50 years, but no one's prepared. *The Verge*. www.theverge.com/2019/4/17/18299563/ai-algorithm-music-law-copyright-human

Deloitte. (2022) 2022 media and entertainment industry outlook. *Deloitte*. [online] Available at: www2.deloitte.com/us/en/pages/technology-media-and-telecommunications/articles/media-and-entertainment-industry-outlook-trends.html [Accessed 23 August 2022].

Economist. (2019, 27 July 2019). How big stars maximise their take from tours. *The Economist*. www.economist.com/finance-and-economics/2019/07/27/how-big-stars-maximise-their-take-from-tours

Economist. (2021a, 2 October 2021). The music industry is an unexpected victim of a plastics shortage. *The Economist*. www.economist.com/business/2021/10/02/the-music-industry-is-an-unexpected-victim-of-a-plastics-shortage

Economist. (2021b). Universal, the world's biggest record label, heads for an IPO. *The Economist*. www.economist.com/business/2021/06/23/universal-the-worlds-biggest-record-label-heads-for-an-ipo

Fulara, R. (2021). Retrieved 2021-08-11, from https://edtimes.in/what-are-slave-contracts-in-the-k-pop-industry-of-south-korea/

Harris, J. (2021, 21 July 2021). Towards Data Science In 2021: A Year in AI (so far) – Reviewing the biggest stories of 2021. Towards Data Science podcast 21 July 2021. https://open.spotify.com/episode/0mgLGLqeMtYcr5CBJINmOn?si=66eade991e244d25

Herman, T. (2018). Boy Bands, TWICE Top South Korea's Gaon Charts Best-Selling Physical Albums List. www.forbes.com/sites/tamarherman/2018/11/20/boy-bands-twice-top-south-koreas-gaon-charts-best-selling-physical-albums-list/

Herman, T. (2019). *BTS* Sell Out 'Love Yourself: Speak Yourself' Stadium Dates in England, France and U.S. www.billboard.com/pro/bts-sell-out-love-yourself-speak-yourself-tour-dates/

Hiller, R. S. (2016). The importance of quality: How music festivals achieved commercial success. *Journal of Cultural Economics*, 40(3), 309–34. doi.org/http://dx.doi.org/10.1007/s10824-015-9249-2.

Hong, C. (2016). How Much Does It Cost To Debut A K-Pop Group? www.soompi.com/article/883639wpp/much-cost-debut-k-pop-group

Ingham, T. (2021, 11 February 2021). If Universal Music Sells Its Spotify Stock Right Now, Artists Get $500 Million. *Rolling Stone*. www.rollingstone.com/pro/features/universal-music-spotify-ownership-artists-1126893/

Kemppainen, P. (2012). The Role of Public Service in Digitization of Radio. *Journal of Media Business Studies*, 9(1), 71–83. doi.org/10.1080/16522354.2012.11073537

Kim, J. O. (2021). *BTS as method: a counter-hegemonic culture in the network society*. *Media, Culture & Society*, 43(6), 1061–77. doi.org/10.1177/0163443720986029

Knutson, R. (2021, Friday, 10 December 2021). Back Stage at a Metaverse Concert In *The Journal – Wall Street Journal*. www.wsj.com/podcasts/the-journal/back-stage-at-a-metaverse-concert/6e2b1b5f-4d03-4e31-b2bb-9b9c321ad942

KpopBehind. (2018). History of *BTS*: Debut, Success and more. www.kpopbehind.com/2018/09/history-of-bts-debut-success-and-more.html

Lee, D. (2019, 23 September 2019). How Untitled Goose Game adapted Debussy for its dynamic soundtrack. *The Verge*. www.theverge.com/2019/9/23/20879792/untitled-goose-game-nintendo-switch-debussy

Leyfield, F. (2021, 1 October 2021). Ed Sheeran made a staggering £31m and paid himself £21 MILLION salary in just ONE year. www.thesun.co.uk/tvandshowbiz/16299007/ed-sheeran-made-million-salary/

Martoccio, A. (2021). Watch *BTS* Take to the Roof for 'Dynamite' at the 2021 Grammys. Retrieved 2021-03-15, from www.rollingstone.com/music/music-news/bts-2021-grammys-dynamite-performance-1139299/

McIntyre, H. (2019). *BTS* Scores The Bestselling Album In South Korea Of 2019 (And Of All Time). www.forbes.com/sites/hughmcintyre/2019/12/19/bts-score-the-bestselling-album-in-south-korea-of-2019-and-of-all-time/

McIntyre, H. (2021). *BTS*'s 'Map Of The Soul: 7' Is Officially Named The Bestselling Album In South Korea In 2020. www.forbes.com/sites/hughmcintyre/2021/01/12/btss-map-of-the-soul-7-is-officially-named-the-bestselling-album-in-south-korea-in-2020/

Mudrick, C. (2021). Intro to the Metaverse. https://newzoo.com/insights/trend-reports/newzoo-intro-to-the-metaverse-report-2021-free-version

Nguyen, D. (2019, 27 March 2019). Choosing The Independent Music Business Model That Works For You. *D4 Music Marketing*. https://d4musicmarketing.com/independent-music-business-model/

Nicolau, A. (2022, 3 January 2022). Warner Music Acquires David Bowie's songbook for about $250m. *Financial Times*. www.ft.com/content/fe392575-9b65-4a4e-805e-95270c2cca24

Pastukhov, D. (2019). The Mechanics of Touring: How the Live Music Industry Works. *Soundcharts*. https://soundcharts.com/blog/mechanics-of-touring

Pelly, L. (2017, December 2017). The Problem with Muzak. *The Baffler*. https://thebaffler.com/salvos/the-problem-with-muzak-pelly

Plant, R. (2022, March 2022). BBC Desert Island Discs In *Robert Plant*. www.bbc.co.uk/programmes/m00159xd

Porter, J. (2022, 20 January 2022). Streaming music report sheds light on battle between Spotify, Amazon, Apple, and Google. *The Verge*. www.theverge.com/2022/1/20/22892939/music-streaming-services-market-share-q2-2021-spotify-apple-amazon-tencent-youtube

Prescott, S. M. (2022). In *Me, Myself and AI*. https://sloanreview.mit.edu/audio/choreographing-human-machine-collaboration-spotifys-sidney-madison-prescott/

Reigart, E. M. (2020). Is Artificial Intelligence Friend or Foe to Radio? *Radio World*. www.radioworld.com/industry/is-artificial-intelligence-friend-or-foe-to-radio

Robertson, D. (2020, 9 November 2020). 'It's the screams of the damned!' The eerie AI world of deepfake music. *The Guardian*. www.theguardian.com/music/2020/nov/09/deepfake-pop-music-artificial-intelligence-ai-frank-sinatra

Roettgers, J. (2018, 23 May 2018). Nielsen's Gracenote Uses Artificial Intelligence to Classify 90 Million Songs by Style. *Variety*. https://variety.com/2018/digital/news/gracenote-music-ai-sonic-style-1202819230/

Ross, M. (2022). Interview with Dr Alex Connock [Interview at Said Business School, University of Oxford, MBA Module 'The Business of Arts, Culture and Entertainment'].

Savage, M. (2019). *BTS* are the first Korean band to headline Wembley Stadium. www.bbc.co.uk/news/entertainment-arts-48487862

Savage, M. (2021). MPs call for complete reset of music streaming to ensure fair pay for artists. www.bbc.co.uk/news/entertainment-arts-57838473

Savage, M. (2022, 22 March 2022). The global music market was worth $26bn in 2021. *BBC News*. www.bbc.co.uk/news/entertainment-arts-60837880

SBSPopAsia. (2016, 2016-10-18). *BTS set new Billboard 200 record with 'WINGS.'* www.sbs.com.au/popasia/blog/2016/10/18/bts-set-new-billboard-200-record-wings

Schreiber, D. and Rieple, A. (2021) Aggrandisement: Helping Micro-Enterprise Owner-Managers Construct Credibility in the Recorded Music Industry. *Journal of Media Business Studies*, 1–25. doi.org/10.1080/16522354.2021.1978263

Sentric. (2016) A [DAB]ble Into Radio Royalties. https://sentricmusic.com/blog/a-dabble-into-radio-royalties/

Simon, J. P. (2019) New players in the music industry: lifeboats or killer whales? the role of streaming platforms. *Digital Policy, Regulation and Governance*, 21(6), 525–49. doi.org/http://dx.doi.org/10.1108/DPRG-06-2019-0041

Spurk, C. and Dingerkus, F. (2017). The need and the opportunities for sustainability – The case of local radio stations in Tanzania. *Journal of Media Business Studies*, 14(1), 38–59. doi.org/10.1080/16522354.2017.1292715

Stringer, R. (2021, 10 March 2021) In Variety Strictly Business podcast with Rob Stringer Chairman of Sony Music. https://variety.com/2021/music/podcasts/rob-stringer-strictly-business-podcast-interview-1234924585/

Tiffany, K. (2019, 11 January 2019) Spotify's most personalized playlist is now for sale to brands. *Vox*. www.vox.com/the-goods/2019/1/11/18178701/spotify-discover-weekly-brand-playlists-personalization

Vanek Smith, S. (2021) *BTS*: The Band That Moves The Economy: The Indicator from Planet Money. www.npr.org/2021/07/28/1021968141/bts-the-band-that-moves-the-economy

Weinberger, M. and Bouhnik, D. (2021) Various information aspects following the emergence of music streaming applications [Information aspects in music streaming apps]. *Online Information Review*, 45(1), 118–37. doi.org/http://dx.doi.org/10.1108/OIR-04-2020-0118

Zaugg, J. (2018) Inside the intensive world of K-POP cram schools. www.cnn.com/2018/10/05/asia/kpop-schools-south-korea-intl/index.html

SECTION D

Pioneers

New sectors building the future of media
production and distribution

CHAPTER 16

Podcasting

A digital-driven content development factory

....

INTRODUCTION TO THE SECTOR

Podcasting is a combination of the words 'iPod' and 'broadcast,' previously known (by some) as radio-on-demand.

Podcasts grew from independent radio production, a niche segment built out of volunteerism, small branded projects and public stations – as the internet facilitated transmission of audio files. Through quality, range and early investment by Apple, podcasting became one of the most creatively exciting sectors in media.

But it is also a relatively small one, valued globally at $11.4 billion in 2020.

- It is forecast to grow fast – by one finance firm on average at 31% annually. Even so, as yet it has "an unfeasible economics model" (Podcasting Market Size, 2021).
- Another firm puts projected podcast revenue at a $94 billion revenue industry by 2028 (InsiderIntelligence, 2021).
- Podcast usage (as opposed to production) is definitely growing. In February, 2022, industry source *Podtrac* said podcast downloads were up by 61% over the same period in the previous year.
- Growth in the Arts podcasts category was particularly strong at 78%, and Sports were up even more, at 122%.
- In the United States, the number of listeners was growing at 6.1% annually in the US to 125 million in 2021, and worldwide listeners were projected to be 424.2 million in 2022, or 20.3% of internet users as a whole (InsiderIntelligence, 2021).
- Of those numbers listening, the younger demographics dominate: amongst consumers aged 35–44, over half listen monthly in the US. For comparison, *Nielsen*

DOI: 10.4324/9781003213611-20

data said US network TV ratings declined by 29% over the same period, and by 82% over the ten years period to 2022.

For most podcast creators, podcasting is not a viable business model. The average podcast has 27 listens per episode (Riverside, 2021). The top 1% have only 3,200 listens per episode – still not enough for significant advertising. But at the other end of the spectrum, *The Joe Rogan Experience* reaches over 7 million listeners.

Even if podcasting is not yet economically significant, there is additional value: creativity. This nascent industry is a source of some of the most original content and in media of the 2020s. Those ideas are changing storytelling, and influencing other sectors. Podcasting is a quintessential creator economy.

THE VALUE CREATION MODEL

Development

At the development stage of the value creation process in podcasts, informal market analysis is essential: what shows exist in the sub-genre of podcasting that the firm or creator plans to enter and what is performing well?

From here, key inputs are ideas generated (like *Morbid: A True Crime Podcast*) combined with the personal brand of the producer or presenter (say, *Smartless:* Jason Bateman) and any brand equity that the production company has (*Dateline: NBC*). Production company *Gimlet* has substantial brand equity, and a podcast from the firm gains automatically higher profile (*544 Days, The Disappearance, Every Little*

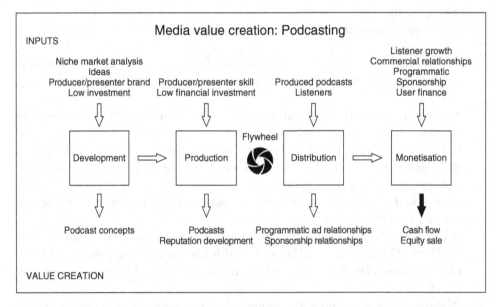

FIGURE 16.1 Successful distribution of a podcast means finding an audience – which then feeds back revenues, facilitating enhanced production volume and budgets

Thing.) Key outputs at this phase are the prototype podcasts themselves, in finished form, because production is cheap.

Value creation in podcasting is about ideas. Like the creator space, this is a democratic media category, with free-flowing innovation. (Like *The Pitch:* where real entrepreneurs pitch to real investors – for real money.)

Podcaster Joe Rogan said: "The beautiful thing about podcasting is it's just talking. It can be funny, or it can be terrifying. It can be sweet. It can be obnoxious. It almost has no definitive form."

There are as many genres within the podcast space as there are in the media as a whole: drama (*Unwell, A Midwestern Gothic Mystery*), documentary (*Slow Burn, This American Life*), sports (*That Peter Crouch Podcast*), conversation (*Everything is Alive*), humour (*How Did This Get Made*), news (*The Daily*) and many more.

"The podcast industry is in a particular moment of creative and innovative renaissance," says one industry report. (InsiderIntelligence, 2021). Podcasts enable the disintermediation of traditional networks – and are a spur to creativity.

An academic study on 'authentic outsiders' in American comedy suggests that the genre itself has had a powerful impact on the kind of talent who can reach the mainstream.

> This new generation of "outsider" comedians is challenging the power of an American television industry which largely excluded them … through the low-budget, less conspicuously mediated form of the podcast, these comedians have been able to manufacture a perceived "authentic" celebrity image, differing from that which is historically possible in television or film.
>
> *(Symons, 2017)*

Genre breakdown

Podcasts, like all media forms, are built on constant viral imitation and iteration, and ever-evolving micro-genres.

* Genre-splitting shows such as *Welcome to Night Vale* (a scripted sci-fi/conspiracy show in the shape of a local news service) *Serial* (an investigative show that spends a season on a single story) and *Lore* (a 'campfire' storytelling show about nefarious activities) spawned many shows in similar breakout formats (Tee Morris, 2020).
* Each constellation in podcast universe has a solar system of shows, each of which influences the others with its creative gravity. In life advice, the *NPR Life Kit* podcast adopts the tropes of the how-to ecology; how to be less indecisive, how to cope with the stressful news cycle.
* Top podcast *Start With This* aims to make listeners cleverer, *Philosophy Bites* teaches them useful metaphysics and axioms and so forth.
* In the media space (useful for readers of this book) *Sway* (from the *New York Times*), *The Verge*, *Equity* (from TechCrunch), *Wall Street Journal Tech News*,

Variety's The Business, Pivot and many others all cover similar issues around the nexus between the media business and tech.

- In sport: *Brian Windhorst and the Hoop Collective* and *The Lowe Post* both by ESPN, *Always Cheating: A Fantasy Premier League Podcast* by Blue Wire, *The Athletic FPL Podcast* by *The Athletic* offer discursive and sophisticated coverage.

Similar ecologies of creativity exist in every niche of spiritual (*On Being*), business (*After Hours*), political (*L'Atelier du Pouvoir*) and artistic life (*The Week in Art*). There are thousands of podcasts in each major genre – far more than there are drama shows or films.

Why is this? Because in common with the creator economy in video (see Chapter 14), the media firm has been dis-intermediated; podcasts are not subject to the 'gate-keeper' of a media firm or backer for their right to exist and be produced.

Production

At the Production stage of the value creation process, key inputs are again the skill and brand of the producer, presenter and production company, and potentially low financial investment for production costs. Outputs include the podcasts themselves and the development of the reputation of the participants, which may enhance other productions.

Podcasts are recorded anywhere and with a wide range of tools, from phone to zoom call to laptop. They are edited on a variety of software options (like *Voice Recorder, Adobe Audition, Hindenburg Journalist, Logic Pro, GarageBand*) and compressed into MP3 using a tool such as *Audacity*. After editing, metatags (ID3 tags) are added, giving basic information to the file, and show notes are created.

Industry range

Podcasts are created by individuals, but also increasingly by news publishers and other media companies.

- On the US most-listened podcasts list in December 2020, many of the country's most significant firms featured: NPR, Cumulus Media/Westwood One, NBC News, WarnerMedia, Fox News (Adgate, 2021).
- News publishers in a range of countries "are making significant investments in news podcasting, hoping to attract younger audiences, build habit, and bring in additional revenue," said a report (Newman and Gallo, 2019) from Oxford's *Reuters Institute for the Study of Journalism*.
- Amongst 49,514 podcasts categorised as news (of which nearly 12,000 were new in 2019 alone) they picked out three sub categories: micro bulletins (1–5 minutes), news round ups (6–15 minutes) and deep dives (20 minutes or more.) They suggest that – true to their respective heritages – news publishers tend to

go for deep dives, whilst broadcasters tend to go for multi-item podcasts. *The Economist* features three stories in *The Intelligence*. *The Wall Street Journal* tells a single story in *The Journal* produced with Gimlet (Newman and Gallo, 2019).

- Production companies Gimlet, Wondery and Stitcher produce a substantial portion of the top domestic shows in the US. Wondery reached the top of the podcast charts in seven countries with its *Dr Death* true crime series in 2019.
- Whilst America dominates, with 40% of global listening, podcasts have global traction. Of the top 200 podcasts in Sweden, 40% are foreign produced, and in Australia that figure is 58%. However, in the US, only 7% of the top podcasts are made overseas (Newman and Gallo, 2019).

Podcasts have been used for an almost infinite variety of cultural purposes.

- In Senegal, the podcast *Xam sa dŭmb, xam sa tey* ("Know your past, know your present") sets up out to bring the nation's history to life. It was created by the national archives working with the Goethe institute. It has fifty, 15-minute episodes online, in both local language Wolof and French.

Creativity is not confined to content within the podcast: it's also around the format itself. Podcasts increasingly contain video, blurring the lines with wider creator content (see Chapter 14) on *YouTube* and elsewhere.

- Video podcasts include *The Joe Rogan Experience*, *Technorama* and *Universe Today*. (Tee Morris, 2020).
- Video game streaming platform *Twitch* can also be used for podcast streaming, as can *YouTube*, *Periscope*, *Twitter* and *Facebook Live*.
- In this vibrant melee of creativity, a lot of firms are "trying to figure out kind of how to create the *TikTok* of audio" (Carman, 2021).

Distribution

Once the podcast is created and produced, value needs to be created, which means it needs an audience. This is the Distribution stage in podcasting, where key inputs are a sufficient set of produced podcasts to gain market traction, and a strong listen count. Key value-creating outputs are programmatic advertising (e.g., with *Spotify* – see below) and/or sponsor relationships. Distribution and production can interact at this point in a flywheel. The more content is produced and distributed, the more listeners can engage with. More engagement means more content can be produced.

Like in the video creator economy, distribution costs are minimal, because the platforms are free. (There are some admin and transaction costs.) In the video creator industry, formats and sizes are specific to each platform – *YouTube*, *Facebook* – requiring bespoke uploads. However, audio files are platform agnostic and can be simultaneously uploaded to all platforms via an intermediary provider.

- A newly uploaded podcast is listed in directories, the main of which are *Spotify*, *Apple Podcasts*, *Podcast Index*, *Google Play*, *Amazon Music*, *iHeart Radio*, *Overcast*, *Castbox*, *Podcast Addict*, *Pocket Casts*, *Pandora Stitcher* and *BluBrry*.
- The technicalities of distribution are being automated with directly AI-driven publishing tools (see AI section below).
- Of these options, *Spotify* is emerging as fractionally the largest, claiming to have overtaken *Apple Podcasts* as the most-used podcast platform in the US, in October 2021, just above Apple's 28 million listeners (InsiderIntelligence, 2021).
- Where the podcast is considered high value it may be an exclusive to one network – for instance, with Meghan Markle's 2022 *Spotify* podcast (Spangler, 2022b). Podcasts can also be discovered via search engines like *Listen Notes*, a database of the material content of podcasts as well as the titles. *Spotify* provides podcasters with statistics on streams (over a minute) and starts (under a minute.) Lower length interactions cannot be monetised.

Alongside those platforms are major producers, who publish podcasts on their own sites, and take advantage of their substantial traffic – such as *NPR*, *The New York Times* and the BBC (with its *BBC Sounds* platform).

- Podcast listeners tend to be younger: of people aged 18–34 in the US in 2019, about 53% were podcast listeners, against only 19% in the 55+ age group (Newman and Gallo, 2019).

Monetisation

Amid all this creativity, a financial reality check is appropriate. Asked in Oxford (April 2022) about the potential of podcasts as an opportunity for the distribution of advertising, three leading executives from the largest global media buying agencies expressed doubt that this media segment had the scale, content quality and brand safety to have real traction in global advertising.

Yet at the Monetisation stage of value creation in podcasting, there is opportunity for both business growth and profit. Key inputs are strength of the listener count and any commercial relationships created. Value-creating outputs are programmatic ads, sponsorships, foundation money and user contributions (see below), resulting in cash flow and equity uplift for the company, including its potential sale.

Podcasts reach customers via a 'push' mechanism following 'subscription' – but unlike in streaming, subscription is usually free. This is one way podcasting is not (yet) effectively monetised like streaming (where subscription is paid, or ad-funded) or social video (funded by programmatic advertising). A 2022 research report said of podcasting "the unfeasible economic model is one of the main concerns for publishers offering content on media streaming platforms." Advertising had not worked because of audience resistance. "But brands are working on alternatives" (Podcasting Market Size, 2021).

Cracking this value conundrum is a challenge for podcasting business in the 2020s. There are eight routes to monetisation – paid production, advertising sales, sponsorship/affiliate sales, programmatic advertising, e-commerce, selling shows for TV/film, listener donations, and selling the business. (See also Creator section in Chapter 14.)

Paid production

By the end of 2020, *Spotify* had 2.2 million podcasts on the platform, with aggregate listening treble the 2019 level.

But its value creation challenge, common to podcast platforms, was lack of content ownership. "There's so much to like [in the business model] and yet … Unlike *Netflix*, the deep problem is they don't own content, up until podcasts. And so, the thing that *Netflix* had, which was content that was sticky and it was original" (Moon, 2021).

- For *Spotify* to add exclusive content, they bought podcast production companies Gimlet Media and Anchor, and invested some $200 million in *The Joe Rogan Experience*. *Spotify* became a direct production funder. From the producers' perspective, value in their businesses had been crystallised by sale.
- Other companies offering similar direct commissioning and monetisation avenues to producers are the BBC and *New York Times*.
- France's top podcast (Chartable chart, March 2022) is *L'Heure du Monde*, produced by newspaper group *Le Monde*.

For producers, being simply paid by a bigger media organisation to produce content, even at the expense of giving away rights to that content, is a direct value creation strategy.

Advertising sales

Podcast advertising is proving its model, albeit from a small start.

- A study in March 2022 by *The Guardian* and research company Tapestry found Podcast adverts achieved more listener attention than other channels; 65% of listeners paid attention versus 38% on radio and 39% on TV, which translated into a 51% propensity to buy, again versus 38% on radio. When a podcast channel was added to the overall mix for brands, trust rose from 45% to 63% (Douglas, 2022).
- Not only that but "listeners tend to be young, affluent, and educated, and generally open to advertising in podcasting" (InsiderIntelligence, 2021).
- A study by Edison Research found that people over age 13 spend 6% of their audio time with podcasts, increased from 2% in 2014 (Adgate, 2021).
- The share of monthly podcast listeners aged 12–34 went from 27% in 2017 to 49% in 2020. The highest number of users using podcasts on a daily basis are

in News, which accounts for 30% of all podcasting revenues. Format-wise, the interview format was also dominant in revenue generation at 30% (Podcasting Market Size, 2021).

Advertisers view podcasts as a platform to reach engaged, self-segmented customers. Combining niche audiences (which drives advertising efficiency) with user-specific addressability of platforms such as *Spotify* drives opportunity for value creation through programmatic advertising.

Programmatic advertising

Because the medium works, programmatic advertising spend is growing in podcasts.

- An industry report estimated $800 million in podcast advertising spend in the US in 2020, rising to $1.7 billion by 2024.
- Not only does podcast advertising reach a potentially attractive audience – but it may be attractive to them in turn. Those keen enough on the genre to listen to 5 hours a week or more were 'super listeners,' amongst whom 49% agreed that "advertising on a podcast is the best way for a brand to reach you" and 54% would actually buy a product after hearing an advert (Adgate, 2021).
- The number of adverts in podcasts is on the rise – to 3.3, on average, per podcast by September 2021.

Platforms are developing programmatic advertising products with equivalent offers to the immensely lucrative, targeted models seen on *YouTube* and Snapchat.

- *Spotify* offers programmatic advertising (like an audio version of *YouTube* pre- and mid-rolls) via its *Spotify Audience Network*. To make that possible, *Spotify* bought Megaphone, the publisher oriented podcast monetisation platform (Carman, 2021).
- The advertiser experience provided by *Spotify* (and their ability to activate pro- grammatic advertising with actual sales leads, in performance marketing) was improved with call-to-action cards, offering click-through experience. "With these investments, we're delivering impact for advertisers and growth for pod- cast publishers like the *Wall Street Journal*, ViacomCBS, and AdLarge," said *Spotify*.
- Similar programmatic offers are found worldwide. In India, HT Media launched an audio programmatic market for the country with AdsWizz in 2021. "Our technology combines the power of programmatic advertising with the power of podcasts, enabling advertisers' easy access to a highly engaged audience," said Ads Wizz, estimating 170.6 million podcast listeners in India by 2023 (Podnews, 2021).

To make all this programmatic effort work and reach scale, *Spotify* also needed bigger shows (like *The Joe Rogan Experience*), increasing power and reach in its ad inventory.

Podcasters in turn use sites *Technocrats* and *Google* to verify audience interaction (Tee Morris, 2020). To complete its audio programmatic advertising investments, and justify advertising buys to corporate clients with hard metrics, *Spotify* added tech companies Podsights (podcast audience measurement) and Chartable (analytics and attribution) (Spotify, 2022).

Sponsorship

Value generation for a podcaster can also be achieved with direct show sponsors.

- KLM Royal Dutch Airlines backed *The Journey*, an award-winning podcast from audio company Airborne, about lives transformed by travel.
- Other examples of sponsored podcasts include Mike Rowe's *The Way I Heard It* podcast and WNYC's *Note to Self* which have been sponsored by such companies as Blue Apron and Squarespace (Tee Morris, 2020).
- The top investors in podcast sponsorship in the US in 2021 were *Better Help* (spending $35.7 million in the first seven months of the year) and *Zip Recruiter*, with $13.6 million.
- Other big consumer brands were *HelloFresh*, *NBC Universal*, *Amazon* and *Capital One*. Strong B2B investors included Simplisafe and Squarespace (Lebow, 2021).

E-commerce and affiliate models

In context of over 4 million podcasts, media sponsorships are still uncommon.

Other models include affiliate programs (referral sponsorships), in which vendors get a code that podcasters can offer listeners for discounts or exclusive deals, paying them commission for sales. Affiliations like this feature on podcast *Happy Hour from the Tower*, and are a good way of hedging risk: if no sales are made, no fee is paid (Tee Morris, 2020).

Shows can simply sell their own goods in direct e-commerce. This can be standard online shopping, or custom merchandising to that podcast – for example, in the US, delivered by *CafePress*. Start-ups such as MikMak are aiming to make shoppable technology available to all podcasts.

Listener donations

A simple way to monetise a podcast is to ask for listener donations, via *PayPal* or similar. This can work well for fan-driven podcasts, or those with a particular political or social thrust.

- Good examples are found in the socially aware *Radiotopia Presents* network; *Adultish* looks a issues like mental health, *S***hole Country* looks at immigrant stories, *Ear Hustle* examines prison life.
- Outside that network, the *Radical Personal Finance* podcast used *Patreon* (see Chapter 14) as a tool to recruit 200 listener-funders for a small podcast.

Selling formats

Podcasts are a useful low-cost testing ground for material that can then be made, at higher cost, into TV shows and film.

Production cost per hour of a podcast could be as little as a thousandth of premium TV drama. Using podcasts as a development 'skunkworks' can make sense for media producers. As *The Hollywood Reporter* said: "Podcasts seem to be the source material *du jour* … whether the inspiration is a work of journalism or narrative fiction, showrunners say that coming armed with an audio sample to a pitch meeting can increase the chances of getting a green light."

Condé Nast Entertainment, the cross-platform production company from the publishers of *Vogue* magazine, amongst others, use podcasts to test creative ideas that can translate to TV and film (O'Connell, 2022) as part of a wider digital multi-platform strategy launched in 2021.

Examples of format sales include *Netflix* horror series *Archive 81*, Apple's *WeCrashed* (about WeWork) and *Gaslit* (based on the *Slow Burn* podcast).

Selling the business

Possibly the best way to monetise podcasts is to sell the business that makes them. The multiples paid on earnings can be high.

- The UK's leading podcast production company Somethin' Else was sold to Sony Music Entertainment in June, 2021 as the driver of the Japanese company's global expansion. "Our new global podcast division is key to our plans for a fast-paced expansion in the market, diversifying our creative abilities and providing a home for exciting content that will benefit millions," said the acquisition statement (Creamer, 2021).
- Amazon bought podcast producer Wondery in December 2020 – a podcast network with a monthly audience of 8 million listeners – for a reported $300 million.
- *SiriusXM* bought Stitcher – which hosts 462,000 podcasts (at March 2022) and has 50 of its own, as well as an ad-funded app and an advertising-free version for $4.99 monthly subscription from E. W. Scripps for a reported $235 million.
- In 2020, *The New York Times* bought Serial Productions, producer of *This American Life* (Adgate, 2021).
- Sports podcaster Bill Simmons sold his business, *The Ringer*, to *Spotify*, for nearly $200 million (via earnout).
- *Spotify* spent $400 million on Gimlet Media, Anchor and Parcast (Leskin, 2020).

AI technologies

AI tools are used in the production, distribution and creation of podcasts. Common themes are Natural Language Processing (NLP) for translation and synthetic voices.

AI in podcast production

- *Adobe Audition* is part of an industry standard suite of tools, with integrated AI. Its Generate Speech tool lets users type text and generate a voice over track using synthesised voices.
- AI-assisted editing tool *Podcastle* automatically converts news content into a podcast, providing instant audio publishing and synthetic voices. Machine learning also allows simultaneous playback and editing. (Normally in non-linear editing, the user does one or the other.)
- *Descript* uses NLP to transcribe podcast recording in real time, cut gaps in the conversation and eliminate words like 'er' and 'um' and thereby speeding up the edit process. Having put audio into text, *Descript* then allows drag and drop editing of the audio from a text document – a massive workflow improvement. Within *Descript*, the *Lyrebird AI* division allows users to create automated synthesised versions of their *own* voices – an overdub tool that means that if a recording misses a key sentence, it can be voice-synthesised into the edit (The Rise of AI Podcast Tools, 2019).
- This has led to concerns of a risk of deepfakes. Machine learning company Dessa deepfaked the voice of leading podcaster Joe Rogan. To mitigate against misuse of synthetic voices, *Descript* made users of its Overdub go through a live recording process, making it impossible to upload third party voices.
- AI research company DeepMind built the *WaveNet* voice synthesis tool, using a deep generative model to imitate any voice at levels of verisimilitude in both English and Mandarin Chinese higher than earlier speech-to-text models, because it uses 16,000 samples per second. It beats earlier concatenative and parametric models of voice synthesis, and on samples of just a few minutes of audio (Fry, 2022). This tool can be used in podcasts to synthesise missing audio from speakers.
- Voice synthesis could also have countless malign uses, like bank fraud, if released onto the market. Audio watermarks stating voices were fake could be one potential solution to that. *Wavenet* has also been used to create realistic classical piano music (DeepMind, 2016).
- *Auphonic* algorithmically polishes audio with intelligent levellers, loudness normalisation, audio restoration and an 80-language speech recognition and transcript editor.
- *Otter.ai* and *SpeechText.Ai* are transcription services

AI in podcast distribution

Spotify Podcast Ads serves advertising based on user actions, and is interactive, so that "users can directly engage with podcast ads without needing to remember, say, the coupon codes … a staggering 81% of listeners have taken action after hearing audio ads during a podcast" (Spotify, 2020).

- *Spreaker* is an audience-building tool that syncs with podcast distribution platforms, enabling dynamic ad creating contextual to podcast material, plus real-time analytics.
- *Buzzsprout* automatically optimises ('magic mastering') and publishes audio, providing promotional tools such as 'visual soundbites' as short videos. It runs over 100,000 podcasts.
- *Podcast.co* has real-time AI-driven transcription (like *Otter* and *Speechtext*) using NLP and machine learning, and an automated distribution tool to assist podcast promotion to multiple networks simultaneously.
- Podcast platform *iHeartMedia* in 2022 aimed to use Veritone's synthetic-voice tool to translate and produce podcasts into other languages – starting with Spanish versions of *Stuff They Don't Want You to Know*, *Tech Stuff* and *Ridiculous History*. Its goal was synthetic voice in 119 languages, plus dialects and accents. It can be used for advertising creation and translation too (Spangler, 2022a).

AI in podcast creation

- Podcast *Sheldon County* was created by PhD student James Ryan in 2018, allowing users to type a random number into a site, which set off a calculation machine designing characters, relationships and action. That is all narrated by a voice synthesiser and turned into an audio file which can be distributed (Vincent, 2018).

Exercise: podcasting

For a podcast to be viable, it needs to have ten clear attributes: central editorial proposition, clear genre, format, target audience, presentation style, marketing/distribution strategy, promotional plan, release schedule or 'cadence,' budget and monetisation plan.

Podcasts can be a consumer-centred media product (B2C) – like *Welcome to Your Fantasy*, from Gimlet, a true crime series about the *Chippendales* dance group. Here the monetisation model is likely to be around advertising or even subscription. (True crime as entertainment is a paradoxical concept: as Steve Martin observed in the hit Hulu drama series *Only Murders in the Building* (2021) "Every true crime story is actually true for someone.")

Or podcasts can be conceived as a business to business (B2B) tool to help a firm transmit to potential customers its enhanced understanding of a particular sector. Here the business model may be a single company's sponsorship – an 'owned media' product (see Chapter 13). A good example: *Deepmind: the Podcast*, a series about the London-based, Google-owned firm's work in multiple fields of Artificial Intelligence.

Either …

- Design a B2C podcast. Create a slide deck showing your plan for a consumer podcast to be released in your country.
- Design a B2B podcast. Create a clear document for your board showing them why their sponsorship of a podcast that your company will put out will win new clients.

If you are in a class, split with each half working on each task. Then when each team pitches, the other half of the class can play the role of the board, asking probing questions about the podcast idea, and then voting on which idea the board will back

CHAPTER SUMMARY

TABLE 16.1 Key themes in this chapter

Podcast	Development	Production	Distribution	Monetisation
Business model	Low or zero investment (apart from time) in content creation.	Low investment in producing content.	Zero investment in distribution (except when using paid promotion strategies).	Programmatic and, affiliate ads, sponsorship, product placement, e-commerce, subscription.
Uses of AI	Low AI usage.	Production tools and custom software integrate AI in multiple ways.	High AI usage by platforms for personalisation, audience segmentation.	Use of AI in advertising optimisation to maximise returns for platform and creator.
Value Creation	Low value creation at ideas stage.	Low value creation at the production phase until audience traction is achieved.	Value generation from audience success.	Strongest monetisation around sale of exclusivity on a strong title, or sale of business.

BIBLIOGRAPHY

Adgate, B. (2021, 11 February). As Podcasts Continue To Grow In Popularity, Ad Dollars Follow. *Forbes.* www.forbes.com/sites/bradadgate/2021/02/11/podcasting-has-become-a-big-business/?sh=1678c6b52cfb

Carman, A. (2021, 27 December 2021). Recode Media In *The Verge's Ashley Carman on Podcasting's Big Year.* https://open.spotify.com/episode/4ftrKVazL7BqVAFLkIj3ge

Creamer, J. (2021). Sony Music buys Somethin' Else. www.televisual.com/news/sony-music-buys-somethin-else/

DeepMind. (2016). WaveNet: A generative model for raw audio. https://deepmind.com/blog/article/wavenet-generative-model-raw-audio

Douglas, F. (2022, 16 March 2022). Guardian study finds podcast ads command more attention than other media channels. *Campaign.* www.campaignlive.co.uk/article/guardian-study-finds-podcast-ads-command-attention-media-channels/1749731

Fry, H. (2022, January 2022). Series 2 In *DeepMind: the Podcast.* www.deepmind.com/the-podcast

InsiderIntelligence. (2021). *Podcast Industry Report: Market Growth and Advertising Statistics in 2022.* www.insiderintelligence.com/insights/the-podcast-industry-report-statistics/

Lebow, S. (2021, 4 October 2021). A look at the biggest US advertisers in podcasting. *Insider Intelligence.* www.emarketer.com/content/look-biggest-us-advertisers-podcasting

Leskin, P. (2020, 12 February 2020). Bill Simmons scores massive sale as Spotify buys his publication, The Ringer, for nearly $200 million. *Insider.* www.businessinsider.com/spotify-ringer-deal-price-250-million-podcasting-bill-simmons-report-2020-2?r=US&IR=T

Moon, Y. (2021, 24 March 2021). HBR After Hours In *The NFT craze and Spotify.* https://hbr.org/podcast/2021/03/the-nft-craze-and-the-future-of-spotify-and-streaming-music

Newman, N., and Gallo, N. (2019). News Podcasts and the Opportunities for Publishers. Reuters Institute of Journalism. https://reutersinstitute.politics.ox.ac.uk/news-podcasts-and-opportunities-publishers

O'Connell, M. (2022, 6 March 2022). Podcasts Are Hollywood's Source Material Du Jour. *Hollywood Reporter.* www.hollywoodreporter.com/business/digital/podcasts-hollywood-the-dropout-wecrashed-1235102186/

Podcasting Market Size. (2021). Published by Grand View Research. www.grandviewresearch.com/industry-analysis/podcast-market

Podnews. (2021, 29 December 2021). HT Media Ltd. launches India's first programmatic podcast marketplace in partnership with AdsWizz www.livemint.com/technology/ht-media-partners-adswizz-to-bring-india-s-first-programmatic-podcast-marketplace-11640770877314.html

The Rise of AI Podcast Tools. (2019). www.podcast.co/reach/ai-podcast-tools

Riverside. (2021, 22 September 2021). Podcast Statistics and Trends (& Why They Matter). https://riverside.fm/blog/podcast-statistics

Spangler, T. (2022) iHeartMedia will translate English Podcasts into other languages using Veritone's synthetic voices. *Variety.* [online] Available at: https://variety.com/2022/digital/news/iheartmedia-podcast-translate-synthetic-voices-veritone-1235184677/ [Accessed 16 August 2022].

Spangler, T. (2022b, 17 March 2022). Meghan Markle Podcast Coming to Spotify This Summer, After Royal Couple Resolves Concerns Over Streamer's Handling of COVID Misinfo. *Variety.* https://variety.com/2022/digital/news/meghan-markle-podcast-spotify-covid-misinformation-1235208317/

Spotify. (2020, 8 January 2020). *Spotify's Head of Global Ads Business and Platform Jay Richman Talks New Spotify Podcast Ads* https://newsroom.spotify.com/2020-01-08/spotifys-head-of-global-ads-business-and-platform-jay-richman-talks-new-spotify-podcast-ads/

Spotify. (2022, 16 February 2022). Spotify Acquires Podsights and Chartable To Advance Podcast Measurement for Advertisers and Insights for Publishers. https://newsroom.spotify.com/2022-02-16/spotify-acquires-podsights-and-chartable-to-advance-podcast-measurement-for-advertisers-and-insights-for-publishers/

Symons, A. (2017). Podcast comedy and 'Authentic Outsiders': how new media is challenging the owners of industry. *Celebrity studies*, *8*(1), 104–18. https://doi.org/10.1080/19392397.2016.1217162

Tee Morris, C. T. (2020). *Podcasting for Dummies*. 4th edition. Published by For Dummies

Vincent, J. (2018). What an 'infinite' AI-generated podcast can tell us about the future of entertainment. www.theverge.com/2018/3/11/17099578/ai-generated-podcast-procedural-storytelling-art-sheldon-county

CHAPTER 17

Esports

A new digital business, but with echoes of twentieth-century models

....

INTRODUCTION TO THE SECTOR

"All the best games are easy to learn and difficult to master." That is called Nolan's Law, after Nolan Bushnell, who was the 1972 founder of *Atari* – one of the original sources of classic games, including *Space Invaders* (Scholz, 2020).

The law fits Esports very well – a media business segment which is the natural offspring of the massive video games sector covered in Chapter 5. The games sector is a $180 billion annual revenue juggernaut. Esports had a more delicate $1.084 billion revenue of its own in 2021 (Newzoo, 2021). But it is growing fast.

- With 465 million people watching them (Wijman, 2021) Esports are amongst the most watched content on the planet.
- In 2021, 23.3 billion hours of games were watched on *Twitch*, plus another 4.5 billion on *YouTube Gaming* and (new to the space) 3.5 billion hours on *Facebook Gaming* (Wijman, 2021).
- Segmentation of 2021 Esports revenues included $641 million from sponsorship (up 11% year-on-year), $192.6 million from media rights, $126 million from publisher fees and $66 million from merchandise and tickets (probably pandemic-affected) (Wijman, 2021).

The Esports sector started in 1972 with a Stanford University *Spacewar!* student competition, where the winning prize was a year's *Rolling Stone* magazine subscription.

- By 2019 the sport was substantially more economically significant. Kyle "Bugha" Giersdorf won $3 million in the *Fortnite* World Cup final that year, which is more

DOI: 10.4324/9781003213611-21

than Novak Djokovic received for winning the *Wimbledon* tennis men's final (Clifford Chance, 2020).

- Investment bank Goldman Sachs saw an investment opportunity. "We believe Esports are at the cross-section of some powerful trends: social connections being formed and maintained online, digital consumption of video, and global growth in the gaming audience." They suggested that Esports revenue would reach $2.96 billion in 2022 (Merwin, 2018).

But for all the hype, viewership and excitement, Esports is also, as yet, a nascent media segment, whose total revenue is roughly equivalent to that of a single hit Hollywood movie, or a passable weekend's trading for Apple. The short-term value in Esports may actually reside not in its ticketing, event merchandising or advertising and sponsorship opportunities, but simply in its marketing potential for video games, a point acknowledged in conversation with an executive from a global games company.

Unlike in the other comparably small and new 'pioneers' sector in this book – podcasting – there is little value creation through intellectual property development in Esports. But there is a potentially more scaleable revenue base, born of the enormous client traction at global scale of video games, and therefore there is probably more value creation opportunity in advertising.

Scale and content

Esports (or 'electronic sports,' in its full expansion) is a live arena event, which is then 'broadcast' globally – in many ways a very twentieth-century media construct, like *Live Aid* (1985), or any given *Manchester United* home match.

In Esports that live event is competitive video gaming, where pro and amateur players compete for cash. Esports depends on elite video games players both competing, and being relatable enough to mass market players that people will join in their hundreds of thousands to watch them, enjoy the show and pick up tips.

In Esports, championships and tournaments are organised by game developers, or third party organisers who have license the rights to the games (SBJ, 2017). The biggest tournaments are held in stadiums and have "the same atmosphere as rock concerts" (Meddings, 2021).

- Esports fall into categories according to the game the players play. They can be based around electronic versions of original sports like *FIFA*, *NBA* or *F1*. They can be fighting games, like *Mortal Kombat* or *Tekken*. Or they can be first-person shooter (FPS) games like *Valorant* or *Counter-Strike*.
- The most popular Esports games are multiplayer: *League of Legends* (or LoL), *Defense of the Ancients 2* (or *Dota 2*), *Call of Duty* (CoD), *Overwatch* and *Fortnite* (Kordyaka et al., 2020). Multiplayer creates better live event action.
- Esports is notably inclusive, especially when compared to 'real' sports. It is global, open to all contestants, and a level playing field regardless of gender and physical ability. (Though it does have constraints around equality of bandwidth,

or latency, on a technical level.) Top players and teams can earn significant sums. The *International Olympic Committee* said in July 2021 that Esports may one day be in the Olympics, potentially as early as 2028.

- Esports often play out on *Twitch*, the (mostly) game-streaming platform at vast scale, making this one of the biggest screen activities globally by view time. *League of Legends* had 29 billion views by April 2020, on *Twitch* alone. In 2012. an estimated 134 million people watched gamers competing. By 2021 that number had leapt to 443 million (Newzoo, 2021). There are not many media sectors trebling their user base in a decade.
- The demographics of Esports are attractive to advertisers, and that may present a viable long-term future for the sector. Some 41% of Esports viewers on *Twitch* are age 16–24, and another 32% are age 25 to 34 (BritishEsportsAssociation, 2021). According to a Newzoo report, the worldwide Esports audience will grow to 920.3 million by 2024, a further compound growth rate of +9.2% on top of what has been achieved already.

Investment

Esports is not yet at scale as a media industry, and not yet be a profitable venture for game developers (Amenabar, 2021). Investment is needed in the sector to organise championships, support professional leagues and promote events. To meet that demand, and attracted by the exponential growth potential in the market, venture capital firms are increasingly investing in Esports.

- In 2021, there was a 1.6 times increase in the total Esports deal value, to $1 billion, in 102 deals (Investgame, 2022).
- The biggest investment made so far was into an Esports team, a Series B fundraise at $50 million led by Valor Equity Partners into Cloud9 Esports, Inc., team with players in several leagues including the *League of Legends* leagues (Perez, 2018).
- The *League of Legends* ecosystem includes 117 teams overall, in 12 regional circuits. Esports tournament-hosting company Gfinity, founded in 2012, stock market-listed for £13.2 million in 2014 (Meddings, 2021) and, in March 2022, was valued at £18.96 million.

But the attention that Esports attracts every year as a market segment is disproportionate to its financial scale. The viewership is also an important marketing tool for games, and that in itself is a financial driver for the sector.

Academic study

From an academic standpoint, Esports is a "unique phenomenon in the modern mediascape" for study, because it bridges the online world and the physical one. (McCauley et al., 2020) It mixes media forms in an almost uniquely versatile way: "concurrently live and taped, tangible and intangible, mobile and stationary, remote and central, social and independent, and immersive and escapist."

The Esports business has many interdependent stakeholders, all "digital, global, and agile": players, teams, fans, platforms, games companies, sponsors, investors, technologists. But it is also a little "Wild West," since eSports is a "new frontier in which existing regulations may not apply" (Scholz, 2020).

And to return to Atari founder Nolan Bushnell, he has concluded that Esports will become a major media business segment: "People would much rather watch or play Esports than watch traditional football" (Meddings, 2021).

THE VALUE CREATION MODEL

The strength of the Esports model is that it has the best of two worlds: globally scaleable digital delivery at every phase of its value creation, combined with the physical and monetisable opportunity of live interaction. There are multiple customer touchpoints, both virtual and tangible, each of them capable of rapid scaling and monetisation.

Drivers of value in Esports are the sheer motivation of the participants at all levels, the 'glocal' market orientation (meaning that best of local and global), the dynamic approach to change, the resource allocation to the coal face of tournaments and teams, and the profoundly digital nature of the activity (Scholz, 2020).

'Secondary stakeholders' like investors influence the industry through investments or pressure (McCauley et al., 2020) such as marketing. "In sum, Esports is commonly

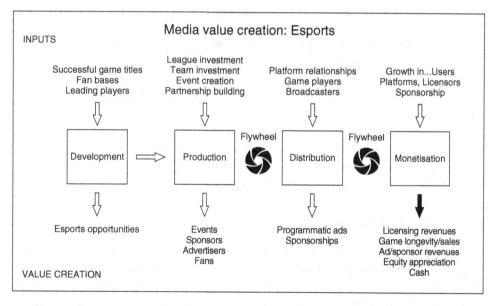

FIGURE 17.1 The greater the distribution scale of an Esports event, the greater its revenue potential, and this in turn drives the scale and ambition of the event production

regarded as one of the newest, most dynamic, and most transformative media industry segments" (Hayduk, 2021).

As a through-line to map the value creation journey in Esports through development, production, distribution and monetisation, we will dissect the *League of Legends*, and bring in other events and commentary to amplify the discussion.

Development

At the development phase of an Esports project, the vital component is a hit multiplayer game, and one which requires training to excel. (Games development is covered in Chapter 5.) Without the hit game to start with, no Esports event is ever possible.

- *League of Legends*, a MOBA game (Multiplayer Online Battle Arena) which was developed and released by Riot Games in 2009, would become by 2021 the most popular Esports game in the world, and the first mover in organised Esports tournaments (SocieteGenerale, 2021).
- Riot Games realised early that Esports success was about eyeballs, and *League of Legends* was the key to unlocking that. In early 2011, Riot organised their own official Esports leagues and began building the tools they needed. Riot Games has geared all their newly released games towards Esports, and this segment of their revenue is growing.
- To get *LoL* into production, investment mattered. With seed capital of $1.5 million (Crunchbase, 2022), Riot Games launched a new business model in *League of Legends*, as a free-to-play game where in-game micro-transaction represent the only monetisation strategy.
- The game quickly gained traction around the world, particularly in China, arousing the interest of games entertainment conglomerate Tencent, which invested $400 million for a 93% stake in Riot Games in 2011 (Pearson, 2022) then bought the remaining 7% in 2015.

Other firms have tried crowdfunding approaches, but research shows it has not usually worked.

- "The surplus of esport projects on crowdfunding platforms [is] reflective of significant lost opportunity costs stemming from founder-funder information asymmetries" said one academic study (Hayduk, 2021).

Production and distribution

In the Esports media segment, production and distribution are one and the same, because the production is itself the distribution, in the form of a live show and a live stream. In fact, Esports has a new paradigm for distribution. "Unlike traditional sports, the vast majority of Esports viewership is online, the same medium where multiplayer game play takes place and through which the Esports audience consumes media content." (Merwin, 2018).

At this phase of value creation, the requirements are a live venue, teams, finance and sponsors, live fans, remote fans, digital/viral marketing and a massively scaleable online distribution platform.

Role of players

Players come in two basic categories: professionals, who are elite gamers working either individually or in a team, to win tournaments; and 'lifestyle' gamers, who are skilled but standalone gamers, broadcasting their games to subscribers. The act of streaming on *Twitch* is not Esports, but those Esports influencers can play in tournaments too.

* The *Twitch* hack of Autumn 2021 revealed that some game players have advertising-driven earnings amounting to hundreds of thousands of dollars per month, as much as major sports stars.
* *Critical Role*, a team of Dungeons and Dragons-playing voice artists, made over $9.6 million in two years, according to the leaked (supposed) figures.
* These earnings would be augmented with additional earnings from sponsorships from games makers or third parties – a function of the 1.7 billion hours of viewing on *Twitch* in September 2021 (Needleman, 2021).
* After Riot's successful launch, there are now *League of Legends* tournaments globally – in the US, Europe, China, South Korea and Brazil.
* The World Championship is the premiere event – with 15,000 attendees at the January 2020 Paris final, and another 44 million watching live on *Twitch* and elsewhere (SocieteGenerale, 2021).

League structure

Franchise models help the games and tournaments scale fast. "Esports organisations can choose to become franchises as permanent league partners, putting an end to relegation, and averting the tumult that a financier-unfriendly framework would result in" (Kordyaka et al., 2020).

Riot Games runs regional leagues, whereas Blizzard Games' *Overwatch League* takes a global approach. Research showed that the best-performing franchises weren't the largest or the smallest geographically – but some kind of middle-ground.

* An academic survey of 216 *League of Legends* players found that "medium-diversified franchises seem to have the most beneficial positions in the eSports market" (Kordyaka et al., 2020).
* The ecosystem that results is "one of the most promising new environments for studying human networks and patterns of interaction" (Hayduk, 2021).

- Massive tournaments are staged offline in venues while also being streamed globally.
- The best known is in the small Swedish city of Jönköping. which hosts the huge *DreamHack* events for thousands of participants each year, who even fly in their own computers. *DreamHack* is the world's largest LAN [local area network] party. "As a result, the event has assumed an important role in the identity of the city to the extent that Jönköping's tourism branding is as 'The City of *DreamHack*'" (McCauley et al., 2020).

The network economies of scale

The bigger the distribution is, the more widely the central costs of Esports are amortised, the more attractive the event becomes to sponsors, the higher the programmatic advertising revenue rises, the stronger the marketing impact becomes for the core video game brand, and the better the show is for attendees. These are the network economies of success in Esports.

As an example of how big an Esports event can be, the 2021 *League of Legends* finals between *DWG KIA* from South Korea (*League of Legends Championship Korea*) and Chinese team *Edward Gaming* (from the *League of Legends Pro League*) saw 73.8 million Peak Concurrent Viewers (PCU), a 60% increase, according to Riot Games (Fudge, 2021).

A study found *League of Legends European Championship* has higher audiences than tennis, basketball and rugby union in the 16–29 age group. And the average *League of Legends* Esports fan is only 23 years of age, a big business opportunity long-term when the average traditional sports fan is aged 42 (Church, 2021).

Fans are not homogenous. It would be a mistake to think they all think the same way about digital and live shows.

- Academic research showed that "Esports consumers are non-monolithic, with segmentations having significant impact on perceptions of value for both traditional and digital media offerings" (Ji and Hanna, 2020).
- That means that successful Esports brands will split their offer into distinctly targeted audience segmentations, both around the different digital distribution options (say, *Twitch* vs *YouTube*), and also in the offline development of powerful live event experiences.
- Obtaining backing from local government, or creating local clubs, or finding local influencers can be helpful, even in a globalised, real-time business, not least in fostering a helpful level of "grassroots growth" (McCauley et al., 2020) in the way that tennis or hockey might approach an audience strategy.

Monetisation

Monetisation drivers in Esports include commercial sponsorship and advertising and live event ticketing, plus IP licensing.

In 2019, the total industry revenue segmented to 42% from sponsorship, 23% from media rights, 17% from advertising, 9% from merchandise and tickets and 9% from publisher fees. The segment growing fastest is media rights, expected in a 2020 study to achieve +39.6% compound growth in the five years to 2022 (CliffordChance, 2020).

As Goldman Sachs put the market opportunity in 2018: "Unlike many existing pro sports, the Esports audience is young, digital, and global: more than half of Esports viewers are in Asia, 79% of viewers are under 35 years old, and online video sites like *Twitch* and *YouTube* have a larger audience for gaming alone than *HBO*, *Netflix* and *ESPN* combined."

Complex value drivers

But fascinatingly, the value drivers, and the money in Esports, are flowing in multiple directions at once.

- Sports leagues are licensing their content to games companies. (And finding additional marketing upside through contact with new audiences and on new platforms.)
- Games companies are licensing their content to Esports leagues. (And benefiting from it by extending the lifespan of their games through generating fan enthusiasm.)
- Broadcasters, often those with the rights to the real sport, are licensing back the rights to show the games content, in an effort (partly unsuccessful) to reach new and younger market segments in an era of digital-first media habits.
- Platforms like *Twitch* and *YouTube* are both paying for right to show the content, and monetising it via advertising. With the enormous traffic, undisclosed revenues from programmatic advertising will be high.
- In a circular economy, leagues and teams paying to play, being paid to play, paying players and being paid for players' contributions.
- There are value generation opportunities even beyond that eclectic selection. "We see further tailwinds to the broader eSports ecosystem – including online video platforms, hardware manufacturers (core and peripheral), and chip makers" (Merwin, 2018).
- Pro players can access real-world paid brand endorsements. League of Legends player Jian 'Uzi' Zihao signed a Nike deal (Fitch, 2018).

This indicates an industry in an early and febrile stage of evolution. In this phase of what may soon become a powerful segment of the media and entertainment business, the biggest financial driver of all may still be the value accretion to the original creator of the game, with Esports as a powerful game-marketing tool.

Combining that with the youthful, fast-growing fan-base, the overall growth of gaming, and the relatively fixed costs of staging an Esports event, should result in Esports being viable and at-scale as a long-term media industry.

IP/rights exploitation

For games creators and publishers, Esports offers a revenue stream from the licensing of IP rights in their games.

"The primary purpose of such licensing may be direct (a distinct revenue stream under the licensing contract) [or] indirect (using Esports to generate interest in the game to drive sales)" – marketing in other words" (CliffordChance, 2020). In terms of direct revenue, *Twitch* paid $90 million in 2018 for the broadcast rights to the *Overwatch League* (excluding China) – a jump from the $300 million *Major League Baseball*'s video streaming operation BamTECH paid *Riot Games* for *League of Legends* for the seven years, 2016–23.

Similarly major sports leagues are re-monetising their rights by licensing them to video games companies, including for Esports. The National Basketball Association does this with the *NBA 2K* game, published by Sega Sports since 2005.

Competition and league sponsorships

Games publishers (like Riot Games) run or licence competitions. Esports then shares some monetisation models with traditional sports – like sponsorship, licensing deals, merchandise and ticket sales, the core difference between Esports and traditional sports lies in the league ownership.

While traditional sports leagues are owned by the teams playing in the specific league, an Esports league is usually owned by the developer, Riot Games in the case of *League of Legends*. This gives the developer a lot of power over structure of the League.

- In 2017, some 65% of all event sponsorship in Esports and 88% of team sponsorships was actually from so-called 'endemic brands' – that is, brands that work in Esports already, and largely the games makers themselves (CliffordChance, 2020).
- The opening 2021 *League of Legends* show was sponsored by Mastercard, with short films from *Imagine Dragons* on an Arcane-themed journey throughout the world of *Runeterra* cities *Piltover* and *Zaun* (Legends, 2021).
- Other sponsors in that league include Coca-Cola. Toyota sponsors the *Overwatch League*.
- A *Counter Strike* event is "a very good opportunity for brands to be very close to the real action within eSports" and put advertising within the experience. "Having an ad on a bus shelter, that is something that we actually do utilise in that game," said Niklos Bakos from in-game advertising firm Advety. "You walk around in the city of Barcelona, you're killing terrorists, basically. But we're putting programmatic ads into that experience. And that's a super way for, for brands to be reaching a lot of activities for gamers." (Hart, 2021).

According to John Needham, head of Riot Games' Esports business, *League of Legends* Esports was not profitable yet in 2021, and the short-term goal was for break even, with any potential profits going back into developing the league (Amenabar, 2021). Esports events do offer multiple opportunities for monetisation both offline and online, both local and at global scale.

Advertising

In-game advertising is a new area, like in games *per se*, where developers or third party agencies can enable adverts inside the game play, by coding them. Mastercard took out *Summoner's Rift Arena* banners in-game in the *League of Legends* 2020 broadcasts.

- Different leagues can have different sponsors even within the same overall game. Multiple ad-tech companies now offer programmatic in-game advertising, including for Esports.
- Affiliate marketing tools enable gamers with followings to promote products they are using, via joining an affiiiate programme which pays a commission on sales leads generated.
- Products advertised could vary from cloud gaming services like *Uplay+* and *GeForce Now*, to game shops like *Ubisoft*, *Epic Games*, *Gamestop* and *Humble Bundle*. Meanwhile ad exchange *Zeropark* acts as a demand side ad exchange for betting platforms who want to generate traffic from gamers, like *Luckbox* and *Parimatch*, and a supply side exchange for traffic providers (i.e., gamers) (Zeropark).

Wider advertising in and around Esports has become an extensive and fast-growing economy.

- In 2021, the *European League of Legends Championship* made a short film with European finance company ERSTE Group around the perennial debate 'is Esports a sport?'
- Car company BMW worked with Esports organisations Cloud9, Fnatic, FunPlus Phoenix, T1 and G2 Esports on a #UnitedinRivalry campaign.
- Other major 2021 campaigns featured Ralph Lauren (with G2 *League of Legends* star Martin Larsson), Intel (with ESL Gaming), NIKE, Kia, Williams Racing and many more. All this is again indicative of a brand and advertising universe that is keen to involve itself in a space with a large, young and hard-to-reach demographic (Hyrliková, 2021).

Team economics

Team owners in Esports are paid by the developer, but need sponsorships too. So the success of an Esports league requires the league itself to earn revenue. This structure caused a public debate between team SoloMid owner and founder Andy Dinh and Riot Games co-founder Marc Merrill (Kollar, 2016). In 2021, Riot changed its

Esports structure for the *North American League Championship Series* to a franchise model.

Streamers and broadcasters

A clear category of winners in the Esports space are the services that stream the gameplay at scale, because they can monetise the content via advertising, having licenced the rights to stream gameplay with the publishers, either exclusively or not.

- Key players in the space are Amazon (with *Twitch*), Google (with *YouTube*), Tencent (with *Douyu* and *Huya*) and *Facebook Gaming*.
- Even traditional broadcasters have got in on the act, by contracting with publishers to broadcast the best gamers.
- But they have come up against the generational shift away from TV and found it hard to convert gamers, with 61% of Esports viewers telling ratings agency Nielsen that they did not watch TV in any given week (CliffordChance, 2020).

Gambling

For betting, the challenge that Esports has is that its players are not known outside the arcane (if large and globally scaled) market of the game and league itself. They have no wider reputation. However, even if the stars are sectorally parochial, there is the opportunity for gambling to become involved (different regulatory environments permitting).

- Entain, the gambling group behind Ladbrokes and Sportingbet entered the Esports market in 2021 with the acquisition of one of the sector's leading betting firms, Unikrn, and development of a platform to allow it to tap into this market with more than 450 million viewers in the 18–35 age bracket.
- Entain's chief executive Jette Nygaard-Anderse said: "People want more betting and gaming content, they want more interactive experience" (Walsh, 2021).
- But in an interview, one leading executive in traditional sports saw clear challenges for the Esports offer, in making sure that it is uniquely innovative and natively digital, rather than simply defaulting to the value chain construction of other professional sports: "I think there's a long way to go."

AI in Esports

There is substantial AI in gameplay (see Chapter 5) driven not least by pure AI research companies like DeepMind. But there are also Esports-specific AI applications.

- AI is being used in gameplay to detect match fixing or cheating (EsportsNewsUK, 2021).
- AI is actually playing Esports. Elon Musk Google have created AI players to beat human opponents at games such as *Dota 2* and *Starcraft 2*.
- *The OpenAI Five* Esports team, a team of five neural networks, beat the *Dota 2* champions in 2019. It had played itself in 180 years worth of games every day using reinforcement learning. "One AI milestone is to exceed human capabilities in a complex video game like *Starcraft* or *Dota*. Relative to previous AI milestones like Chess or Go, complex video games start to capture the messiness and continuous nature of the real world (OpenAI, 2018).
- AI is being used to coach professional players. Tools like SenpAI can assess player stats and suggest strategies in *League of Legends* and *Dota 2*.
- AI is used in Esports betting to gather and evaluate data at scale and speed. PandaScore's platform collects data points in *League of Legends*. "The system continually learns based on history and incoming data to provide the most current breakdowns and predictions about who will win, lose [and] accomplish certain tasks" (iGB, 2021).
- Esports Technologies (a US-listed company) is building systems to model odds in Esports competitions using AI, to inform betting in parallel with streaming platforms like *Twitch* and *YouTube* (EsportsTechnologies, 2022).

Class discussion questions

- Which participant in the Esports value chain is most investable, and why? (Options include games, game developers, leagues, games publishers, players, live events, venues, accessories/hardware, teams.)
- How can Riot Games make Esports viewing engaging for someone who doesn't play *League of Legends*?
- How will Esports become a sustainable business model?
- You are briefing an Esports team on ways to exploit AI to (legitimately) improve performance. What will you propose?

CHAPTER SUMMARY

TABLE 17.1 Key themes in this chapter

Esports	Development	Production	Distribution	Monetisation
Business model	Investment in game titles is a sunk cost by the time they are exploited for Esports.	Large investments required for league and team creation, and live event staging.	Multifaceted footprint from live events to broadcast, via streaming on multiple platforms.	Advertising including in-game, sponsorship, licensing in multiple directions, programmatic revenues on streaming.
Uses of AI	Low AI usage.	Production tools and custom software integrate AI.	High AI usage by platforms for personalisation, audience segmentation.	Use of AI in advertising optimisation to maximise returns for platform and creator.
Value Creation	Low additional value creation at the development stage.	Value creation begins as game becomes an Esports event or series, and licensing deals are struck.	Value creation when games, leagues, teams reach scale and streaming traction. Triggers interest from advertisers.	Strong value creation for games developers if a league gains traction. But real value remains in game marketing.

BIBLIOGRAPHY

Amenabar, T. (2021). League of Legends Esports still hasn't turned a profit. That's okay, says Riot. Retrieved 2021-11-01, from www.washingtonpost.com/video-games/esports/2021/11/01/league-worlds-2021-profit-lol/

BritishEsportsAssociation. (2020). Pearson International BTEC & British Esports Association Virtual Roadshow. https://britishesports.org/press-releases/british-esports-partners-with-pearson-btec-qualification/

Church, B. (2021). League of Legends is growing. Traditional sports better watch out. https://edition.cnn.com/2020/08/19/sport/league-of-legends-esports-growth-spt-intl-cmd/index.html

CliffordChance. (2020). *Play by Play – An Introduction to Esports, monetisation and IP Rights.* www.cliffordchance.com/content/dam/cliffordchance/briefings/2020/06/thought-leadership-publication-play-by-play-an-introduction-to-esports-monetisation-and-ip-rights.pdf

Crunchbase. (2022). *Riot Games – Funding, Financials, Valuation & Investors.* www.crunchbase.com/organization/riot-games/company_financials

EsportsNewsUK. (2021). AI Data and its applications in Esports. *ESports News UK*. https://esports-news.co.uk/2021/03/31/ai-data-and-its-applications-in-esports/

EsportsTechnologies. (2022). *A Scalable Platform Powering iGaming Solutions*. Retrieved 21 March 2022 from https://esportstechnologies.com/technology/

Fitch, A. (2018). Uzi signs endorsement deal with Nike. *ESI Sports Insider*. https://esportsinsider.com/2018/10/uzi-nike-endorsement/

Fudge, J. (2021). Riot Games reveals Worlds 2021 Finals viewership numbers. *The ESports Observer*. www.sportsbusinessjournal.com/Esports/Sections/Media/2021/11/Worlds-2021-Finals-AMA.aspx

Hart, A. (2021, 5 May 2021). Marketing Today with Alan Hart In *Adverty's Niklas Bakos: Marketing Today with Alan Hart 5 May 2*. www.marketingtodaypodcast.com/258-the-future-of-advertising-in-video-games-with-advertys-niklas-bakos/

Hayduk, T. M. (2021). Kickstart my market: exploring an alternative method of raising capital in a new media sector. *Journal of Media Business Studies*, 18(3), 155–78. https://doi.org/10.1080/16522354.2020.1800310

Hyrliková, H. (2021). The best Esports advertising campaigns of 2021. *Esports insider*. https://esportsinsider.com/2021/12/best-esports-adverts-2021/

iGB. (2021). How artificial intelligence drives new experiences in Esports betting. https://igamingbusiness.com/esports/esports-betting/how-artificial-intelligence-drives-new-experiences-in-esports-betting/

Investgame. (2022). Gaming Deals Activity Report 2021. https://investgame.net/news/gaming-deals-activity-report-2021/

Ji, Z., and Hanna, R. C. (2020). Gamers First – How Consumer Preferences Impact eSports Media Offerings. *International Journal on Media Management*, 22(1), 13–29. https://doi.org/10.1080/14241277.2020.1731514

Kollar, P. (2016). The past, present and future of League of Legends studio Riot Games. www.polygon.com/2016/9/13/12891656/the-past-present-and-future-of-league-of-legends-studio-riot-games

Kordyaka, B., Jahn, K., and Niehaves, B. (2020). To Diversify or Not? Uncovering the Effects of Identification and Media Engagement on Franchise Loyalty in eSports. *International Journal on Media Management*, 22(1), 49–66. https://doi.org/10.1080/14241277.2020.1732982

Legends, L. o. (2021). League of Legends Esports Media Center – "League of Legends Esports Breaks World Championship Viewership Record." www.lolesportsmedia.com/League-of-Legends-Esports-Breaks-World-Championship-Viewership-Record

McCauley, B., Tierney, K., and Tokbaeva, D. (2020). Shaping a Regional Offline eSports Market: Understanding How Jönköping, the 'City of DreamHack,' Takes URL to IRL. *International Journal on Media Management*, 22(1), 30–48. https://doi.org/10.1080/14241277.2020.1731513

Meddings, S. (2021, Sunday 25 April 2021). Atari founder Nolan Bushnell: Esports will be bigger than the World Cup. *Sunday Times*. www.thetimes.co.uk/article/atari-founder-nolan-bushnell-esports-will-be-bigger-than-the-world-cup-68fjh6qqm

Merwin, C. (2018). Esport from wild west to mainstream. Published by Goldman Sachs. www.goldmansachs.com/insights/pages/infographics/e-sports/report.pdf

Needleman, S. (2021, 10 November 2021). WSJ Tech News Briefing In *Twitch Hack Revealing Streamers' Earnings Isn't the Full Picture*. www.wsj.com/podcasts/tech-news-briefing/twitch-hack-revealing-streamers-earnings-isnt-the-full-picture/e94ae0a0-e043-4626-93c6-27c38b15ca96

Newzoo. (2021). Global Esports & Streaming Market Report. https://newzoo.com/insights/trend-reports/newzoos-global-esports-live-streaming-market-report-2021-free-version

OpenAI. (2018). OpenAI Five. https://openai.com/blog/openai-five/

Pearson, D. (2022). Tencent acquires Riot Games for around $400 million. www.gamesindus try.biz/articles/2011-02-07-tencent-acquires-riot-games-for-around-USD400-million

Perez, M. (2018). Esports Company Cloud9 Raises $50 Million In Series B Funding. www.for bes.com/sites/mattperez/2018/10/15/esports-company-cloud9-raises-50-million-in-series-b-funding/

SBJ. (2017). An Introduction to the Esports Ecosystem. *Sports Business Journal*. Retrieved 2017-08-04, from https://archive.esportsobserver.com/the-esports-eco-system

Scholz, T. M. (2020). Deciphering the World of eSports. *International Journal on Media Management*, 22(1), 1–12. https://doi.org/10.1080/14241277.2020.1757808

SocieteGenerale. (2021). League of Legends, the game that made Esports take off – Société Générale. Retrieved 2021-07-28, from www.societegenerale.com/en/league-legends-game-made-esports-take-off

Walsh, D. (2021, Friday 13 August 2021). Gambling Giant Entain puts £50m bet on Esports. *The Times*. www.thetimes.co.uk/article/gambling-giant-entain-puts-50m-bet-on-esports-dgtg6x6l3

Wijman, T. (2021). *The Games Market and Beyond in 2021: The Year in Numbers*. https://new zoo.com/insights/articles/the-games-market-in-2021-the-year-in-numbers-esports-cloud-gaming/

Zeropark. *Zeropark blog*. https://zeropark.com/blog/affiliate-marketing-esports-gaming/

CHAPTER 18

The Metaverse

A virtual world that does not yet exist still has growing momentum

....

INTRODUCTION TO THE SECTOR

By aggregating revenues from the games industry and other sources, and extrapolating forward the building of the project, Bloomberg suggested the Metaverse may be an $800 billion market in 2024 (Bloomberg, 2021).

Citibank goes even further than that, calling it a potentially $8–13 trillion opportunity by 2030, which will cover everything from virtual advertising and social commerce to smart manufacturing and healthcare (Boyle, 2022).

Yet in three different senses those projections are wildly ambitious, because the Metaverse does not exist, and no one can agree what it is.

- First, from a literal point of view, it never will exist – by definition a virtual world currently envisioned not to have a conventional, physical reality.
- Second, as software, the Metaverse has not been built yet.
- Third, and more fundamentally, as one senior social media executive put it in an interview: "Nobody actually knows what the Metaverse is."

Asked 'What is the Metaverse?' – the *Megatron Transformer 11b*, an AI, said:

> The more we can make virtual worlds more social, the more likely they will be accepted as part of our reality. It all comes down to augmented and virtual reality technologies which enable us to overlay interactive computer graphics and interactive digital objects onto real-world environments.

DOI: 10.4324/9781003213611-22

That is a useful potential description of a nascent business sector. *Variety*'s Kevin Tran called the Metaverse: "Less a particular virtual place than it is an umbrella term, denoting the digital experiences that we will all eventually have when technology allows for us to virtually interact in ways that are not currently possible" (Tran, 2021).

Despite the conceptual uncertainty, massive investment, collective intellectual energy and major planning by brands and advertising agencies are all predicated on the Metaverse becoming 'reality' in the mid-2020s.

Candice Mudrick, at industry specialists Newzoo, wrote: "Although it's far from a unified concept, most would agree that we are collectively hurtling towards greater participation in simulated worlds that are even more limitless than our real one" (Mudrick, 2021). She quotes industry leaders' answers to what the Metaverse is: "Persistent, shared, 3D virtual spaces in a virtual universe," said Roblox. "A persistent, infinitely scaling virtual space with its own economy and identity system," said Jonathan Lai of *a16z*.

So if a definition of the Metaverse is edging into view, what will be the business model?

THE VALUE CREATION MODEL

Value creation through the Metaverse is at present an imprecise science. But we can provide some basic architectures.

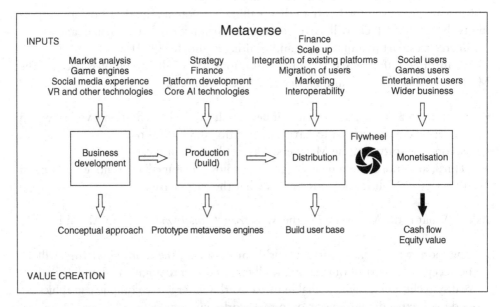

FIGURE 18.1 Winners in the Metaverse are likely to be the very largest tech companies with the infrastructure to scale up virtual worlds

Business development

The business development of the Metaverse will require not only market research, but also a market creation exercise, selection of games engines or other software, social media know-how and a network at vast scale, plus VR (or similar systems) for users, payment mechanics and many other technologies. The key output will be one or more viable, conceptual approaches. The Metaverse as currently envisioned is not how it will end up. One report on the immersive sector observed: "Creative projects have a tendency to change direction in the course of development. Prototyping and audience testing can either validate or negate early assumptions and intuitions" (Chitty, 2020).

To what extent the market in a virtual world will replicate the dynamics of offline markets is as yet unknown – but the likelihood is that it will, just as, say, programmatic advertising replicates the economic mechanisms of a traditional county fair, with buyers, sellers and an auction ring.

Key principles

Even if we cannot study it forensically, five clear points are cited by leading social media executives as requirements for a functioning Metaverse.

- Presence – meaning that the user feels present within the environment.
- Persistence – meaning that the Metaverse does not stop when the user leaves, like when they hang up a phone call, but is a continual environment.
- Scaling – the Metaverse needs to scale infinitely, more than the current cap of roughly one hundred players per zone available in multiplayer, online games.
- Economy – it needs to be possible to trade in the Metaverse, between games and not just within them.
- Interoperability – meaning that some people can be on laptops whilst others are on phones, and so forth. Users may want to enter on multiple gaming platforms with different companies, games and systems. But they might want to use the same avatar and items (such as playing a game of *Fortnite* and *NBA 2K* with the same character), meaning that the systems will have to be interoperable. This has not been solved yet. At present, a *Facebook* account absolutely does not have access to *Snapchat*.

Key players

Candidates amongst existing companies to create the virtual environment which the Metaverse will occupy fall into five categories:

- Games developers, with existing platforms that in many ways already achieve it: such as Epic Games (makers of *Fortnite*) *Roblox* and *Unity* (a development tool used industry-wide). "The primary Metaverse revenue opportunity for video game makers consists largely of existing gaming software and services market as well as rising sales of gaming hardware" (Bloomberg, 2021). Developers with scaled-up user bases for online games like *Grand Theft Auto Online* will have the early edge in the space. *Roblox* believes it will already reach 4 billion hours of participation per month, by 2023 (Ball, 2020). Ryan Gill of games company Crucible said: "If web developers are the architects of the internet as we know it (web 2.0), then game developers are the architects of the Metaverse (web 3.0.)" (Mudrick, 2021).

- Major technology companies such as Apple (with a rumoured head-mounted VR/AR system in development), Amazon (with its wide footprint in customers' online lives) and hardware company NVIDIA with its *Omniverse* product (Sinha, 2022). When announcing the planned acquisition of games publisher Activision Blizzard in 2022, Microsoft CEO Satya Nadella positioned that deal as a step towards the Metaverse (Lewis, 2022).

- Theme park companies such as Disney, which – perhaps not coincidentally – chose a former theme park manager Mike White to head its Metaverse strategy, following its own announcement that it is building the 'Disney Metaverse.' One industry observer said: "Disney has been turning its IP into immersive experiences ever since its first theme park opened in 1955" (Lee, 2022). A venture capital industry blogger observed: "For decades, the only real way to experience a digital world with agency and an individual sense of self was to go to the theme park. Games have been on the cusp of these experiences for years, but in 2020, they're well under way" (Ball, 2020). In a similar vein, Epic Games and toy company Lego plan to build a 'family friendly' version of the Metaverse (Rubio-Licht, 2022). (Some might say that a 'Disney Metaverse' would by definition fall foul of the interoperability test cited above for a true Metaverse.)

- Social media companies: Meta have stated the intention to create the Metaverse and invested in it (see below). Other networks such as *TikTok* owner *Bytedance* and *Snapchat* already have relevant technologies, particularly the layering of Augmented Reality onto real world situations. But as with all previous waves of technology, it may be a start-up that leapfrogs all existing companies to create a Metaverse product.

- Entertainment companies are keen to enter the space. Film and TV studio Viacom CBS's in-house 'futurologist' Ted Schilowitz described the Metaverse as "the evolution of the visual and communication tool set that we've been using since the beginnings of recorded cinema" (Tran, 2021).

No singular vision

Music, fashion, retail, tourism, sports, cars, consumer goods, cosmetics, education and TV/film have all in some way already jumped into the Metaverse (Mudrick, 2021).

But not everyone in tech buys into the hype. *Tesla* and *Space X* entrepreneur Elon Musk said in 2021: "I don't see someone strapping a frigging screen to their face all day and not wanting to ever leave … I currently am unable to see a compelling

Metaverse situation … Sure, you can put a TV on your nose. I'm not sure that makes you 'in the Metaverse' " (Musk, 2021).

Finally, it is clear that there will be multiple Metaverses – one in the West and one in China – and possibly more or less commercially partisan Metaverse rivals. The Chinese one may be built in a more online/offline combination, on a vision so far led by Tencent, with real events combining with the virtual world. Tencent is producing content that may be less reliant than Western models on user-generated contributions, because of the different regulatory environment (Mudrick, 2021).

There is also the prospect of an 'eduverse' specifically based on education. Start-up Labster, with 5 million students and 3,000 universities and high schools signed up, raised $47 million on that concept in 2022. And the Indian government has invested $10 million in a 'smart classrooms' concept (Palmer, 2022).

Production

At the production phase, a business going into the Metaverse will require a clear strategy, substantial finance, a platform and core technologies. The output will be prototype Metaverse engines and experiences capable of being seamlessly iterated across many platforms. Players will be able to not only have avatars, but also own other assets in the Metaverse – like cars, houses and pets, plus potentially protect their true identity with blockchain-style decentralised identifiers (Mudrick, 2021). (It is worth remembering that early iterations of social media companies – such as *WhatsApp* – also emphasised anonymity, only to later dial that back.)

As conceptual work on the Metaverse begins to firm up, and video game makers "continue to elevate existing titles into 3D online worlds that better resemble social networks, their market opportunity can expand to encapsulate live entertainment such as concerts and sports events as well as fighting for a share of social-media advertising revenue" (Bloomberg, 2021).

In October 2021, *Facebook* renamed itself to Meta and stated that it was investing $10 billion in a migration of the business towards a Metaverse vision. This means backing their move with substantial uses of AI. Jerome Pesenti of Meta said: "We want AI models to understand the entire world around us. And with the advent of the Metaverse, we have a unique challenge and a unique opportunity to make that happen" (Meta, 2022).

Meta and other companies are dealing with new AI challenges like the physics of rendering 'egocentric perception' (otherwise known as POV) which is about seeing worlds from a first person perspective. As one social media executive said: "You can have an AI recognise a rollercoaster. But put an AI on a rollercoaster and it's much harder to recognise." Training AI to see the world as we do is necessary for a first-person-navigated virtual world.

Real-time generative AI models are being designed to allow users to create worlds from simple speech. Dynamic world creation, rich avatar and non-playing character experiences, rapid generation of levels, maps and worlds – and of course realistic metahumans – will all be key AI contributions to the Metaverse (Mudrick, 2021).

Meta's 'builder bot' product development seeks to do some of that. (Meta, 2022) Meta's Chief Product Officer Chris Cox said that *Horizon Worlds*, launched in December 2021 for its Oculus headsets, had rapidly acquired 300,000 users, suggesting latent demand, which might accelerate if, as planned, the product came to phones (Dent, 2022).

Software company Adobe is similarly engaged in building basic tools for the Metaverse that will plug into its existing offers (Yeomans, 2022).

Distribution

At the distribution phase, the key inputs for a Metaverse platform will be finance on an extraordinary scale, sufficient to power global network distribution, the integration of existing platforms and migration of existing users (a powerful driver for extant social media or scaled games companies) and the functioning interoperability of systems with other emerging Metaverse standards. The critical output at this point will be the engaged user base – measured, for instance, as Daily Active Users – who may be engaged in new and potentially dynamic new ways.

- Relatable and emotionally intelligent AIs from companies like Replica and Pandorabots create the possibility of 'AI friendships,' using neural networks and natural language processing. This could be a key vector of AI development for the Metaverse (Lai, 2022).

For the user, the Metaverse will constitute a far more immersive and physically engaging experience than current entertainment of all kinds.

- A 2018 experiment by the market research agency Ipsos MORI and The Royal Shakespeare Company staged Shakespeare's most violent play, *Titus Andronicus*, in virtual reality. "On average, heart rate was raised to levels equivalent to that of a 5-minute cardio workout across the total duration of the performance" (Bailey, 2018).
- 'Live' virtual concerts in the Metaverse do not even have to be live. Virtual influencer Hatsune Miku events are staged as if real, with a backstage waiting area for guests, who can actually join at any time (Mudrick, 2021).

Key dimensions of the internet will need to change in order to truly deliver the Metaverse experience. Latency (the time it takes a data signal to travel from one point to another on the internet and back again) needs to drop from the current 75–150 milliseconds (acceptable for video calls and gaming) to less than 12 milliseconds – for truly immersive and realistic experience (Boyle, 2022). 5G phone technology may provide some of this benefit, when fully implemented.

Monetisation

The final stage of the Metaverse value creation process will be the derivation from the user base, both individuals and corporate, of monetisable models.

These will yield value, in terms of cash flow and equity value enhancement. Models are likely to be re-iterations of familiar business tools: advertising, e-commerce, in-'game' consumption, data. As in past waves of technology, the tools may be new but the commerce familiar.

There are many signs already of new twists on existing business models:

- Brands are "tip-toeing into immersive VR experiences, also known as the Metaverse," an inaugural 2022 Internet Advertising Bureau event on brands in gaming heard (Wood, 2022).
- This is partly to follow the audience; 46% of US gamers are female, 71% of US mothers play games, and amongst Generation Z, 80% are gamers. Brands like *Acura, Balenciago, Gucci,* have experimented in the Metaverse. In 2021, *American Eagle* launched a "Members Always Club" activation in Roblox, where gamers could play tennis or visit the on- site swimming pool, while also having the chance to try on the entire spring collection with their avatars (Wood, 2022). It remains to be seen whether fashion brands can achieve commercial traction with these innovations.
- Digital fashion is being created in the Metaverse; in a March 2022 survey by creative agency Virtue Worldwide, 46% of people in a survey said that they expected over half of their wardrobe to be digital within five years (Serrano, 2022).
- Following previous online concerts, in 2022 Warner Music announced that it was looking to host live music concerts in the Metaverse (Miot, 2022). And tech platform Unity partnered with a rave events company, Insomniac, to create Metaverse events.

Class discussion questions

- Make the case for a surprising potential monetisation opportunity in the Metaverse that is not possible in the 'real' world.
- Put yourself in the position of CEO of a specific real-world games publisher. What is your Metaverse strategy?
- Bearing in mind the dark side of social media after 2016 – disinformation, bad actors, hate speech, data breaches, content moderation failures – could similar risks affect the Metaverse? What moderation tools should companies implement in order to prevent this? What guard rails should governments and regulators implement?
- Which AI technologies are pivotal to implementation of the Metaverse?

BIBLIOGRAPHY

Bailey, P. (2018, 2 May 2018). Shakespeare still shocks – even in Virtual Reality. Published by Ipsos. www.ipsos.com/en-uk/shakespeare-still-shocks-even-virtual-reality

Ball, M. (2020, 8 March 2020). Digital Theme Park Platforms: The Most Important Media Businesses of the Future. *MathewBall.vc*. www.matthewball.vc/all/digitalthemeparkpl atforms

Bloomberg. (2021). *Metaverse may be $800 billion market*. www.bloomberg.com/professio nal/blog/metaverse-may-be-800-billion-market-next-tech-platform/

Boyle, K. [et al.] (2022). Metaverse and Money. Published by Citi. https://static1.squarespace. com/static/5d388244fb247f00017de2f7/t/625f47c72786ac74b1f0e1d4/1650411482490/ Citi+GPS+Report+--+Metaverse+and+Money%2C+Decrypting+the+Future.pdf

Chitty, A. (2020) *The UK creative immersive landscape 2020: business models in transition. Audience of the Future.* [online] Available at: https://audienceofthefuture.live/wp-cont ent/uploads/20201126_DC_153_UKCreativeImmersiveLandscapeReport_Digital_v1.pdf [Accessed 23 August 2022].

Dent, S. (2022, 18 February 2022). Meta says its VR platform has grown by ten times since December. *Engadget.* https://engt.co/3Bb3kBd

Lai, J. (2022) Meet me in the metaverse. *andreesen horowitz.* [online] Available at: https:// a16z.com/2020/12/07/social-strikes-back-metaverse/ [Accessed 23 August 2022].

Lee, A. (2022, 17 February 2022). The bridge-builder: Why Disney tapped a former theme park executive to lead its metaverse strategy. *Digiday.* https://digiday.com/marketing/the-bridge-builder-why-disney-tapped-a-former-theme-park-executive-to-lead-its-metaverse-strategy/

Lewis, R. W. L. (2022, 21 January 2022). Why gaming is the new Big Tech battleground. *Financial Times.* www.ft.com/content/2d446160-08cb-489f-90c8-853b3d88780d

Meta. (2022) Inside the lab: building for the Metaverse with AI. *Meta.* [online] Available at: https://about.fb.com/news/2022/02/inside-the-lab-building-for-the-metaverse-with-ai/ [Accessed 29 August 2022].

Miot, S. (2022, 28 January 2022). Warner Music Wants to Host Live Music Concerts in the Metaverse. *PCMag UK.* https://uk.pcmag.com/digital-life/138401/warner-music-wants-to-host-live-music-concerts-in-the-metaverse

Mudrick, C. (2021). Intro to the Metaverse. Newzoo report. https://newzoo.com/insights/ trend-reports/newzoo-intro-to-the-metaverse-report-2021-free-version

Musk, E. (2021, 22 December 2021). *Elon Musk Sits Down With The Babylon Bee.* www.yout ube.com/watch?v=BaRKd4U6Ixg

Palmer, M. (2022, 4 April 2022). Forget the metaverse – Labster raises $47m to build the 'eduverse.' *Sifted.* https://sifted.eu/articles/labster-edtech-raise/

Rubio-Licht, N. (2022, 7 April 2022). Epic Games and Lego team up to build a 'family-friendly' metaverse. *Protocol.* www-protocol-com.cdn.ampproject.org/c/s/www.protocol. com/amp/epic-lego-metaverse-kids-2657118621

Serrano, S. (2022, 3 March 2022). New report from Virtue, in collaboration with The Dematerialised, expects digital fashion to go mainstream within 5 years. *Campaign.* https:// campaignme.com/new-report-from-virtue-in-collaboration-with-the-dematerialised-expe cts-digital-fashion-to-go-mainstream-within-5-years/

Sinha, D. (2022). Top 10 Companies working on Metaverse and its developments in 2022. *Analytics Insight.* www.analyticsinsight.net/top-10-companies-working-on-metaverse-and-its-developments-in-2022/

Tran, K. (2021). Metaverse & Media, Special Report. *Variety Intelligence Platform.* [online] Available at: https://variety.com/vip-special-reports/metaverse-and-media-how-techs-hott est-trend-will-impact-the-entertainment-industry-1235116381/ [Accessed 29 August 2022].

Wood, C. (2022). How the gaming universe is preparing marketers for the metaverse. *Martech. org.* https://bit.ly/3RBnvNU

Yeomans, J. (2022, 20 March 2022). Adobe boss Shantanu Narayen seeks to conquer the metaverse. *The Sunday Times.* www.thetimes.co.uk/article/adobe-boss-shantanu-narayen-seeks-to-conquer-the-metaverse-8n2hntmm2

CHAPTER 19

Future of the media business

Challenges and opportunities for media management in the age of AI

....

RELENTLESS EVOLUTION IN THE MEDIA BUSINESS

As Logan Roy, the fictional media industrialist character at the centre of the *HBO* hit, *Succession*, says: "The future is real. The past is made up." The media is a sector which constantly looks forward, and even reinvents history to suit that forward facing narrative.

It is instructive to reflect on some examples of how quickly media companies have found themselves rendered obsolete by competition.

- In 1975, photo film company Kodak had 90% of the US market. The brand was so universal that a good photo was actually called a 'Kodak moment.' Kodak was a verb, in the way that we now talk about 'Googling.'
- For fun that year, Kodak engineer, Steve Sasson, made a bulky gadget to save images electronically, taking out US Patent 4131919A for an "electronic still camera" (Azhar, 2021).
- But, as Kodak already 'owned' the value chain in photography, its top brass didn't see a need to challenge their own model by adopting his reinvention of the film category. Kodak chose not to capitalise on Sasson's design. Consequently, it missed the digital photography market, which would destroy its film business.
- Kodak filed for Chapter 11 bankruptcy in 2012. (Two years earlier, *Blockbuster Video* had gone bankrupt after missing the video streaming opportunity.)
- In the wake of that debacle, Kodak's digital imaging patents were sold to intermediary companies (Skillings, 2012). Those companies were dealing with tech giants that would dominate the decade; Apple, Google, Samsung, Adobe, Facebook and Amazon.

DOI: 10.4324/9781003213611-23

- By 2021, an estimated 1.2 trillion photos were taken annually and the global camera smartphone market was $273.9 billion, growing at 7% per year (Ocean, 2021). This was Kodak's missed opportunity, one to which its technology had contributed, as the company that created the world's first consumer digital camera.

Centrality of technology

What is the point of bringing up that 50-year-old story? In fact, there are two.

The first is that entire media sectors have already been reshaped by digital – cinema exhibition, newsprint, physical magazines, some theatre, books, business publishing, home video and DVD sales or rental, airline magazines, some commercial radio, photography businesses – and this will continue to happen.

Many of these segments might have been in any twentieth-century media business textbook, but found themselves legitimately consigned to the cutting room floor in any twenty-first-century study of media business in the age of AI. People don't buy magazines much any more, or rent DVDs. Generation Z don't much listen to the radio either – they prefer podcasts and streaming.

The second point is that today's giants may not even be tomorrow's top tens. Unassailable market position can very quickly evaporate, if a company misses a technology, and suffers a collapse in value. Even for the six companies that bought some of the Kodak digital photography tools – Apple, Google, Samsung, Adobe, Facebook and Amazon – it is not axiomatic that these current champions will invent the future.

- The global top ten brands in 2000, ranked by *Interbrand*, were *Coca Cola*, *Microsoft, IBM, GE, Intel, Nokia, Ford, Disney, McDonald's, Marlboro*. But just three survived the list to 2020 (*Coke, Microsoft, McDonald's*) (Statistics&Data. org, 2021).
- The best companies know that one major miss (*Blockbuster Video* not embracing streaming) or legal mistake (UK newspaper *News of the World*, closed down after the 2011 phone hacking scandal) may rescind their *raison d'être*.
- Meta CEO Marc Zuckerberg said: "You need to disrupt yourself before your competitors do." Someone wittily tweeted in 2014: "*Facebook* is being pretty aggressive in making sure it's the next *Facebook*" (Ingram, 2014).
- Like Kodak, *Skype* was also a verb ('I'll *Skype* you') when it was bought by Microsoft in 2011, for $8.5 billion. After a poorly received design refresh, it lost market share to *Zoom*, which was the pandemic-defining software tool of 2020–21.
- *Zoom*'s market capitalisation reached $100 billion by July 2021 (Levy, 2021) – a huge tranche of equity value Microsoft investors may felt they should have realised, given *Skype*'s earlier market dominance. (By August 2022, it was just $24 billion, partly eroded by competition from *Teams*, owned by Microsoft.)
- Interviewed in 2021, leading European media/tech investment banker, Hugh Campbell of GP Bullhound, put the challenge of continual, radical technological

evolution like this: "If you're not a technology company, you're not really a company."

The dynamism of media is both the challenge and joy of studying the sector.

Next generation

This book deliberately looked at very different media business segments through a single value creation construct, from development, through production and distribution to monetisation.

Within each segment, there are analogous stories of radical change. *Instagram* has been challenged by *TikTok*, *Netflix* by *Disney+*. A dominant player will be challenged by a new arrival with a better product (say, the *iPhone*) a better interface (the *iPhone*), or a better creative idea – again, like the *iPhone*, whose 2007 launch revolutionised three industries at once: phone, software and music (Jobs, 2007). Many failed to spot the threat. Steve Ballmer, 2007 CEO of Microsoft, said of the *iPhone*: "Five hundred dollars? ... That is the most expensive phone in the world, and it doesn't appeal to business customers, because it doesn't have a keyboard" (Hardwick, 2016). Ballmer was wrong, and the *iPhone* became the most successful consumer product of all time.

The rest of this chapter looks to the future of media and entertainment business models, in light of evolving technologies. It considers how editorial creativity will interplay with AI analytics. It looks at the level of automation likely to drive creativity

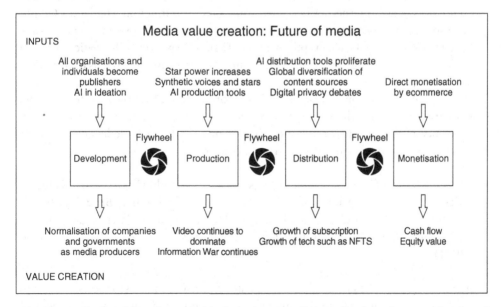

FIGURE 19.1 Successful media enterprises in the future are likely to directly scale up as a function of their sales, exploiting powerful flywheels across the entire value creation process

in future, the interface between content and e-commerce – and other key factors in a new era.

Ten themes are chosen, each alluded to in other chapters. There follow some questions for class discussion, so that readers can think about which brand will be the *Kodak*, *Skype*, *Yahoo!* or indeed the *iPhone*, *Netflix* or *TikTok* of the future.

Primacy of IP grows with technology solutions like NFTs

IP will remain core to value creation in all media sectors. IP will be iterated across new platforms, and monetised in different ways – subscription, in-game ads, in-game purchases, live events, Metaverse events and social media-driven e-commerce. But IP ownership will remain the most dependable equity driver for media businesses, and with blockchain may become more transparent, harder to infringe and more valuable.

- The arrival of NFTs (non-fungible tokens, unique digital assets underpinned by blockchain) can tilt the balance of copyright identification, and therefore monetisation, towards the content originator This could dynamise creativity, putting money in the pockets of artists worldwide.
- Seven in 10 adults pay for digital content each month, a total of $300 billion annually – so the market is available (Kemp, 2022).
- Deloitte's 2022 media industry overview said: "The sudden rise of NFTs and their success in bringing scarcity and exclusivity to digital goods will drive new models of customer engagement and loyalty. They'll also lead to more digital product innovation, greater empowerment for their creators." (Deloitte, 2022).
- The number of cryptocurrency owners increased by 37.8% in 2021 alone; one in ten working-age internet users owned some (and two in ten in Thailand.) Crypto is also heavily biased towards upcoming generations; only one in twenty people aged between 55–64 own crypto (Kemp, 2022). (Crypto saw a dramatic decline in valuation in mid-2022, with even 'blue-chip' Bitcoin losing two thirds of its value.)

The challenge for proponents of NFTs is to normalise and de-risk the technology, which currently carries the insurgency badge of a new, alternative market entrant. For evidence of that outsider reputation, here is how leading US media commentator Kara Swisher described one leading NFT innovator:

- "*Beeple* is one of its most visible success stories ... an unlikely virtuoso. His recent '*Everydays*' have the look of pulpy sci-fi ... a child holding *Buzz Lightyear*'s bloodied head, a double-headed Clinton-Trump robot ... Then, again, maybe he's exactly the right person to usher in this bizzaro frontier of NFTs" (Swisher, 2021).

To go mainstream, NFTs need a less edgy poster child. They need storied, mainstream brands like *Disney* or *Netflix* to embrace them. With that change, each fragment of creativity could be reliably monetised on consumption, producing a revolution in the equitable allocation of returns from IP creation.

Major impact of AI

AI and other technologies will continue to dynamise distribution and production short-term, and radically impact content creation in the longer term, as discussed extensively in other chapters.

Natural language processing will drive universal translation, opening up the internet to the 3 billion people whose first language is all but invisible online. Computer vision will enable automated video-to-text interpretation at scale, and production workflow will radically change; editing will be faster, or even automatic. Distribution algorithms will facilitate ever more targeted provision of content to individuals, especially within streamer-owned walled gardens, which gain data collection permissions at enrolment.

- A consequence of further AI-driven personalisation may be further erosion of broadcasters, as advertising efficiency segments mass audiences into ever more granular categories.
- But the 'water cooler' success of major titles (*Squid Game* on *Netflix*, or the FIFA World Cup) may augur a different future. Here, mass audiences are algorithmically aggregated for popular content to a moment of live transmission, producing a reinvention of broadcasting.

In media creativity, since AI agents are trained on real-world datasets, disputes will proliferate around content ownership, with multiple parties able to credibly claim input. Court cases will revolve around whether synthetic content is owned by any one of four possible parties: the source of the AI training data, the algorithm creator, the algorithm funder or the human artist (if there even is one).

- "New mechanisms for the allocation of responsibility for the production of semantic artefacts will probably be needed ... A better digital culture will be required, to make current and future citizens, users and consumers aware of the new infosphere in which they live and work ... and hence able to understand and leverage the huge advantages offered by advanced digital solutions such as *GPT-3*" (Floridi and Chiriatti, 2020).

Production will turn on its head.

Movies will be created in game engines and virtual studios before a frame of footage is even shot, meaning that the clapper board for 'take one' will be closer to the last stage of the content production process, than the first. (This is already the case on large virtual studio productions like Disney's *The Mandalorian* or HBO's 2022 hit, *House of the Dragon*.) Notwithstanding the charms and nostalgia value of analogue, companies which disavow AI production technology could lose business efficiency and equity value.

- *Disney* has invested heavily in 18 new studio sound stages in the UK (some of them virtual) (Ramachandran, 2021). *Netflix* and *Amazon* are building similar relationships at Shepperton and Pinewood Studios.
- Transitioning to an AI-driven approach is complex. One UK government official in the field explained the difficulty organisations have. "You cannot just sprinkle kind of AI gold dust on a solution …You have to understand your company's data, you have to understand what that data means, you need to clean it, you need to analyse it … And that journey allows you to get to the point where you're using these technologies."

Star power increases, but synthetic voice and video complicate it

There are three likely changes to the star economy.

First, demand has already driven growth in the rates paid for stars by long-running streaming shows, upending the traditional hierarchy between film and TV. Big stars such as Al Pacino (*Hunters*), Chris Rock (*Fargo*) Nicole Kidman and Meryl Streep (*Big Little Lies*), Henry Cavill (*The Witcher*) Jonah Hill, Jennifer Lawrence and Leonardo di Caprio (*Don't Look Up*) now appear on streaming-first shows or films. This is a material rebalancing.

Second, stars have leveraged increased demand, by owning their own rights through production businesses, then selling them, based on the expected cash flow from partially unknown future projects.

- Reese Witherspoon sold production company *Hello Sunshine* to private equity investors for a reported $900 million, with only a limited catalogue of historic rights. The investment was viewed as a bet on the future shows and other business opportunities likely to be created by Witherspoon's star power and good creative taste (Belloni, 2021).
- Basketball star turned media entrepreneur LeBron James's multimedia production firm *SpringHill Company* sold a large stake to *Nike, Epic Games* and *Fenway Sports Group* (owners of the *Boston RedSox* and *Liverpool Football Club*) on a $725 million valuation – again predicated on future projects as much as catalogue (Hayes, 2021).

Third, AI systems will expand and complicate star exploitation in the near future, with IP and ethical issues around their image usage unsolved.

- Some viewers objected to discovery that in *Roadrunner*, a documentary about deceased US chef/TV personality, Anthony Bourdain, statements he had made in writing were turned into audio with synthetic voice by director Morgan Neville, after inputting ten hours of Bourdain's speech into a machine learning system as training data (BBC, 2021).

- AI was also used to de-age Robert De Niro in the *Netflix* drama *The Irishman*, by the George Lucas company *Industrial Light & Magic*, which involved scanning images of his younger face. James Earl Jones' Darth Vader voice was synthesised, in 2022.
- Digital Domain scanned Josh Brolin's facial movements to map onto the character Thanos in *Masquaerade* (Sweeting, 2020).

AI will be used to bring stars back from the dead for new roles, with creative, ethical, legal, taste, copyright, financial and other issues yet to be solved.

Radical global diversification of stories and storytelling

Globally, differential media growth rates, will change the balance of media we see.

- In 2020, Africa and Middle East, content spending grew 46.3% to $2.8 billion. Saudi Arabia, with hitherto limited media, began investing substantially in expansion of distribution (cinemas) and production (facilities and locations) as part of a partial, wider liberalisation of its society.
- In Asia, content spending grew 19.8% to $27.7 billion, with expansion of film production and streaming (Sun, 2021) amongst other industries in China. The Chinese cinema industry was in rapid expansion with home-grown product, at the same time as Western cinema chains faced potential bankruptcy.
- Latin American content spending grew 32.9% to $5.2 billion.

Equally important, globalisation of streamers and their need for audience growth outside the saturated US market is driving local content growth, which then intermittently achieves success globally, changing cultural perceptions.

This will benefit content makers in Africa (Mitchell, 2022) and South Korea – where even before breakout hit *Squid Game*, *Netflix* committed a $500 million investment in new shows in 2021 for its 4 million subscribers.

- "Great Korean stories are nothing new … in fact storytelling is deeply rooted in Korean culture," said Minyoung Kim, VP of Content for Korea. "But today we live in a world where *Parasite* is an Academy Award Best Picture winner, *BlackPink* plays *Coachella*, and over 22 million households tune into a horror TV series, *Sweet Home*" (Merican, 2021).
- Prior to the 2022 Ukraine war, Russian streamers were seeking to export content. That came to at least a temporary halt. Latin American hits have travelled.

America still dominates global content investment, with $149.3 billion spent on streaming (Datastream, 2021). But with every entry of a new entertainment culture into the mainstream global zeitgeist, international cultural understanding can potentially grow. Given wider geopolitical challenges in the 2020s, therein may be a social good.

Direct monetisation, via e-commerce, of democratic production

The dial will not be turned back on democratisation of media production. Owning a smartphone with a 4k camera capable of creating movies good enough for cinema transmission, an increasingly large segment of the world's 7.75 billion people will continue to grow into semi-professional creator roles. It remains an extraordinary sociological shift that billions of people can now produce, disseminate and even monetise content (including with e-commerce) without any professional mediation.

- Live social commerce is growing fast in China, with two shoppers in three saying that they had bought from a live stream in the past 12 months.
- "In 2020, the first 30 minutes of *Alibaba*'s Singles Day presales campaign on *Taobao Live* generated an impressive $7.5 billion in total transaction value" (McKinsey, 2020).
- Social commerce streamers Li Jiaqi and Viya generated $3 billion of sales on a single day in October 2021 (Santora, 2022).
- Live commerce is taking off in the West as well. *Tommy Hilfiger* have staged events. *Walmart* ran a live stream with seven times more viewers than expected and increased *TikTok* followers by a quarter. Via start-ups like *NTWRK*, and *Buywith*, viewers watch hosts on e-commerce platforms (McKinsey, 2020).

Subscription remains the most highly rated monetisation tool

Through the efficient maths of customer lifetime value (see Chapter 3) companies with sustainable income (annual recurring revenue or 'ARR') are more highly rated than those with lumpy, unpredictable cash flows. This is because customer acquisition cost is more efficiently amortised through long-term cash flows than one-off purchases. This fact of economic life will incline more content businesses to move away from programmatic digital advertising to subscription revenue as their primary income.

- In video games, *Xbox Game Pass* and *Xbox Live Gold* have been popular – 25 million users (Warren, 2022) – and are likely to be countered by a rumoured *PlayStation* rival service.

Content protection will grow. The technology of streamers in all categories gives them potential command of customer details and IP addresses, which will enable them to both minimise piracy and monetise content more efficiently for themselves, their producers and, potentially, wider consumers.

- A Latin American academic study showed that cutting piracy in a market will actually increase competition by 11%–15% (Rodriguez Ovejero et al., 2019).

Normalisation of companies and governments as media producers

At the start of the book, we discussed how the media industry is no longer the coherent space that it might have been recognisable in text books of a generation ago.

Like the dinosaurs in *Jurassic Park*, the media has broken through the electric fences. It is now roaming free across many other industrial prairies. Every retailer, and every government is a content company.

How these businesses manage their roles as producers of content in volume will define the shape of production industries as a whole.

- The signs are that e-commerce companies like *Pretty Little Thing* (UK) and *Zomato* (India), or governments from Ukraine to China, will continue find the economics of dis-intermediating agencies and media companies compelling, and grow as direct producers in their own right.
- The UK government already has a published social media playbook (Gov.uk).
- The Russian government has extensive control of many media outlets; "Now it sees reporters as public servants first, and journalists second – if at all" (Kovalev, 2017).

Meanwhile as big companies take the approach of Unilever's award-winning *U-Studio* (discussed in Chapter 13) that will potentially constrain growth of the agency sector. How this pattern plays out, with media business control being directly undertaken beyond traditional media companies, is significant commercially, and also to democracy and the accountability of institutions.

Digital privacy debates continue to profoundly shape the media market

A 2021 UK and US survey found that "consumers are more concerned about data privacy and security than they are about gun violence, natural disasters, crime, drug use and job security."

- Mobile phone privacy is so compromised that phones can be used as a hacking device, even if your camera and microphone are disabled. "The gyroscope on your iPhone, put there to detect motion and orientation, is sensitive enough to pick up acoustic vibrations and therefore can eavesdrop on conversations" (Schneier, 2018).
- Once the preserve of the FBI, installing a fake cell phone tower to intercept phones "became so easy that hackers demonstrate it onstage at conferences."

That potential information security compromise is just the tip of a much bigger iceberg of data breaches and imperfect privacy management across media and social media. This creates an imperative for media brands to re-tool their businesses towards a much more privacy-centric approach, and away from models driven by the exchange of customer data for free services.

- Francis Haugen was the whistle blower who came forward in 2021 with a critique of *Facebook*'s business model. Haugen noted that *Google* was running a system where humans and machines were operating in a form of harmony that might be a model for other companies. "So each time they change their ranking algorithm, it's not a decision that's made blindly by an algorithm. It's not like they just look at the performance of the metrics. They literally have these people called raters ... they will go in there and very carefully compare the search results and give you a judgment. And that's a system where humans are deciding where the system goes forward" (Haugen, 2021).
- Whether she made a fair relative assessment of *Facebook* and *Google* or not, this approach feels likely to succeed in reconciling the challenges of programmatic and other forms of digital advertising which require user data to efficiently target advertising, whilst mindful of the parallel exigencies of user privacy.
- In 2021, Apple made privacy changes to the iPhone operating system which required consumers to opt in to data sharing in certain circumstances. A US academic observer, Scott Galloway, said of those changes: "One of the great brand moves in history was anticipating the increasing relevance of privacy ... Violating privacy is central to the business model of Apple's rivals, and thwarting that has left them befuddled" (Galloway, 2022).

Understanding the algorithm is the new skill which boards are going to need:

- Alan Rusbridger, former editor-in-chief at *The Guardian* newspaper (UK), in 2021 on the *Facebook* oversight board, gave a sense in 2021 of how far there is to go. "These questions about how *Facebook* chooses what to go in your feed and what to promote, and what not to promote, and whether Facebook is engineered in order to create polarized disagreement ... I think, probably, our job as a board is to get as far as we can in understanding that. And at the moment, we're just in the foothills" (Rusbridger, 2021).
- One of the ways the *Facebook* oversight board – and similar bodies in other platforms and media companies, and even individuals – will need to navigate is by properly understanding the underlying AI tools in content recommendation. Those tools are often 'black box' AI systems. Rusbridger continued: "The easy thing is to say, 'let's see the algorithm.' But having the technical capability to understand what you're being shown" is more challenging.

To satisfy the need at both a customer and societal level for responsible digital privacy, customers, workers, regulators and boards will need to develop the expertise to properly understand the algorithms underpinning media companies' use of their data. Since the algorithm of a platform is its most protected IP, clashes of interest are inevitable.

Information warfare proliferates

Even before the February 2022 war between Russia and Ukraine, information war was widespread. But at that date, it became existentially pressing for democratic governments and platforms to combat misinformation (material that is wrong) and disinformation (material that is deliberately wrong).

AI tools amplify potential disinformation, as they deploy mass-personalisation and dynamic content optimisation for the digital marketing of falsehood.

- Nicole Perlroth's book, *This is How They Say The World Ends*, is required reading for anyone looking at the evolution of media and tech in the 2020s in context of cyber- and information wars.
- One specific threat identified is a dystopian combination of media production and black ops. "AI-enabled malign information campaigns will not just send one powerful message to 1 million people, like twentieth century propaganda. They also will send a million individualized messages – configured on the basis of a detailed understanding of the targets' digital lives, emotional states, and social networks" (US National Security Commission on Artificial Intelligence Final Report, 2021).
- Francis Haugen points out the existence of 'adversarial harmful networks,' like the *QAnon* movement which came to prominence in 2019–21. These are groups and content streams that are deliberately constructed to engage and enrage.

In the face of all of this, for the platforms, perfecting AI in content moderation (from text analysis to deepfake identification) will be crucial (see Chapter 6), as will be addressing anomalies in distribution, such 'rabbit hole' algorithmic content selection.

- Networks will be scrutinised by regulators and advertisers. These bodies will look for any tendency of recommendation algorithms to point user predilections towards radicalisation.
- One of the primary technologies for protecting the truth may be the use of blockchain to show the origin, and therefore the veracity, of news items. (See the BBC section in Chapter 8.)

Reputation: the new equity

The levelling playing field for industry professionals, corporations and creators driven by the smartphone adds another dimension. Reputation management will become increasingly important. All content will be both visible, searchable and a determinant of reputation and employability. This is already visible in 'cancel culture' – the near-instant, and potentially catastrophic impact of, say, an ill-judged tweet on an individual's reputation and livelihood.

Reputation is starting to be measured by AI. Natural language processing and semantic analysis are functioning on a global scale (see Signal AI analysis section in Chapter 9), thereby changing the nature of PR and communications companies.

Reputation is also evaluated, using AI search tools, by brands and employers before choosing to work with companies, influencers or individuals. Influencers will not be offered brand relationships if they have associated – even fleetingly – with malign content. Freelance creatives risk losing work as firms check social media before hiring.

- "Reputation plays a decisive role in overcoming barriers of entry to networks, and obstacles to employment in artistic-creative projects. Thus, it is crucial to learn how reputational capital can be built, developed, preserved and expanded" (Eigler and Azarpour, 2020).

Summary

We could compile these trends into the original media value creation model with which we have worked in this book.

What becomes clear is that at every stage of the process – Development, Production, Distribution and Monetisation – certain common factors are in evidence:

- AI technologies are driving change in processes. This is seen in the development process, around how ideas are devised and executed ideas. And it is seen in the technical delivery of content production, its distribution, and its monetisation.
- The flywheel effect is a staple of the scaleable internet business models like social media platforms. More production drives more distribution and more monetisation. This regenerative process is the *de facto* business strategy objective of many media companies.

As we think about the media business, the marriage of intelligent technologies with the virtues of a circular economic model will become ever more important.

Class discussion questions

- Are the ten future media business trends identified above the right ones? What different ones would you pick?
- Identify a media company in your country which missed technology changes in the market, including AI. Consider its mistakes, and propose a recovery plan.
- Find a use of AI in any other industry which could also be deployed in the media.

Analysis: Blockchain and NFTs in a Hong Kong production company

Background

Award-winning production company Phoenix Waters Productions aimed, in 2021, to bring Hong Kong entertainment to global audiences – by incorporating blockchain and NFTs into their financing and production. Was this an attractive business model?

British banker of Chinese descent Bizan Tong combined a finance career at Barclays with a film production company, but after making independent film *The Escort*, he moved to Hong-Kong (Alderson, 2021) and went full-time in entertainment.

There he joined up with former broadcasting company ATV, and directed suspense thriller *Lockdown* (Shackleton, 2020), a UK/Hong Kong film and shot during the pandemic in the UK, US, Hong Kong, Italy and Japan (Frater, 2021a).

Lockdown also took Phoenix Waters Production into Non Fungible Tokens. With tech company Marvion, Tong auctioned five limited-edition "hybrid NFTs" of the theatrical cut of *Lockdown* (Shackleton, 2022).

The next project was Cantonese-language Hong-Kong 12 x 30 minute crime series *Forensic Psychologist*, that started shooting in January 2021 (Shackleton, 2020), distributed by Endeavour Content (Wiseman, 2021). Tong also developed an English-language version with UK producer Debbie Mason, co-founder of London production company Kudos (*Life on Mars*, *Spooks*) (Shackleton, 2020).

Blockchain

Interested by the NFTs experience on *Lockdown*, Phoenix Waters integrated blockchain and NFTs into projects:

- For Hong Kong zombie movie, *Chungking Mansions*, Tong and his team added blockchain marketing and Fusion NFTs memorabilia (Tokenizer, 2021).
- In Asia's first NFT drama series, *Crypto Keepers*, about crypto users and bankers (Shackleton, 2020), Phoenix Waters teamed up with Duncan Wong's CryptoBLK to offer the audience NFTs that let them vote on the second season storyline (Shackleton, 2022).
- Metaverse Blockchain Fusion NFT company Coinllectible bought a stake in Phoenix Waters' Hong Kong and UK production companies. The plan was to use Fusion NFT and blockchain technology to disrupt the arts and entertainment sector (Cosmos, 2022; Frater, 2021b).
- There were more innovative shows, like *Music Monarch*, an NFT-only music competition where artists around the world would have their works curated on the blockchain for viewers to vote through the use of NFTs.
- Crime film *Karma* would have interlinked short stories from across the globe, curated entirely on the blockchain, and the film would be available as NFTs (Frater, 2021b).

Class discussion questions

There is lots of interest in blockchain in the entertainment business.

- How could the technology open up payment opportunities for creators?
- With NFTs, how could a producer be paid all the way through the royalty lifespan of projects?
- With NFTs, how could an audience get 'agency' in shows through decision-taking power in the stories?
- Will the Phoenix Waters combination of great stories, Asian star power and blockchain be a winning combination?
- Would you invest in blockchain led entertainment projects? Either way, give your reasons.

BIBLIOGRAPHY

Alderson, G. (2021) The Filmmakers Podcast. https://thefilmmakerspodcast.com/filmmaking-in-a-pandemic-with-bizhan-tong/

Azhar, A. (2021) Exponential: How to Bridge the Gap between Technology and Society. London: Penguin.

BBC. (2021) AI narration of chef Anthony Bourdain's voice sparks row. www.bbc.co.uk/news/technology-57842514

Bellamy, M. (2021, 5 August 2021) In Recode Media with Peter Kafka on Puck, sale of Hello Sunshine. https://open.spotify.com/episode/3KuXKPJszGFPn2NB2LGefh?si=46f9cf15a fff455b

Cosmos. (2022) *Coinllectibles™™ Completes Acquisition Of Phoenix Waters Productions (HK) Limited and Phoenix Waters Productions Ltd (UK)* www.prnewswire.com/news-relea ses/coinllectibles-completes-acquisition-of-phoenix-waters-productions-hk-limited-and-phoenix-waters-productions-ltd-uk-301476517.html

Datastream. (2021) Visual Capitalist. www.visualcapitalist.com/datastream/

Deloitte. (2022) 2022 media and entertainment industry outlook. *Deloitte.* [online] Available at: www2.deloitte.com/us/en/pages/technology-media-and-telecommunications/articles/media-and-entertainment-industry-outlook-trends.html [Accessed 23 August 2022].

Eigler, J., and Azarpour, S. (2020) Reputation management for creative workers in the media industry. *Journal of Media Business Studies*, 17(3–4), 261–75. doi.org/10.1080/16522354.2020.1741148.

Floridi, L. and Chiriatti, M. (2020) *GPT-3: Its Nature, Scope, Limits, and Consequences.* (Report). *Minds and Machines: Journal for Artificial Intelligence, Philosophy and Cognitive Science*, 30(4), 681. doi.org/10.1007/s11023-020-09548-1

Frater, P. (2021a) 'Lockdown' Pandemic Thriller Unlocks Studio Era for Asia Television's AMM Global (EXCLUSIVE). Retrieved 2021-03-15, from https://variety.com/2021/film/asia/lockdown-pandemic-thriller-unlocks-studio-era-at-asia-television-1234928099/

Frater, P. (2021b) Omnific Blockchain Studio Launches With NFT-Backed 'Karma' Film and 'Marvion' Music Show. Retrieved 2021-11-08, from https://variety.com/2021/digital/asia/omnific-blockchain-studio-launches-1235107197/

Galloway, S. (2022, 18 February 2022) Apple: Thief. *No Mercy/No Malice.* www.profgallo way.com/apple-thief/

Hardwick, T. (2016) Former Microsoft CEO Steve Ballmer Admits He Was Wrong About the iPhone. *Mac Rumors*. www.macrumors.com/2016/11/07/former-microsoft-ceo-steve-ball mer-wrong-iphone/

Haugen, F. (2021, Monday, 20 December 2021) Sway, New York Times In Why Facebook Whistle-Blower Frances Haugen Thinks She'll Outlast Mark Zuckerberg. www.nytimes. com/2021/12/20/opinion/sway-kara-swisher-frances-haugen.html

Hayes, D. (2021). LeBron James' SpringHill Company Sells 'Significant' Minority Stake To RedBird Capital, Fenway Sports, Nike & Epic Games. *Deadline*. https://deadline.com/2021/10/lebron-james-springhill-company-sells-significant-minority-stake-redbird-capital-fenway-sports-nike-epic-games-1234855800/

Ingram, M. (2014) Mark Zuckerberg has learned what Steve Jobs knew: You need to disrupt yourself before your competitors do. *GigaOM*. https://gigaom.com/2014/02/20/mark-zuc kerberg-has-learned-what-steve-jobs-knew-you-need-to-disrupt-yourself-before-your-comp etitors-do/

Jobs, S. (2007, 9 January 2007) Steve Jobs Introducing The iPhone At MacWorld 2007 www. youtube.com/watch?v=x7qPAY9JqE4

Kemp, S. (2022) *Digital 2022: global overview report*. https://datareportal.com/reports/digi tal-2022-global-overview-report

Kovalev, A. (2017) In Putin's Russia, the hollowed-out media mirrors the state. *The Guardian*. www.theguardian.com/commentisfree/2017/mar/24/putin-russia-media-state-government-control

Levy, A. (2021) Zoom's lightning-fast ascent to $100 billion made big acquisitions a sudden priority. www.cnbc.com/2021/07/24/zooms-fast-ascent-to-100-billion-made-acquisitions-a-sudden-priority.html

McKinsey. (2020) *It's showtime! How live commerce is transforming the shopping experience* (McKinsey Digital, Issue. www.mckinsey.com/business-functions/mckinsey-digital/our-insig hts/its-showtime-how-live-commerce-is-transforming-the-shopping-experience

Merican, S. (2021) Netflix Will Invest $500 Million In Korean Content This Year. *Forbes*. www.forbes.com/sites/saramerican/2021/02/26/netflix-will-invest-500-million-in-korean-content-this-year/

Mitchell, W. (2022) Perspectives on 2020: EbonyLife Media CEO Mo Abudu on Netflix deals and African stories. www.screendaily.com/features/perspectives-on-2020-ebonylife-media-ceo-mo-abudu-on-netflix-deals-and-african-stories/5155854.article

Ocean, R. (2021, 20/20/2021) Global Smartphones Market is anticipated to grow at a CAGR of 7.6% over the projected period of 2022–2030. *Taiwan News*. www.taiwannews.com.tw/en/news/4636438

Ramachandran, N. (2021). Disney to be First Client at 18 Sound Stage Shinfield Studios in U.K. – Global Bulletin. *Variety*. https://variety.com/2021/film/news/disney-shinfield-stud ios-uk-1235131847/

Rodriguez Ovejero, J. M., Stammati, L. and Torres Figueroa, M. P. (2019) The impact of piracy on the structure of the Pay TV market: a case study for Latin America. *Journal of Media Business Studies*, 16(1), 40–57. doi.org/10.1080/16522354.2019.1572449

Rusbridger, A. (2021, Friday, 7 May 2021) In Sway with Kara Swisher: Inside the Decision on Trump's Facebook Fate. www.nytimes.com/2021/05/07/opinion/sway-kara-swisher-alan-rusbridger.html

Santora, J. (2022) Key Influencer Marketing Statistics. *Influencer Marketing Hub*. https://inf luencermarketinghub.com/influencer-marketing-statistics/

Schneier, B. (2018) Click here to kill everybody: security and survival in a hyper-connected world. New York: W. W. Norton & Co.

Shackleton, L. (2020) Hong Kong broadcaster ATV returns to production with UK's Phoenix Waters. www.screendaily.com/news/hong-kong-broadcaster-atv-returns-to-production-with-uks-phoenix-waters/5155926.article

Shackleton, L. (2022) NFTs: just a craze, or a gamechanger for the content industries? www.screendaily.com/features/nfts-just-a-craze-or-a-gamechanger-for-the-content-industries/5166362.article

Skillings, J. (2012) Kodak sells its imaging patents for $525m. *CNET*. www.cnet.com/tech/tech-industry/kodak-sells-its-imaging-patents-for-525m/

Statistics&Data.org. (2021) *Top 15 Best Global Brands Rankings.* Retrieved 18 February 2022 from https://statisticsanddata.org/data/most-valuable-companies/

Sun, N. (2021, 8 June 2021) Alibaba, Baidu and Tencent learn Netflix lessons in content fight. *Financial Times.* www.ft.com/content/ac4ebc50-457b-4131-99b0-669340d3389b

Sweeting, P. (2020). Artificial intelligence and media: a special report. *Variety.* https://variety.com/vip-special-reports/artificial-intelligence-and-media-a-special-report-1234783682/

Swisher, K. (2021, 22 March 2021) Sway In *What the Heck are NFTs? Let's Ask Beeple.* www.nytimes.com/2021/03/22/opinion/sway-kara-swisher-beeple.html

Tokenizer, T. (2021) https://thetokenizer.io/2021/09/16/coinllectibles-plans-to-roll-out-fusion-nfts-for-phoenix-waters-productions-new-film-chungking-mansions-accepting-doge-and-trx-as-payment/

US National Security Commission on Artificial Intelligence Final Report. (2021) www.nscai.gov/2021-final-report/

Warren, T. (2022) Microsoft's Xbox Game Pass service grows to 25 million subscribers. www.theverge.com/2022/1/18/22406059/xbox-game-pass-subscribers-25-million-microsoft-activision

Wiseman, A. (2021) Endeavor Content Joins Hong Kong Crime Series 'Forensic Psychologist'; First Look Images. Retrieved 2021-12-10, from https://deadline.com/2021/12/endeavor-content-joins-hong-kong-crime-series-forensic-psychologist-first-look-images-1234888617/

Index

Printed in the United States
by Baker & Taylor Publisher Services